RAILROADING RELIGION

RAILROADING RELIGION

MORMONS, TOURISTS, AND THE CORPORATE SPIRIT OF THE WEST

DAVID WALKER

THE UNIVERSITY OF NORTH CAROLINA PRESS
CHAPEL HILL

This book was published with the assistance of the
Authors Fund of the University of North Carolina Press.

© 2019 The University of North Carolina Press
All rights reserved

Designed by April Leidig
Set in Arnhem Pro by Copperline Book Services, Inc.
Manufactured in the United States of America

The University of North Carolina Press has been
a member of the Green Press Initiative since 2003.

Cover illustration from *Crofutt's Trans-continental Tourist's Guide . . . over the Union Pacific Railroad, Central Pacific Railroad of Cal., Their Branches and Connections by Stage and Water . . .* (New York: G. A. Crofutt; etc., etc., 1873); courtesy of the Department of Special Research Collections, University of California, Santa Barbara.

Library of Congress Cataloging-in-Publication Data
Names: Walker, David, 1979– author.
Title: Railroading religion : Mormons, tourists, and
the corporate spirit of the West / David Walker.
Description: Chapel Hill : University of North Carolina Press, [2019] |
Includes bibliographical references and index.
Identifiers: LCCN 2019011574| ISBN 9781469653198 (cloth : alk. paper) |
ISBN 9781469653204 (pbk : alk. paper) | ISBN 9781469653211 (ebook)
Subjects: LCSH: Mormon Church—History—19th century. | Mormon Church—
Public opinion—History—19th century. | Railroads—West (U.S.)—History—
19th century. | Tourism—United States—History—19th century. |
Corinne (Utah)—History—19th century.
Classification: LCC BX8611 .W335 2019 | DDC 289.3/7309034—dc23
LC record available at https://lccn.loc.gov/2019011574

CONTENTS

INTRODUCTION
The Irony of Religious Industry 1

CHAPTER ONE
Corinnethians and the Death Knell Thesis 11

CHAPTER TWO
Brigham Young and the Railroad Connection 47

CHAPTER THREE
Godbeites and the Capital of Dissent 83

CHAPTER FOUR
Steamboats and the Rise of Atrocity Tourism 115

CHAPTER FIVE
Patrons and the Plays of Mormon Culture 147

CHAPTER SIX
Tourists and the Making of an American Mainline 185

CONCLUSION
The Recreation and State of Religion in 1893 235

Acknowledgments 249

Notes 251

Bibliography 305

Index 331

FIGURES

Railroads and key sites of the Great Salt Lake Region, ca. late 1800s viii

John Gast, *American Progress* (1872) 20

Panoramic view of Corinne (1869) 40

Mormon construction camp at Echo Canyon (1868) 75

Joining of the rails at Promontory (1869) 81

City of Corinne steamer (ca. 1875) 122

"Scenes in the Endowment or Initiation Ceremonies" (ca. 1904) 132

Railroad scene at the Salt Lake Theatre (ca. 1900) 161

Salt Lake City montage (ca. 1870) 169

Deseret Museum advertisement (ca. 1875) 172

Pulpit Rock stereoview (1869) 200

Pulpit Rock postcard (ca. 1910) 201

Page from a railroad scrapbook (1874) 210

Grant Bros. guides and guests at Temple Block (ca. 1890) 212

Utah Exposition Palace Car (1888) 216

"Promised Land" map (1891) 223

"On the Beach at Garfield" (ca. 1898) 229

Lake Park pavilion and train (ca. 1887) 230

Saltair with bathers (1893) 240

Saltair with train tracks (1893) 241

Page from Isaac Hoffman's railroad scrapbook (1894) 244

RAILROADING RELIGION

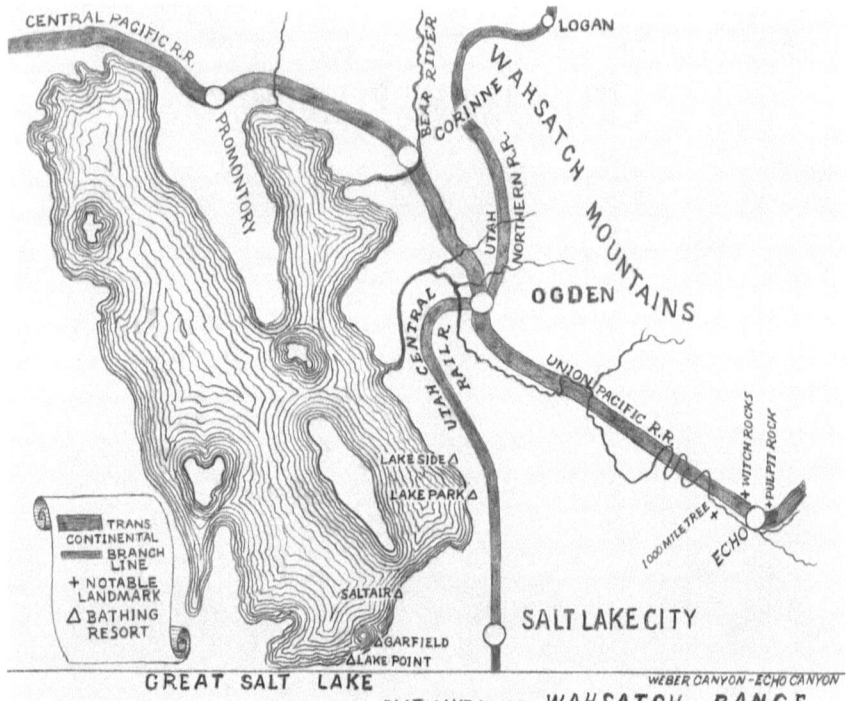

Railroads and key sites of the Great Salt Lake region, ca. late 1800s. (Drawn by Leonardo Nuñez; adapted from Alfred Hart, *Pacific Railway Panoramic Guide* [Chicago: Horton and Leonard, ca. 1870])

INTRODUCTION

The Irony of Religious Industry

✦

IN 1868 AND EARLY 1869, monitoring closely the progress of the transcontinental railroads, several businessmen set out to build The Greatest City of the West. At least that was their plan: they would inhabit a spot along the most likely train route in the Great Basin, and they would advertise it as the best possible junction for the Central Pacific and Union Pacific. Corinne, their metropolis-to-be, was located in Utah's Bear River Valley, near the Idaho and Wyoming borders, where residents would have easy access to fresh water as well as northern trade routes. The area's Shoshoni former residents were mostly gone, said the businessmen, and the land was ready for white settlement. All of this made Corinne a viable industrial hub and a safe investment for American capitalists and settlers, according to its promoters. But above all they promised that Corinne would be a stronghold for anti-Mormon Christians.[1]

This was a time of great national concern about 'Mormonism,' the religion (or, as Corinne's founders described it, the *ir*religion) of the Church of Jesus Christ of Latter-day Saints.[2] Only a decade after Republicans vowed the eradication of Mormon polygamy (1856) and Democrats launched a military expedition against Utah (1857), both parties set their sights westward again, with eyes now toward post–Civil War national integration and expansion.[3] The self-described 'Corinnethians' hoped to capitalize on that focus, and they adjusted their promotions accordingly. By their telling, Corinne would be a place free of control by Mormon president Brigham Young, free of theocracy, free of despotism, free of polygamy, free of sedition. It would be rather a place of freedom for (most) religious groups, capital, industry, farms, and families—a place into which 'normal' Americans might move and out of which their values might grow.[4]

Corinne "is the only chance left by God and nature to plant a loyal American population . . . and bring Christianity into peaceful contact with the barbarians of Utah," according to booster J. H. (John Hanson) Beadle. "At no very distant day Salt Lake City will have a rapidly-growing rival here. It will be a Gentile [non-Mormon] city, and will make the first great trial between Mormon institutions and outsiders."[5] All Corinne needed was a bit of land, the railroad, and the nation's attention. The rest would take care of itself: outsiders would come to work on the lines, to work in the mines, to work in the town, and to settle. According to this plan, they would expose Mormondom to the lights of American scientific observation, politics, and economics, thus diminishing the social power of polygamy, theocracy, and church restrictions on Mormon-Gentile commerce. Salt Lake City would be sucked into Corinne's orbit, rather than the other way around. And Mormonism would be detoothed, if not destroyed.

They failed on all counts. But they did so in highly informative and ironic ways, and their efforts reveal the rise of both 'religion' and 'Mormonism' as objects of national inquiry, territorial contestation, touristic fascination, and bureaucratic management in the West. This book reconstructs that story of intriguing failure. Drawing from diverse nineteenth-century sources and engaging influential theories of secular modernity and recent trends in religious studies, *Railroading Religion* describes the dream for and failure of Corinne to destroy Mormonism and spread a distinctly secular America, showing how railroads and affiliated industries both mobilized and incorporated multiple religious interests and—indeed—mainlined Mormonism in time.[6]

IF J. H. BEADLE'S TOWN-FOUNDING DECLARATION—*Corinne will destroy Mormonism!*—inaugurates this story of industry and religion in the American West, a very different scene ends it. In 1893 boosters of Bear River Valley settlement placed a large advertisement at the World's Fair in Chicago, but they found themselves unable—and in fact unwilling—to mobilize much anti-Mormon sentiment. By then Corinne was understood to be (at best) a poor and culturally sidetracked suburb of Salt Lake City, itself an ascendant hub of railway traffic, tourism, and religious observation. Many newer Corinnethians took a different promotional tack, lauding Latter-day Saint (LDS) pioneers for their industriousness and colonial savvy, claiming the ecumenism of their material culture, and reassuring Gentiles that they had nothing to fear from Mormon neighbors. The culture wars were over, they implied, even if (or, as we shall see, precisely *because*) the religiosity of Mormonism itself remained a matter of open debate.

Since 1869 and by 1893, Corinne's leaders, their conversation partners, and their combatants had refigured the value of Mormonism in the American

West. What happened between these moments is the story of *Railroading Religion*. Three basic narrative emphases, weaving throughout the chapters of this book, connect 1869 and 1893. The first engages the changing cultural, intellectual, and legal conditions that informed a promotional shift away from anti-Mormonism and the discourse of Mormon irreligion. This was a pivotal era for Utah and the Utah-based Church of Jesus Christ of Latter-day Saints. The church, prosecuted since the 1850s for its distinctive legal, political, economic, and marital practices—and finding itself to be an object of increasingly common concern among bureaucrats, industrialists, and homesteaders upon conception of a transcontinental railway—adopted a series of changes that enabled, in time, Utahn statehood (1896) and the seating of Mormon senator Reed Smoot (1903-7). Ecclesiastical alterations—especially the abandonment of polygamy, the dissolution of the Mormon political party, the redistribution of church property, and (of greatest focus here) the development of railroad connections—contributed to, and were accompanied by, a softening of anti-Mormon rhetoric. Bear River offers a demonstrative site of this national story. It is a case study in how Mormonism shifted from an exiled 'problem' to a regional force.[7]

The second strand seeks to complicate easy conclusions from the first, emphasizing the unexpected relationship between commerce and religious discourse. An investigation of how settlement promoters elevated claims to religious dangers and religious possibilities in Utah runs the risk of unsurprising conclusions: namely, that Corinne's boosters and their ilk altered their promotional tactics merely to capitalize on shifts in a national bigotry. What is less predictable—what was never inevitable, what was always contested, and what tells us a great deal more about settlement and religion in the West—is the way in which national sentiments were shaped, the media through which Corinnethian salesmen attempted to evoke them, and the degrees to which their attempts garnered transcontinental response. I suggest that several interrelated institutions and processes mobilized religious discourse in nineteenth-century America, foremost among them land grant initiatives, railroad promotions, and the tourism trade. As conditions changed in northern Utah and in the nation, a shifting cast of Bear River promoters appealed to, and entered discussions within, these venues. There and in associated political lobbies they found many people similarly concerned about the fate and function of religion in an expanding and technologically advancing West. Some of these were, like the Corinnethians, committed to Mormonism's destruction. But others worked to protect LDS bureaucrats and businesses, mediating between pro- and anti-Mormon interests and managing intergroup intercourse. In time their overlapping discussions helped to delineate the terms and boundaries of normative religiosity in the United States. The example of Bear River Valley boosterism thus demonstrates the bureaucratic formation of religion in modernity. It shows how religion has become a category constituted through local and national collision and adjudication, in specific and sometimes surprising venues.

The third strand connecting the chronological brackets of 1869 and 1893 considers the failures and ironies of promotions and institutional practice. Here I consider not only the final fact of Corinne—that is, how it was never much more than a hell-on-wheels railroad outpost—but also how its very limits identify gaps in the logic of comparative religions and the emergent 'secular' state. (I place secular in quotation marks here because, as many recent scholars have shown, Western presumptions of church-state separations were often influenced by Reformation apologetics and thus commensurate with the public power of privacy-professing Protestants. I will argue that Corinne points not only to the types of persistent church-state, private-public interrelations and Protestant-republican-capitalist collaborations identified by such scholars but also to scholars' tendencies, sometimes, to overestimate both their ubiquity and the automaticity of their effective or affective power.) This is not a story of success, at least not for Corinne's founders. Despite showy exhibitions and editorial responses to the promotion of Bear River Valley as a Gentile railroad hub, no land grants were secured, nor were many stable settlements or industries established. Few actual Bear River communities flourished, and the valley has witnessed more displacement than placement, more uprooting and withering than planting and growth. We might refer to the Bear River Valley from 1869 to 1893 as a persistent frontier of failure. It marked the limits of the so-called Mormon establishment and the so-called Protestant establishment alike, not to mention the ends of Shoshoni reservation and settlement rights, of territorial law, of touristic interest, and of arable land. Various groups carved out various modes of settlement and coexistence in the spaces between our canopylike promotional snapshots and their sometimes alkali-saturated grounds of being, but still: this is a rather muted account of ordinary social enterprise, warts and all.

This book recounts Corinne's multisited failure to incorporate its brand of Gentile secularity in and for the West. Crucially, however, as I tell the story, the chief narrative voice and historical substance of this Corinnethian failure is *irony*. In describing Corinne's shifts and shortcomings, I seek also to explore how religious agents work with and against their critics and, in particular, how 'Mormonism' formatted itself to best certain economic and political interests. *Railroading Religion* is therefore equally—if not ultimately—a tale of a particular Mormonism's successes in a modern bureaucratic world. And by my telling this was (and is) a world necessarily but unsteadily reliant on cultic-corporate relations and opportunities for institutional subcontracting. This is a world reliant, too, on interreligious critiques: a place wherein politicians pit proximate religious groups against one another to managerial ends; where business leaders, while mediating among those groups, recognize also the commercial advantages of religious curiosity and cultural ambiguity; and where Mormons have entrenched themselves in American religious imaginaries as exempla of cultural pasts and possibilities.

Bear River's ironic failures allow historians to observe how precisely the strategies of settlement—colonial, exclusive, Protestant, and violent—often worked against their ambitions of capitalist growth and secular expansion. The most lasting and significant aspect of Bear River social formation in these years was arguably the ways in which it evoked institutions and discourses characteristic of nineteenth-century America, especially transcontinental management companies and their religions of opportunity. Thus this book follows the multiple ways in which people articulated and elevated 'Mormonism' in battles over western land and technological progress, the significant fact that 'religion' became the site of general national debate, and the sometimes surprising ways in which that debate did, or did not, change the conditions of western battles themselves.

IRONY IS AN AFFAIR OF inverted efforts and effects, and it invites readings along different vectors. Restated more explicitly from the vantage of Salt Lake City rather than Corinne, the interwoven strands of this story argue that, although railroads, congressional debates, lobbying efforts, federal land policies, and tourism concerned Mormons, they did not cripple Mormonism. Quite the contrary. Latter-day Saint Church officials in Salt Lake City were well aware of railroading anti-Mormonism and the aspirations of Corinne, and they made their own preparations for railroad arrival. More than that: they invited it, welcomed it, and had long advocated for it, not only because railroads would ease Saintly travel to and from Utah but also because they would bring new business, new trade, and new territory for religious encounter. "Speaking of the completion of this railroad," Brigham Young said to a Salt Lake Tabernacle audience in 1867, "I am anxious to see it, and I say to the Congress of the United States, through our Delegate, to the Company, and to others, hurry up, hasten the work! We want to hear the iron horse puffing through this valley."[8] To this end Mormons negotiated labor contracts and industrial locations with railroad directors: they sold materials and graded paths, donated land and buildings, built branch lines, and informed station placements. Mormons also negotiated Mormon culture and identity with railroad officials, who found themselves increasingly reliant on LDS contracts and connections and, thus, willing to lobby on Mormons' behalf in the backrooms of Washington, the publishing houses of other major cities, and the dirt roads of aspiring towns like Corinne. In time these groups forged a terrain of mutual promotion and benefit, much to the chagrin of leading Corinnethians and contrary to their rhetoric of inevitable secularization.

It is wrong and misleading to suggest—as Corinnethians at the time charged and as some historians have since maintained—that Brigham Young and other LDS officials dreaded the transcontinental's arrival on account of its inevitably counter-Mormon, counterecclesiastical, or counterreligious influence. "I don't care anything for a religion which could not stand a railroad," Young reportedly declared, and Mormonism "must, indeed, be a — poor religion, if it cannot stand one railroad."[9] The church president had little cause for disappointment, in any case. By the end of the train-building era, Mormonism had 'stood' not one but many railroads, and few could consider it 'poor' by most economic, social, or political measures. LDS leaders, moreover, learned from their railroading enterprises the managerial strategies and promotional campaigns most conducive to defending church legitimacy and longevity in the West, well into the twentieth and twenty-first centuries. The transcontinental era had mainlined Mormonism for good.

A NOTE ON SOURCES and the structure of my study: I am attempting here to do a type of history that is cognizant of some notion of lived reality—in Corinne, in Utah, in the West generally—that we know is always also a discursive fact and function. Moreover, I am dealing with groups that *couldn't stop talking about themselves*: federal authorities, business interests, tourists, Mormons. My pursuit, therefore, has led me to consult a vast array of documents and archives. These include newspaper accounts, novels, ethnographies, guidebooks, advertisements, ledger books, paystubs, stock statements, probate records, photographs, scrapbooks, diaries, letters, sermons, excommunication reports, denominational histories, school curricula, maps, tickets, and research notes, as pertaining to land grants and settlement practices, corporate policies and developments, church and missionary endeavors, government decrees and deliberations, political lobbying, tourist rites, museum displays, architectural designs, and the interpretive priorities of historians themselves. Many of these materials are uncommon to works of American religious history, but I argue that they might well be considered evidence in the history of religions and indeed that they are particularly productive for the history of religion in the West.

Because it informs also the shape of my chapters, I will restate this interpretive wager—that the stuff of religious studies may be located in such diverse and often mundane negotiations—from a different angle. I mean not only that such exchanges yield data for scholars' acts of comparative religions, or even that we may observe powerful mechanisms of subject formation and religious discipline there. Both statements are true, but I mean also that ordinary Americans articulated and advanced therein their own theories of religion. Although occasionally inchoate, these theories are themselves comparable to theories operating in the field of religious studies or in historiography generally, the likes of which have shaped the reception history and archival status of 'ordinary' 'American' 'data' in the first place. History entails historiography, and historiography creates history. Religious theorizing is not simply the etic stuff of the academy or even the government, in any case. Important as those venues are, their own tools and heuristics frequently intersect with the intellectual labors, taxonomies, adjudications, and anthropological representations of local groups otherwise testing systems of settlement and corporate infrastructure. *Railroading Religion* is structured according to this logic and this argument. The first part of each chapter traces the emergence and operation of certain theoretical concerns in specific nineteenth-century contexts, and the middle part generally considers how contemporary scholarly categories echo or obscure, complicate or correct them. The last part then returns to Utah in order to observe anew its shifting religious constructions and finally to suggest also how western history and religious studies might once again learn from each other. By this pattern readers will encounter engagement with influential historiographies of capitalism, western colonialism, Mormonism, and American religions generally—as well as with key theories of secularism, technological sublimity, sacred space, bureaucracy, ritual, and tourism—as necessarily component to the stuff and story of these chapters.

Chapter 1 analyzes the railroading promises of Corinne in light of contemporary religious theories and antipolygamy legislation. Of particular interest is what I am calling the 'death knell thesis': the notion that trains and capitalism, by opening the West to free enterprise and liberal thought, would modernize Utah and destroy Mormondom. Railroads, according to the logic of this thesis, were chaplains of culture and catalysts of true religion; and Corinne, in the vision of its boosters, would house the first belfry of Mormonism's death knell. Chapters 2 and 3 then explore Mormon responses to these and related designs for industrial secularization and manifest destiny. LDS Church officials mobilized in several ways—through prerailroad preparations, trade embargos, business initiatives, emigrant promotions, railside ecclesiology, land grants, and labor contracts—to secure certain arrangements in Utah, as well as to code and defend them precisely as 'Mormon' and 'religious.' Together these efforts belie traditional notions of 'sacred space' by revealing more concrete geographies of religious authority and industry in the West. Arguments for Mormon precision and legitimate religion were made both against Gentile outsiders *and* against intrachurch dissenters, in any case. Among the dissenters were the so-called Godbeites (chapter 3), schismatic opponents of Brigham Young's economic policies who, through interactions with Corinnethians, congressmen, and capitalists, induced LDS officials to find new balances between openness and enclosure in the railroad age.

The product of such ecclesiastical argumentation and reformation was an orthodox Mormonism; but neither its visibility as such nor its intelligibility as 'religion' was the work of Utah residents alone. The second part of this book tracks more specifically the roles of tourism and railroad agents in the local consolidation and national mainstreaming of Mormonism. Chapter 4 treats Corinnethian attempts to mobilize positive and negative sightseeing around Corinne, chapter 5 observes Mormon countermeasures in Salt Lake City and along new church-owned railroads in Utah, and chapter 6 analyzes transcontinental businessmen and tourism agents' efforts to mediate between them. Both discursively and materially—as both a cultural curiosity and an exemplar, target and attraction, comparate and conversation partner—Mormonism was sustained precisely through the collective efforts of these and related travel boosters, train builders, and religious tourists: this, notwithstanding their occasional or ostensible cross-purposes. In time, their collaborations frustrated Corinnethian aspirations and ensured Mormon longevity by creating new common grounds in America.

Attempts to railroad religion thus had ironic results, yielding dynamic and expansive religious institutions. Rather than eradicating or diminishing religion (in general) or Mormonism (in particular), western railroads helped to create them—and to create new modes of their social incorporation—in the world. They did so by occasioning new means of religious encounter and shaping new media by which to understand encounters as religious. An appreciation of this process necessitates paying close attention to the shifting religious observations and negotiations that occurred under railroad auspices and along train lines in Utah.

INTRODUCTION 9

TRACING CORINNETHIAN UPBUILDING projects over twenty-five years, *Railroading Religion* shows how certain venues mediated popular discussions of religion in nineteenth-century America. It demonstrates how Mormonism itself figured—and how it figured itself—in regional politics and expansion, too. Through an examination of what Mormons and non-Mormons variously understood as 'Gentile' interests in land grant applications, settlement schemes, congressional considerations, and above all railroad programs, this book narrates the construction of normative religion on a local and national scale.

In time Mormonism was domesticated in America through the combined efforts of church officials, politicians, travelers, and businessmen. But I wish to be clear that this is *not* a simple story of secularization. The beauty of the Corinnethian project—and its challenge to modern secularity studies—is that its boosters were archetypal Protestant secularists, speaking precisely and strategically the language often identified as regnant in nineteenth-century America: that of righteous Protestantism, privatization, belief, republicanism, church-state separation, monogamous patriarchy, and laissez-faire capitalism. So too did Corinnethians espouse a theory of industrial secularization of a semi-Weberian sort: the idea that western capitalism and railroad development would destroy Mormonism. Corinne's failure thus affords us an opportunity to complexify common notions about secular ascendance and the power of religious rhetoric.

Railroading Religion shows how Mormons established mutually beneficial contracts with railroad companies and politicians via fluency in bureaucratic idioms rather than the verbiage of Protestantism, republicanism, or capitalism per se. Noting railroad officials' attempts to mediate between pro- and anti-Mormon interests in the West, I argue that the transcontinental tourism industry proved to be a modern mechanics of religious development and national intelligibility. Intelligibility entailed, among other things, the cultivation of new ideas about Mormon sacred space, the likes of which worked to Mormons' and railroad agents' mutual benefit. Mormon leaders rewrote Mormon history to emphasize the righteous inevitability of Utahn settlement, and railroads advertised Utahn travel as simultaneously an opportunity for Orientalist gawking, a Coney Island experience in the West, an occasion for reflection on the nature and history of religion, and a domestic counterpart to Holy Land tourism.

Whereas Corinne's boosters assumed the destruction of Mormonism through infrastructural development and private enterprise, western bureaucracies proved to be fertile environments for Mormon interests. *Railroading*

Religion tells this story. Along the way it argues also for a broad field of comparative religious studies and adjudication in the late nineteenth century, demonstrating the popular generation and circulation of religious theory, and adding new characters to our list of religious virtuosi: town boosters, land grant administrators, political lobbyists, railroad agents, and tourists. For, it was their overlapping strategies of possession that defined the ritual process of western settlement.

CHAPTER ONE

Corinnethians and the Death Knell Thesis

✦

"THE FIRST WHISTLE of the locomotive in the Salt Lake Valley will sound the knell of Mormonism."[1] This notion—articulated here by a western travel writer in 1868—became a refrain of sorts, and it echoed in anti-Mormon discourses throughout the country. From congressional halls to newspaper columns to church pulpits, nineteenth-century Americans postulated the demise of Mormonism during the railroad age. Some wrote laws and underwrote companies accordingly. And others, as in Corinne, Utah, chartered new towns.

The 'death knell thesis' (as I will call it here) was keyed to several interlocking, popular theories about religion, economics, politics, law, and sex in modernity. By its terms, railroads would add economic stakes to extant 'human interests' in Utah, even as they provided better means through which to pursue those interests. Corporate success and national integration simultaneously required and constituted local stability, it said. And stability, in turn, entailed humanistic understanding and humanitarian work—including the diagnosis of barbarism and the fight against theocracy—which would be facilitated by intergroup contact and commerce along railroads. One reporter articulated the looping logic in this way: railroads, having increased Americans' "commercial interest" in Utah, and having combined it with humanitarian and political ones, "will as surely as truth is truth, and right is right, crush out the vile thing" called Mormonism and "rid the country of the foul blot."[2] The death knell thesis thus recapped—sometimes through economic argument, and often through the accretion of railroad puns—the assumption that Mormonism could not withstand the arrival of ministers, miners, traders, businessmen, and legislators in Utah, as each of these would bring "contact with our more enlightened civilization" in their own particular ways.[3] Brigham Young would lose control over the social, economic, and political affairs of the territory, it said. The period of Utah's isolation and estrangement would come to an end; men would become familiar with new thoughts and new vocations; women would be exposed to eligible bachelors and enticing fashions; outdated sensibilities and superstitions would wither; and freedom would reign.

"Mormonism may henceforth be considered on the down grade," announced an Illinois reporter in May 1869, ten days after the completion of the transcontinental railroad. "The last spike in the Pacific railroad was the first nail in the coffin of Mormonism." A congressman from Nevada largely agreed with the sentiment: "Every locomotive bell resounding through the gorges of the Wahsatch mountains is sounding [polygamy's] death knell." So too did a prominent Mormon apostate agree: "The construction of the Pacific Railroad" will deliver "the death-blow to Polygamy" and enable people's escape from church oppressions.[4] The ubiquity of the death knell thesis, the diversity of its proponents, and the stability of its terms is enough to imply substance as well as veneer, but it is the historian's task to unpack this circular notion and to situate its interlocking aspects in time and place. Only thus can we understand why it was that, when one group of anti-Mormons attempted to plant a town in the midst of all that rhetoric, politicking, enterprising, and sectarianism, they found little traction. Corinnethians discovered that there was no there, there.

The Anti-Bigamy Act and the Business of Religious Legislation

Speeches by Justin S. Morrill—Vermont representative and namesake of the first federal anti-Mormon legislation, the Morrill Anti-Bigamy Act of 1862—provide introductions to the premises of anti-Mormon industrial theory. They are a fitting place to begin this story of Corinnethian aspirations and railroad knells for other reasons, too. Discussions of the Anti-Bigamy Act drew certain themes in colorful directions, and railroad companies were later imagined as implementing partners for the act's initiatives. In such conversations and contract language we may identify the circulation of influential theories of religion and important concerns of religious comparison.

Five years before the passage of the act, Morrill outlined its concerns before Congress. Mormonism was un-American in several respects, he said. Most glaringly, it was religious and political in manners unbefitting the modernity embodied and advanced in America. Mormonism was monarchic rather than democratic, affording little to no opportunity for dissent or freedom of thought; likewise, it was barbaric rather than enlightened. LDS leaders were "as hostile to the republican form of government as they are to the usual form of Christianity," he said. According to Morrill, Mormons adopted "kingly government, in order to make their patriarchal institutions more homogenous," and they assumed the rhetoric and "guise of religion" to similar intended effect.[5]

Among the congressional concerns of the 1850s was the putative monopoly of Utahn resources by a handful of Mormon 'patriarchs.' Wood, water, and real estate were "monopolized not only by the Mormons," Morrill reported, "but by a few Mormons—the Governor [Brigham Young] and his apostles." So too were obstacles to overland travel and national expansion considered unacceptable: "The Governor and the leading elders . . . extort considerable tribute from the emigrant travel passing through to California." Revenue from bridge and ferry tolls, combined with membership tithes, funded other initiatives by which Mormondom placed itself at odds with American values and expansion: the development of independent legal structures, the expansion of leaders' domestic dominions, and the maintenance of a church militia. This was what theocracy looked like, Morrill thought. LDS leaders had yoked together the interests and offices of religion and statism.[6]

A military expedition in 1857–58 lessened certain but not all congressional concerns. President James Buchanan then ordered some 2,500 troops across country to investigate claims of Mormon barbarism and sedition, and they removed Brigham Young from the governorship of Utah Territory—a position he had held since 1851—and established a military camp outside Salt Lake City. But the 'Utah War' arguably resulted in little more than the excitement of Mormon militiamen, who hastily constructed fortifications in the Wasatch Mountains' Echo Canyon in case of armed confrontation, and a boon to Mormon merchants, who sold expensive provisions to soldiers during their stay and then purchased their supplies cheaply when they left. The U.S. military failed to persuade Mormons of the moral benefits of monogamy, in any case. Opposition to polygamy—or, rather, to polygynous marriage between one man and plural women, a practice publicly adopted by the LDS Church in 1852—thus remained the flagship of anti-Mormon activism well after 1858, even as it continued to catch other interests and initiatives in its wake. Polygamy was argued to be both catalyst and fruition of Mormon patriarchy and religious primitivism, the seed and shell of aberrant sensualities. On these grounds Congress attacked it: Mormonism developed its rhetorical strategies and bureaucratic infrastructures in order to beget and defend a kind of basic, hedonistic, sensual polygamy.[7]

Talk of polygamous patriarchy served anti-Mormon initiatives in two principal respects. First, it evoked sexual and gender politics in a limited way, that is, without necessarily challenging sexism operative elsewhere in American systems of enfranchisement, employment, property holding, and violent crime. Such talk implicitly contrasted such sexism with presumably worse Mormon instantiations instead.⁸ Polygamous Mormonism threatened white womanhood and insulted women's "known virtue," according to Morrill, his activist compatriots, and countless novelists and newspapermen. It made literal slaves of women within LDS domestic labor camps. Mormon "harems" thus upended the natural order of the home, the very microcosm and seedbed of virtue, and they denied women the joyful achievement of simple, direct maternalism. A woman's place was in the sphere of the home, and that sphere should be monogamous.⁹

No less dangerous than Mormonism's attempt to reshape domestic spheres were its claims to religious antiquity, warrant, and worldliness. To speak of patriarchy and polygamy together was to evoke the father figures of the Hebrew Bible and, thus, to force reconsideration of the genealogy of Western religious cultures. Mormons were well aware of the evocation and its challenge, and they deployed the category with provocative intent. Why shouldn't professed descendants of Israel reclaim the marital practices of Israelites, or 'the blessings of Abraham,' even as they claimed Christianity and the blessings of Jesus? In order to negotiate Mormon assertions of ancient religious lineage and sociopolitical warrant—and in order to meet Mormons' challenges to principles of biblical sufficiency, textual interpretation, church-state separation, and marital sanctity—concerned American policy makers necessarily theorized religion. They did so by rethinking their personal and national relations to Christian and Jewish origins, and by comparing Mormonism to different world religions.¹⁰

Congressmen's theories of religion were interwoven with their concerns about Mormonism, and the standard model identified Islam as Mormonism's best point of comparison. This association deflected the Mormon provocation to specific genealogical consideration, in a way, albeit through evocative concessions necessitating certain clarifications. On the one hand, the Mormons-to-Muslims comparison avoided judgments regarding the state of Mormon Jewishness and Jewish religious legitimacy, thus allowing congressional sidestepping of one familiar yet impolitic option: an acceptance of LDS claims to Jewish roots fueled by basic anti-Semitism, pursued in order that both traditions might be singly distanced from a Christian religious norm. Similarly, it avoided a second impolitic possibility: the substitution, via congressional adaptations of popular anti-Catholicism, of a Catholic comparate for a Jewish one.¹¹ At the same time, broadening the comparative pool beyond Jewish and Christian exempla entailed additional burdens of religious classification, and it conceded also Mormonism's relevance to global religious politics.

Morrill said that Mormons—with their "seraglios," "despotic" leaders, and "fanatical" adherents—were American "Turks" not American Jews, let alone

American Christians.¹² This was not an atypical rhetorical move. Early American reports on Mormonism had long likened it to Islam, and vice versa; since at least 1831 charges of 'American Mohammedanism' had echoed in various contexts and to multiple effect, with spikes in use predictably preceding the 1857 Utah War and the 1862 Anti-Bigamy Act. For most the comparison of Mormons and Muslims consisted in evocations of a putatively shared militarism, theocracy, polygamy, or sensuality and in references to their novel scriptures similarly devised by postbiblical and countercultural prophets. Anti-Muslim stereotypes had little relation to Islam as practiced by most Muslims, of course, and they bespoke an ignorance of America's own Muslim populations. But the purpose of the comparison was to signal Mormonism's alarming western installation of the same Oriental barbarisms that had supposedly threatened Christianity throughout the Middle East, Africa, and Asia. It "symbolically aligned" the "oriental and occidental frontiers," to quote historian Timothy Marr, thus "discrediting both religions through the association of their mutual distance from palatable Protestant practice." Indeed talk of American Muslims and American Turks evoked 'otherness' of distastefully religious and racial sorts, thereby mobilizing against Utahn Mormons (a predominantly Anglo population) racist and cultural stereotypes without necessarily claiming religious equivalence or ethnic descent. This is true equally in literary and political instances. In both, Mormon-to-Muslim comparisons used easy, ready-to-hand, and often superficial templates and similarities to pursue projects of deep, enduring cultural importance.¹³

Elaborately reductive in practice if not always intent, the putative Muslim connection invited new conversations while short-circuiting others, in any case rendering Mormonism more intelligible, less American, less white, and less biblical by making Mormons differently exotic and noteworthy. In this particular congressional instance, the Islamic reference accompanied noteworthy articulations of religious modernity and sincerity (as differentiated from barbarism and imposture), American Christianity, appropriate church-state relations, and the legal criteria for intervention in putatively religious institutions.

With respect to American church-state law, Morrill argued that First Amendment protections did not apply to polygamy because it was not an institution of religion. Polygamy was a crime—an offense to modern law and morality alike—and "the fullest latitude of toleration in the exercise of religion could not be understood to license crimes punishable at common law."¹⁴ Criminal acts could not be religious, and religious acts must not be criminal. This was common knowledge, according to Morrill. Thus any attempt to institute polygamy or theocracy—a form of governance unacceptable for territories under federal jurisdiction, Morrill said, given congressional church-state restrictions—was nothing but an act of "burlesque" perpetrated by "artful men" seeking "to hide under the name of religion."[15] Congress needn't question the sincerity of religious beliefs or call beliefs irreligious, but it had every right to denominate undesirable acts matters of irreligious imposture and to treat them as such. Proper religion consisted in intangibles held in good faith or in acts and institutions consonant with American common law and legislative statutes.[16]

Morrill summarized several of his arguments thus: "Under the guise of religion, this people has established, and seek to maintain and perpetuate, a Mohammedan barbarism revolting to the civilized world." Mormons' particular "guise of religion" was insultingly fanciful—people might as well claim that "burglary or rape" was "an act done in accordance with the religion of the prophet Mercury, or the prophet Priapus," he said—and yet it was recognizable to worldly persons, being comparable to 'Mohammedanism.'[17] As such, the crimes that Mormons instituted were 'barbaric' and 'uncivilized.' Latter-day Saints were unfit for survival in modern America, a nation founded upon truer and higher—and many said more Christian—fruitions of sociopolitical evolution.

IF MORRILL OUTLINED the basics of congressional religious theories relative to Mormonism, other lawmakers fastened them to the railroading death knell thesis by emphasizing their component notion of modernity—or Mormons' nonmodernity—and by stressing the functional equivalence of modernity, evolution, and industry. Among the more vocal members of this group was Representative William Waters Boyce (D-South Carolina)—a sometimes controversial figure whose notions of industrial religious intervention came to characterize the mainstream of mid- and late 1860s legislative thought.

During March 1858 considerations of anti-Mormon legislative possibilities, the southern Democrat Boyce agreed with his northern Republican colleague Morrill, and with other congressmen, on two basic points. First, Boyce concurred that First Amendment protections did not apply to the strange case of Mormon (ir)religion. The enlightened framers of the U.S. Constitution could not have expected that "an American Mohammed would rise up in the United States in the middle of the nineteenth century and promulgate a new dispensation, made up of Christianity and Oriental sensuality," Boyce said; and so they gave no guidelines for its treatment. Second, Boyce agreed that Mormonism's "sensuality"—its putative institutionalization of licentiousness and barbarism—and its location—in the middle of the country—equated to necessary intervention on the part of modern politicians. Under different circumstances politicians might usefully consider inaction, Boyce supposed, simply waiting and watching as Mormonism withered from its own incoherent Eastern-Western, Muslim-Christian hybridity. But Utah's location atop transcontinental trade and transportation routes, and thus Mormons' ability to harass California-bound emigrants or disrupt the eastward return of their capital gains, precluded that option.[18]

Boyce's more distinctive contribution to the conversation—and a point of disagreement between him and Morrill—was to encourage legislative, judicial, and military caution premised precisely on the 'facts' of Mormonism's sensationalism and centrality. He thought that strict legislation and enforcement of antipolygamy statutes ran the risk of dispersing Mormons throughout the country, where, by becoming "confederated with the Indian tribes" into "a race of American Arabs, they will become enemies of the human race," attacking emigrant trains and stunting economic development throughout the West. The terms of Boyce's concern speak to long-standing governmental interests in dominating western indigenous populations. They also speak to the ways in which 'Indians' were imagined as a third party within Mormon-Muslim comparisons, a party whose perceived proximity to Mormonism influenced both the degree and tenor of Arab evocations themselves. But Boyce's principal point was that it was better to keep Mormons contained in their own Great Basin reservation, even with their capacity for isolated overland disruptions. And better to surround them with industry than to scatter them through intervention.[19]

The best policy for the elimination of the 'Mormon problem,' according to Boyce, was the legislative encouragement of internal improvements: better roads, more telegraph wires, and, in time, a railroad. Envelop Mormons with economic and infrastructural development, he proposed, and give non-Mormon travelers, emigrants, and businessmen multiple options for traversing the Great Basin. Results would be positive. The religious facade of Mormonism would crack as Mormon men pursued out-group opportunities for commerce and conversation and as women pursued their "divine mission" of in-group, virtuous domestication. Boyce argued before the House of Representatives that "the greatest danger to the integrity of the Mormon faith is prosperity. The greater their material, moral, intellectual development, the less hold a false faith will have upon them. . . . In short, the more they become civilized, the less they are Mormons." Just as "the Turks, the Mormons of Europe, are perishing from contact with civilization," so too will prosperity destroy Mormonism. "Civilization is death to Mohammedanism or Mormonism."[20] Boyce's prediction was that prosperity and industry would bring civilization, civilization would bring schism, and schism would bring opportunities for more development. Mormonism, such as it existed around 1860, would be no longer.

Boyce's appeal represents a shift toward the railroading death knell thesis. Although Boyce agreed with Morrill and others that Mormonism constituted a threat to American morality and expansion, his proposal—rather than direct anti-Mormon military or political action—was the encouragement of (ostensibly) nonsectarian internal improvements and (definitely) non-Mormon business interests. Modern industry and pure capitalism would destroy premodern, hybrid forms of religion, economics, and politics.

CONGRESSIONAL ACTION IN THE 1860S, during and immediately after the Civil War, blended Morrill's interventionist priorities with Boyce's industrial assumptions, all the while retaining a shared language of religious barbarism. The Anti-Bigamy Act—passed and signed into law in 1862—banned bigamy, threatened offenders with fines and imprisonment, voided Utahn legislative acts protecting polygamous practice, and limited church property ownership in any U.S. territory to fifty thousand dollars. The goal was to reduce LDS Church control of territorial resources and real estate and, in the words of the act itself, to criminalize "the practice of polygamy, evasively called spiritual marriage, however disguised by legal or ecclesiastical solemnities, sacraments, ceremonies, consecrations, or other contrivances," without thereby "affect[ing] or interfer[ing] . . . with the right 'to worship God according to the dictates of conscience.'"[21] Congress, however, made neither financial appropriations nor official appointments for the law's enforcement. Some expected that the Pacific Railway Act, which passed the same year and authorized the construction of a transcontinental railroad across the American West, would obviate the need by substantially altering Utahn social, demographic, political, economic, and religious climates. By this logic, railroad agents would become covert officers of Anti-Bigamy Act provisions.

After signing the Anti-Bigamy Act into law, Abraham Lincoln agreed to an interview with T. B. H. Stenhouse, a Mormon newspaperman who had traveled to Washington to ascertain the president's legislative intentions. Stenhouse claimed that during the interview, Lincoln voiced a reticence to enforce the act, likening Mormonism to an intractable log in the middle of an agricultural field: "Stenhouse, when I was a boy on the farm in Illinois there was a great deal of timber on the farms which we had to clear away. Occasionally we would come to a log which had fallen down. It was too hard to split, too wet to burn and too heavy to move, so we plowed around it. That's what I intend to do with the Mormons." Although the story is likely apocryphal—Stenhouse's contemporary recollections are less colorful, containing no agricultural references and indicating only a basic interest in peaceful relations—the metaphor is nevertheless apt.[22] Having registered its disapproval of LDS practices and institutions, the federal government planned to proceed with the business of territorial development in the spaces around the church and to maneuver its machinery there as possible and necessary. It was a political path of least resistance, in many respects; preoccupied with the Civil War, Lincoln and his subordinates were content to let Mormon matters rest for a time, thus avoiding active and costly conflict on multiple fronts. But it was also a path of industrial trust and territorial assumption. The Civil War Congress subcontracted the tasks of western economic development, national cohesion, and religious regulation to capitalists and speculators.

The Pacific Railway Act and the Religion of Business Legislation

Proponents of the 1862 Pacific Railway Act sought to make it "worthy of favorable consideration by capitalists" and to convince businessmen that transcontinental railroads would be both "profitable to themselves, and of great value to our country."[23] In its final form, the plan granted several key benefits to two railroad companies: rights of way through public lands, with extinguishment or settlement of Indian titles and squatter claims as necessary; between sixteen thousand and forty-eight thousand dollars in government bonds for each mile of track built, depending on terrain; and, most controversially, alternate sections of public domain on each side of the route, which the railroads could then sell to fund the project. The Central Pacific and Union Pacific Railroads—responsible for building lines east from California and west from Nebraska, respectively, with plans of meeting at a spot yet to be determined in the middle—received some ten square miles of public domain per mile of track, thus becoming major western landholders and landlords. The act was a watershed instance of American public-private cooperation, different both in scale and in effect from earlier attempts at internal improvement through land grants.[24] It was distinct by measure of rhetorical content and project drift, too. The act overlapped significantly with concurrent cultural and religious interests, alternately bisecting, encompassing, and combining them in discussion and practice.

It is in certain respects unsurprising that discussions of the Pacific Railway Act, one of the largest land-granting acts of American history, conveyed many contemporaneous social concerns. As historian Richard White has noted, land grants have throughout the nation's history "served as a sort of seal of approval

John Gast, *American Progress*, 1872. (Chromolithograph published by
George A. Crofutt; courtesy of Prints and Photographs Division,
Library of Congress, Washington, D.C.)

for social consensus"—or at least as an indication of governmental priorities and efforts at consensus building.[25] Applications for and announcements of grants are thus robust sources for the identification of arguments about 'public goods,' in the sense both of the resources deemed available to government agents and of the social programs considered most needful of their help or most beneficial for local and national development. The Pacific Railway Act is no exception, and its discussions show a Civil War Congress deeply concerned with the West as a site of necessary national expansion and limitless individual prosperity that must be saved, as such, from undeserving indigenous and foreign populations alike. In practice, the land-granting priorities of the act often ran up against those of the other principal land acts of 1862, the Homestead Act and the Land-Grant College Act, which promised grants, respectively, in support of small farms and schools of agricultural education. Yet the amassing of acreage by absentee industrialist landlords was seen (if it was seen at all) as a necessary step in the direction of western connectivity and the very accessibility of America's new homesteads, farms, and markets. The famous chromolithograph *American Progress* expresses well the hopes and presumptions of this legislative trio in their most nationalistic and racialized inflections: American industry would work hand in hand with American settlers to spread American liberties and American public schools throughout the West, scattering undomesticated animals and Indians before them.²⁶

Religious ideas and rhetorics ran throughout popular and political discussions of the 1862 land-granting acts in ways both precedented and unique. Earlier such acts in the country's history had similarly echoed religious concerns, referring, for instance, to Indians as savage barbarians with consequently negligible sovereignty claims; internal improvements as instruments of America's divinely authorized expansion; yeoman farmers as exempla of Protestant self-mastery; and public schools as bastions of nonsectarian Christian morality. However they generally avoided allocating resources specifically for or against religious groups as such. (To be clear: this is not to say that religious groups and initiatives have not benefited from federal land-grant policy but rather to state that their benefits have been bestowed in sometimes indirect or unobvious ways. The government decided not to allocate lands directly to religious organizations in the Land Ordinance of 1785 or the Northwest Ordinance of 1787, for instance, but rather to set lands aside for the support of public schools. Insofar as these schools were in turn expected to teach general religious and moral values, though, they became sites of renewed contention and occasions for new institution and coalition building among different religious groups. Similar processes followed upon the Land-Grant College Act of 1862.) The Pacific Railway Act is unusual in that—in good part because of its perceived overlap with the Anti-Bigamy Act—the potential religious effects of its land grants and industrial charters were discussed openly and often. Whether by virtue of railroad tracks' very physicality, because of religion's assumed relationship to technological modernity generally, or through the trickle-down land-distributing efforts of presumptively moral railroad companies themselves, the Union Pacific and Central Pacific were explicitly expected to serve religious interests by carving up Mormon lands and making available other lands for more 'mainstream' communities. The Railway Act catalyzed powerful constructions of religion as a 'public good' of and for the industrializing West.²⁷

CONGRESSIONAL DISCUSSIONS of railroad construction mentioned Mormonism in important respects and contexts, often outlining the anti-LDS presumptions of the act. Mormonism came up when politicians debated the most expedient route to the Pacific Coast, for example—specifically when some outlined a modified Overland Trail route along the Platte River, through the South Pass, and around the Great Salt Lake.²⁸ Representative Francis Preston Blair Jr. (D-Missouri) noted that the only obstacles anyone had encountered there were "the destruction of the grass by the Mormons, and the artificial barricades with which they have defended" Echo Canyon and other "passes of the mountains" during the so-called Utah War. But continuing Mormon presence was a point in favor of that route, by his account, more than against it. Samuel Curtis (R-Iowa) developed the argument in this way: the central route was easygoing through "the Mormon settlement," he said, "where we have a population of at least forty thousand, and an army of two or three thousand, with which we must have constant communication." The American government would benefit from improved communication with Salt Lake Valley residents and administrators, particularly given their self-professed distance from other national groups. The fact of an established military presence—troops having been stationed in Utah since the 1857–58 Expedition, tasked variously with ongoing projects of emigrant escorting, mine hunting, infrastructure protecting, Indian chasing, and Mormon watching—only made industrial proximity and communicative expediency more appealing.²⁹

Railroads could have aided the suppression of Mormon crimes in the past, and they would help with similar tasks in the future—while enforcing new antibigamy legislation, for example. The Utah Expedition had been a costly venture, and in the words of one congressman, the U.S. government continued to spend considerable sums in the "management of the Indians, Mormons, Pacific commerce, mails, &c."³⁰ The transcontinental railroad would cut such costs significantly, at the same time securing the Pacific Coast from possible schism or colonization. The railroad "is essential for national defense," said Senator Stephen Douglas (D-Illinois). "It is essential, if we are to have foreign wars, in order to protect the Pacific coast. It is essential, if we are to have Indian wars."³¹ Senator Jefferson Davis (D-Mississippi) agreed, and he added, with reference to the Utah War: "If this road had been built, it would not have been necessary to have made that expedition across the country, *if indeed it could have been possible that the Mormons would have taken the attitude of rebellion at all.*"³²

The final notion became basic to 1860s Mormon policy, even after Davis's departure from Washington. Rebellion is difficult when groups are connected by railroad, it said; or, to reverse the order: railroads have a pacifying, unifying, even moral effect on peoples. "The railroad itself is likely to perform a missionary work among the Mormons, more pacific and less expensive than the carrying of troops and munitions of war," wrote one Baltimore reporter.³³ Railroads were considered to be agents of culture and Congress alike.

During the buildup to the Civil War, congressmen spoke often about the unifying and moralizing potential of railroad industry. "The evil of our time is sectionalism," said Senator William H. Seward (R-New York) in 1860. But the railroad can help "bind the Northeast and the Northwest, and the Southeast and the Southwest, and North and South, and East and West, by a physical, material bond of indissoluble union." Railroads are "facilities for communication, commerce, and affection," Seward said, and they "bind together and assimilate discontented and ill-assorted communities." Through railroad-building projects, northern and southern states could (according to Missouri representative J. R. Barret) join "into a united effort for national progress, national defense, and national welfare," thereby creating (said California senator Milton Latham) a "solid arch, spanning our distant oceanic shores, upon which the whole fabric [of a national culture] may rest as upon an iron foundation."[34] Separation and barbarism would be destroyed, and a common national ethos would roll westward over the continent.

That Mormonism would be altered beneficially by this "fabric" was a point of general, hopeful agreement. Representatives Godlove S. Orth (R-Indiana) and Aaron F. Stevens (R-New Hampshire) expressed well the religious, economic, and political presumptions of the death knell thesis when they proclaimed, in celebration of the Union Pacific Railway's charter, that "the progress and completion of this work will ... tend to solve political problems which have troubled, and do yet trouble, the wisest statesmanship. The Territory of Utah, with its one hundred thousand deluded human beings—with its mis-named religion, a shame and a blot upon our fair name—will be pierced and crossed by the Pacific Railroad," and thereafter "the sensuality of the Mormon, shall give way to the progress of civilization, commerce and Christianity."[35] Many of their colleagues in the Civil War and Reconstruction era congresses concurred. But some politicians had even grander religious plans, setting sights well beyond the Pacific: "The route to India will be opened, science and knowledge will be transmitted to the heathen shores of Hindos, and those that sit in darkness will rejoice in the light of revelation. The power of steam, the extension of railways, and intercourse by electricity, will unite the world."[36] Industry and technology would spread culture, awakening, unity, and modernity near and far.

THUS WHILE POLITICIANS considered plans by which to enforce the Morrill Anti-Bigamy Act, some people fixed on railroad companies as both substitute armies and peacemakers and as part of a larger program of constructive religious action. Railroads were imagined partly as implementing partners of the act's initiatives, as agents destined to bring about their fruition following years of procrastination and inefficiency. Yet they were imagined also to obviate the necessity of legislative implementation, thus defending further delay of action. Either way, railroads, railroad agents, and railroad riders would do what others could not: choke out the Mormon menace. A San Francisco journalist stated the principle this way: "The remedy against the evils of Mormonism is not to be found in Federal legislation; it must be looked for in the increasing power and progress of a civilization radically hostile to Mormon ideas," as spread, for example, through "the establishment of railway stations at short distances from the Mormon towns."[37] Legislation *could* aid in the latter respect, of course, but this was foremost—or at least first—the business of businessmen.

The Technological Sublime: A Sentiment in Training

Congress's willingness to subcontract matters of religious regulation to transcontinental railroad builders was consistent with the popular association of technology, morality, and religion found elsewhere in American culture. These associations were both specific—wielded, that is, by particular religious groups to specifically denominational ends—and general—phrased often in nonspecifically Protestant terms of divine mechanics and the ideal correspondence between private reason and public systems. In either case bolstered by the discourse of manifest destiny, the transcontinental companies rode high their net gains to the West Coast and back.

Railroads and associated technologies have been invested with religious significance in numerous arenas of American history and historiography. As scholars have often noted, many religious activists joined congressmen in applauding new media of communication and transportation, experiencing them as signs of Providence and using them to expedite missionary work; and others thrilled in humanity's machine-aided and godlike power to transcend erstwhile limitations of time and space, for instance, when speeding across distant lands recently prepared for national expansion. Merchants' magazines advertised haymakers and steam engines as harbingers of the millennium, while Spiritualists saw telegraphy as proof and metaphor for other interdimensional modes of communication.[38] Pastors and laypeople evoked Isaiah 11:16's "highway for the remnant of [God's] people" and Revelation 10:6's "there should be time no longer" when speaking of railroad travel or the hastening of Jesus's return.[39] Attributing the powers of modern technology to Divine Grace, human ingenuity, or both, such champions interwove motifs of manifest destiny and manifest divinity, celebrating simultaneously the conquest of nature and the fruition of God's design.

Champions of tech-savvy religiousness and the widgets of missionary expansion were often generically or specifically Protestant. This was true not only because businessmen sought the aid of Protestant pastors when endeavoring to indoctrinate laborers into what sociologist Max Weber termed a particularly Protestant work ethic, a life characterized by sober industriousness and modest comportment. Neither was it true only because Protestant groups rallied to rebrand certain religious preferences and principles—readings from the King James Bible, celebrations of state disestablishment, and critiques of ecclesiastical hierarchy, for instance—as 'nonsectarian' and thus as worthy of financial support in public schools planted along new western transportation routes. The peculiar proximity of Protestant and technological interests in the Americas was forged also through epistemological affinity and the mutual embrace of the secular.

Recent scholarship by Talal Asad, Tracy Fessenden, Pamela E. Klassen, John Modern, and Winnifred Fallers Sullivan, among others, has shown how secular principles of democratic order in nineteenth-century America and the West were characterized by and constituted through Protestant power—in the Foucauldian if not also juridical sense. American politicians, literati, businessmen, lawyers, physicians, metaphysicians, and Protestant apologists often shared the desire to differentiate between 'public' (political, legal, and economic) and 'private' (religious) aspects of life, with each operating according to complementary principles of republican or common-sense reasoning. By their divisions Protestantism itself remained both the implicit model of 'right religion' and also a de facto and de jure fixture of political life, for—according to this logic—it was liberal Protestantism and Protestants that most successfully eschewed the types of public cultic activity, magical thinking, and theocratic governance that characterized Catholic or pagan societies. Riding the waves of mass media and technological development, then, and seeing in the machine an effective analogue for divine order, each with its own legible logic, these Protestant politicians pushed westward their calls for republican self-mastery and religious privatization. Expanding such nineteenth-century 'secular' ideals was thus simultaneously—if not centrally—an affair of particular religious interest.[40]

Relationships among Protestants, politicians, corporations, and technocrats were not necessarily easy or celebratory, though, such connections notwithstanding. To dig deep into the history of any single datum used to support the idea of a generalized Protestant, progressive, protechnology consensus is to reveal considerable corporate contention and multiple conflicting interests.

Take, for example, the case of the Western Railroad Corporation from 1838. The company, having difficulty completing its lines in western Massachusetts, not only applied for aid from the state legislature but had its agents send a message to area ministers begging their "assistance on this great work" by "deliver[ing] a Discourse before your Congregation, on the moral effect of railroads in our wide extended country." Much to the directors' disappointment, however, the request called forth rather more outrage and embarrassment than pan-pulpit support; ministers and newspaper reporters charged company men with overstepping their corporate bounds and with conflating church, company, and government in a manner unbefitting disestablishmentarian principles and religious freedom. The Western Railroad thus learned that, while many general statements respecting the religious effects of mechanical development and technological expansion were considered palatable, outright directions to ministers and scripts for sermonic pronouncement were not. At least not yet.[41]

How best to explain such moments of friction and religious hesitation vis-à-vis the railroading advances of corporate America? One interpretive possibility, deployed sometimes by students of the secular, derives from a large body of scholarship on the so-called 'technological sublime' in America. This literature and lens—arguably the most influential frame for understanding relations between religion and technology in and across the fields of American studies, American history, and American religious history—posits, provocatively, that nineteenth-century Americans responded to telegraphs, steamboats, and railroads with a mixture of awe and anxiety, wonder and terror—a *mysterium tremendum et fascinans*, as phenomenologist of religion Rudolph Otto would have it. Generally Americans were enthusiastic about mechanical development, but according to this scholarly line, their championship sometimes contained also an undercurrent of existential concern that machines might sap life of a measure of interpersonal intimacy, authenticity, and quietude; that they might be worshipped directly in place of God; or that they might pollute nature and otherwise destroy an ordained order among humans, the divine, and the environment. Some people were trepidatious, that is, but their trepidation itself might be explained as an integral part of a larger religious response complex to technological advance.[42]

The rhetoric of the technological sublime is indeed peppered throughout nineteenth-century literature, periodicals, sermons, and journals. Nathaniel Hawthorne wrote both of a train whistle sharpening his appreciation of nature (in *The American Notebooks*) and of a railroad as the idol and chariot of hell-bound, environment-destroying convenience-seekers (in "The Celestial Railroad"); and Mark Twain suggested that steamboats resembled fire-breathing demons to the ignorant and uninitiated. Meanwhile Walt Whitman's

"Passage to India" shared with Civil War era congressmen an excitement about technology-enabled encounters with the religious Far East, albeit with a more ambiguous sense of the proper direction or evolution of influence; railroads evoked longing for "The Past!" he wrote, even as they prepared new paths to messianic harmony by connecting people to each other and to ancient wisdom.[43] Such double-sided language is ubiquitous, and—although its meaning was not always consistent—even the most gestural of references to the technological sublime arguably partook in a culture wherein more and more people evoked almost mechanically the moral mandates of machines.

The technological sublime, however, was never really a pure state or a sui generis sentiment, and neither do its supposed trepidations map well onto the corporate reticence of (say) Massachusetts pastors in 1838—except, I would argue, as a form of mischaracterization acting as ideological cover. By challenging the basic and pure explanatory power of the technological sublime, I mean not simply that it consists in ambivalent feelings or the conjoining of euphoria, hope, and terror—the kind of tense experiential or artistic reconciliations of pastoral and technological powers expressed by the favored subjects of Leo Marx, David E. Nye, and other like scholars of sublimity. Rather, I mean that technology, mass media, and politics shape notions of the natural and the pastoral in the first place, and so too of the right or wrong, awed or terrified religious sentiments purportedly catalyzed by encounter between things 'modern' and 'premodern' or by overlap between things 'corporate' and 'churchly.' The technological sublime was a corporate project, one that partook in the amplification of particular Protestant and republican ideals about mirrored legibility across public and private spheres and about the reassuring senses of connectivity and calculability. Assertions respecting certain groups' fears of the railroad were often component products of nineteenth-century progressives' work to cultivate right religious sentiment relative to the apocalyptic powers of technology by stressing the awesomeness of mechanical connections and by projecting reticence on either the unlettered or unprincipled.

By the Civil War era—as more northeasterners and midwesterners rallied behind the idea of network building through Chicago and the Great West, and as many Protestant denominations designed novel missionary enterprises along new western highways—businessmen, bureaucrats, and pastors had all come to recognize that 'positive' religious responses to and for railroads had to be trained. This was done, for instance, through the increasingly normative practice—itself derived from customs common among American tollcollectors since the eighteenth century—of granting reduced-price fares to clergy members or by limiting passenger services or charging conductors with scripture readings on Sundays. Or else it was done by offering free lands to large denominations in order that they might build churches in major western towns, thereby making good on public expectations that government land grants be routed somehow to religious ends, or through other lobbying efforts less ham-handed than that of the Western Railroad.[44] Crucially, though, such groups also recognized that 'negative' responses could be usefully and lucratively feigned, for instance, in an emergent romantic literature about "The Past!" and the 'ancient wisdom,' 'frontier virtues,' and 'pre-technological nature' to which trains promised new access and analytical purchase, on the one hand, or about the 'superstitious misunderstandings' purportedly underlying more fearful opposition, on the other. We will encounter several novel corporate constructions of western antiquity, awe, superstition, and haunting alike in the chapters that follow. But the point here is that many railroad officials and champions partook both in the fabrication of the overarching complex concept of 'technological sublimity' and also in the sublimation or shoehorning of inconvenient responses under one or the other of its purportedly complementary sentiments.

Increasingly throughout the second half of the nineteenth century, critiques of technological millennialism—whether rooted in corporate suspicions and revelations of backroom dealing (as in 1838 Massachusetts) or in anticolonial concerns about death and survival (as among Whitman's idealized primitives or Twain's backwoods bumpkins)—were less often allowed continuing popular recognition as such than as expressions of a kind of quaint or questionable religious conservatism, on the one hand, or as the superstition-inflected misrecognition of sublimity itself, when acting in its terror mode, on the other. Between such 'confusions' and the blind idolatry of Hawthorne's hell-bound railroad-riders was said to be the middle ground of the progressive middle class: the space of true modern religion, and of its righteous balance of awe and concern. This was ideological argumentation and social construction of a most powerful sort. Indeed it was far *more* powerful, in this particular corporate admixture, than either the purportedly unified technoreligious secular or the purportedly Janus-faced technological sublime on its own.

The historiography of the technological sublime is thus itself inadequate to explain how and when railroads had religious effects or affects, insofar as it fails often to trace either as constructs of the corporate. Meanwhile the historiography of the secular seems sometimes to occlude temporal or institutional gaps in its proposed consensuses or else to plug them by recourse again to the concepts of the sublime or the subliminal. However the two point well, together, to the fact of the secular *as* practice rather than *in* practice. That is to say, in this case, that they point to techno-Protestant subjectivity as a practice never precisely of achievement but rather of periodic managerial debate, a debate variously promoted and incorporated over time and space.[45]

THE TRANSCONTINENTAL RAILROAD companies were chartered, through an act of government, during a swell of such ideological presumption respecting the righteous investment of middle-class moral sentiment in network-building technologies, particularly for the West. They drew continuing strength from it, too, especially as large Protestant denominations signed on to the project of railroading religion and partook in the corporate construct of the technological sublime, that is, as denominations proclaimed anew their particular commensurability with technological modernity and predicted therefore the imminent demise of superstition.

The Church on the Railroad: Denominational Mainlines

If technology and railroading projects were conducive to and cultivated through the spread of nonspecific Protestantism, they were also occasions for specifically Protestant denominational efforts. American Presbyterians were one group that harmonized denominational interests with the death knell thesis in part by deploying the rhetorical move described above. Claiming a particular religious affinity for modern network society and projecting superstitious sentiment on the Latter-day pagans of Utah, Presbyterians proclaimed themselves the quintessential church of the railroad era West.

Sheldon Jackson was the chief architect of Presbyterian expansion in the railroad era. Indeed, he was more than that: Jackson reorganized American Presbyterianism specifically *for* the railroad era, and both anti-Mormonism (generally) and Corinne (specifically) featured prominently in his western designs. In the terms of the death knell thesis, his was among "the orthodox churches of the land" that, according to one reporter, awaited "the opportunity that the railroad will give" to "throw themselves against the spurious monster of Utah."[46] The other "orthodox" churches included the American Methodists, Baptists, Episcopalians, and Congregationalists. These denominations shared Presbyterians' basic concern with the West as a site of simultaneous religious peril and promise, a concern paradigmatically expressed by Lyman Beecher's 1835 *Plea for the West*: that it be fortified through institutions of Protestant morality, discipline, and education against the anarchic and un-American influences of Catholicism, barbarism, immigration, and unbelief. (Later in the century Josiah Strong's best-selling book *Our Country* added Mormonism to this list of "perils.")⁴⁷ After 1869 each of these denominations raised funds through its home missions society for railside work in the West, and each considered railroads to be an opportunity, means, and blueprint for religious formation. In both respects they encouraged an association with transcontinental railroads likely responsible for the easy adoption, in later years, of 'mainline' as a synonym for 'orthodox' and 'mainstream' Protestantism. 'Mainline' Protestants commonly plotted western churches in conjunction with railroading campaigns against disorder.⁴⁸

According to legend, Jackson stood atop an Iowa hill in April 1869, looked westward at "the great unchurched areas," and prayed for those "destitute" regions without "a single Presbyterian church." By then the Central Pacific Company, building eastward from Sacramento, had reached the flats of eastern Nevada, and the Union Pacific, building westward from Omaha, had reached the northeastern shores of the Great Salt Lake in Utah, near Corinne. The final route was yet to be determined, and so were the locations of the main railroad hub and other major company towns. Nevertheless Jackson determined that he would frequent them wherever they may be, making "the Union Pacific Railroad [his] mission ground" and thus "win[ning] the West for Christ."⁴⁹

Jackson's proposed "Church on the Pacific Railroad" was designed principally for working and managerial classes of Anglo settler-colonists affiliated with orthodox Protestant denominations. Especially targeted were east-to-west migrants who might forget the staples of eastern virtue—sober comportment and Sabbath observation among them—and fall to drinking and stealing and "making gold their god."⁵⁰ Jackson realized that the industrial settlements of the West were not inherently moral places; it was with good reason, after all, that newspapermen popularized the term "hell on wheels" to describe the shantytowns of "saloon keepers, gamblers, desperadoes of every grade, [and] the vilest of men and of women" that bloomed briefly at labor camps along the transcontinental line.⁵¹ Organized effort was required to fulfill the heavenly potential of railroad extension, and Jackson's mission was to convert mining towns and other hell-on-wheels outposts to hubs of networked piety.

Only in a secondary sense was Jackson's transcontinental scheme concerned with American Indians or other so-called exceptional populations, the Presbyterian missiological category that included also Hispanos, New Mexicans, and Mormons. Nevertheless, Mormonism emerged as a special concern for Jackson—and also for his donors—for several interrelated reasons. Its Utahn headquarters sitting astride the projected rail route, and its followers being themselves predominantly white, the LDS Church, Jackson feared, might sway the souls and minds of his primary target population. One supposed aspect of Mormon life and doctrine was thought to be particularly appealing to westward-bound migrants, as well: its materialism. According to many Presbyterian apologists of the era, Mormons failed to understand proper public-private and spirit-matter divisions, with LDS leaders exercising control over political and economic affairs and with church members speaking of God as a material being and of salvation as a matter of priestly agency. Insofar as western migrants might already be inclined to deify mundane things, Jackson was encouraged to expend special energy keeping them from Mormon delusions. Jackson worked to teach them instead the sole possibility of both national and individual salvation through liberal economics and Calvinistic self-discipline.[52]

POSITIVE THAT ANGLO COLONISTS would benefit from—and Mormon leaders would fear—the incursion of rail-riding ministers into lands of erstwhile unruliness and materialistic superstition, Jackson convinced representatives from the presbyteries of Missouri River, Des Moines, and Fort Dodge, Iowa, that the time was ripe for ecclesiastical expansion. Jackson argued, and they agreed, that Presbyterianism was especially well suited to the railroad age: its ecclesiastical polity allowed for congregation-level adaptations to distinctive frontier concerns while retaining a regional identity and national systems of support and authority; and it had well-established arms of colportage, education, and fund-raising. Moreover, the denomination drew its membership from "the cream of society," and western businessmen would surely advocate for congregation building and the pacific participation of their workers. Jackson anticipated also the support of railroad officials, men with their own vested interests in the settlement and middle-class piety of company employees, and he secured from them reduced-fare clergy passes as well as the promise to donate lands in major towns for church buildings.[53]

Meanwhile, American Presbyterianism stood updating in one major respect, in addition to needing new missionary districts and officers corresponding to railroad advances. The West being large, and its populations being far-flung and often rowdy, newly appointed ministers could use "a slight dash of Methodist extemporaneousness." By this Jackson meant a willingness occasionally to embrace itinerancy and discard sermonic formality, preaching in taverns and town halls as necessary until railroad companies made good on their land grants and until congregations, boards, synods, and assemblies could support regular meetings.[54]

Appointed superintendent of missions for Iowa, Nebraska, Dakota, Montana, Wyoming, and Utah, Jackson was authorized to devise systems and appoint personnel by which—to cite the headline of one denominational reporter—

the West might be "occupied for Presbyterianism." The basic plan, as Jackson explained it, was for church agents to "occupy every important point on the line of the Union Pacific Railway extending from the Missouri River across the plains and over the mountains to Nevada," forming churches in both new and newly accessible towns as quickly as possible. Jackson assigned three people to different stretches of transcontinental track: one took areas between Omaha, Nebraska, and Julesburg, Colorado; another those between Julesburg and Rawlins, Wyoming; and a third, the Reverend Melancthon Hughes, those between Rawlins and northern Utah. These were considerable jurisdictional distances even in railroad terms; Hughes's area, for example, was some 290 linear miles. Therefore, their actions were to be cursory, preliminary, and strategic. After choosing one town as his base, each missionary was to visit other settlements as quickly as he could, preach there at regular intervals, ascertain community interests and resources for permanent church formation, and report back to his superiors. Jackson and others would then follow their lead, traveling to towns of reported promise, moving how and where the train moved. "The train whistles, and I must be off westward," Jackson wrote to an eastern readership during one such trip, after reporting on Presbyterian prospects at Cheyenne, Wyoming. Meanwhile, Jackson worked to raise money among that same readership in order to backfill his and his compatriots' paths with the infrastructure of Presbyterianism: schools, churches, pastors, pastorates, presbyteries, synods, and missionary overseers.[55]

Jackson was an extremely effective architect of ecclesiastical infrastructure, and his railroad plan substantially affected Presbyterian appearance and distribution in America. By his count Jackson and his three supervisees organized twenty-two churches "in that memorable year" of 1869, almost all of which survived it and the 1870s to follow. (As of 1876 there were some sixty-seven church communities and thirty-six church buildings in the area of Jackson's oversight.) Their efforts also catalyzed the creation of new ecclesiastical offices and the expansion of others. Jackson himself was promoted from superintendent to district missionary; and after the northern Old School and New School Presbyterian churches reunited in 1870, they gratified Jackson's hilltop vision by making western expansion a key component of their joint operation. The newly formed Board of Home Missions built on Jackson's foundations by further redistricting and subdividing the western mission fields and by staffing them more fully. It created the Presbytery of Colorado to include churches in Utah, Montana, Wyoming, and Colorado, for example; and it appointed new superintendents to the mission fields of Nebraska and Dakota. By 1897 Jackson was a nationwide denominational hero, and the general assembly honored his western labors by appointing him moderator.[56]

Jackson's fund-raising methods were also far-ranging and fruitful. When Jackson became supervisor of missions for Iowa, Utah, and neighboring territories in 1869, the position came with no salary, and he understood that the presbyteries and church boards had few available resources to help him. But Jackson managed to raise over ten thousand dollars between May 1869 and December 1870, and he recorded another eight thousand dollars in donations for 1870–71. Contributions to Jackson's "Raven Fund" came from people compelled by his project of (in the words of one Illinois-based donor of five dollars) "spreading the gospel of Jesus along the great Pacific Railroad."[57]

Donors' interest was piqued largely through reports of western projects printed in the East, where articles on Mormon irreligion were regular features of church newspapers and western missions reports. One series by the Reverend Frank F. Ellinwood was also followed closely by Jackson, who clipped and saved it in his personal scrapbook alongside reports on his own efforts. The subject was that "vexed question" of admitting Utah and its Mormons to the status and rights of statehood, and Ellinwood argued that they were unacceptable as they were: polygamous and theocratic, with large families, "strange mystic ceremony," and fanatical ignorance all precluding national incorporation. "What shall be done with Utah?" Ellinwood asked. "How shall our Government disintegrate a social mass so formidable and bound together" by civil, ecclesiastical, fraternal, and secretive ties? For his part, Ellinwood hinted at the possibility of another civil war lest Christian missionaries find some better way of combating Mormonism. But Jackson was confident that the railroads—and, in time, the hopeful city of Corinne—would help him ring both Mormon death knells and Presbyterian church bells.[58]

The Corinnethian Congregation: Beadle's Call to Arms

Corinne's founders were well aware of national presumptions, political rhetoric, and denominational initiatives respecting the moral and Morrill work of the railroads, and they hoped to leverage them into local business and public policy, by planting a new metropolis precisely at the site of their overlapping interests. The earliest town planners and residents represented diverse vocations and religious backgrounds. There were, for instance, Catholic military men and miners, Congregationalist territorial appointees, Episcopalian Wells Fargo agents, Jewish retailers, ex-Mormon merchants, and denominationally unaffiliated reporters, not to mention also the populations that they often elected to ignore: Chinese launderers, Indian traders, and white laborers variously interested or uninterested in religion. But J. H. Beadle—the newspaperman and booster most responsible for crafting religious common grounds and significance for Corinne—expressed a conglomerate ethos when he wrote: "We are Methodist, our first friends Episcopalian, our warmest supporters Hebrew, and we still desire the help of the Catholics." Beadle's Corinnethians had in common a certain 'Gentility'—non-Mormonism—and a basic familiarity with western business and development schemes. And they were not tone deaf. Watching as the Central and Union Pacific lines approached on either side of the Great Salt Lake in early 1869, they set up camp at one possible junction point along their anticipated route, singing the praises of a non-Mormon railroad hub, hoping to catch the attention of politicians, businessmen, railroad agents, missionaries, and homesteaders alike. "All parties 'close up' and front the common foe," Beadle wrote. "Don't waste a shot!"[59]

Beadle's call to arms involved elaborate arguments about world religions in general, American religious history in particular, Mormon origins, racial identity and progress, national commerce, western development, and secularity—each component of which echoed or elaborated similar themes from popular and political discussions. Such arguments were developed in multiple venues over time, but their most complete articulation was his *Life in Utah; or, The Mysteries and Crimes of Mormonism* (1870), a book published within two years of Beadle's arrival in Utah.[60]

BEADLE, BORN IN 1840 IN INDIANA, was a midwestern Republican of a self-consciously (if not conflictingly) Jacksonian ilk; he was a supporter of the Civil War Congress's nationalizing economic initiatives on the grounds that they, though industrial development and settlement incentives, might maintain the American West as a self-determining site of democratic individualism, simple virtue, and frontier manliness. Like Justin S. Morrill and William Waters Boyce before him, Beadle saw in Mormonism a blight on the countryside and the resurgence of forms antithetical to the Republic: autocracy, theocracy, polygamy, and barbarism. Like them too, he saw in Mormonism a likeness to 'Mohammedanism,' particularly "in the relations of the sexes." But Beadle expanded on congressional theories regarding Mormons' monstrous attempts to mix Islam with Christianity. Drawing from a long history of Christian polemics, he did so by positing a number of other influences and precedents, 'Oriental' and otherwise, and also by explaining their particular assemblage in light of American religious contexts and global racial developments. Beadle saw in Mormonism evidence of Manicheism and Gnosticism, as well as Voodoo, 'Fetichism,' and Buddhism.[61]

Beadle's American religious history sought to understand why premodern thoughts and practices would resurface then and there, in nineteenth-century America. His argument was that uniquely American and generally positive conditions of liberty, disestablishment, ethnic pluralism, and frontier democracy, combined with the revivals and schisms of the so-called Second Great Awakening, served also as seedbeds for social aberrance and speculative confusion. "America is the paradise of heterodoxy," he wrote, a place where "wild, strange and even abominable religions flourish unchecked, side by side." Such heterodoxy was to be expected, even celebrated, in America; "where every man is free to choose as he will, it is reasonable to suppose that many will choose but poorly." The problem with Mormonism, Beadle argued, was that it combined the worst elements of American religious experimentation—the most alarming "jerks," enthusiasms, and social transgressions of early nineteenth-century camp meetings, for example—with the basest possible desires for immediate revelation and personal divination. Mormonism told common American people that their lives and circumstances had meaning, but it also encouraged them to imagine themselves as privileged and unbeholden to mundane limitations. This is the point at which it began to transcend the natural, the understandable, and the appropriate, Beadle said. It "controverted the inherent American idea" of liberty when "it turned back to sensualism for its inspiration, and to despotism for its model."[62] Mormonism elevated prophets, built kingdoms, and otherwise formed obstinate social blocs in areas of democratic promise. Similarly it instituted polygamy and resuscitated heresy. Mormons' Oriental and theocratic responses to America's western liberties were fundamentally unacceptable, according to Beadle.

Mormon innovations and regressions would not have survived as long as they had, Beadle wrote, if not for their isolation. Fearing "contact with vital Christianity," Mormons have "long managed to avoid whatever contact would weaken their organization," most recently by moving to the Great Basin and refusing Gentile society, commerce, and industry. Hence the situation of Mormonism in 1850s and 1860s America, according to Beadle: having grown beyond its marginal Second Great Awakening status and having established its warlike mentality and corrupted Christianity deep within the American West, Mormonism developed the practical, Oriental, and theocratic aspects of its hybrid assemblage, thus further racializing and distancing itself from a palatable mainstream. In Utah, Mormons had solidified their "system of voting solidly, at the dictation of a few men"; and they had intensified efforts at in-group solidarity through hostility to exogamous trade and social intercourse.[63] Mormons threatened Americanism from within by importing persons, practices, and ideas from without.

BEADLE'S ANALYSIS of Mormon development within global and American religious history culminated in a crescendo of death knell promises and Corinnethian promotions. Corinne was the answer to the Mormon question, he said, and it was the rightful fruition of previous anti-Mormon efforts and white colonization projects in northern Utah. By consolidating "Gentile power ... in the northern counties, along the railroad," Corinne's inhabitants would "eventually liberalize that section of Mormonism," drawing residents away from Brigham Young's stronghold and into the open arms of liberal capitalism, nationalism, monogamy, and true Christianity.

Lest Beadle's readers be concerned about Indian as well as Mormon populations in Utah, Beadle alleged that the Bear River Valley had been 'cleared' for Anglo Americans some seven years earlier by General Patrick E. Connor. Stationed in the northern Great Basin after the 1857 Mormon War to protect overland mail and immigrant routes, General (then Colonel) Connor directed a regiment of California Volunteers in 1863 to attack and kill over 250 Shoshonis in the upper Bear River Valley, just north of the future Corinne; and he later promoted mining interests there and in southern Utah with hopes of also supplanting Mormon populations with Gentile workforces. Beadle applauded the Indian-killing and Mormon-hating soldier as having inaugurated "the 'golden age' of Gentiles in Utah," and several of his writings celebrated Connor's approval of the Corinnethian venture—noting indeed that Connor himself would be a part-time resident, and that the town-founders had considered naming Corinne "Connor City" in his honor. Readers of Beadle's various 1869 and 1870 publications could hardly fail to recognize that they were being invited to pick up and carry Connor's torch along the railroad. Beadle's Bear River call-to-arms was less overtly militaristic than Connor's had been, to be sure, but the Corinnethian project entailed related arguments regarding the nature of true religion, civilization, and whiteness in the West. The Valley's Indians now gone, or so he claimed, Beadle invited an Anglo readership to displace also the Mormons and thus ensure the properly white, Christian, and American future of Utah.[64]

The town of Corinne was in many ways well equipped for the tasks of Mormon destruction and railroad rule, according to Beadle, even without taking into account its trail-breaking heritage. Located where railroads necessarily crossed one of Utah's rare freshwater resources, the Bear River, Corinne was surrounded by "the finest farming land," and it was also a convenient hub for Montana and Idaho business. Once Gentile bankers and businessmen had assembled there and made Corinne a new center for farming and mining trade, they would cut into the small-town commercial monopolies maintained elsewhere by LDS churchmen. Corinne would be "an anomaly in politics" too,

Beadle said: "a little republic in the midst of a theocracy" from which democracy would spread with commerce.[65]

Beadle, in harmony with basic death knell logic, said that industry, capitalism, and politics would all bring "contact with vital Christianity" and that Corinne, soon to be a commercial railroad hub, would be vitally Christian as well. He acknowledged the possible counterintuitivity—among westerners at least—of a railroad town being also a center of morality and religious piety, given that many 'hell-on-wheels' outposts tended to boast as many bars and brothels as residents. But Beadle reassured readers that any such disorder would be surpassed quickly en route to permanent urbanity. Sheldon Jackson's Presbyterian missionary efforts would only expedite that surpassing. So too would the support of soldiers like Patrick E. Connor and the inevitable investments of railroad managers and government agents in city infrastructure. Corinne was determined to be "the political and religious antipodes of Salt Lake City" in all ways: to be "on her good behavior," to maintain a "good reputation," and to be "morally . . . an exception to railroad towns."[66]

THE FINAL TASK of Beadle's *Life in Utah*—having described Mormon religious hybridity, decried its regressive orientation, proposed plans for its breakup or redirection, and nominated Corinne as key to Utahn futures—was to outline a more palatable form of religious hybridity worthy of American modernity and Corinnethian congregation. Beadle suggested that the best way to combat Mormonism might be through the active, self-conscious combination of different and more modern trends, or the making of better social and religious hybrids.

According to Beadle, Mormonism itself posed no lasting problem for mainstream denominations in America. But its strangely mottled appearance did "indicate a new or modified phase of religion" there nonetheless. Beadle predicted the rise of "a distinctly American Church" in the nineteenth century: a progressive combination of the best traits of all Gentile American religions, one capable of defeating Mormonism's inverted assemblage of barbarisms and heresies. As he wrote: "Each nation has developed one central, theologic and ecclesiastical idea, and we are not yet so fully completed and individualized, as to be without the same want and yearning. Perhaps one of the present sects will modify and *advance* to the needed place; or from the spirit of union in *many*, may come the ascendant and satisfying *one*." From Presbyterianism the "American Church" might take "universal suffrage," a principle "peculiarly suited to the genius of our whole people"; from Methodists a "hearty simplicity and earnest work" ethic; from Baptists a "hearty pioneer[ing]" character; and from Unitarians a certain "philosophy and taste." In any case, "the Church of the future must be both intellectual and emotional; it must look to the future for its hope, and to our own land for its governing polity, and not to worn out systems which have proved too weak for earthly means."[67] Beadle imagined America as a place of palatable pluralism with the spirit of progressive ecumenism, with both characteristics being measured in terms of proximity to democratic ideals and common law traditions. And Corinne would be the spearhead of its western establishment.

In Beadle's articulations of 'the Salt Lake City Mormon' vis-à-vis 'the Corinnethian Gentile,' we see the further outlining and application of comparative religious frameworks and notions of normative Protestantism. Put differently, Beadle's 'Corinnethian' was a perfect embodiment of the historiographic 'secular.' Situated in a key location of expansion and encounter, the model Corinnethian articulated—with recourse to key terms and contemporary data, and in forums of national interest—arguments for Gentile Christianity and national identity similar to those traced by the aforementioned scholars. According to this model, Mormons were inauthentically or insufficiently religious insofar as their 'religion' consisted of barbarous theocracy, violence, resource monopoly, and polygamy. By contrast, the sociality of the Bear River Valley, alternately marked and unmarked as religious, was imagined to be broadly ecumenical in its focus on private piety, domesticity, internal improvements, and moral American citizenry. Only the latter would be publicly productive, worthy of government support, suitable for business, and capable of railroading Mormonism.

IF CHRISTIANITY was part and parcel of basic Gentility, liberal economics, and politics, by Beadle's telling, it would also come to Corinne and northern Utah via more traditional agents, in time: missionaries, churches, and Christian schools. Beadle seldom stressed the particularities of Gentile subdivisions in isolation from each other, preferring instead to speak of an aggregate Corinnethian Christianity inclusive of all non-Mormon Protestants—and sometimes also Catholics and Jews, to the degree that they similarly denounced theocracy and tribalism. But his announcements of generally Gentile futures, published in numerous newspapers and pamphlets throughout the spring of 1869, caught Sheldon Jackson's attention; and Jackson made Corinne a centerpiece of his specifically Presbyterian plan to evangelize the Pacific Railroad and convert western whites to Christ. Willingly echoing Beadle's promises of Mormon destruction and metropolitan Gentility in denominational newsletters and fundraising materials, then, Jackson proclaimed Corinne to be the answer to Mormonism and the inroad for western Presbyterianism alike. He instructed Melancthon Hughes, his missionary agent for the Wyoming and Utahn stretch of the Union Pacific, to begin his work there posthaste.

The early flag-planting, church-building efforts of Corinne's Presbyterians reveal much about the intersections of railroading anti-Mormonism, town planning, and religious formation in the West. They illuminate also the social realities and institutional effect of Beadle's putative ecumenism while simultaneously pointing to economic and demographic conditions seldom mentioned in Beadle's metropolis-promising pamphlets. Both locally and nationally, denominational officials used Corinne as a site and fulcrum for their own projects of religious upbuilding, even as Corinnethians used them to ostensibly similar effects. The cumulative result of these and other railside efforts, cross-purposed though they may have been at times, was the peculiar situation and scaffold for western religious construction.

WITH ENCOURAGEMENT from Sheldon Jackson, Melancthon Hughes quickly settled on Corinne as his base of missionary operations in the West. "I learned that Corinne . . . is the largest gentile town in Utah, and the most important point perhaps this side of Laramie," he wrote to his supervisors. Admittedly, he was not the first to learn about it—a certain Reverend Foote of the Episcopal Church had just been to Corinne to secure a lot for a future place of worship—but Hughes saw no reason why they shouldn't fix their Presbyterian hub there, too. If Corinne was to become the transcontinental railroad junction, there would be ample room and resources for both them and the Episcopalians. And in the meantime the ministers would cooperate, Hughes wrote. He and Foote agreed to visit the town twice a month and to share facilities on Sundays: the city hall for now, and perhaps an Episcopal Church building after that. This was apparently Beadle's ecumenism in action: two Protestant groups jointly occupying the town for Christianity and for America.[68]

Two weeks after his arrival, Hughes addressed to Jackson a story of ecclesiastical operation that reveals much about early town priorities and provisions. "Last Sunday I preached at Corinne in the City Hall," he wrote, referring to the sixteen-by-eighteen-foot room that, though built of rough-hewn boards, was one of the town's few walled and wooden structures in the spring of 1869. Hughes's letters show that Corinne was still little more than an idea then. There were only three or four hundred railroad-anticipating residents in March 1869, when Beadle began his town-boosting efforts in earnest, and most of its buildings were platformed and fronted tents. There were, for instance,

Panoramic view of Corinne in 1869. (Photographs by Andrew J. Russell; courtesy of Oakland Museum of California, Oakland)

saloons, restaurants, groceries, brothels, washhouses, and a newspaper printing shop in these, and also a dealer of tents themselves. A particularly large tent served as the town gambling hall, and it was from this one that Hughes borrowed benches for his first service, returning them afterward "in time for an evening game of keno." Like the city hall, the town was rough around the edges—but Hughes agreed with Beadle that its appearance would soon match the purity and grandeur of its designs. "People are waiting for the [railroad] question to be decided," he wrote, and "a church may soon be organized there if the town prospers." Corinne needed only the railroad connection to make industry, architecture, gentility, Presbyterianism, and Christianity bloom.[69]

Jackson rewrote Hughes's account of Corinne, for the benefit of an eastern readership, by combining its revelations of social and architectural transience with the whitewashed rhetoric of Beadle's writings. Summarizing first one of Beadle's pamphlet proclamations, Jackson wrote that "the friends of Corinne claim the following:- It is the probable point of junction between the Union and Central Pacific Railroads. It is on the only navigable stream between the Missouri and Sacramento rivers, distant from each other eighteen hundred miles, and also at the railroad crossing this river," and "it is the only desirable and natural location for a city on the Union Pacific Railroad west of Laramie, a distance of five hundred miles." Adding to these considerations the fact that

Corinne was "the only place in Utah were where the Gentiles can procure land and do business free from the petty annoyances of Brigham Young," there was little chance of its failure.[70]

Jackson went on to praise Hughes's work among Corinne's Presbyterians, here adding a bit of strategic humility to his boosterism. "The strictly religious element in the community is very feeble," he admitted, and Hughes found himself "regularly borrow[ing]" some "rough benches" for services "from the gambling saloons nearby." But such was frontier life, Jackson wrote, and prospects there were good. "In this community," he concluded, "like similar communities in the far west, there are a few who love the Lord Jesus, and a few others, who, although not communicants, yet, from the force of early religious training, greatly desire that churches may be planted and sustained in their midst." These people would rise to the cause in time, and other Gentiles would follow suit. Thus religion would ascend in Utah if Presbyterians succeeded, and Presbyterianism would win if Corinne did.[71]

Jackson's readers were asked to aid the trainside mission, if not by steering the tracks toward Corinne, then by sending support. "Come over and help us," pleaded the missionaries, here issuing the 'Macedonian Cry' on behalf of Beadle, the Corinnethians, their neighbors, and the "unnumbered hosts of deluded Mormons" in Utah.[72]

"The Child Is Born": Corinne's Fate on the Line

Along with Hughes's and Jackson's missionary correspondence, J. H. Beadle's numerous editorials and articles afford much insight into the evolution of Gentile railroading expectations and Corinnethian promises; and so too does the scrapbook that he kept to chronicle early town efforts. Two articles written in late October 1868, when the Central Pacific and Union Pacific seemed destined to meet somewhere along the northern shores of the Great Salt Lake, express the anticipations of the moment: "The rapid approach of the U.P.R.R. towards Salt Lake Valley has awakened a lively interest among those who propose to make an early real estate investment in the 'great central city of the future.'" Somewhere, he wrote, most likely "between the mouth of Weber Canyon and the northwest point of the Lake, at the most convenient spot for staging and freighting to Montana, Idaho, Oregon and Washington, is to be a city of permanent importance, and numerous speculators are watching the point with interest. But the location is still in doubt." The one certain thing was that the junction site would be home to a "Gentile city."[73] Cooperating land agents, railroad men, industrialists, merchants, missionaries, settlers, and politicians would ensure as much. Of this Beadle was positive.

For a time it seemed as if Union Pacific agents were on board, not only with the selection of a lakeside point for their roundhouses, offices, and transfer stations, but also—true to railroads' reputation as harbingers of Protestant progress—with making it a Gentile stronghold. At the most basic and material level, the company priority was simple: to grade and build its line as far west as possible before joining with the Central Pacific, whose agents were themselves trying to push ever eastward, both railroads hoping to collect maximum land-grants and proceeds in the process. Extending themselves to their utmost for the time being, they planned to fix their official transfer point later, either at the place where their lines actually met, or elsewhere, at a mutually favorable location nearby, with postmeeting readjustments made as necessary. Both companies were willing to entertain townsite proposals and cooperate with regional and national development projects, but they also wanted to land, in the end, at locations favorable to branch-line connectivity and freighting business.

Corinne had a good chance of being the de facto meeting point for the Central and Union Pacific lines, or the mutually agreed-upon postmeeting hub, or even—Beadle's greatest dream—both. Its main rival in the hub contest of spring 1869 was Ogden, a well-established and predominantly Mormon settlement between Corinne and Salt Lake City. Favored especially by the Central Pacific, Ogden's eastern location allowed for maximum federal compensation as well as easy connection with Salt Lake City (to the south) and Idaho and

Montana (to the north). However the Union Pacific reached Ogden well before its rival, and as of early March 1869, it was already building northward toward the Bear River, toward Corinne. Speculation then flourished about where the lines would end up meeting and about the non-Mormon settlement opportunities afforded by a non-Ogden junction. Towns mushroomed in hopeful expectation. Corinne's hopes and population grew.

"As yet the U. P. R. R. Company has offered no inducements or given any promises" about where it might fix its hub, Beadle reported with some frustration in March.[74] Redoubling then his efforts to make Corinne "the site of *the* great Gentile town of the valley," Beadle appealed in several ways to both company directors and local railroad agents. With an eye to the former he wrote of Bear River Valley's arable land, its good water supplies, its proximity to the Montana trade, and its potential as launching point for an Oregon branch of the Union Pacific. To those wishing to develop Utah's tourism trade—often an important revenue source for railroads—he wrote of Bear River's proximity to the Great Salt Lake and Salt Lake City. Imagine the following scenario, Beadle said: "A man steps off the [railroad] cars at Bear river" and onto a steamboat, on which he "makes a tour of Salt Lake and is landed in the Jerusalem of the Mormons. The trip overland has novelty enough without counting the strange people" there. Proceeds from such sight-seeing excursions would be substantial. For those less interested in "counting" on Mormonism's continuance, though—or for those more concerned with the dismantling of Salt Lake City than with its sideshow encapsulation—the "great Gentile town" would accomplish their aims, too. It would bring about "the successful and peaceful solution of the Mormon problem," Beadle said, by eclipsing the Mormon city in demographic, economic, and political force.[75] In any case the railroad was sure to make money in Corinne: "They can certainly sell more lots, if that be their object," than in any other location.[76]

ONE OR MORE OF THESE arguments captured the attention of John O'Neil, surveyor for the Union Pacific Company, and James A. Williamson, a recently designated agent of the Union Pacific committee for townsite lots and land sales. Picnicking with them on the banks of the Bear River on March 4, 1869, Beadle and other would-be Corinnethians offered toasts to the transcontinental railroad, to President Ulysses S. Grant, to Vice President Schuyler Colfax, to the eradication of polygamy, and "to the United States[,] May their jurisdiction soon be extended over Utah." Afterward O'Neil laid out the town lots on the west bank of the river, at the site of the railroad's crossing. For his part Williamson promised to help administer and promote local affairs, offering even to bestow upon the town the blessing of his daughter's name: *Corinne*.[77] A short while later he also agreed to donate a plot of railroad land to Sheldon Jackson's Presbyterian mission in Corinne, thereby affirming again railroads' presumed commitment to serve Gentile and Protestant religious ends.[78]

All good signs, thought Beadle!

"THE CHILD IS BORN," Beadle announced on March 15, 1869, "and her name, as you see, is Corinne." The matter was finally decided, according to the Beadle-backed *Salt Lake Weekly Reporter*: "The Gentiles and the Railroad Company are agreed at last; there is to be one metropolis and its name is Corinne." Granted the railroad lines had not yet met—they would do so on May 10 on Promontory Summit, twenty miles west of Corinne—but the town evidently had the backing of Williamson and O'Neil, as well as the missionary likes of Sheldon Jackson. Such was grounds enough for a cheer and a blessing: "All hail to the future Corinne! And for ourselves we say in the language of the Apostle: 'O, ye, *Corinnethians*, our mouth is open unto you, our heart is enlarged. Now, for a recompense in the same, *be ye also enlarged*. Our flesh hath no rest till we come unto thee. All the Saints salute you. . . . Grace be with you all. Amen.'"[79]

Corinne seemed to have won. At least for a few days, it did.

The Decision Is Made

By late March 1869, the U.S. government had tired of watching its pet companies race to still-undetermined locations, building subpar roads and grading extraneous paths in the process. Congressmen intervened, demanding answers and accountability. That J. H. Beadle took this as a good sign is unsurprising; he was optimistic that congressional proponents of the death knell thesis would fix the Union Pacific–Central Pacific junction point at Corinne, thus cementing the informal toasts and pledges made with railroad agents along the banks of Bear River. As he had been saying for months, "With everything concentrated on one point, the popular energies, the influence and business of the railroad, the weight of the Government, a good town may be built."[80] But Beadle would soon discover the faultiness of this logic and encounter the limits of popular rhetoric, the ethereality of governmental policies, and the realities of industrial influences and business concerns. Railroad company men and U.S. congressmen decided his town's fate with little care for Beadle's appeals, Jackson's denominational plans, or O'Neil's and Williamson's picnic promises.

ON APRIL 8 AND 9, just as the Union Pacific started laying track at Corinne, representatives of the Union and Central Pacific companies met in Washington, D.C., to discuss their Utahn plans. In time the parties came to agreement on the location of the railroads' meeting place and junction point. It was an agreement designed to satisfy both Union Pacific interests in maximum reimbursements and Central Pacific desires for a terminus close to the Wasatch range. Neither Beadle nor Jackson, however, would be happy with it.

By the terms of their agreement—accepted, passed, and announced by Congress one day later—the railroads would meet at Promontory Summit, west of Corinne, but then establish their official junction near Ogden, east of Corinne, with the Central Pacific reimbursing the Union Pacific for all tracking built between Promontory and Ogden, including at Corinne.[81] Corinne itself was multiply bypassed.

By act of Congress and agreement of railroad directors, then, Corinne became a stopover along the Central Pacific rather than the great railroad hub of the West. It retained hopes of tapping the Montana trade, securing branch railroad connections, building tourist attractions, and developing new agricultural ventures, but dreams of being "the Chicago of the Rocky Mountains" faded.[82]

The line had been sold out from under them. And Corinnethians, having done their best both to echo and institutionalize national presumptions respecting religion and western progress, were left wondering why.

CHAPTER TWO

Brigham Young and the Railroad Connection

✦

EARLY IN 1869—as Union Pacific employees finished construction at Echo City, forty miles east of Ogden—Brigham Young worked his own way to Ogden, hoping to intervene directly in the junction question. By then it was clear that the Union and Central Pacific lines would meet somewhere north or northeast of the Great Salt Lake. Knowing that Gentiles planned to build an anti-Mormon metropolis at the hub and learning also that some had been speculating in land at Ogden, the president of the Church of Jesus Christ of Latter-day Saints devised a plan by which to thwart their efforts. Young "met with the [Mormon] proprietors of the 5 acre lots at Ogden" located at the likely site of a railroad stop, and according to church records, "those brethren who owned the land where the railroad station was to be built signed the agreement to sell" to Young and the LDS Church rather than to non-Mormons or their railroad companies.[1] He did this not to withhold these lands from railroads himself, however. Quite the contrary, Young wished rather to aid and expedite the incorporation of railroads within Mormonism—and of Mormonism through railroads.

The tracking of Brigham Young's land deal in Ogden is crucial to understanding the events concluding chapter 1. Young offered these plots—amounting to some 131 acres total, along with buildings, roads, and supplies—for free to the transcontinental railroad companies, provided that they locate their junction there, in the Mormon city. He sweetened the deal further by contracting with the Union and Central Pacific railroads to provide Mormon labor along their lines and by pledging to build a branch railroad to Ogden from Salt Lake City, for which he would accept construction materials in partial payment for labor contracts. Thomas Durant, vice president of the Union Pacific, was impressed. There "was not another man on earth could have done the same," he reportedly said.²

The plan worked, with the Union Pacific and Central Pacific choosing Ogden over Corinne as their hub, and with the U.S. Congress following suit. *This*, then, is what transpired behind the act—a surprising occurrence, from the Corinnethian perspective—of Corinne's bypassing. Having established particular geographies of religious authority in the Great Basin, Brigham Young and his colleagues oversaw the incorporation of railroads within them, and working in contracted collaboration with transcontinental company men, they laid groundwork for the continuing industrial success of Utahn Mormonism itself. Saints bent and built railroads to their benefit.

The Mormon Land System: Origins and Precedents

Founding Mormon prophet Joseph Smith Jr. struggled, during his fourteen years of church leadership (1830–44), to find a formula for Saintly cohesion in America. Among his social, political, economic, mythic, ritual, and spatial innovations, four were especially important to Great Basin futures. These were the 'Plat of Zion,' a blueprint for Mormon town-building; the 'United Order,' an attempt at centralized, communalist economics; 'theodemocracy,' a notion of rightly regulated politics; and 'the priesthood,' a constellation of ecclesiastical offices capable of implementing the above. Each of these constructs was utopian in both the Greek and colloquial sense. These were ideal social arrangements, forms that—while imagined to transcend the contingencies of time and space—yet existed nowhere, not least because midwestern Mormons often needed to recalibrate them in response to their own shifting needs. The Plat of Zion, United Order, theodemocracy, and priesthood nevertheless formed together the ideological and practical canopy under which Brigham Young attempted, after Smith's death, to place Mormonism in Utah. And Young's efforts, in turn, set new standards around which to debate the real and ideal form of Mormonism in America, especially during the railroad era.

I stress here, at the outset, that I am not suggesting that this cluster of innovations was rightly or quintessentially Mormon, per se. As we will see, it was multiply contested and variously imagined, and many Mormons sought meaning outside it or in different combinations of early church practices. Rather, the point is that this grouping set the stage for the development and incorporation of certain railroading interests in Utah, the likes of which in turn informed its perceived place in—if not precisely *as*—Mormon orthodoxy over time.

Joseph Smith devised the Plat of Zion in 1833, while living in Ohio. It was to be the model for future Mormon settlements, especially—but not only—in Independence, Missouri. Among its chief features were: orientation by cardinal directions; a grid-system division of land, featuring blocks, lots, and streets of uniform lengths and widths; a central area for public buildings and temples; and an area outside the residential section for farms and animals. Houses were to be located on alternate sides of city blocks, with each house set back from the street at a uniform distance. Smith's instructions—written along the edges of the map—were to settle "from fifteen to twenty thousand people" in such a town, with one family per house, one house per plot, and (generally) twenty plots per block. "When this [town] is thus laid off and supplied," wrote Smith, "lay off another in the same way, and so fill up the world in these last days." Thus Mormons would build and populate a central City of Zion, with other like cities around it; and by means of that network they would constitute the greater kingdom of God.[3]

In many ways the City of Zion would resemble other frontier towns laid out according to the U.S. Land Ordinance of 1785, with rectangular surveys, gridded blocks, and areas reserved for public programming. Yet it would be different in crucial respects. Zion was designed to have smaller lots, for instance, and also more distinct village-farmland boundaries than midwestern towns generally. Moreover, Smith's plat—anticipating as it did ecclesiastical buildings on downtown lots withheld for them by area politicians—reclaimed the importance of direct governmental support of religion through mechanisms of land granting, rather than indirect support through grants to schools or businesses. In these latter ways the Plat of Zion harkened back to the older northeastern settlements of Pilgrims and Puritans, and it reclaimed the importance of uniform, visible saintliness for westward expansion.[4]

According to historian Feramorz Young Fox, the Plat of Zion represented a compromise between Mormons' desire to eliminate poverty "by bringing about approximate economic equality" among Saints and their "defensive needs" for tight-knit settlements.[5] Respecting their economic hopes, Joseph Smith and the Saints had by 1833 attempted to institute the United Order and the Law of Consecration and Stewardship in communities at Kirtland, Ohio, and in Jackson County, Missouri. By this system Saints voluntarily deeded property to the church in exchange for an "inheritance," "stewardship," or "allotment"—in other words, for access to land, buildings, tools, and further goods equal to their need and capacity for productive use. Through direct purchase, deeded acquisition, or the benevolent sharing of Saints, the church hoped to ensure ease of assembly and mutual sustenance for all.[6]

But the communalist United Order system faltered from its beginnings. Plagued by several factors—land speculation schemes and high real estate prices; the imbalance of need, ownership, and benevolence; and the opposition of non-Mormon locals among them—the order collapsed, at least in Ohio and Missouri. It remained thereafter an ideal expression of a more generalizable Mormon communitarian ethos, an arrangement kept alive more in spirit than fact, held aloft in subjunctive anticipation of a world unencumbered by hostile factors.

The Plat of Zion was, then, an urban blueprint drawn in full recognition of past, present, and prospective difficulties of implementation. Neither plat nor instructions mandated consecrated donations to the church. Nor did they discuss the sharing of lots or buildings outside central blocks. Still they assumed the rough equivalence of acreage holdings by family, and they assumed also a centralized system of territorial acquisition and distribution, either by ecclesiastical leaders or by cooperative land agents. These were tall orders in a world of cultural pluralism, class stratification, and piecemeal settlement patterns. Therefore the plat expressed above all a hope for exclusively Saintly congregation around a central city, in small communities with defined external boundaries.

Zion and its plat were, however, 'utopian' not merely in the sense that they had no literal or descriptive application. The City of Zion was simply impossible as platted: the numbers didn't (and couldn't) add up, neither to the ideal population nor to the ideal town length and width; and there were internal inconsistencies respecting lot locations and sizes. The Mormon blueprint was paradoxical in other ways, too, particularly insofar as it assumed great hierarchical organization to ensure maximum equalitarianism and parity of property.[7]

As Joseph Smith and Mormonism moved westward, he and it built an elaborate priesthood system, and they expanded their ecclesiastical constellation accordingly. Regions (as of 1834) were divided by stakes, which were subdivided (after 1839) by wards, whose congregations (as of 1835) included male priesthood members of two types, Aaronic and Melchizedek, with different rights and responsibilities. For their part women were said sometimes to partake in priesthood by virtue of marriage or (after 1842) by membership in the Female Relief Society, a short-lived vehicle for acts of charitable outreach, moral reform, healing, teaching, and temple work. (Brigham Young officially dissolved the Relief Society in 1845, one year after Joseph Smith's death.)[8] Ward-level activities were ideally overseen by a bishop and two counselors, who were in turn overseen by a three-person Stake Presidency and a twelve-person High Council, which were overseen by a Presiding Bishopric. In areas of smaller church membership, Saints were organized into branches and districts, which were grouped by mission, which were monitored (as of 1835) by a Quorum of Twelve Apostles and a Quorum of Seventy. Apostles were supervised by the First Presidency, which consisted of the church president and his two counselors. The First Presidency—along with (as of 1841) the Quorum of Twelve Apostles and another Council of Fifty officers—directed demographic, ritual, political, and economic activities for the church at large. Meanwhile local bishops presided over the consecration of properties, the collection of tithes, and the allotment of public resources.[9]

Joseph Smith's preferred term for this complicated, hierarchical, and dynamically expansive bureaucracy—the goal of which was to ensure maximum access to temporal and divine rights for Saints, at least according to their sex, familial status, location, and ecclesiastical office—was "theodemocracy." By this he meant to identify Mormons as a people of God (Israel), committed to government by God and God's agents (theocracy) and by the people themselves (democracy). "Rather than seeing these systems as being competitive or contradictory," explains historian Patrick Mason, "Smith and his followers viewed them as complementary; indeed, many argued that they were in fact part of an organic system of government that permeated not only earthly but also heavenly realms." Theodemocracy embraced certain standards of American republicanism. The Constitution was considered to be an inspired document, for instance, with freedoms of assembly and religion held sacred and with the notion of yeoman pastoralism held high. But theodemocracy critiqued also republicanism's perceived shortcomings: excessive individualism, economic dislocation, the failure to acknowledge God as supreme lawgiver, and the continuing prevalence of state and mob violence constraining religious liberties. "While Smith agreed with the liberal premise that the state existed to guarantee and protect individual liberties, he insisted that no current government was living up to their fundamental duties." Thus "Smith and the Mormons embraced a more robust application of revealed religion in the public sphere as the answer to the secular government's hostility to minorities' rights (namely their own)," even as "anti-Mormon critics denounced the prophet as a tyrant and his politics as theocratic despotism."[10] Hence Smith's candidacy for U.S. president in 1844, as well as his more local attempts (as in Kirtland, Ohio; Independence and Far West, Missouri; and finally Nauvoo, Illinois) to centralize and control Saintly settlement free of governmental or cultural intrusion. Thence too, on the Gentile side, a proportional rise in anti-Mormon sentiment and hostility, culminating in mob violence and the murder of Joseph Smith himself.[11]

"UTAHpian Spiritual Views":
Mormon Politics and Land Policies in the Great Basin

Most important to our narrative is not that actual Mormon settlements varied with respect to the Plat of Zion—although that is certainly true. Nor is it that theodemocracy was a complicated conjunction with paradoxical application; nor even that violence was enacted frequently (if irregularly) by Mormon officials and settlers, government agents, lawyers, and anti-Mormon mobs in the Midwest. Rather it is a related series of factors. First, that Mormonism was a 'proximate other' to many northeastern and midwestern frontier groups. Not only was it ideologically and ethnically similar to American Protestantisms generally, but its emergent patterns of urban planning and divinely ordained republicanism—recognizably divergent as they were—recalled internecine conflict over western settlement and politics as the stuff of religion.[12] Second, Utahn relocation allowed for the reconceptualization of Mormon settlement and political templates in Mormon practice, that is, for a new and selective application of in-group utopian models and for corresponding reconfigurations of priesthood offices and bureaucratic responsibilities. Third, such relocation and reconfiguration were contested ventures. Challenges occurred at one level among Mormons themselves, for instance, among those who insisted that the right place for Mormonism was *not* Utah. Meanwhile, other Saints objected that Brigham Young had unduly empowered certain offices, such as the Quorum of Twelve, and disempowered others, such as the Female Relief Society; and still others argued that theodemocracy could be multiply interpreted and applied.[13] But westward-moving and Utah-bound Mormonism faced opposition from non-Mormons, as well, to the degree that Gentiles reapproximated and appropriated 'The West'—and thus also Mormonism—in time.

As practiced in Utah, theodemocracy meant the governmental system administered by LDS ecclesiastical officials, in the absence of federal authority in the Great Basin, around 1847. Ranking churchmen functioned as surveyors, mayors, councilmen, judges, and tax collectors, and there was little functional distinction between the personnel and perspectives of church and state. This system was nominally reduced and disbanded after the Treaty of Guadalupe Hidalgo in 1848 and the Compromise of 1850, but the administrative arm of 'Deseret'—Mormons' proposed Great Basin state—persisted as a shadow government alongside and within Utah's nationally approved territorial legislature for years thereafter. For his part Brigham Young met separately with ecclesiastical committees on affairs of economy, law, settlement, and social programming, but from 1851 to 1858 he served also as authorized governor of

Utah Territory. Other Deseret personnel and provisions were similarly integrated into Utah's official government.[14]

Much of the legal and extralegal activity in Deseret and the early Utah Territory pertained to the division and use of lands and natural resources. And much of this, in turn, occurred in rough accordance with the ideals, if not specifics, of the 1833 Plat of Zion. Thus Mormon theodemocratic politics in Deseret (circa 1848–51) and Utah (1850 and thereafter) amounted, in large part, to the pursuit of a truly and duly platted Zion. And many of Brigham Young's corresponding decisions reshaped the modes and morphologies of Mormonism.

Not only did Young's Saints bring Smith's blueprint overland with them to the Great Basin, but (writes historian Richard H. Jackson) "the establishment of Salt Lake City under the direction of Brigham Young followed Smith's plan more closely than any town established by Smith himself."[15] There were of course differences, informed, for instance, by midwestern experiences and western aridity. In Salt Lake City ten-acre blocks were divided into eight lots, each one and a quarter acres in size (rather than twenty blocks at half an acre each, per the original plan); a single block (rather than several blocks) was laid aside for public buildings and a single temple (rather than twelve temples); streets were widened to allow for sidewalks and irrigation ditches; and space was made for stables and barns in the city. But in many other respects Young proceeded as if the Salt Lake Valley were a blank slate onto which Smith's utopic plat might be planted unencumbered by the need for interagency negotiation and cultural translation. This was despite the presence of native Utes, especially along the southern end of the Wasatch Front near present-day Utah Lake; of Shoshonis, north of Salt Lake; and of itinerant "mixed-bloods," in the middle.[16] Settlements in these areas required different orientations, often with forts built to defend Mormons against any Indian attacks incited by their own intrusions, or with different architectural concessions to smaller populations. But Salt Lake City was the Plat of Zion almost incarnate and relatively immediate.

Approximately one week after the famed arrival of Mormon pioneers on July 24, 1847, church officials initiated the survey and division of land in "Plat A." (Plat B followed one year later, and others after that.) Brigham Young, church apostles, and other ranking LDS officials claimed lots and blocks close to the city center, and other emigrants settled around them. Subsequent arrivers received "allotments" either from Brigham Young and Heber C. Kimball—self-appointed but unanimously sustained committeemen of general apportionment— or by lottery, "casting lots, as Israel did in days of old."[17] Wilford Woodruff and his fellow pioneers recalled Young's directions to the flock thus: "He . . .

said that no man who came here should buy land," for "the Lord has given it to us without price." Therefore "every man should have his land measured out to him" by church authorities "for city and farming purposes. He might till it as he pleased, but must be industrious and take care of it," and he would not "be suffered to cut up his lot and sell a part to speculate out of his brethren." Most settlers paid only $1.50 for their one-and-a-quarter-acre city lot assignments: a $1.00 surveyor's fee, plus a $0.50 recorder's fee. This was slightly less expensive than the lowest official national land fees, at some $1.25 per acre, but maximum holdings were also smaller. And proceeds went to church-appointed personnel rather than the federal government.[18]

With almost nine hundred Mormon emigrants applying for city and farm land by the fall of 1848, "the clerk literally did a 'land-office business'!" Or so joked historian Fox, whose exclamation relies on knowledge of certain facts of American land law. Most saliently: Salt Lake City had no federally recognized land office at that time, and thus the Mormon distribution system, organized and busy though it was, was not at all legal. From the federal perspective, Mormons were squatters, and neither they nor their church government could buy, sell, deed, or transfer title to 'public' acreage. This is not to say that Mormons were altogether aberrant, from the national perspective, nor that they had zero rights; squatting was common practice in the Americas, and federal land laws were designed accordingly, with 'preemptors' allowed early opportunity to purchase legally their lands after formal governmental integration, survey, and offer. But until the opening of a *real* land office in Utah, thousands of Mormons necessarily trusted in the functionality of their ecclesiastical settlement policy, the stability of their communities, the righteousness of Brigham Young's patronage (if not precisely his territorial ownership), or the ability to square their practices with governmental standards to come.

And trust they did, at least to the degree necessary to operationalize a distinctive land system built on *trustee*ship. Indeed, among Joseph Smith's and Brigham Young's many titles was trustee-in-trust of the LDS Church.[19] Here Mormons called upon their own particular history of United Order communalism, not to mention the more generically American, ethnocentric assumption of manifest destiny. Church leaders, they thought, should be able to claim territory, hold properties in trust, and grant access or allotments as necessary for the assembly and expansion of Israel. For several years, then, the Utahn Mormon church distributed land, held lotteries, issued receipts, and adjudicated disputes as its leaders saw fit—as if it were legal, as if in a land office.

Congress did not grant Utah an official land office until 1869, to correspond with railroad connections in Utah. But in the intervening years Brigham Young's territorial government took several steps to legalize and expand its ecclesiastically directed land system. For instance, in 1850–51 Governor Young approved "An ordinance creating a Surveyor General's Office" and "An ordinance in relation to County Recorders." The first of these mandated that future state and territory surveys "correspond with the original survey of Great Salt Lake City," and also that the surveyor general issue certificates of legal possession to residential claimants as before, by application or lottery. Meanwhile, the second ordinance, in setting standards for registering "all transfers or conveyances of land" by or between Utahn residents, similarly aimed to ease de facto title acquisition upon extension of national land laws to Utah, by ensuring that future land office claims might be traced to and aligned with original surveys and allotments. In both cases Utahn territorial laws translated older ecclesiastical systems into official land management policy.[20]

Utah's legislature also incorporated Mormon regulations respecting timber rights, mineral lands, and water use, and it passed additional laws to similar effect, granting extensive properties and "exclusive rights" to church authorities. Such standards were rationalized in the same terms, as were Plat A and the United Order—trusteeship, divine direction, benevolent patronage, and communal good—but they raised eyebrows later in Congress. (Recall Representative Justin S. Morrill's complaint that wood, water, and real estate were "monopolized not only by the Mormons, but by a few Mormons—the Governor and his apostles.")[21] Influential historians have found reason to defend the church against such eyebrow-raising. Fox, for example, reports that "the grants were intended not as a conferring of unconditional title, but as a means of social control terminable at the will of the granting power." This is true enough. But insofar as "the granting power" *was* at that time the church/government and President/Governor Young, and as early grants *did* go almost entirely to Young, Ezra T. Benson, Heber C. Kimball, George A. Smith, and their LDS cohort, these require further comment. Historians must consider closely Morrill's own 1857 quip that Young's land policies were "convenient for the maintenance of his *Utah*pian spiritual views." Young and his colleagues made their Mormonism a matter of Utahn imagination and land management alike.[22]

The timberland grant to Apostle George A. Smith was representative of Deseret and early Utahn procedures: it was a high-level grant with trickle-down presumptions, partly private and partly public in operation. Smith received "exclusive control" to the canyons "on the east side of the range of mountains west of Jordan," with the expectation that he (with church support) would build access roads and a sawmill. Others were allowed to take boards and timber from the area, but only after receiving Smith's consent and remitting to him appropriate tolls and payments—a portion of which would be forwarded to the public treasury.[23] Meanwhile Brigham Young granted himself "exclusive control over the timber, rocks, minerals, and water in the City Creek Kanyon" north of Salt Lake City, for which he paid five hundred dollars to the territorial treasury. This differed from Smith's grant insofar as it reserved fewer rights of public access to wood and stone. But it too evoked semidemocratic obligations of trusteeship by guaranteeing that water, at least, would "be continued pure unto the inhabitants of Great Salt Lake City."[24] Indeed water was held to be an especially sacred resource in Utah, in Young's grants and elsewhere. It was set apart from strictly private ownership or appropriation, and even where "exclusive control" was granted, the public and protective purpose thereof was generally specified. ("There shall be no private ownership of the streams that come out of the canyons," decreed Young, for "these belong to the people: all the people.")[25] Subsequent legislation confirmed water's status as a state- or territory-controlled resource, the right of access to which could be appropriated, granted, restricted, or sold as determined by public officials.

The relevant point here is that the mechanics of resource management in Utah were not divorced from Brigham Young's priestly position, the norms of communitarian trusteeship, or the structures and locations of Mormon power. Quite the contrary, they reified and relied upon them—and in retrospect they further reveal them. 'The public' was presumptively and prescriptively Mormon in Utah, and it remained so throughout the 1850s.

Sacred Space and the Placement of Western Religion

To be clear: I am pursuing a particular line of argumentation here, namely, that Mormonism in the late Midwest and early Utah periods was constituted largely in and through bureaucratic mechanisms of land management and resource distribution. (This is a story about how Mormonism became a particularly landed religion.) I intend to show below how certain such bureaucracies were set in iron during the railroad era and—beyond and below that—how particular railroad era Mormon loci became 'sacred' *not* because of inherent natural qualities but because of mutual agreements forged among Mormons, businessmen, politicians, and tourists to stage there key modern social-structural differentiations and to beg alongside them the principles of secular discernment. (This is a story about how Mormon lands were leveraged toward railroad connections and, then, how railroads mobilized Mormonism—as a discursive object and an object of both visible and visitable concern—in a way that justified again Mormons' secure place in American maps and markets.) Before proceeding along this track, however, it may be useful to differentiate my sense of these modern, Mormon techniques of religious placement vis-à-vis the category of sacred space and related historiographies of western religious geography. The pursuit of terms and trains of historical thought is, to my eye, the interpretive presumption and, I hope, the consequence of my research. By treating religion, geography, place, and the West as interrelated nouns and processes, and also (in a later chapter) by tracing the very ascendance of popular counterparts to academic theories of geographical determinism and sacred space, I wish not only to tell a story about religion in the American West but also to relate how that story should change our notions about the nature and meaning of religion in *the* West.

ABOUT THE IMPORTANCE of land to religion in the West, a familiar story says: although multiple and diverse, the most famous types and antitypes of 'western religion'—indigenous spiritualities, Mormonism, and naturism—afford a distinct centrality to geography and its forms. My concern is not that this statement is necessarily wrong but rather that it is seldom connected to another of the more common academic assertions about the nature of the West: that American lands west of the 98th meridian share concerns of federal territorialization, industrial development, and water acquisition. Such statements appear often together in volumes on 'Religion in the American West,' but one finds little sustained investigation of their practical overlap and continuity, for instance, through consideration of how technologies of territorial development or drives to increase agriculture have informed the degree to which Americans voiced or recorded claims to natural sublimity at different times and places. Specificities of geography, territory, and religion's coconstruction in the West have received less ink than have general announcements of the centrality of sacred space, topographical religious response, and the like. And thus readers, insofar as they expect fulfillment of the implied promise of such regional religious histories, are forced to the margins for material data regarding conditions for the actions and imaginings of western religions.[26]

Rote affirmations of the 'centrality of sacred space' shortchange the theoretical and historical potential of western religion studies in several ways. One is their propensity to see religions gathering instinctively and incessantly around sites of 'the sacred's manifestation.'[27] Without denying the existence of special signs and centers in many religions, including Mormonism, the assumption here is that human concerns and interests always inform the ways in which landforms are viewed, mapped, and inhabited, and thus that topographies do not beget locative religious actions and systems without social interest and argument. Therefore, since people inevitably discuss the authenticity and ownership of particular religious spaces and forms, scholars might focus on the acts and occasions for discussion rather than on the veracity of their religious assessments. Neither nature nor technology is inherently sublime in any particular way, though each is implicated in the articulation of the other's purportedly right or wrong religiosity. (As we will see in the case of Utah's 'Pulpit Rock,' technology corporations invented sites and strata of natural sublimity in order to flatter modern senses of cultural difference and refinement.) Another methodological takeaway is that spaces are not necessarily sacred on account of a priori qualities, but rather through conscious human acts of placement and 'setting aside.' Place, as opposed to space, can easily be conceived in verbal and procedural form, and thus scholars—like Jonathan Z. Smith—have increasingly called for studies of the methods by which religions, religious rituals, and religious myths have 'taken place' in particular locations at particular times.[28]

The payoff of these discussions, here and in western religious studies more broadly, is that we can envision different ways to explore geographical and regional histories of religion: ones that avoid reliance upon tropes of a priori 'sacred space' or ex nihilo 'topographical response' and that instead seek data on the material conditions in which such tropes are themselves articulated and heard. Resultant data may consist of foundational social concerns about land, water, climate, and the potential for settlement, but that fact should not be surprising, nor should it be considered a necessary return to 'space' and strict 'geographical determinism' as starting points. We must be prepared to recognize various ways in which land, sociographical concerns, and religion have comaterialized in the West, particularly as diverse mundane conditions have occasioned the articulation and adjudication of 'western religiosity,' 'authentic religion,' and 'the sacred' in the first place.[29]

OCCASIONS FOR CLAIMS to religion in both Salt Lake Valley and Bear River Valley did change over time, and so did related claims to sacred spaces and spatial potential in general. As Utah underwent economic integration, railroad construction, LDS Church disestablishment, and statehood, one can—and I will—observe the way religion, as a human process, speaks to historical change and modal diversity. But what is of interest to me is the *consistency* of this story as well, and my attention is especially arrested by the continuing mutual dependence between formulations of religion and determinations of land ownership, technologies of land distribution and transportation, water rights, infrastructural financing, and tourism. Such concerns—so typical of the American West west of the 98th meridian—are also integral to a longer cataloging of 'religion.' Western religious studies therefore returns historians and religionists alike to the particular announcements and contestations of geographical possibilities effected in the name of sacred space and divine purpose. At the nexus of these concerns we find, in Utah, a locational moment—the placement of western religion—that was also a locomotive moment. We find a Mormonism that consisted *not*, as certain scholars might have it, in the experiential encounter with and return to sacred time and space, that is, in the unmediated and sublime encounter with hierophanous topographies and the responsive foundation of settlements and rituals around them.[30] We find rather a certain group, led by Brigham Young, regulating the perception and distribution of resources in a new environment and then justifying such perception, distribution, and environment alike as naturally Mormon. Moreover, we find that both their efforts and justifications were accelerated and amplified by the approach of the Union and Central Pacific railroads and, then, by the gradual intertwining of LDS Mormons' and railroad officials' complementary designs for western temporal and geographical establishment. *This* is the story of Mormonism's placement in the West.

Expansion, Extraction, and Exclusion: Modes of Mormon Colonization

Salt Lake City was only the first LDS settlement in Utah. From it many others stemmed and grew. These settlements were of several sorts and aims, and a good number developed in haphazard and informal ways. But the earliest crop shared similar and more directive methods of dispatch: Brigham Young and his advisers organized companies to settle areas of strategic interest; the Deseret General Assembly or the Utah territorial legislature assigned them municipal charters; local leaders took charge of distributing land, diverting water, and developing wards; and church authorities visited the colonies to monitor their progress. Leaders and members of 'colonizing companies' sometimes petitioned or volunteered for the honor, while others were nominated or called during church meetings. Many of the persons called were newcomers whose emigration to Utah had been sponsored by the church's Perpetual Emigrating Fund Company, the ecclesiastical arm (founded 1859) responsible for raising money and supervising overwater and overland journeys from Liverpool, New York, New Orleans, and elsewhere. Colonists repaid their debts to the church through communal labor on canals, forts, buildings, and the like.[31]

Official Mormon colonies were of three basic types in the prerailroad age. The first took the form of missions to area indigenous groups. The second were single-commodity extractive and manufacturing communities. And the third were permanent settlements designed for predominantly (if not exclusively) Mormon residence but diverse economic activity. All three worked together to expand Mormon interests in the Great Basin and to establish networks of exchange later mobilized for and modernized by railroads.

SALT LAKE VALLEY was (in the words of one historian) "an indefinite borderline between Shoshoni and Ute Indians," the two recognized "landholding tribes" living to the north and south, respectively.[32] When Mormons moved to the valley in the summer of 1847, representatives of both groups met with them, and Shoshoni delegates especially claimed that they "were the owners of the land" and demanded "powder and lead" in exchange for settlement rights. The official church record and pioneer journals agree on the response, though they disagree about whether it was voiced by Brigham Young or someone else on his behalf: "'The Land,' said the speaker, 'belongs to our Father in heaven, and we calculate to plow and plant it; and no man will have power to sell his inheritance, for he cannot remove it; it belongs to the Lord." By extension there would be no "paying the Indians for the lands" either, "for if the Shoshones should be thus considered, the Utes and other tribes would claim pay also."[33] Here we see how the rhetoric of theodemocratic trusteeship was used not only in defense of Mormon allocation systems. It was also used to dislocate and dispossess prior residents.

But Mormons did offer certain services in exchange for land. They promised to act as intergroup buffers and mediators between Shoshonis and Utes, for instance, as well as between them and other white settlers or government agents; and they promised trade, education, and religious instruction. Such services were not without value for certain Indians, in certain places, at certain times. Some of the Mormon colonies in Sanpete County, in south-central Utah, began, in fact, by invitation from the Ute chief Walkara. Walkara wanted closer and more controlled contact with whites and their resources, and in 1849 Young, with his support, assigned missionaries to trade and teach area Utes about agriculture and the Book of Mormon.[34] (According to official Mormon doctrine—which held uneven interest among Mormons themselves, particularly on this topic—American Indians were "Lamanites," peoples descended from an Israelite patriarch but fallen into darkness and ignorance; and Mormons would help "redeem" them, making them again "white and delightsome," as part of the in-gathering of Israel and the establishment of a New Jerusalem.)[35] Young expanded his missions program in 1851, setting up "Indian farms" in Millard County and Utah County as well as Sanpete County. "Originally," writes Arrington, "their assignment was to grow produce to be used in pacifying the Indians; later their work expanded to include teaching the Indians themselves how to farm" in fenced plots and permanent quarters.

In both respects their efforts corresponded with national reservation policies at the time, and thus when Garland Hurt was appointed federal Indian agent to Utah in 1855, he tried further to 'domesticate' Utes, Shoshonis, and others in fixed agricultural settlements.[36]

None of this is to say that American Indian, Mormon, and national governmental relations were harmonious, neither within or among groups, or that intentions were ever mutual, consistent, or clear. Quite the contrary. For their part federal congressmen and Indian officials (Hurt included) distrusted Mormon missionary motives, fearing not only the intermingling of (ir)religious barbarisms but also the formation of hostile, anti-American alliances between Mormons and natives. (Recall here Representative William Waters Boyce's concerns about Mormon "confeder[ations] with the Indian tribes" creating "a race of American Arabs" capable of wreaking havoc upon emigrant trains, the "human race," and the greater West.)[37] Such concerns were not altogether unfounded, their racist expressions excepting. As tensions mounted between Mormons and the federal government in the late 1850s, and on the eve of the 1857–58 Utah Expedition, Brigham Young and his agent Dimick Huntington *did* try to get Indian leaders to ally with the Mormon "Heavenly Father" and his patriarchal representatives in Utah rather than any governmental "Great Father" from Washington. Huntington authorized Shoshonis, Utes, and Paiutes to raid emigrant trains and federal camps, seizing "Beef Cattle & horses that was on the Road to Calafornia." And it was in this context that Mormon militiamen and Indian accomplices killed some 120 westward-bound emigrants along the Old Spanish Trail in southern Utah, on September 11, 1857, in the infamous Mountain Meadows Massacre.[38]

Indian groups also distrusted Mormons, with similarly sound reasons. Indeed they had far sounder reasons: Mormon Indian policy had fluctuated wildly since 1847. On the one hand Mormons' farming, trading, and missionary efforts—questionably philanthropic as they were—extended only to "good Indians," itself a shifting category from LDS perspectives.[39] And even they were undermined and interspersed constantly by violence. True, Brigham Young advised trade in 1849, and he expanded his Indian farm programs in 1851. In 1853 and 1855 he advised disgruntled Saints to be generous and forbearing with natives, as "it is better and cheaper to feed and clothe the Indians, than to fight them."[40] But in the intervening years of 1850 and 1854, he *did* fight them, raising expeditions and encouraging killings by Mormon settlers.

Mormon officials also belied rhetorics of territorial cohabitation and trusteeship ("The land . . . belongs to our Father in heaven," said Young, and "our Father the Great Spirit has plenty of land for you and for the Mormons") with memorials to Congress requesting the extinguishment of Indian titles, the removal of Indian tribes, and the bestowal of exclusive ownership rights on Mormons.[41] In particular Mormons pleaded for the establishment of a reservation in the Uinta Basin (which the LDS press called a "vast 'contiguity of waste,' and measurably valueless") and the establishment of a land office in Salt Lake City, in order that Mormons might make formal entries for former Indian lands. The notion was considered seriously in Washington, and in 1864 Congress set aside the Uinta Basin as an Indian reservation and passed "An Act to extinguish the Indian Title to lands of the Territory of Utah suitable for agriculture and mineral purposes."[42]

Congress may have supported the removal and replacement of Utah's native populations, but enforcement of its reservation and title-extinction acts was delayed—as was the Anti-Bigamy Act—on account of railroading considerations. In effect Congress was uncomfortable officially 'vacating' lands in Mormon areas until there were measures in place by which non-Mormon white people might also have equal or easy access to them. And railroads were expected to fill that role.

Reservations and land offices would thus be on hold until the railroad came. But in the meantime—and unofficially—Congress sanctioned the 'removal' of Utahn Indians in other ways, especially by overlooking or authorizing white-on-Indian violence. Mormons fought Indians in the south, as in the Black Hawk War. And newly arriving Gentiles fought Indians in the north, as when Colonel Patrick E. Connor and his California Volunteers massacred over 250 Shoshonis and Bannocks in the Bear River Valley, forcing them farther north into Idaho. The administrative assumption was that, once the Indians were gone and railroads were present, white settlers could get down to the *real* business of making the West white and delightsome—even if that required new Mormon-Gentile fights about the precise, practical nature *of* whiteness and delight. And for their part Connor and the future Connor-loving Corinnethians welcomed the contest.

IF OUTSIDERS SOMETIMES FEARED camaraderie between Mormons and natives at Indian farms, they were more often troubled by settlements of other sorts. The second type of Mormon colony obtained in nonagricultural areas, built around industries designed specifically to obviate trade with Gentiles. These were centers of commodity production and processing, for instance, of iron and coal, cotton and flax, molasses and sugar. The ideology behind such economic missions and "home manufactures" was self-sufficiency. "We do not intend to have any trade or commerce with the gentile world," declared Young shortly after moving to the Great Basin in 1847, "for so long as we buy of them we are in a degree dependent upon them. The Kingdom of God cannot rise independent of the gentile nations until we produce, manufacture, and make every article of use, convenience, or necessity among our own people.... We shall need no commerce with the nations. I am determined to cut every thread of this kind and live free and independent, untrammeled by any of their detestable customs and practices." Again in 1853: "Produce what you consume," and "let home industry produce every article of home consumption." "Iron missionaries" at Cedar City, lead miners in Nevada, and wool spinners in Salt Lake Valley provided raw materials for Salt Lake City bells, nails, andirons, bullets, and clothing.[43]

Self-sufficiency did not preclude outgoing sales and exports, however, or the provision of way stations for overland travelers. Mormons learned early that there was money and power to be gained through toll roads, bridges, and outfitting businesses tailored toward California-bound, gold-seeking forty-niners, for example—of which an estimated ten to fifteen thousand passed through Utah that year. Miners bought high-priced Mormon wares and stock (such as flour, vegetables, horses, and mules), exchanged theretofore rare and expensive commodities (such as wagons and coffee), and provided specie and circulating media by which LDS leaders funded new public works and outreach programs (such as the Perpetual Emigrating Fund). But Mormon officials learned something else from such migrants as well—namely, the transience and instability of precious-metals mining communities. Therefore, even as the church profited immensely from what one historian has called the "Harvests of '49 and '50," Brigham Young and others officially discouraged Saints from abandoning basic Deseret colonization work.[44]

THE THIRD TYPE of Mormon colony—often contrasted by church leaders with forty-niners' presumptively anomic ghost towns—was certainly the most numerous. These were the permanent settlements, designed and chartered as satellites of Salt Lake City, for which new arrivals and enterprising pioneers alike were recruited. Most of these were located in the southern Great Basin through 1857, for Young mistakenly thought northern areas cold and inhospitable. LDS settlements spread through Cache Valley and Box Elder County, both north of Ogden, only when Young later sought there new homes for groups dislocated during the southern Indian wars and the 1857–58 Utah Expedition.

Most permanent settlements started as forts and lined encampments. But as they grew they were often recalibrated and realigned. Land was surveyed and allotted, central blocks were set aside for public buildings, and bishops oversaw the construction of canals and the adjudication of water rights. By the 1860s northern, southern, and eastern Utah were all dotted with gridlike Mormon settlements and wards.[45]

Claim Jumping and Train Hopping:
The Coordination of Land Office and Railroad

LDS officials applied often in the early 1850s, and again in the early 1860s, for the extension of federal land laws to Utah and the establishment of a legal land office in Salt Lake, in order that Mormons might obtain full title to 'their' lands.[46] But congressmen and federal officials repeatedly delayed, awaiting "the time ... when a respectable portion of the people of Utah" was greater, that is, when there were more Gentiles present. "There can be no doubt that the true policy of the government in regard to Utah is to encourage the emigration to that Territory of a population less hostile to the United States than the present," wrote the surveyor general of Colorado and Utah in 1864, several years after the Utah War. Thus "Gentile emigration must have the chance of acquiring title to the land, and must be protected in that title."[47] By his and other accounts, the government had done a good part of its job by chartering the railroad, and the railroad would in turn even the settlement score.

With sights set on approaching trains and knowing that the government was likewise focused, several Gentiles attempted to 'jump claims' throughout Salt Lake City in 1866–67. Some squatted in public squares, fields, and parade grounds, while others seized previously claimed lands in private, residential areas. All such cases displeased the Mormon majority. Prior settlers fenced fields, tore down new shanties and buildings, threw intruders into lakes and rivers, and chased them out of town. On one occasion eviction turned murderous: Dr. J. King Robinson, having staked claim to an area near a warm spring—a place theretofore used as a bathing resort by some Saints—was later beaten to death.[48]

Claim-jumping incidents forced public statements from Brigham Young. The gist of his message was that, while Mormon pioneers would forgive no incidents of (white-on-white) property theft, they would welcome any newcomers that located and improved 'open' land:

> If you undertake to drive a stake in my garden with an intention to jump my claim, there will be a fight before you get it; if you come within an enclosure of mine with any such intent, I will send you home, God being my helper. You can occupy and build where you please, but let our claims alone. We have spent hundreds of thousands of dollars in taking out the waters of our mountain streams, fencing in farms and improving the country, and we cannot tamely suffer strangers, who have not spent one

day's labour to make these improvements, to wrest our homesteads out of our hands. There is land enough in the country; go to and improve it, as we have improved our possessions; build cities, as we have done."[49]

J. H. Beadle and his fellow Corinnethians took precisely the latter tack, finding and building their own city. But the government maintained faith that railroads would force cracks also within and between Mormon settlements proper.

Citing the transcontinental railroad as a harbinger of change and a missionary of culture, the chairman of the House Committee on the Public Lands argued in favor of extending land laws and land offices to Utah in 1868–69, thus: "The Central Pacific railroad will pass over the country, and the work may take fifteen thousand employees in that region. The influx of such a column of operatives must be felt in the social condition of Utah, and many that may go there in the road service and by general immigration will doubtless remain.... It is the opinion of this office that our laws in respect to the disposal of the public lands should be promptly extended over that Territory and a land office established."[50] Congress agreed that non-Mormon railroad workers would settle in and around Salt Lake City, shaping its culture and assuring demographic change. Therefore it approved the measure. Salt Lake would soon have a land office in fact as well as function.

Reconciliation and Retrenchment:
The Mormon "Modus Operandi" in the Land Office Age

If government officials and Gentile jumpers thought that land offices, land laws, and railroads would together weaken Mormonism and unravel LDS settlement systems, they were mistaken in every respect. Quite the contrary occurred: the extension of federal land laws to Utah in many ways empowered the First Presidency, ward bishops, and county officials. For, these parties found new ways to fix and prescribe Mormon settlement systems, forcing both public and private resolutions around the persistent ambiguities of theodemocracy and Utahn colonization.

True: railroads and land offices *did* push Mormon norms into open debate; and debate did, in turn, reveal moments when LDS utopic templates stood aside messy and multiple social formations. But in so doing they raised also the stakes of normative identification and adoption, surfacing old concerns and forcing new reactions among Saints. Church officials mobilized an orthodox Mormonism in, for, and through land offices and railroads.

The land office in Salt Lake City opened March 9, 1869, one month before transcontinental agents and U.S. congressmen determined western railroad junctions, and it inaugurated a period of complicated reconciliation between Mormon and federal settlement systems. This was not simply because Mormon allotments and preemption claims needed to be externally validated and replaced by legal titles. Standard LDS city, plat, block, and lot sizes also differed from federal standards (six-mile-square townships, 640-acre sections, and 160-acre quarter-sections), and titular confirmations necessitated intersystem alignments. "The land laws applicable are not made to fit Utah, but seemingly to bother and perplex us," wrote Apostle and Church Historian George A. Smith.[51] To ensure the proper retention and registration of lands by Mormons, and in anticipation of surveyors' attempts to reitemize and reapportion them by townships and sections, Mormon officials and bishops developed what Elder Amos Milton Musser called "the Modus Operandi."[52]

The Mormon Modus Operandi had a few basic principles and bureaucratic players. The first of these resembled the Mormon trusteeship system in miniature. A single agent would act on behalf of several brethren by entering a full preemption claim for 160 acres, paying $1.25 per acre, then subdividing it among actual residents, dispensing quitclaims and receiving proportional payments from each. As George A. Smith advised other Utahn Mormons, "In all cases where there are several owners to a piece of ground, it is wisdom to pre-empt and pay for it at once. Some confidential man interested should do it with as little previous understanding with the other parties interested as possible. But with an intention to do right with it, which will be to distribute to each man his proportion at cost and expenses." Smith hoped thereby to avoid inter-Saint conflicts or jealousness, but often one of the residents themselves (rather than a confidential third party) operated as general agent for his neighbors. In any case it was of paramount importance to Smith that Saints obtain secure title to their lands, dividing it among themselves with a minimum of strife and confusion, allowing absolutely no room for Gentile claim jumpers.[53]

The second version of the Modus Operandi worked like the first, albeit with a mayor or probate judge filing as trustee for a larger community. Such an official, usually a high-ranking churchman, would then parcel out land to others, usually his fellow congregants, by application and allotment.[54] By 1871 the probate-distribution system was well established in Ogden: "The Mayor of this city has entered all the land that this City stands upon," wrote J. T. Little, "and every person that owns any lot or lots should make their application to the Probate Judge to get a title." Meanwhile Gentiles complained that Mormons had incorporated all desirable land within city boundaries and that city mayors and judges blocked exogamous settlement by withholding titles or claiming trespass.[55]

But if the system seemed smooth (to Mormons) and solid (to non-Mormons), it was not always. At least, it required serious "instruction." Amos Milton Musser wrote in his journal that he spent "June, July + August [of 1869] ma[king] several trips north to Weber + Cache counties to ~~attend to preempting &~~ instruct some 77 persons how to preempt + afterwards enter + thus pay for . . . many ¼ sections of land. As the people were unacquainted with the Modus Operandi I had to assist them in performing this service." Musser taught Ogden-area Saints, bishops, and mayors to claim as much land as possible, in accordance with new federal laws as interpreted by the Mormon priesthood, thereby extending both their bureaucratic networks and their responsibilities. Finally, as Musser concluded: "Most of this land was afterwards sold to President Brigham Young."[56] Mormons acted either as trustees for each other or deeded land directly to the trustee-in-trust.

BY THE TIME the Union Pacific Railroad Company laid claim to its official land grants in Ogden, in June 1869, it found much of the area preempted and settled by Saints. Musser, Young, and George A. Smith had paid special attention to the would-be railroad land, and they instructed local leaders to do likewise. "The brethren have been very busy for the last two months entering their farms and homesteads at the U.S. land office," wrote Smith in late June, "as a land office is now open and our citizens can now take the benefits conferred upon them by the Pre-emption and homestead laws, as far as our territory has been surveyed by U. S. Surveyors. The R'Way Company about three weeks ago, laid their claim on alternate Sections with twenty miles of their line pursuant to Congressional grants, but as a general thing the brethren had their claims entered prior which debars the R'Way company from getting title to lands previously Settled and improved."[57] The railroad found itself in receipt of many Utahn acres, to be sure, and its agents had the option of selling them to Mormons or non-Mormons as they saw fit. But in several critical instances it necessarily relied on local settlers and officials to resell properties adjacent to its tracks. And that is precisely what occurred in Ogden, when Brigham Young offered to transcontinental agents a fortune in already improved, intra-urban land, buildings, and materials. Mormons beat them to those lands, combined and improved them, and then offered them back to the companies, in exchange for snubbing the Modus of the Corinnethians.

Conferences and Cooperation:
Planning to Embrace the Railroad

By wooing railroad officials with land—some of which they might have received anyway from the federal government, if it weren't for Saintly organization—

Mormons hoped to demonstrate and maintain control over Utahn geographical *and* human resources. LDS leaders knew already from experience with gold-seeking forty-niners that they could benefit from Gentile trade without themselves becoming precisely Gentile. Around 1869 they sought to do likewise through structured social and economic preparations for, and then relationships with, railroad companies and modern industry. Latter-day Saint leaders in Utah worked to secure Mormon labor systems throughout Mormon lands.

Notwithstanding popular presumptions of Mormon technophobia, Brigham Young advocated railroad building in the West as early as 1847, and by 1854 Utah's territorial legislature had petitioned Congress for a Pacific-bound track passing through Weber Canyon, through Salt Lake City, around the southern end of the Great Salt Lake, to California.[58] Public Mormon excitement about transcontinental railroad projects peaked again around the 1862 passage of the Pacific Railway Act, and indeed Brigham Young subscribed then for five thousand dollars in Union Pacific stock—a sum sufficient to warrant his placement on the company's large board of directors, a mostly ceremonial appointment that nevertheless presaged more substantial partnerships to come. From then until 1869 Young pronounced pleasure: "Speaking of the completion of this railroad, I am anxious to see it, and I say to the Congress of the United States, through our Delegate, to the Company, and to others, hurry up, hasten the work! We want to hear the iron horse puffing through this valley. What for! To bring our brethren and sisters here."[59] Meanwhile he and other Saints wrote letters, diary entries, and other informal notes applauding technological advance and—to cite one Illinois church member, she in turn citing Isaiah, Revelation, and the Mormon scripture Doctrine and Covenants—heralding a time when "the 'high way will be cast up,' . . . 'time is no longer,' and distance is overcome." Railroads would ease Saintly gathering, fast-tracking the upbuilding of Zion.[60]

While LDS leaders voiced optimism, however, in October 1868 they also organized a special conference for Saints concerning "the railroad problem," in which they "attempted to prepare their followers for . . . changes . . . that the railroad would produce."[61] At this conference Apostle George Q. Cannon acknowledged that a certain death knell thesis had become popular among anti-Mormons, by reading aloud an editorial that prophesied the downfall of Mormondom in the railroad age and summarizing it thus: "We are told openly and without disguise, that when the railroad is completed there will be such a flood of so-called 'civilization' brought in here that every vestige of us, our church and institutions, will be completely obliterated." This was laughable, he thought. But yet it was not a laughing matter. The remainder of the session was spent discussing appropriate measures of preparation and defense, including old and new techniques of commodity production, consumption, trade, labor organization, trusteeship, and community enfranchisement.[62]

CANNON, YOUNG, AND THEIR COHORT used the occasion of railroad arrival to promote many of the institutions and social programs with which people now associate an 'orthodox Mormonism.' Indeed their very orthodoxy is a function of the degree to which they were made to intersect with and serve church needs in the railroad era. These include emigration assistance programs, women's committees, and department stores, but perhaps the most recognizable are proscriptions against consuming coffee, tea, alcohol, and tobacco. Though they dated back to 1830s church dietary codes called 'the Word of Wisdom,' drinking and smoking norms gained broad traction and attention only in the late 1860s, when they were advanced as part of an initiative to help new Saints emigrate to Utah over the railroads. Quite simply: Utahn church members were asked to stop drinking coffee and alcohol, to save the money they would have spent on them, and to donate that money to the church, so that the church could then buy railway tickets, enticing emigrants and maintaining demographic predominance in Utah.[63]

"Many a sister's coffee money went into the railroad fund of the P.E.F.," writes Leonard Arrington; and he is right to link the rebirthed Word of Wisdom with an expanded Perpetual Emigrating Fund and the LDS sisterhood.[64] As for the Perpetual Emigrating Fund, the church launched a major fundraising campaign for its in-house travel agency on the eve of railroad arrival. Amos Milton Musser spent "much of [his] attention" on "The P.E.F. Co." while traveling to teach Saints about settlement opportunities and the Modus Operandi, and other LDS representatives approached Salt Lake City businessmen "to ascertain what [they] should do for the Emigration Fund."[65] Meanwhile George A. Smith happily reported in June 1869 that the church was able to subsidize and welcome a "company of immigrants from Europe," who "reached Ogden" after only "23 days from Liverpool," and that "Latter day saints emigrants are brought from New York to Ogden . . . for fifty dollars each in six or seven days."[66] The railroad was doing a solid emigration business even before its completion, with support from the Perpetual Emigrating Fund and its contributors. And, in turn, emigrants were integrated quickly into established communities and labor forces, while avoiding the grogshops and listlessness of the hell-on-wheels bunch.

If railroads changed Mormon tastes in one way, via renewed dietary codes, the Relief Society and Young Ladies' Retrenchment Associations did so differently, but with similar benefit to the Perpetual Emigrating Fund. Recall here the Corinnethian prediction that railroads would bring to Utah not only eligible bachelors but also enticing fashions detrimental to polygamous survival. ("Polygamy will cease to exist when Mormon wives come into competition, in the matter of dress, with the other women of the world," according to this argument, especially when "their millinery bills begin to pour in upon their husbands. The Pacific Railroad, with the Gentile immigration encouraged by it, will soon make the distinction between the possession of one wife and that of two very serious, to say nothing of the indefinite number of wives popularly attributed to the leading saints in Utah.")[67] Leading female Saints—including Eliza R. Snow and Brigham Young's other wives—organized to prove their predictions wrong. Partly through the Relief Society, which was reestablished in late 1867 for this purpose, and through the Young Ladies' Department of the Cooperative Retrenchment Association, first convened in early 1870, they worked in accordance with President Young's dual charge: "to set your own fashions," avoiding "extravagance in dress, in eating, and even in speech," thereby setting "an example before the people of the world worthy of imitation"; and to "visit the sick and the helpless and the needy, . . . learn[ing] their wants" and providing them comfort. Among the articles of resolution for the Retrenchment Association was to "adopt the wearing of home-made articles, and exercise our united influence in rendering them fashionable."[68] Women thus encouraged home manufactures, plainness of dress, and simplicity of diet, and "the fruits of their labor were commonly devoted to the P.E.F."[69]

Women's activism in Utah was not confined to the worlds of fashion, millinery, temperance, or emigrant aid, however. Despite its limited official charge, the reconstituted Relief Society was used by many Mormon women as a vehicle for healing rites, preaching, and other acts of leadership associated sometimes with the original society in Nauvoo. Moreover, its leaders advocated strongly for women's suffrage in Utah, and in early 1870 they won that right. Eliza Snow was ecstatic, not least because women had the opportunity to debunk publicly and vocally the notion of female enslavement in Mormondom:

> Our enemies pretend that in Utah woman is held in a state of vassalage—that she does not act from choice but by coercion—that we would even prefer life elsewhere, were it possible for us to make our escape. What nonsense! . . . Were we the stupid, degraded, heart-broken beings that we have been represented to be, silence might better become us; but, as women of God—women filling high and responsible positions—performing sacred duties—women who stand not as dictators, but as counselors to their husbands, and who, in purest, noblest sense of refined womanhood, being truly their helpmates—we not only speak because we have the right, but justice and humanity demand that we should.[70]

The fact of woman suffrage in Utah belied popular arguments in the East, and it forced anti-Mormons to recalibrate rhetoric about patriarchal oppression and female servitude. Soon Corinnethians would argue that *all* women were unfit for the franchise, insofar as they lacked mental capacities for political understanding; and that Brigham Young had pushed for enfranchisement legislation in 1869 especially to secure a larger Mormon voting bloc on the eve of Gentile railroading. Only in the latter respect did they have a point.[71]

IF WOMEN'S ORGANIZATIONS, the expansion of the franchise, frugality, and subsidized emigration worked to offset the disruptions of Utahn national connections, perhaps "the Mormons' main defense against the coming railroad" was "economic cooperation." As historian Ronald W. Walker has noted, "The ideal of a self-sufficient Zion, with a roughly equal distribution of wealth and a one-man rule following the pattern of [the United Order of] Enoch, seemed in peril" in 1868–69. For, "despite [Brigham Young's] continuing pleas throughout the 1860s, the Saints continued to buy eastern 'store-bought goods' instead of 'homemade,'" and "they seemed quietly but alarmingly ready to reject Young's leadership" on economic matters.[72] Railroad arrival only exacerbated Young's concerns by threatening to flood Utah with cheap goods as well as labor. To counteract such threats, and to shore up his leadership and authority, Young and the First Presidency advocated wage reductions among local workers—"in order that Utah might be able to compete with the manufactures of the States."[73] Meanwhile, building outward from the distributive mechanisms of the United Order, they worked to establish a church-run wholesale business capable of regulating the import, export, purchase, and exchange of most goods: the Zion's Cooperative Mercantile Institution (ZCMI).

At the October 1868 church conference on "the railroad problem," LDS leadership announced a general boycott of all Gentile businesses and trading establishments, and it voted also that "those who dealt with outsiders should be cut off from the Church."[74] The ZCMI would thenceforth constitute the principal mode of merchandizing in Mormon towns. By its design, LDS merchants would turn over their inventories to the central ZCMI in return for stock, and retail cooperatives or branch ZCMIs served as outlets for imported and deeded goods. These and other participating firms were instructed to hang or paint signs of "the Mormon insignia of the 'All-Seeing Eye,'" along with the words "Holiness to the Lord" and "Zion's Co-operative Mercantile Institution," on their storefronts; that signage would indicate to "even the most naïve among the faithful . . . which shops were Mormon."[75] The goal was to evict hostile Gentile merchants and restrict entry for others. By the end of the month George A. Smith reported happily that "the Resolution of Conference not to patronize our enemies evidently had some effect on the temper as well as the business of the outsiders. Our leading merchants are sustaining the Co-operative movement handsomely." Some Gentiles sold out to the ZCMI, while others stayed and opposed the movement.[76]

One nonparticipating Gentile firm is of particular interest, given future Corinnethian connections: the Walker Brothers, "Wholesale Dealers, Importers, and Jobbers of Foreign and Domestic Dry Goods, Clothing &c." in the 1850s and 1860s, as well as bankers and mining promoters by 1870. Samuel Sharp, Joseph Robinson, David Frederick, and Mathew Henry Walker had come to Utah with their Mormon mother in 1852, but aside from making contributions to the Perpetual Emigrating Fund (one thousand dollars in 1867, for instance), they were noncommunicant at best.[77] The church officially "cut off" the brothers in 1861, and LDS leaders warned Saints against business with them. Not all obeyed, of course—the Walkers' biographer writes that "many of the faithful would sneak in through the back door, and goods purchased there would be marked in such a way as to conceal that they had come from the Walker Brothers"—but the Walkers were nevertheless compelled to seek business elsewhere. To that end they supported the foundation of Corinne, set up a (short-lived) store there, and partnered with Patrick E. Connor in mining projects.[78]

A few other merchants joined the Walkers in considering Corinne to be a viable alternative to Salt Lake City's regulated economics, taste cultures, and settlement systems in the spring of 1869, after the Mormon railroad conference.[79] But the church was not worried—or so said its leaders. "By industry we thrive," announced Daniel H. Wells in an April sermon on cooperation, productive business, and Corinne. By this phrase he meant two things: that "industry, in the mechanical and agricultural pursuits, is the foundation of our independence," and that cooperative exchange and inter-Saint dependencies would ensure stability for Salt Lake City and greater Mormondom. In both senses LDS cities had better chances of survival than Corinne: "I heard recently of a city that the outsiders are endeavoring to start, called Corinne, which it is said is to be the great city of the interior West. Who are going there to expend their labor?" No one, answered Wells: Corinne was a paper town occupied more by the speech patterns of transient boosters than by actual and productive citizens, the defections of some merchants notwithstanding. "There may be a rush there, for a short time, of speculators, loafers, and rowdies; but if these are the only classes of people who go there—as there is good reason to believe—this great city that is to be, like others of the same class, will soon die out, and the people be scattered to some other places."[80]

The sermon's logic was sound, thought Wells and his apostolic cohort. Corinne would be a "mushroom town" at best, for there was no future in a place that defined itself as 'everything that Mormonism was not.' Nevertheless Young, Wells, Smith, Musser, and others made moves to undergird their own oppositional rhetoric with railroad goods: money, bureaucracy, mobility, ties, iron, and power. And soon they would forge new sense for the phrase "By industry we thrive."

"By Industry We Thrive": Contracting with the Transcontinentals

Brigham Young and his cohort knew at the time of the 1868 railroad conference that they occupied a position of power, all rhetorics of besiegement and protectionism notwithstanding. For one thing Mormon officials controlled the bulk of agricultural and forestland in Utah, and they stood to make significant profits by selling food and lumber to the railroad companies. Moreover they had access to another good in abundance: labor. Brigham Young perceived that the best defense against demographic and economic upheaval—indeed, the best way to turn national railroads to proactive local profit—was to limit the importation of both materials and work crews along the Utahn stretch of the transcontinental line. While Saints generally were instructed to conduct business only through authorized channels, then, Young worked also to ensure that railroad officials likewise contracted directly with church agents for local products and laborers.

Thomas Durant, vice president of the Union Pacific Company, approached Brigham Young about a possible labor contract with Mormon settlers in the spring of 1868, as the westward-bound line built across Wyoming toward the Great Basin. "Are you disposed to take contract for a portion or all our grading between head of Echo Can[y]on & Salt Lake[?]" asked Durant by telegraph, in May, referring to the same canyon in eastern Utah where Mormons had constructed fortifications during the Utah War. "If so please name price per cubic yard according to character of material," and "we propose to give you the preference on work near your settlements if your reply is satisfactory." Young jumped at the opportunity to secure preferential hiring for church members in Utah, and he replied the same day: "I would like to contract for the grading you mention." Engineer and operations superintendent Samuel Reed traveled then to meet Young in Salt Lake City, and the two men settled on preliminary terms: Mormons would grade some fifty to ninety miles from the head of Echo Canyon, through Weber Canyon, toward the Great Salt Lake, up to a terminus yet to be determined. If the railroads decided on a southern route, Young's contract would cover all work through Salt Lake City to the southern shore of the Great Salt Lake. If they chose a northern route, it would cover work through

Ogden, to the northern shore of the lake, and as far west as the Union Pacific might extend its line before meeting the Central Pacific.

In short order the contract was broadened to include also excavation, hauling, tunneling, and bridge masonry work. Brigham Young promised up to five thousand able-bodied men, provided that the Union Pacific supplied basic tools and transportation for his laborers at cost and provided also that it made regular payments: 30₵ (or more) per yard for excavations, $15 per yard for tunneling, $8 (or more) per yard for masonry construction, $2 (or more) per day per worker, and so forth, with exact amounts owed to be tabulated on a monthly basis. The total consideration was some $2,310,000, and Young claimed also the right to charge for overtime and additional laborers.[81]

Brigham Young's contract with the Union Pacific was a formally capitalistic relation between two semipublic corporations and western landlords. On the LDS side, Young fulfilled his obligations by appointing as project administrators three of his sons—Joseph A. Young, Brigham Young, Jr., and John W. Young—who in turn initiated subcontracts with approximately one hundred local bishops, church authorities, and businessmen. These subcontractors then "handled [their subcontracts] in much the same way that other cooperative projects were undertaken," that is, by calling local congregants to service work. Payment plans dictated that the Union Pacific deduct from its monthly bills the basic cost of tools and transportation provided to Mormon laborers and that it pay the balance directly to Young, who would divide it among LDS subcontractors after withholding a tithe for the church and an additional sum for the Perpetual Emigrating Fund. (P.E.F. agents worked meanwhile to bring additional would-be railroad workers from Europe to Utah—or at least to Nebraska, from which the Union Pacific agreed to transport them at cost.) Finally, Brigham Young's subcontractors would pay their workers in cash, tithing credit, ZCMI script, or debt relief, according to preference and availability.[82] Not all Mormon laborers were happy with the arrangement; some complained about losing workers on nonrailroad projects, others about forced deployment far from home, and still others about delays in payment.[83] But for many people—especially teamsters, sawmill operators, P.E.F.-funded emigrants, and farmers impoverished by recent grasshopper blights—the railroad work was welcome. By their accounts the Union Pacific brought good wages, high trade values, debt relief, and a veritable "money harvest" to Utah.[84]

Church leaders appreciated the Union Pacific's willingness to let them determine the demographic makeup of most "work [teams] near your settlements."[85] This would mean, they thought, that they could avoid the employment of many Chinese and Irish laborers and thus also the establishment of new 'ethnic' settlements in Utah. However they wondered aloud, still, whether the nature of railroad work and their inevitable run-ins with Gentile laborers

Mormon construction camp at Echo Canyon, Utah, 1868.
(Courtesy of University of Iowa Libraries, Iowa City [Levi O. Leonard Papers])

and hell-on-wheels encampments would pollute the Saints. "Can a person work on the railroad," asked Wells, "and be associated by the wicked without being contaminated by them?" The answer was a resounding "O yes, if he is so disposed. An elder of Israel should wrap himself as with a mantle, from sin, whether he goes to preach the Gospel to a wicked world, or whether he goes to labor among the wicked."[86] For Wells, Mormon railroad camps were occasions for the articulation of elements of an LDS orthodoxy, including hard work, temperance, Sabbath observation, tithing, and restraint from swearing. And as such they would be beacons unto the world as well as boons to the economy and buffers against invasion.

Notwithstanding the grumblings that some registered in their journals,[87] most Mormon laborers also applauded their heaven-on-wheels rail camps as if they were small, temporary Zions. "A birds eye view of the railroad camps in Echo canyon would disclose to the beholder a little world of concerted industry unparalleled, I feel safe to assert, in the history of railroad building," reported the *Deseret News* in July 1868.[88] And one canyon worker penned a song expressive (also prescriptive) of LDS excitement:

> Hurrah! Hurrah! For the railroad's begun!
> Three cheers for our contractor, his name's Brigham Young!
> Hurrah! Hurrah! we'er honest and true,
> For if we stick to[,] it's bound to go through.
>
> Now there's Mr. Reed, he's a gentleman true,
> He knows very well what the "Mormons" can do;
> He knows in their work they are lively and gay,
> And just the right boy's to build a railway.
>
> Chorus.—Hurrah! Hurrah! &c.
>
> Our camp is united, we all labor hard;
> And if we work faithfully we'll get our reward;
> Our leader is wise and industrious too
> And all things he tells us we're willing to do . . .
>
> We surely must live in a very fast age;
> We've traveled by ox teams, and then took the stage;
> But when such conveyance is all done away
> We'll travel in steam cars upon the railway.
>
> Chorus.—Hurrah! Hurrah! &c.
>
> The great locomotive next season will come
> To gather the Saints from their far distance home;
> And bring them to Utah in peace here to stay,
> While the judgments of God sweep the wicked away.[89]

If managed properly, the Reed-Young contracts would mobilize rather than endanger a Mormon ethos. Surely God and nation would smile upon Saintly rail camps.

WHEN BRIGHAM YOUNG SIGNED contracts with Samuel Reed, Thomas Durant, and the greater Union Pacific, the route of the road was not yet determined: not only was there no agreed-upon junction for the Union and Central Pacific, but both companies were undecided about whether to build north or south of the Great Salt Lake. For his part Brigham advocated a southern route and a Salt Lake City connection, and Mormon merchants similarly "donated" "large somes of money . . . to the company . . . to have it come to the city."[90] On the company side, Samuel Reed worked to maintain positive business relations with the Saints—and also to "ke[ep] Young and his men out of the hands of the Central Pacific, which also tried to recruit him"—by flattering them and implying the strong likelihood of precisely that course. This was not outright deception, on Reed's part, at least not at first. The Union Pacific *did* investigate the southern route, and as late as September 1868 George A. Smith optimistically reported that "the Eastern Company have surveyors on the south side of the lake." But by the preceding summer—indeed by the time Mormons had begun their grading work at Echo Canyon, cheering "Mr. Reed" as "a gentleman true"—company brass had inclined themselves toward the north. Chief engineer Grenville Dodge visited Brigham Young personally to break the news: the Union Pacific had chosen the northern route, for it was shorter, flatter, and better forested.[91]

Angered by Dodge's news, Brigham Young turned from the Union Pacific westward to the Central Pacific, "which had already decided upon the northern route" as well, but which "kept this information from the Mormons in order to secure their assistance in speeding up the construction of their line."[92] Brigham contracted (covertly) with them, too, for approximately $1 million in grading and construction work, in hopes of persuading them to stick south. But despite his efforts the matter was soon publicly decided in favor of the northern route. Thereafter Mormons focused anew on influencing the pace and placement of that route near Ogden, Corinne, and Promontory and on building a branch railroad to it from Salt Lake City.[93]

A WORD OF CLARIFICATION is in order, lest it seem that Brigham Young was duped and bowled over by the railroads. This is not true. Although Mormons failed to win approval for the more arduous path through Salt Lake City, they prospered much during the long and confusing process of northern construction, and they navigated effectively the spaces between the tangled arms of a would-be transcontinental octopus. Consider Mormons' contracts with the Central Pacific: they were made officially in the names of Ezra Benson, Lorin Farr, and Chauncey West, so that Brigham Young and the LDS Church would not breech the terms of their exclusive Union Pacific contract. ("Perhaps you can see the difference tween tweedle dum an' tweedle dee, but I cannot," complained Dodge, even as he dispatched an associate to keep peace with Young.)[94] Perhaps more telling yet is Young's willingness to capitalize on intracompany power struggles and intercompany competition: the Mormons willingly graded and constructed miles of purposeless, dead-ended, or parallel track as Union Pacific officials Dodge, Seymour, Durant, and others fought among themselves over practical and political matters and as they jointly fought the Central Pacific for mileage and subsidies. "Prest. Young's contract is proceeding satisfactorily" with the Union Pacific, gloated George A. Smith, "as is also the contract of Benson, Farr and West with the Central Pacific"; and although "a portion of [one] job overlaps for fifty miles a job previously let by Gov. Stanford," the railroad "has been the means of distributing among the inhabitants of Utah a million of dollars received for payment for work on the same, and there is about another million due us." Mormons made do in a world of bureaucratic and corporate inefficiency, willingly subcontracting responsibilities or even duplicating energies toward the general systemic up-building of Mormondom.[95]

Granted, the million-or-so dollars owed by the Union Pacific to the Mormon Church in the spring of 1869, partly for work done above and beyond the necessary, was never paid in full. The church eventually settled for a payment significantly lower than the amount billed. That resolution, however, constituted neither a true loss for the church nor callous mistreatment by the Union Pacific, and it should not be considered evidence of naïveté or bad negotiation on Brigham Young's part either. Quite the contrary. The Union Pacific had by then already paid out some $1,350,000 in cash and company scrip, on top of $230,000 in equipment; and it had provided a good amount more in subsidized travel. Of the $940,000 still claimed by the church (down from an initial claim of $1,138,800), approximately $204,000 consisted of overage charges that were debatable at best. Finally—after Brigham Young sent two of his principal subcontractors, Joseph A. Young and Bishop John Sharp, to negotiate a final payment with Union Pacific officials in Boston—the two parties agreed to settle the bill via a feat of mutually agreeable accounting. The church would accept $50,000 in cash to John Sharp, $230,000 in Union Pacific notes payable within seven months to Brigham Young, $10,000 in immigrant transportation costs, $50,000 for freight transportation, and, most important, $600,000 in rolling stock and railroad materials. The last sum would be used in building a branch line from Salt Lake City to Ogden, to be called the Utah Central, a railroad that would be owned and operated directly by the LDS Church.

Brigham Young's settlement terms thus guaranteed that, even though the Union Pacific might pass to the north of Salt Lake City, he extracted from it the necessary means to connect the Mormon city with the mainline. All told this was a victory for the LDS Church. Not only did Young's negotiations pave the way for the church's own railroad, but they enabled and indeed ensured future good-faith relations with *the* railroad, the Union Pacific.[96]

WHILE THE LDS CHURCH watched the Central Pacific and Union Pacific debate their futures—and while its leaders engaged in profitable negotiations with both companies—there was one point on which Brigham Young was unwilling to countenance indecision. That was the final junction town. If it was not to be Salt Lake City, Mormons were at least determined to make Ogden the place where the Central Pacific and Union Pacific—and soon also the Utah Central—would locate their transfer stations.

Despite their best efforts, Mormons watched as "there grew up at the respective termini mushroom towns," or hell-on-wheels encampments that flared up and died down as Gentile contingents of the Union Pacific's construction force moved on. "The first in the territory was called Bear river," wrote George A. Smith, referring to a site in southwest Wyoming where "some heavy contracts requiring many hands" necessitated the employment of many Gentiles. By Smith's account the town fizzled when "the graders ignored the County authorities and undertook to govern themselves; a party organized themselves as a vigilance committee and commenced to hang the other half.... A skirmish ensued and some twenty or thirty were killed and wounded on both sides," and "soon after the track was laid past the place and the town vanished." Other towns sprouted and vanished likewise, but, Smith wrote, only when they reached better-established and more orderly Mormon regions could their violence be tamed.

Smith much preferred that railroad towns not mushroom where they could not be contained by Mormon authorities, and he agreed with Brigham Young that Ogden was best equipped to tame the hell-on-wheels lawlessness that moved along the tracks. "The Ogden city fathers were able to maintain good order and to suppress much of the lawlessness manifested at every other terminus," said Smith, not least because the city "has been incorporated for many years," with "a Mayor, aldermen, Councillors, recorder, police and other appendages of city government" working alongside Mormon bishops to maintain its Plat of Zion–inspired orderliness. "The strictness of the municipal arrangements at Ogden was very uncongenial to the feelings of many who had enjoyed, for a considerable length of time, freedom from all wholesome restraints, and as the only alternative they hurried on to some point, where they could again inaugurate their drinking saloons, gambling houses and dancing institutions."[97] In other words Ogden managed to maintain its Mormon Modus Operandi even when it first functioned as a terminus, that is, as the Union Pacific first began to build through the town in early April 1869.

The principal concern for the church, then, in early April, was that the Union Pacific might look beyond Ogden to Corinne: a place that seemed to grow larger each day after the frontline camps moved north and west from Ogden, toward the Union's still-undetermined meeting point with the Central Pacific. Wrote Smith:

> At Corinne 27 miles north of Ogden . . . all the floating material that has followed the railroad seems to be concentrating; and here murder, bloodshed and crime are rampant; forming a striking contrast between this and the hitherto temperate, peaceful and orderly condition of the inhabitants before the introduction of the railroad. Corinne is evidently the head quarters for libertines and thus far has been very successful in gathering from all parts of the territory those who had proclivities for free drinking and free fighting.[98]

Other Salt Lake Mormons took notice too, of course. Therefore—just as Corinnethians seemed to capture the interest of Union Pacific surveyors and Sheldon Jackson's missionaries, and as J. H. Beadle heroically proclaimed Corinne "*the* great Gentile town" of the West—they did their best also to poke fun at Corinnethian aspirations and terms-of-art. "Corinne, built of canvas and board shanties, . . . is fast becoming *civilized*, several men having been killed there already," reported the *Deseret News*; and "there is not less than three hundred whisky shops" in the area, "all *developing the resources of the Territory*, and showing the 'Mormons' what is necessary to build up a country and make it self-supporting and permanent."[99] Smith and the church newspaper may have considered Corinnethian aspirations overblown and worthy of ridicule, but their humor was belied by fears of Union Pacific disloyalty, and also by recognition that the death knell thesis was serious business indeed.

Thus it was that, when Brigham Young intervened in the melee of corporate indecision respecting "the Chicago of the West," he did so to ensure that the Central and Union Pacific returned precisely to Ogden, to a point directly between Salt Lake City and Corinne. Thus it was also that Ogden's many land transfers and corporate connections numbered high among Mormons' great transcontinental triumphs. The Mormon Modus Operandi secured thriving industrial ties by and through which Mormonism itself could continue to thrive from that point on.

Ogden: The Hub Is Born

Brigham Young did not attend the Central Pacific and Union Pacific's rail-joining festivities at Promontory Summit on May 10, 1869, for he knew already

The joining of the Union Pacific and Central Pacific rails at Promontory, Utah, May 10, 1869. Brigham Young didn't attend the celebration, but other Saints did. The image itself is by Mormon photographer C. R. Savage, who traveled and trained with A. J. Russell of the Union Pacific corps. One of the bottle-holding men may have been Francis A. Hammond, an LDS laborer on Benson, Farr, and West's contract with the Central Pacific. Benson, Farr, and West themselves were also present. (Courtesy of the Church History Library, The Church of Jesus Christ of Latter-day Saints, Salt Lake City [PH 3747])

that the de facto junction would be Ogden.[100] Moreover, Young had made plans already for a church-owned railway company to connect Salt Lake City and Ogden. The Utah Central Railroad Company was chartered in March and dedicated in May 1869, with Brigham Young as company president and Joseph A. Young as general superintendent.

Officials of the LDS Church held a ground-breaking ceremony for the Utah Central, the first formally Mormon railroad, on May 17 in Ogden. The celebration took place next to the Union Pacific depot there, on lands that had already played a significant role in aligning church and railroad interests. From there, church laborers extended the Utah Central line southward toward Salt Lake City, across lands already claimed through the Mormon Modus Operandi. Workers deployed skills learned while building the transcontinentals, now building their own road with tools and tracks received in partial payment for their work, and linking up locomotives likewise deeded to Brigham Young by the Union Pacific. Some received cash for their labor, while others were paid in company stock, railroad tickets, or goods and credit from the ZCMI. Many more worked for tithing relief or as an act of indenture to the P.E.F. and Brigham Young for subsidizing their Utahn emigrations. The entire operation was closely integrated, in any case, and it moved along quickly. With such land, labor, stock, and capital at its disposal, the church opened its line for travel in January 1870.[101]

The Utah Central's 'joining' ceremony mimicked that of the transcontinentals, albeit with a Mormon bent. Company and church president Brigham Young drove the last spike, made of native Utahn iron, with a mallet engraved with the words "Holiness to the Lord." (Young did not miss his target, as Thomas Durant and Leland Stanford had infamously done at Promontory.) The road was dedicated in prayer, and Brigham Young declared publicly his gratitude to the Union Pacific, several of whose officers were in attendance. "You have refused us no favor," he said, offering to us always "kindness . . . as companies, as superintendents, as engineers, as conductors and etc.," not to mention also the materials without which "this road would not have been and this track would not have been laid to-day." Finally, Young "also thank[ed]" the LDS Mormons of Utah, "the brethren who have aided to build this, our first railroad. They have acted as Elders of Israel, and what higher praise can I accord to them, for they have worked on the road, they have graded the track, they have laid the rails, they have finished the line, and have done it cheerfully 'without purse or scrip.'" This was a holy corporate undertaking indeed.[102]

"OUR OWN R ROAD!!" exclaimed Amos Milton Musser in his diary, pleased that his land deals had helped yield such dividends. *By industry we thrive.*[103]

CHAPTER THREE

Godbeites and the Capital of Dissent

✦

During Mormon celebrations of transcontinental completion and the Utah Central's charter, Salt Lake City merchant William S. Godbe toasted "the railroad" as "a mighty engine for the promulgation of the gospel of 'Peace on earth and good will to man.'"[1] This was a sentiment that Brigham Young shared—or so he then thought. Within five months the church president would learn that Godbe had a distinctly different vision for Mormon development in the railroad era. And because of it Godbe was excommunicated.

Church authorities excommunicated Godbe and his colleague Elias L. T. Harrison on October 25, 1869, nine days after they published "The True Development of the Territory," a thorough critique of Brigham Young's economic priorities and measures for Saintly consolidation. In it Godbe and Harrison had argued that laissez-faire capitalism and mining were more conducive to Mormon wealth—and, indeed, to Mormon religious legitimacy—than Young's favorite programs of cooperative merchandizing, home manufactures, and agriculturalism. For it, they were then charged with "harboring the spirit of apostasy," promoting ideas "obnoxious to the policy of Brigham Young," and sowing discontent among Saints. "They have introduced views + sentiments in direct opposition to the principles of the Gospel," wrote Amos Milton Musser, leading member of the Deseret Agricultural and Manufacturing Society and unofficial Mormon land agent, in his journal. "They have sought to promote the development of the 'precious' metals in our midst + thus invite among us an element that would, if strong enough, destroy us." A public trial followed, and the Salt Lake Stake High Council found Godbe and Harrison "in open + avowed opposition to the Gospel + the interests [of] the Kingdom of God."

Consequently "they were unanymously cut off from the Church + turned over to the buffittings of Satan."[2]

WILLIAM GODBE AND OTHER so-called 'Godbeites' of the 'New Movement' were astute observers of the railroading programs advanced by Brigham Young, national politicians, and the Corinnethians. Indeed by working wherever these programs collided or overlapped, Godbeites effectively questioned the railroad era priorities of the LDS Church, simultaneously shaping both local and national debates about spiritual economics and the place of religion in modernity. Godbeites claimed to represent a liberal, laissez-faire, republican, privatized, and thus properly Protestant brand of Mormonism fit for secular currency and amenable to American incorporation. Along the way—via complicated interactions with Corinnethians and government officials and following the formation of a schismatic Mormon church—they helped catalyze instead the redefinition of orthodox Mormonism, even as they illuminated its various and divergent conditions. The New Movement thus responded to Brigham Young's railroad plans in ways illustrative of several industrial mechanisms engaged in the formation of modern American religions.

To be clear from the beginning: the Godbeites, like the Corinnethians, failed in their efforts to supplant or displace what they called 'Brighamite' Mormonism. But they did so in interesting and related ways, with complicated and sometimes ironic results. Godbeites tapped into national networks and reconfigured local politics, for a time. They situated themselves amid key players—Saints, congressmen, Corinnethians, capitalists, and Protestants—at the crossroads of important American trends, highlighting each in turn. The fact that Godbeites failed, finally, to unite these networks and trends to sit atop them triumphantly tells us less about Godbeites' incoherence, as individuals or a group, than it does about the bureaucratic management of western religions, about secularism's necessary but unsteady reliance on interreligious critiques, and about the economic mainstreaming of mainline Mormonism.

"A Mormon Protestantism"

A decade before transcontinental connections William Godbe was one of the wealthiest men in Utah. He was also on close working terms with Brigham Young, having played an important role in the development of Salt Lake City's commercial district, in which Godbe operated a general merchandise store and from which he organized shipments of eastern goods to other western

Mormons. Such activity met with Young's approval, at the time, provided that (as Young once reminded Saints from the pulpit of the Salt Lake Tabernacle) Godbe and other LDS merchants did not "forget their God and their religion in trying to get rich," inflating prices or otherwise forgoing neighborly responsibilities in favor of self-aggrandizement.³ Meanwhile Godbe invested in Wyoming mines, likewise an acceptable but risky enterprise from Brigham Young's perspective: acceptable so long as Godbe refrained from precious metals mining and promotion in Utah itself, but risky insofar as it attracted opportunistic Gentile speculators to nearby lands. Such businesses subsequently proved contentious when Young, anticipating adverse effects of impending railroad connectivity, decided that risks outweighed rewards. But in the early and mid-1860s the church president supported Godbe's enterprises, and Godbe returned the favor by lecturing publicly on key acts of LDS devotion: pursuing personal righteousness and global salvation, restoring spiritual gifts and prophesy, and upholding the ancient principle of plural marriage (Godbe himself married four women between 1855 and 1869). By most accounts William Godbe was a pillar of the 1850s and mid-1860s LDS community.

Other would-be Godbeites were also considered model Mormons prior to the railroad age. Among them were Elias L. T. Harrison, architect, literary enthusiast, and philosopher; Edward W. Tullidge, newspaperman, playwright, and historian of Utah events; and, somewhat later, Fanny Stenhouse and T. B. H. Stenhouse, writers, socialites, and cultural go-betweens for Mormons and Gentile easterners. All were Britons who, like Godbe himself, had been converted during the 1840s and 1850s missionary milieu of social criticism and evangelical fervor in England and then had moved to Utah in the 1850s and early 1860s seeking new religious and economic opportunities. Similarly committed to the idea of Mormonism as a restorative and yet modern movement, they celebrated it for reacquainting people with the signs and wonders of the biblical era while also enshrining the proofs and protections of individualism. By their collective accounting Mormonism focused—or *did* focus, in its original instance—on personal progress, private belief, and direct relationships with the Divine. Above all, they said, Joseph Smith's promises of democratic priesthood rights assumed humans' capacity for independent thought and inspiration respecting affairs of state, spirit, and family.⁴

The Mormonism of Harrison, Tullidge, Godbe, and the Stenhouses' estimation was a self-consciously individualist, intentionally ecumenical, and generally Protestant affair. It was also an economically liberal one: a tradition that allowed, philosophically if not logistically, for as much free exchange among individuals as it did among humanity and divinity. Such presumptions, however, proved increasingly disconnected from reality in 1860s Utah, or so it then seemed to the future Godbeites. By their accounts Brigham Young's efforts to enforce Mormon communitarianism stood to threaten Saints' spiritual development and economic freedom.

Communitarianism was not a new impulse among Saints, of course. Mormon groups had long experimented with in-group financial arrangements, communal property holding, patterns of consolidated settlement, and 'theodemocratic' politics to maintain them. But Godbe especially thought that Brigham Young had taken matters too far during the prerailroad years of economic and ecclesiastical centralization. He resented the establishment of the Zion's Cooperative Mercantile Institution, and he opposed ecclesiastical sanctions against mining—all of which handicapped economic integration with the East and limited merchants' markets. Godbe's fiscal frustrations were counterbalanced only by his steadfastly positive appraisal of Mormonism itself as a movement, rightly conceived, for individualism and liberality. Thus by 1868 Godbe and his more philosophically inclined friends shared the seditious thought: that Young had insulted Mormons' intelligence and Mormonism's divinity alike by claiming unto himself an infallible, extrahuman wisdom and by reducing priesthood itself to a shallow office of temporal direction and dictation. Godbe thought that Brigham Young had cheapened the Mormon gospel, all the while impoverishing most Mormons, for the sake of a fragile and outmoded clannishness.

For all of Brigham Young's flaws, however, Godbe and his colleagues did not wish to unseat him from the church presidency, at least not at first. Far less did they want to leave Utah. They saw themselves rather as reformers of a true church in its proper place, on the eve of its rightful integration into American society. Wishing above all to restore Mormonism's fundamental spirituality through new discourses and practices of materiality, they therefore reperiodized Mormon history, prescribing LDS futures by redescribing church pasts. Godbe and others deemphasized the temporal foci of Joseph Smith's gospel, for instance, and characterized early Mormonism as a spiritually vital time of "close and constant intercommunication between this and the Heavenly worlds," in which "visions and divinely-given dreams" were "widely diffused amongst us."[5] They also praised Smith's successor for having "played the part of a Mormon Moses to perfection" after Smith's death, ferrying Saints to a place of safety in a time of need. Brigham Young "was inspired to bring this people to these mountains," wrote Harrison, and all Mormons owed him a debt of gratitude for laying out cities, building infrastructure, and otherwise ensuring the earthly stability of the church. But such work being then complete, there was no further need for "Mosaic performance in this age and country," let alone a "papal" system of ecclesiastical commerce and coercion. It was time for Mormons to return to their liberal roots in order that they might grow in(to) a liberal nation.[6]

But if proto-Godbeite narratives expected Brigham Young to find his way back to the true path, that hope receded as Young's railroading platform unfurled. Tullidge, the chief chronicler of the New Movement, recalled with special frustration Young's responses to Pacific Railway construction, characterizing them as axiomatic of Mormons' increasingly unholy preoccupations with 'temporalities' instead of spiritual matters. By his account railroads and Mormon railroading projects inaugurated the era of Brighamite mismanagement and, thus, of the Godbeite movement itself. "Since he could not prevent [the railroad's] accomplishment," wrote Tullidge, Brigham Young "purposed to make it serve his own ends," by becoming "the chief contractor in the construction of the Utah branch of the line" and by drawing his coreligionists into closer contact with him through telegraphic and mercantile connections. "It was an attempt to use the machinery of civilization, usually designed for breaking up isolation, to make isolation complete and organized; to establish Mormonism within civilization, but intact, as a wheel within a wheel, an *imperium in imperio*; an isolation of a higher and more complex character, unlike that which had hitherto existed, and was dependent upon geographical conditions merely, was to be secured."[7] Tullidge complained that Brigham Young's contractual innovations constrained the would-be 'liberal,' 'civilizing' mechanics of railroads in Utah. More than that, Young had repurposed industry to ironic effect, maintaining cultish cohesion amid transnational connections.

Tullidge was not without insights, and he identified well certain operations of Mormon bureaucracy relative to national economic forms. He saw clearly that Brigham Young controlled the chief means of production in Utah, having certain abilities to direct and dispose of land, lumber, and labor, and that the LDS Church acted like a private enterprise, contracting with other private enterprises to meet certain community needs while also amassing profits. Indeed Tullidge recognized in Mormon railroading a certain type of capitalism. However it was neither good nor pure, by Tullidge's accounting, but rather a monstrous system guilty of primitive operation and categorical confusion between profit and prophet. Brighamite industry existed, Tullidge thought, for purposes of cultic exaltation through selective exposures to market access. And that defeated the entire purpose of capitalism.

What Tullidge and other would-be Godbeites imagined and theorized was what Max Weber would later describe as *modern*, rational capitalism, a system characterized not only by corporate development and control of productive forces but also by free labor, free trade, and scientific management.[8] To the degree that Mormonism implemented the former but not latter conditions, Tullidge, Godbe, and company fought for a more 'advanced' capitalism, assuming by it the direct concomitance of economic diversification, liberalism, individualism, and intelligence. In so doing they approximated the ideology of Corinnethianism, which added to this proto-Weberian constellation the also-Weberian prospect of religious decline or rather Protestant ascendency.

Of course Tullidge and Godbe considered themselves properly Protestant and thus resistant to any of industrial modernity's religious downsides. "A Mormon Protestantism was at length a fact," Tullidge wrote some years later, looking back at the origins of the Godbeite New Movement. He meant by this to analogize William Godbe and Martin Luther in their fights against 'papal' authorities, but also to signal Godbe's approval of American Protestant norms for distinguishing public from private life. By their estimation Mormon Protestantism—indeed, Mormonism originally and rightly conceived—was a democratic faith perfectly coincident with economic liberalism, rational capitalism, and national development. Thankfully, "Providence was moving to demolish the worst part of Brigham's work *that the better part might be preserved!*" The catalysts of such Protestant providence in Utah were, by Tullidge's account, the self-same objects of Brighamite mismanagement—namely, railroads, mines, and Gentile businessmen. Their arrival had marked the moment of acceptable intra-Mormon critique.[9]

WILLIAM GODBE'S 1869 TOAST to the railroad is more clearly significant in light of these providential considerations. Standing in Ogden, at the halfway point between Salt Lake City and Corinne, Godbe imagined that trains would effectively bridge eastern and western religious cultures, yielding the renewal of an arguably original and liberal Mormon ethos, the contraction of temporal priesthood authorities, and the expansion of exogamous trade opportunities. Insofar as he had perceived 'Brighamite' ecclesiastical efforts to the contrary, his dissatisfaction with Mormonism leadership had grown. Thenceforth Godbe resolved to articulate, in increasingly public venues, a reformed Mormonism differently commensurate with railroads and especially immune to their death knells.

Tullidge, Harrison, and the Stenhouses stood ready, with Godbe, to reclaim railroad platforms as their own and to announce from them the dawning of a New Movement. Little did they anticipate the many frustrations to come, wrought by the de facto operations of the modern bureaucratic state and its favored corporations. To their great surprise Godbeites found them to be peculiarly amenable to and indeed dependent upon certain religious forms and functions, the simultaneous mobilization and management of intercultural conflict and the selective incorporation of the supposedly premodern. Bureaucrats and railroad barons alike had separate but overlapping interests in keeping 'Brighamites' at the table, and they considered Godbeites useful mainly insofar as they served as a type of political capital and bureaucratic bargaining chip.

"The Right Place to Strike"

The pro-laissez-faire Mormons advanced their critiques in the *Utah Magazine*, based in the Godbe Exchange Buildings.[10] They did so slowly at first. But with increasing frequency and fervor in the fall of 1869, *Utah Magazine* writers suggested that Brigham Young had overstepped his ecclesiastical rights and responsibilities. Well beyond counseling "free acceptance of doctrines" and directing church ordinances, they said, the president had asked Saints to forgo personal relationships with divine intelligence, and to ignore their own common sense, when determining proper comportment in private or public, mind and market. Brigham Young's plan of closed-market, farm-based trade was stifling chances for the elevated national profile and prosperity of Mormon people and limiting the spiritual freedoms concomitant to right economic practice.[11]

"The True Development of the Territory"—the October 1869 article for which Godbe and Harrison were excommunicated, and thus also the founding document of what then became known as the Godbeite New Movement—was an essay in praise of mining. In it the *Utah Magazine* agitators argued that Utah had "mountains of coal, iron and lead, and enough copper and silver to supply the world," and that it was criminal to neglect their extraction and exportation. These were fighting words. And they took aim at Brigham Young himself, for it was he that had discouraged mining efforts in favor of farming (for most) and railroad building (for some). Young had thought—rightly—that mining was a tenuous and irregularly profitable venture, and he was also concerned—more contentiously—that the discovery of precious metals would lead to stampedes of gold-rushers and the moral decline of Mormon people.[12] The Godbeites' rejection of this tenet was no small affair, especially given their stated willingness to consult and hire Gentile partners. Godbeites were "turned over to the buffittings of Satan" in large part because, in Amos Milton Musser's words, "they have sought to promote the development of the 'precious' metals in our midst + thus invite among us an element that would, if strong enough, destroy us."[13]

An additional anecdote demonstrates the seriousness with which LDS officials took the religious challenge of Godbeites' promining columns. Approximately one year after Godbe's excommunication, some leaders challenged church members to defend their patronage of the Godbeite periodical—which by 1870 was renamed the *Salt Lake Tribune*. George Darling Watt, a sometime stenographer for Brigham Young, was among those challenged. Recalling the exchange in a letter to his wife, Watt emphasized the types of answers deemed acceptable, if they and other Saints wished to retain their subscriptions:

> The teachers ask me the following questions.... *"Do you take the Salt Lake Tribune[?"]* I do. *"What do you think of it?"* Its mineral department is an exaggeration, and used to flood the country with people from abroad to rob the Mormon people of their Legislative and municipal rights.... *"Why do you take it then?"* To inform myself as to its purpose and intent, and to be prepared to ward off impending danger to myself and family and to my friends and the social and religious institutions with which I am connected and which I prefer to uphold and defend.... *"What do you think of the Godbe religion?"* They have no religion.[14]

This was a catechism of religious affirmation and denial, the likes of which was repeated often, Watt implied, by those unwilling to claim closer affiliation with the rebellion. It rightly identified some of the terms by which proper Mormonism was debated, in any case: temporality, mineral development, and religion. Both Godbeites and Brighamites insisted that right religion consisted in right economic practice and right evaluations of mineral wealth.

SUPPORTERS OF THE NEW MOVEMENT imagined a Mormon state of prosperity consisting in interrelated social, economic, political, and ecclesiastical efforts. Tullidge wrote—here, with a wink to Brigham Young's conception of Utah as "the place" for Mormonism—that "the agitation for the opening of the mines was the 'right place' to strike for Utah's social redemption," and so "we struck there first, before proclaiming any spiritual or religious movement."[15] But the line between the economic and religious fronts of Godbeites' offensive must not be overdrawn. Mining *was* for them a necessarily, if unfortunately, religious issue. Raising questions there and elsewhere about the "right place" of priesthood authority, and by asking whether church officials could legitimately regulate industry or dictate commerce, New Movement members could reasonably consider their economic agitations to be religious and vice versa. Brigham Young had linked the material and spiritual conditions of Mormonism in one way, by establishing ecclesiastical regulation of trades, but Godbeites argued that such connection worked to their mutual detriment. New Movement members sought differently to determine proper relations between things material and spiritual, economic and ecclesiastical, secular and sacred. "We are nothing, if not spiritual," the leaders announced.[16]

From 1869 through the early 1870s, Godbeite publications insisted that open communion, open businesses, and open markets were favorable for the Mormon people as a whole and that outside connections and capital could catalyze inside wealth. "In the development of our mineral riches . . . lies the only hope for our mechanics to get decent wages and deliverance from the miserable 'trade' system. With the Great Railway at hand, we can ship them to the East and West, get our pay in cash, and the men working them can get the same kind of pay."[17] Supporters of the New Movement thus agreed with Brigham Young that railroads brought opportunities for Mormon deliverance, but they took this to mean something decidedly different.

Political Platforms

If mining was the right place to strike against Brigham Young's leadership, and if railroad connections precipitated that action, then railroad platforms themselves were the right place to talk politics and plot reformation with eastern visitors. This was especially true in 1869, when numerous Republican politicians toured the country by train, stopping in major cities to give speeches, ascertain political climates, and decide how best to reconstruct the West. With respect to Utah and the Mormons, that meant assessing recent social and economic developments and deciding whether to renew antichurch and antipolygamy offensives or to let railroads run their supposedly pacifying course. Awaiting them at Utah's stations were Corinnethians, Saints, and Godbeites, each with a different view on the matter.

Approximately three weeks before their excommunication, the soon-to-be Godbeites had occasion to discuss their economic philosophies with Vice President Schuyler Colfax, who was then undertaking just such a transcontinental tour through Salt Lake City. Though Colfax's general dislike of Mormons was by then well established, Godbe, Harrison, and others hoped that they could alter his opinion of some if not all Saints. Colfax's visit seemingly raised the stakes of intrareligious argument and the opportunity for sect-state alliance, notwithstanding secularism's philosophical presumptions of church-state division. And initial conversations seemed promising. Indeed, based in part on their private railside interactions, the Godbeites banked on their chances for government embrace and secular success. Their "True Development" article ran two weeks later.

Colfax's 1869 tour was the first opportunity to argue Godbeite platforms before prominent American statesmen. Other opportunities for political recognition came soon after that, in 1870: during elections for city and territorial representatives and amid political debates regarding the Cullom Bill, a national antipolygamy measure designed to augment and enforce the Morrill Anti-Bigamy Act. In discourses surrounding all such events there was a replay of earlier efforts at (anti-)Mormon explanation, including congressional pronouncements on comparative religions and theories of industrial acculturation. There were, however, changes in personnel and subdivisions of affiliation, and in 1869 and 1870 the Godbeites were actively involved in voicing the logics of religious reform through internal schism and external deregulation.

THE TRANSCONTINENTAL political tour of Schuyler Colfax—former Speaker of the House, now vice president under Ulysses S. Grant—brought him to Salt Lake City in October 1869.[18] During his stay there Colfax "declined the hospitalities of the [Mormon] people here" altogether, according to Apostle and Church Historian George A. Smith. Instead he was "run"—managed—by founding Corinnethian O. J. Hollister, a man soon to become Colfax's brother-in-law and later his biographer. By all accounts Colfax spent the bulk of his time with Hollister (who had been appointed collector of internal revenue for Utah by the Grant administration in April 1869), General Patrick E. Connor (who Colfax thought would make a good governor for Utah), and other prominent Utahn Gentiles. The significant exception to his Gentile-centric visit was Colfax's willingness to meet with the 'liberal' Godbeites of the *Utah Magazine*.[19]

Colfax gave a speech from the porch of the Townsend House hotel in Salt Lake City on October 5. The essential argument was familiar from decades of congressional religious theory relative to Mormonism, albeit with slight variations. First there was the standard distinction between belief and acts. Only beliefs, creeds, and other "matters between [the faithful] and God alone" were protected under laws of religious liberty, Colfax said, whereas behaviors were subject to laws of general application. Colfax pointed to Hinduism for an analogy: "The Hindoos claim, as part of their religion, the right to burn widows with the dead bodies of their husbands. If they were to attempt it here, as their religion, you would prevent it by force." As with suttee in Salt Lake City, then, so with polygamy in America: it would receive neither special treatment nor exemption from laws passed by Congress. "Our country is governed by law, and no assumed revelation justifies any one in trampling on the law."[20]

Colfax's second argument brought him into the thickets of intra-Mormon religious dissent. This was an exegetical argument, based in Mormon scripture, against the legitimacy of polygamy *as* a Mormon practice. "I do not concede that the institution you have established here, and which is condemned by the law, is a question of religion," Colfax said. "But to you who do claim it as such, I reply," that federal antipolygamy legislation "only reenacts the original prohibitions of your own Book of Mormon." The vice president referred to a passage in Jacob 2, a denouncement of David's and Solomon's multiple partners and a prescription to have "but one wife," arguing thence that polygamy was not an original Mormon practice and that neither the Anti-Bigamy Act nor any other antipolygamy law was inconsistent with basic Mormon religiosity.[21] True Mormons had no grounds on which to stand, polygamously speaking.

Colfax's reply resembled those of nonpolygamous, non-Utahn Mormon sects. The 'Josephites,' in particular, could not have agreed more with Colfax. More properly called the (Reorganized) Church of Jesus Christ of Latter Day Saints, the Josephites were a Mormon group led by Joseph Smith's first wife, Emma Hale Smith, and their children Joseph Smith III, Alexander Hale Smith, and David Hyrum Smith. None of these Smiths had accepted the legitimacy of the prophet's polygamy revelation. None of them had joined the 'Brighamite' church or relocated to Utah, either, but rather they had stayed in the Midwest, reforming communities of adherence there to (what they perceived as) early church texts and principles. These midwestern communities did not always keep track of developments among the Utahn contingent, but railroads changed that. Josephites then read more about 'Mormonism' in the national press, and—disapproving of many of the details—they anticipated the possibility of inexpensive trips to missionize their former brethren. In July 1869, Alexander Hale Smith and David Hyrum Smith themselves undertook a five-month mission to Utah and southern Idaho, and they stopped several times in Corinne. Indeed they were welcomed there with open arms. Corinnethian boosters including O. J. Hollister and J. H. Beadle hoped thereby to aggravate Utahn Mormons and undermine Brigham Young's authority, and they provided the brothers with ample space, both in the town and in its newspaper, to preach the illegitimacy of polygamy and the corruption of the LDS lineage. Given their common connection to O. J. Hollister, it is possible that the Smiths also met with Schuyler Colfax during their time in Utah. In any case their missions overlapped both temporally and argumentatively.[22]

Vice President Colfax did not explicitly campaign for the Smith brothers or the Josephite community during his 1869 Utah visit, but it is clear that he had them in mind. Indeed even before visiting Utah, while still en route to the Mormon settlements, Colfax wrote to President Grant that the "schism, led by the young Smith's who are for obedience and the law, ags't Polygamy, & for loyalty to the U.S.," might widen "beneficently" with government support.[23] The government had every right, he thought, to choose religious sides, enlivening and perpetuating schism through rhetorical if not legal means. Secular politicians naturally catalyzed and capitalized on religious distinctions, in any case pitting proximate groups against each other to managerial ends.

VICE PRESIDENT COLFAX'S Salt Lake City speech was considered an act of Josephite support and governmental sectarianism by several Utahn observers. And George A. Smith was bemused if not angered by the fact: "He took the position of the Smith boys quoting from the book of Mormon," he said, referring to Colfax's hotel-front exegesis. "Some of the folks called him Elder Colfax from his having quoted the book of Mormon & Doctrine & Covenants as his base of operations."[24] That the vice president of the United States of America argued for particular understandings of both true religion and proper Mormonism was unsettling, to some Mormons.

For their part the would-be Godbeites were decidedly *not* discouraged by politicians' willingness to adjudicate right religion. To the contrary they saw an exciting opportunity to curry favor with the government while arguing also for a different type of Mormonism. There was, however, a problem. Unlike the Josephites, Godbe and company were not generally opposed to polygamy, and therefore their symbolic and political capital was different. Godbe and others nevertheless hoped that politicians would value their economic opposition platform as much—if not more—than the Josephites'. Indeed they had reason to think that Colfax himself would prioritize it, given that he had concluded his hotel address with statements of basic affinity:

> What you should do to develop the advantages your position gives you, seems obvious. You should encourage, and not discourage, competition in trade. You should welcome, and not repel, investments from abroad. You should discourage every effort to drive capital from your midst. You should rejoice at the opening of every new store, or factory, or mechanic shop, by whomsoever conducted. You should seek to widen the area of country dependent on your city for supplies. You should realize that wealth will come to you only by development, by unfettered competition, by increased capital.[25]

If Josephites stood to agree with Colfax's antipolygamy exegesis, Godbeites appreciated his economics. Nascent New Movement members saw an alignment of Mormon-government interests running beyond objections to bigamy. The truest Mormons, they thought, believed above all in the free market principles espoused by Colfax.

Tullidge, Stenhouse, Godbe, and others recognized that Colfax had sided with an antipolygamy, pro-Corinne Gentile contingent upon his arrival in Utah, even as he feigned Mormon exegesis in order to fan the flames of intra-Mormon dissent. The vice president "came up to Utah, that time, with a war program very nearly perfected in his mind," wrote Tullidge, and he "sought to rekindle the smouldering fire of a radical Gentile antagonism" by pledging "the support of the Government to all intents and purposes." But the would-be Godbeites presented Colfax with another option. They "entrust[ed] the Vice President with the secret that a number of influential Elders, who were capable of controlling the commercial issue of the times, and able to affect Mormondom by the local press, were actually on the eve of revolution."[26] T. B. H. Stenhouse then urged Colfax to follow the example of President Lincoln before him, 'plowing' around the Mormons a bit longer: "leave the Mormon Elders to solve their own problems" and "let us alone with this business."[27] Protestant elders had the power to reform Mormonism from within, and in short order the New Movement would manifest many of Congress's railroading dreams, thereby demonstrating the soundness of their economic and religious presumptions. Godbeites urged Colfax to stay an established course.

THE MONTH AFTER Colfax's visit, the newly disfellowshipped New Movement leaders restated their platforms on true Mormonism and the civilizing impetuses of commerce. "Let Vice-President Colfax . . . and the entire nation be assured that there are 'genuine' Mormon elders, who do not fear civilization, railroads, and the liberalizing genius of the American people," Tullidge wrote in an article titled "Do We Fear Civilization?" "The inference that Mormundom will be exploded by the American nation coming up to Utah with her civilization and destiny, bringing with her the age of railroads" applied only to false Mormons and false Mormonism, he said, meaning "the ruling and conservative few, whose policy leads to absolutism, and whose tendencies are anti-progressive." By contrast liberal Mormons were advocates of free presses, free speech, free commerce, and all attendant ideals: "[We] Mormon elders have resolved to maintain henceforth and forever in Utah a free press, free thought and a platform of human rights. The press never fears civilization, thought, progress and individuality. . . . The same is true of the merchant-class; for Commerce is the natural enemy of despotic rule, both in Church and State. There is no fanaticism or servility in commerce. Hence, you find to-day on the side of liberty and expansion some of the most enterprising merchants of Utah." Tullidge concluded, "We do not fear civilization, then, for we have come from the most civilized nations; we do not fear railroads, for we have ridden upon them a thousand times." The Godbeites asked only that Colfax and other easterners support them in their efforts at civilization and internal reform.[28]

Congressmen did indeed take notice of the Mormon schism, and so too did more local groups of Gentile politicians, as at Corinne. The next year saw many debates among Corinnethians, congressmen, Godbeites, and other Mormons about whether Godbeites themselves were useful coalition partners and about whether their New Movement enabled or obviated future government efforts to constrain Mormon power in general. Such debates had mixed aims and even more mixed results, as we will see. But in the meantime Godbe, Harrison, and other Godbeites embarked upon a rather different project of comparative religions, national networking, and spiritual commerce as well.

The Church of Zion

Godbe, Harrison, and company took as their broadest task the modernist separation between religion and commerce, private and public, spirituality and temporality. Following their October 1869 excommunication for "obnoxious" arguments in favor of mining and church divestment from business affairs, they pursued similar sacred-secular divisions from a different angle, in their own church. The Godbeites announced the foundation of the 'Church of Zion' in November 1869.

That the Church of Zion held its inaugural meetings in the old Walker Brothers store points to reciprocal dependences between 'liberal' religion and 'liberal' economics. Making 'true religion' a matter of private choice and individual concern offsets economic norms by differently weighting the moral significance of participation therein. For this reason among others the spirit of the Godbeite Zion would never stray far from the structures of capitalism. But inside those structures the Godbeite spirit strayed very close indeed to the spirit of spiritualism. Many Godbeites adopted spiritualism as both mode and motif of religious explanation, finding in 'spirit phenomena' and 'mediumship' a useful language for Mormon renewal, apostolic succession, and national intelligibility.[29]

It was partly with reference to spiritualism and its practices—séances, planchettes, and other modes of purported communication between living and dead—that Godbeites translated their Mormon visions to other Mormons. Spiritualism afforded a comparison-case and reminder of early Mormonism, by Godbeite estimations. It was a murky mirror by which many Mormons might remember the effervescent days of Joseph and by which they might recall their own, pre-Utah concerns with 'spiritualities' rather than 'temporalities.' Such analogies assumed, wrongly, that Utahn Mormons had failed to find opportunities for prophetic practice and ecstatic experience within contexts of 'Brighamite' communitarianism and territorial regulation, but the point was nevertheless clear: Godbeites valued deregulation and direct exchange in matters of religion and economy alike. Godbeites found in spiritualism a language and method by which to articulate their own Mormon lineage, in terms contemporary to 1860s America—and they pointed to it when characterizing proper Mormon presence for non-Mormon audiences, as well.[30]

At the first Church of Zion meeting, held December 19, 1869, before a capacity crowd of supporters, reporters, and curiosity seekers, Godbe and Harrison claimed visitations from "Angelic beings," among them Joseph Smith, Jesus, Peter, James, and John. These luminaries had encouraged Godbe and Harrison to uphold "reason, enlightened and purified by the Holy Spirit" at all costs and to espouse "a grand system of theology" encompassing "all the great principles connected with the past and future history of the globe from the beginning to the time when it will be celestialized." The Godbeites endeavored to comply, and, they said, the Church of Zion was the vehicle by which they would "return [the Church] to her true order—the guidance of Prophets, Seers, and Revelators, the administration of Angels, and the manifestations of the Holy Spirit," rather than the management of the ZCMI. Neither Harrison nor Godbe, however, stated publicly the provenance of their angelic visitations, at that time. That they had come through sittings with a trance medium during a business trip to New York City was mentioned only later, as Godbeites explored more fully the overlapping histories and concerns of Mormonism and spiritualism and as they argued anew for the possibilities of ecumenical spiritual commerce.[31]

By mid-1870 the Church of Zion—the "Harrison-Godbe-Planchette church," as Brigham Young jokingly called it[32]—had owned its spiritualism more completely. Church members held séances, and they appointed Amasa Lyman, a spiritualist sympathizer since his Mormon missionary days in San Bernardino, California, their official president. At the same time church leaders downplayed the particularity of Joseph Smith's 'mediumship' and the exclusivity of Mormon truths. They invoked a great pantheon of inspired seers and forerunners, Emanuel Swedenborg and Andrew Jackson Davis among them, and they preached the fundamental compatibility of spiritual Mormonism with other world religions and liberal faiths.[33] This was a bold play for a broad audience and an expansive Zion, two means by which Godbeite merchants and their church might find homes in an integrated national economy. But it yielded little positive coverage in the non-Mormon spiritualist press, and to Godbeites' additional disappointment, it entailed risks and losses in local membership. According to the Corinne-based *Daily Utah Reporter*—a close and bemused observer of the ecclesiastical movement—some Salt Lake Saints "begin to think they have been sold" after Godbeite Joseph Salisbury "rose in their meeting" in June 1870 to declare "that all the doctrines Harrison and Godbe had taught . . . had been taught by Andrew J Davis fifteen years ago."[34] Disaffected attendees perceived in the Church of Zion less a Mormon reform movement than an overture to spiritualism.

The Church of Zion soon faltered, its membership gravitating back to the LDS Church or, less frequently, out to spiritualism. But the general idea of a 'liberal' or 'Protestant' Mormonism gained traction even as people lost interest in Utahn spiritualist specificities. Indeed Godbeites' free market arguments received broad and sustained hearings, yielding long-lasting social, political, and religious results elsewhere. And neither Corinnethians nor Salt Lake Saints could afford to dismiss them quite so easily.

Local Coalitions

In February 1870, leading members of the New Movement met with prominent Utahn Gentiles and Corinnethians at the Walker Brothers' old store. This was the site of Godbeite church services, around the time when they introduced discussions of spiritualism. But the agenda for this event was different: attendees gathered to form a coalition political party, later to be called the Liberal Party, in opposition to Brigham Young's governmental and mercantile interests. Its intended constituency was to be "citizens of Utah," regardless of religious affiliation, "who are opposed to despotism and tyranny in Utah, and who are in favor of freedom, liberality, progress, and of advancing the material interests of said Territory, and of separating church from state."[35] It was an attempt, from the hardline Corinnethian perspective, to fan the flames of Mormon division and promote Corinne's free markets. From the New Movement perspective, less concerned with the success of a Bear River metropolis per se, the Liberal Party allowed for the pooling of contra-Brighamite resources and the demonstration of liberal Mormonism's compatibility with national, republican priorities. Each group used the other, and their cross-purposed actions afford subtle insights into the formations of a particular secular.

THE FIRST PUBLIC MEETING of the Liberal Party was a failure by almost all accounts. Conveners had announced the event—the agenda for which was the nomination of party officials and candidates for mayor, treasurer, and other Salt Lake City offices—by invoking a broad base of support. "Come one, come all," the placards said, "the people of Salt Lake City" are all welcome! This invitational wording, however, proved problematic. For, many people did indeed come, albeit not all in the spirit intended: antagonists arrived in greater numbers than supporters, due in part to Brigham Young's and Amos Milton Musser's encouragements.[36] In short order the meeting slipped from the control of its would-be presiders, and mainline Saints appointed their own candidates for all available positions. They replaced Liberal Party nominees at every turn, in every slot. Thus, for example, whereas the Liberal ticket included both Corinnethian Nat Stein and Godbeite Anthony Godbe as candidates for city council, LDS interlopers substituted for them the likes of church stalwarts Heber P. Kimball and Henry Grow. Among participants and observers, some saw this as an act of outright aggression against free speech and assembly, while others perceived it as "practical joke . . . carried out in the spirit of merriment." For his part O. J. Hollister joked about being "out generaled" by Brigham Young and the Saints. In any case the day ended with a coup d'état by the prochurch "People's Party," a flexing of Mormon muscles at the first sign of meddling, middling politics.[37]

For Corinnethian overseers of the assembly, the failure was also an opportunity for coups of their own, and for the reexpression of secularist sneers relative to Mormonism. Citing the hostility of the Mormon capital to liberal thought or democratic action and implying, moreover, a generically Mormon incapacity to separate matters spiritual from political, Nat Stein, O. J. Hollister, and other Gentiles urged—and secured—the relocation of key meetings and administrative operations to Corinne. As Edward Tullidge later recalled, "Since [Corinne was] nearly a deserted place, its founders believed that it would become the nucleus of the Gentile force, and be not only able to carry Box Elder County," where Corinne was situated, "but also to greatly influence the elections in Weber County," home to Ogden.[38] He overstated the case somewhat—Corinne claimed hundreds of residents in early 1870, retaining an active freighting business with the northern mines—but the logic was accurate. Corinnethian removal occurred in hopes of establishing a countywide political stronghold and, with it, a voice in territorial politics.

Relocation to Corinne affected Liberal Party priorities as well as geography. Granted, the most drastic and unilateral efforts by the most radical and anti-Mormon Corinnethians fell short. Foremost among these was an attempt by Dennis J. Toohy, an attorney and sometime editor of Corinne's *Daily Utah Reporter*, to dictate the terms of Liberal continuance by blocking all Mormon membership and appointing founding Corinnethian John Hanson Beadle as the party's candidate for Congress. Tapping the moment if not the moniker of coalition politics, Toohy announced a "Mass Convention of the Gentiles of Utah" to be held in Corinne on July 4, 1870, during which he planned to secure Beadle's congressional nomination. "His name is a tower of strength all through the Territory," Toohy wrote, "and in town and city, in mining camp and settlement his nomination [will be] received with rejoicing."[39] Beadle for Congress!

The *Daily Utah Reporter* considered J. H. Beadle most appealing for the same reason that he was least acceptable to more liberal Liberals: his unwavering, undiluted, small-town anti-Mormonism, coupled with his unwillingness to "compromise with Mormonism or apostates of any creed."[40] Crucially, in the present instance, this meant noncompliance with the Godbeites, the leadership of which Toohy and other Corinnethian writers described as insufficiently different from Brigham Young. Harrison and Godbe were "verging onto the same precipice" and "trying to frame another arrogant despotism," they wrote, insofar as they still invoked revelatory communication with angelic beings, set up "another priesthood," persisted in polygamy, and furthered "the same old paraphernalia of humbugs" as did other Mormons.[41] Tooby and Beadle considered Godbeites' claims to proper Protestantism to be altogether laughable.

There were, however, other Corinnethians more optimistic about Godbeitism and the continuing benefits of public political cooperation with it. Among these was O. J. Hollister, Schuyler Colfax's host during his 1869 visit to Salt Lake City, who had been present for Tullidge's railside overture to the vice president and who witnessed his cautiously optimistic response. Hollister himself sympathized with Toohy's and Beadle's strident rhetorics of church-state division and anti-Mormonism, but he had come to recognize also that Corinnethianism and Corinne, as a mode and model of secularism, depended, still, upon the religious. They depended, that is, not only upon the fact and specter of debatably religious communities but also upon their work of mutual critique and, then, upon the possibility for others' shifting governmental selections among them.

Hollister had published widely, albeit pseudonymously, his support of the Godbeites since the time of the Colfax meetings. Indeed Hollister's "Douglas" bylines in the *Chicago Tribune* were a significant source of information respecting the New Movement, most of it cautiously hopeful in tone, all of it describing Godbeitism as a positive effect of railroad interventions and a harbinger of liberalizations to come. Representative is the following text, part of the same entry in which Hollister announced the July anti-Mormon conventions in Corinne: "Since the completion of the railroad, now fifteen months ago, there has been a great loosening of the hidebound old carcass obstructing the progress of civilization in the West. . . . Encouraged by the thickening signs of a new era, prominent men of the hierarchy itself seceded from it, organized a liberal church, and through pulpit, rostrum, and press, devoted themselves to exposing its absurdities and abuses. . . . These schisms are daily gaining strength, and proportionately weakening and demoralizing the adherents of ecclesiastical despotism."[42] Hollister thought the Godbeites imperfect, to be sure, and he wrote elsewhere against their adherence to polygamy, revelation, and spiritualism. But even these offenses he called "babyisms, if not barbarisms": things to be outgrown naturally in time. Such sins were relatively minor, considering Godbeites' advocacy of mining, commerce, free speech, and republicanism.[43]

Hollister's overarching message—public as well as private—was that "a little encouragement will bring them to the right point sooner than they otherwise would get there." Thus, even while he did not necessarily want to work with Godbeites any more than Toohy did, Hollister saw Godbeitism as doing important dirty work of secular administration. With strategic pushes by U.S. politicians, he thought, Godbeites were bound both to regulate themselves and Mormonism generally in ways useful for the telos of western liberalism, toward capitalism, immaterial religion, and individualistic reason. Public political alliance between Gentile and (ex-)Mormon liberals could thus be mutually advantageous.[44]

MUCH TO TOOHY'S IRRITATION there was a strong Gentile contingent that agreed with Hollister, and these favored continued collaboration with Godbeite Liberals and operation in Salt Lake City. Thus at Corinne's conventions on July 4 and 16 the "committee of Salt Lake City" refused to fall in line behind Toohy and Beadle or to forge parity of purpose between the Liberal platform and the Corinnethian charter. To Toohy's mind it was a frustrating demonstration of Corinne's political marginality even as Gentiles convened (finally!) on its soil. But even worse was the demonstrated disunity of Corinnethians themselves.[45]

As far as Toohy was concerned, Hollister's procollaboration stance constituted a betrayal of true, radically secularist Corinnethianism and a failure of nerve. In particular the above note of Godbeite congratulations, when published alongside Hollister's call for "Anti-Mormon" unity at the Corinnethian conventions, seemed confused and self-defeating to him.[46] Toohy saw no possibility for united anti-Mormonism absent anti-Godbeitism, and he saw no hope for Corinne save radical Gentile politics and legislative intervention. He may have been right on both counts, too, but the fact was that Hollister represented a newer and more complicated field of anti-Mormon activity.

Hollister's 'secular' was a complex world of various death knell theories, coalition politics, congressional committees, and industrial lobbying. It was a world partly effected by the efforts and failures of both Corinnethians and Godbeites, their ostensibly overlapping dreams of bureaucratic rationalization notwithstanding. His (and thereafter theirs) was a new West in which groups subdivided and recombined with greater frequency, if not force, and in which religion was produced and reproduced according to the competing efforts of proximate and approximating others. From then on, anti-Mormonism would be a more multipartite affair overall, despite the brief formation of a supposedly singular Liberal Party. And from then on, modern bureaucracies would prove highly productive places, religiously speaking.

The Cullom Bill

For present purposes the most climactic evocations of Godbeitism occurred in Washington, D.C., as congressmen and lobbyists considered the 1870 Cullom Bill—the first anti-Mormon and antipolygamy legislation seriously considered since the Anti-Bigamy and Pacific Railway Acts of 1862. The Cullom Bill's provisions reflected both local and national concerns at the time, and they point to realignments along the transcontinental (anti-)Mormon axis, including around Corinne. Surrounding conversations featured standard reiterations of religious and industrial theory, too, even as they showed them operating in new contexts and combinations.[47]

When Godbeites approached Vice President Colfax in 1869 during his transcontinental stopover in Utah, they counseled political patience by prophesying religious schism. Promoting themselves as internal opponents of Brigham Young's economic policies and friends of modern liberalism, the Godbeites hoped to curry governmental favor as well as industrial support. The subsequent announcement of the Cullom Bill came to them, therefore, as a shock. But their spirits were buoyed again by the business community: Godbeites soon found that there was an anti-Cullom contingent in Congress, consisting mainly of railroad men. These legislators willingly aligned themselves with the Mormon opposition party, in rhetoric if not in fact, by arguing similarly for railroading moderations of anti-Mormon battle cries, citing liberalization along the mainlines.

But congressional champions do not always make cultural victories, and the Godbeites were only brief beneficiaries of their Washingtonian evocators. In the end, what we see in Cullom Bill debates is not only the importation of Godbeites' economic critiques and the persistence of Liberal Party debates respecting secularism but also the ephemeral governmental life-spans of cultural go-betweens. By observing bureaucratic mechanisms relative to religious and industrial legislation, we are better equipped to understand the ironic echoes of the death knell thesis. Indeed we may observe also key discursive and logistical conditions of Mormonism's modern success, for it was Godbeitism, recoined as governmental capital, that bought time for LDS ascendance.

IN ADDITION TO criminalizing polygamy and incorporating aspects of the Morrill Anti-Bigamy Act, the Cullom Bill, advanced in the House of Representatives by Shelby M. Cullom of Illinois and drafted in part by R. N. Baskin of Salt Lake City, proposed heavier penalties and easier burdens of proof. Anyone seen "cohabitat[ing] ... with more than one woman as husband and wife" or who is seen "recognizing, acknowledging, introducing, treating, or deporting himself toward" multiple women as if they were wives would be subject to imprisonment for one to five years and fines of one hundred to one thousand dollars.[48] Polygamous alliances of any kind would be dissolved, and there were no exemptions for preexisting unions or statutes of limitations for future offenses. Thenceforth marriage would be "a civil contract," to be solemnized by government-approved justices. Meanwhile polygamists were barred from elective office and from voting for civil representatives, and they were not allowed to serve as grand or petit jurors. The Cullom Bill proposed oaths of loyalty and monogamy for all such offices and civic forums, and in some cases mere belief in polygamy was grounds for refusal. Thus the bill, in a significant departure from the Ant-Bigamy Act and most congressional argumentation on the subject, proposed penalties for religious beliefs as well as behaviors.

The Cullom Bill contained several provisions specifically designed to reverse railroad era Mormon initiatives. Cullom suggested that the U.S. government override the 1869–70 bill for women's enfranchisement in Utah, for instance, on the grounds that it was counterproductive to the goods of national progress, family health, and, counterintuitively, women's freedom.[49] The bill also denied American citizenship to foreign-born polygamists, in hopes of counteracting the electoral advantages of new emigration drives. Third, Cullom proposed that no "person living in or practicing bigamy, polygamy, or concubinage" shall "be entitled to the homestead or pre-emption laws of the United States." This meant not only that polygamous persons would be denied rights to public lands but also that most titles already approved in Utah were subject to contestment. Brigham Young's land and land grants alike could be declared illegitimate, and in Ogden as elsewhere, "the land opened by polygamists would revert to government control."[50]

Cullom's final provisions concerned military might. The federal marshal for Utah Territory and his deputies, in collaboration with the U.S. district attorney and his deputies, were authorized to call upon nearby military camps for "a posse to aid" them "in the execution of any writ, order, process judgment, or decree"—and the president of the United States could also dispatch up to forty thousand troops to Utah. Overall, the bill advocated disenfranchisement, disestablishment, and displacement under threat of war.

The Cullom Bill was austere in tone and broad in scope, even when compared—as it often was—with acts of southern Reconstruction. As such it received much press and discussion, with different congressional, Corinnethian, Godbeite, and LDS groups responding differently to different provisions. As such it was gradually dismembered and finally abandoned, too; although passed by the House, the bill stalled in the Senate. Nevertheless its debate and reception history point to American consensuses about religion and modernity, to the rise of an industrial religious lobby, and to the conditions under which (anti-)Mormon discourses were produced and processed.

Beadle and Godbe in Washington

The Cullom Bill was referred to the House Committee on Territories (of which Cullom was also chairman) immediately upon introduction into Congress in February 1870. Such referrals were standard practice. But in this case committee conversations were noteworthy: witnesses, called to testify to the necessity of various provisions, demonstrated not only the formulations of governmental religious expertise but also the bureaucratic operations of relative social theories. Moreover, both J. H. Beadle and William S. Godbe traveled to Washington in order to play on opposite sides of the lobbying fray.

Beadle, speaking before the territorial committee as one of five key witnesses, testified to the importance of the bill in its entirety. Particularly appropriate, by Beadle's estimation, were sections concerning the disenfranchisement of all polygamous persons, the disempowerment of Mormon courts and juries, and the increased powers of the U.S. marshal. Such allowed for the proper enforcement of federal laws against polygamy, Beadle said, the likes of which had lain dormant since the Anti-Bigamy Act of 1862. Moreover, they allowed for the rise of a Gentile district in the Utahn north, particularly around Corinne.[51]

Unsurprisingly, much of Beadle's testimony reads as a pitch for Box Elder County, which he described as a freer, more active, and more promising site of Gentility than the rest of Utah. Thus, for example, while another witness described the "impossib[ility] for a Gentile to pre-empt any land" due to Brigham Young's "great many grants,"[52] Beadle implied that non-Mormons lived relatively happy and land-rich lives in northern Utah. The areas neighboring

Corinne had low population density, he said, and—as he wrote concurrently in his *Life in Utah*—the entire area might soon be vacated of its polygamists, given a little help from Congress and the passage of the Cullom Bill. "The first effect will in all probability be, that actual polygamists," perceiving a true threat to their institution, "will at once retire from the northern sections and concentrate in the South," thus leaving Corinne and its environs free for Gentiles. Corinnethian Gentiles deserved congressional support, he said, and to this end he hoped that "this bill will pass both Houses, and, by the time this meets the eye of the reader, become a law."[53]

The territorial committee was, however, less interested in the specifics of Beadle's boosterism than in his more general opinion of the death knell thesis, that industrial and religious notion long associated with Corinnethian promotions and Anti-Bigamy Act postponements alike. Committee member Charles Waldron Buckley (R-Alabama) asked Beadle: "It is alleged, and with some degree of force, that polygamy will cure itself, if simply let alone; that with the opening up of railroads and the settling of the county around them, these people will be brought into contract [sic] with American institutions, and polygamy and its kindred abominations gradually fade away before the advancement of a higher civilization. What is your opinion upon that point?"[54] Beadle begged to differ with the notion in such an application. "It never would," he replied. After all he and other Corinnethians had fought to deploy death knell rhetorics along these lines already, expecting transcontinental assistance but receiving little. They had failed, that is, to make of Corinne Utah's railroad hub, all the while watching instead as Brigham Young *did*, indeed, contract with railroads. "[Mormons] could almost completely nullify all these outside influences," said Beadle, thereby "perpetuat[ing] polygamy indefinitely" so "long as such absolute power is left in the hands of the Mormon hierarchy." At the very least it would take some thirty or forty years for Mormon polygamy and theocracy to dissolve under the influence of the railroads and related trade. Neither Corinne nor the nation could wait that long.[55]

Beadle asked Congress to pass and enforce the Cullom Bill as soon as possible and to ignore any versions of the death knell thesis used to opposite argumentative effect. Against "those who have relied so much on the 'peaceful solution-Gentile development' idea," that is, Beadle argued that "'development' and 'peaceful solution'" are only good "when backed up by good laws." Radical Gentility, aggressive capitalism, legislative intervention, and judicial force must be deployed in tandem. Mormon powers should be diminished, Gentile rights should be upheld, and railroads should be contracting with true Christians only.[56]

WHILE BEADLE PROTESTED the misuse of the death knell thesis for purposes of legislative moderation rather than Mormon destruction, however, one of Utah's newest theorists of religious industry arrived in Washington to argue precisely thus. This was William S. Godbe, a man who, though supposedly a Liberal Party affiliate of Beadle's, had been maligned enough during the Corinnethian secularism debates to know to avoid him. Godbe toured the capital with a lobbying mission exactly antithetical to Beadle's—namely, to persuade politicians of the folly and superfluity of the Cullom Bill.

Godbe was not alone in that effort, though. As he made the rounds and presented his case in hotels and homes across the capital, others spoke also on his behalf in Congress. Franklin Head, former superintendent of Indian affairs for Utah, testified before committee members that "the railroad has brought [Mormons generally] into contact with the civilized world outside, and new agencies will be brought to operate upon them." Drawing committee attention especially to Godbe and Harrison's New Movement, he continued: "this very schism is the result of completing the railroad through that Territory." Head considered the Godbeites to be a sign of Mormon civilization and liberal development, and he urged that the government allow them and the railroads to run their course, a bit longer, before intervening.[57]

But aren't Godbeites polygamists? asked Representative Buckley. If so, what use are they in the governmental battle against barbarism? Head's reply sounded as if from the *Utah Magazine* itself, or from the Godbeite appeal to Vice President Colfax. He argued that Godbeites were the most significant of Mormon reform groups because they struck at the heart of Brighamite power, touching upon a matter arguably more important than plural marriage: "the question of union of church and state" and "the right to dictate in temporal matters, regarding business and trade, &c." Besides, he said, Godbeites' polygamy was not like other Mormons' polygamy. The New Movement "acknowledges the revelation in regard to polygamy, but claims that the revelation has been misinterpreted. I had a long conversation with Mr. Godbe on that very point," and "his idea is that the marriage referred to in that revelation is entirely a spiritual affair—nothing carnal about it." Granted most members of the New Movement would not have agreed with this assessment, but some of them were indeed moving away from the principle at the time.

Head concluded his response with reference to another discussion with leading Godbeites, this time concerning the Cullom Bill especially: "In conversation with Godbe and [Henry W.] Lawrence, speaking of this bill, the latter said—and he is a very fair and candid man—that the result of any such legislation, or of any legislation which could be considered unfriendly and oppressive, would be to weaken their party, and to heal up the schism more than anything else that could possibly be done." Head testified that, since Godbeites evidenced railroads' positive religious influence and since aggressive legislation might disrupt and upset them, the government should table or soften the Cullom Bill.[58]

The best way to support liberal development in Utah was *not* to support radical and anti-Mormon legislation, according to Head, but rather to be patient, placing governmental trust in God, Godbeites, and the railroad. For his part Beadle considered the idea sacrilegious, muddying the waters of railroading religious theory and in many ways defeating the purpose of Godbeite affiliation. But Godbe could not have been better represented if he were there himself.

GODBE HIMSELF *was* able to secure personal audiences with Congressman Cullom, Vice President Colfax, and President Grant somewhat later in March 1870. And legend has it that Godbe was singularly persuasive. By Tullidge's account, Godbe and Cullom "went through the 'Cullom Bill,' section by section, Mr. Godbe suggesting revisions and toning it to better suit the peculiar conditions of the Mormon people. At length, half provoked, the Hon. Member from Illinois exclaimed, 'My G—d, Mr. Godbe, you would strike out all the points of my bill!' But the Utah advocate plead the cause of the Mormon people with so much earnestness and feeling that all the animus of prosecution was killed." Tullidge insisted that "at that moment, Mr. Cullom was touched with conviction," and by convincing Cullom to allow his bill to suffer modifications in the House and failure in the Senate, Godbe and the Godbeites had "saved [Utah] from collision with the U.S.A."[59] Godbe converted Cullom to the cause of caution and compassion, with legislative reductions and military disarmament as consequences.

The facts are rather more complicated. Although Godbe's lobbying and the rhetorics of Godbeite promise played a role in the defeat of the Cullom Bill, ensuing debates show them to have been two of several factors. The Cullom Bill did not die in the House committee, after all, but was many times reintroduced to discussion, each time undergoing slightly modified debate and each time inviting commentary by ever-growing groups of interested 'experts.' It was a tedious, confused, long-winded, and swirling affair, with legislative paperwork routinely shuffling across desks, through lobbies, down halls, and back. This, in order that politicians might take them up again, in what was arguably the most overburdened, inefficient, inexperienced, and yet influential congressional era in American history.[60]

This was the very epitome of bureaucratic irrationality in governmental action. And that is precisely the point. In modern ouroboric tedium lie many modern religious constructions, and if anything it was the administrative swirl itself that defeated the bill, to ironic religious effect. For, the Cullom Bill died not by provisional strippings and streamlinings so much as by the conglomeration of discourses, the tetherings of riders, and the proliferations of specificities, all of which allowed for the national education of and about Mormonism. This was life through death by committee.

Railroad Men Intervene

The Cullom Bill underwent discussion in the general House of Representatives, following positive reintroductions there by Cullom and his committee, in February and March 1870. The congressman most predictably opposed to it was Utah's territorial representative, William H. Hooper, a mainstream (though nonpolygamous) Mormon and member of the LDS Council of Fifty.[61] But perhaps most vocal in their opposition to the bill were Representatives Thomas Fitch (R-Nevada) and Aaron A. Sargent (R-California). Both of these men represented railroad interests, and both assumed anti-Cullom stances similar to, but more industrially concerned than, Franklin Head.

Fitch and Sargent argued that, well intentioned though the Cullom Bill may be, and sincere though the Mormons may themselves be, aggressive legislation could unleash cycles of violence and fanaticism among would-be martyrs and their could-be compatriots. Indeed many members of this Reconstruction era Congress shared their concerns about the hostility with which Mormons might receive the new antipolygamy bill and about the potential human and fiscal losses of another domestic conflict. But Fitch and Sargent added to those concerns an especial fixation on the transcontinental railroad. Such fixation was unsurprising to anyone who knew the congressmen, both of whose careers were backed heavily by Central Pacific agents and lobbyists—Sargent's career especially, he having penned the Pacific Railway Act that passed in 1862, the same year as the Morrill Anti-Bigamy Act, and having defended railroad building as a military necessity, then and thereafter.[62] By the end of their speeches none could doubt their commitment to the railroads.

More than a dozen times in their adjoining 1870 statements, Fitch and Sargent registered apprehension about "the temporary obstruction, if not the complete destruction, of the great overland railroad" should the Cullom Bill precipitate outrage among, or warfare against, the Mormons. True the railroad would facilitate military transport to Utah, said Sargent, but only as long as it remained open and operational—and "the first movement of the Mormons, when they shall believe that we are in earnest by an attack like this, will be to tear up hundreds of miles of the Pacific railroad and to destroy all the property upon it within their reach." "Of course we could finally conquer them," Fitch added, "because we could exterminate them"—but "it would cost us millions upon millions of treasure" to do that, and "it would cost us the interruption of that travel which is permanently growing in importance, and which promises, if undisturbed, to fulfill the dreams of Columbus and make America a new highway to the Indies." Absent the railroad, the mercantile and demographic lifeblood of California and the entire West would be cut off; and with it American manifest destinies would die. "I am not willing to look upon the ruin of the great road which forms the keystone of the arch of the highway around the world," declared Sargent. "I am not willing to destroy the channel through which my people hope to receive the life-currents of empire."[63] Railroad health was of primary importance for the body politic, according to Fitch and Sargent.

But if the railroad was a matter of concern sufficient to inform government policy on religion, Fitch and Sargent still thought it capable of precluding interreligious conflict. Joining territorial witness Head in this respect, these and other congressmen reiterated arguments popular since at least 1862, when the first antipolygamy bill passed alongside the Pacific Railway Act—namely, that modern industry and national connectivity would have a gradually civilizing influence on Mormonism, if only trains were allowed to run their course. And relative to 1862 they had more evidence with which to back their plea. By 1870 non-LDS politicians could cite the Godbeite schism and Gentile travel to Utah as signs of positive change, provided that they were willing to sidestep the abundant ironies of their invocation. For Fitch and Sargent, less concerned with Utahn religions per se than with their discursive value for prorailroad politicians, the New Movement was proof, effect, and harbinger of railroads' religious efficacy. Godbeites were reason enough to stay the hand of anti-Mormon legislation, obviating the Cullom Bill—and thereby buying time for railroad barons to benefit further from emerging relationships in the Great Basin.

The Act Runs Its Course

Cullom Bill conversations raised national awareness about Godbeite Mormonism, winning Godbe and company a few advocates in Congress and securing for them lasting places in Utahn lore—at least insofar as it was narrated by Godbeites. But such attention also broke the movement, weakening Godbeites' political influence even as it raised their profile. Positive Gentile press for the New Movement in the Cullom era had necessitated avoiding, minimizing, or defending Godbeites' own polygamy. Thus for their part Fitch and Sargent avoided the issue entirely, while Head spoke of it as insignificant relative to economics and O. J. Hollister's columns spoke of "babyisms" to outgrow in time.[64] But Corinnethian members of the Godbeites' own Liberal Party alliance eventually refused such apologies, Hollister included. Instead they and other Gentile Liberals seized party power and upheld more complete antipolygamy and anti-Mormon platforms, thereby funneling support back into the Cullom-esque initiatives from which their Godbeite colleagues had become known, ironically, as obviating actors. Legislative attention was therefore a double-edged sword for the Godbeites, making of them both mediating go-betweens and inadvertent conduits for crossed political interests.

The Cullom Bill discussions split the Liberal Party, and an emergency meeting, called in March 1870 to discuss possible modifications to the bill, did little to save it. Assembled Godbeite and Gentile representatives were unable to reach consensus, even though Gentiles agreed to "join in any effort to have the land and [male] disfranchising clauses so modified as not to injure any who were disposed to be loyal to the government," in hopes of avoiding widespread rebellion and property damage.[65] By contrast the Godbeites desired a more complete detoothing of the bill, for reasons both specific and general. Most specifically they objected to the absence of exemptions for preexisting polygamous families; they argued that the bill, its rhetoric of benevolent paternalism notwithstanding, would "in reality ma[k]e [women] the sufferer and the scape-goat" of anti-Mormonism, flooding Utah with "dishonored wives and dishonored mothers" abandoned by "unprincipled men."[66] More generally the Godbeites urged commitment to the philosophy of gradual cultural modifications through industrial modernization. Unfortunately for them, though, the Corinnethians had seldom been practical or philosophical gradualists, and, relative to the Fitch-Sargent, Head, and Godbeite schools, their death knell sentiments coexisted comfortably with most forms of legislative and military aggression. The era of Liberal political alliance was thus short-lived.

THE CULLOM BILL ITSELF was also short-lived, as it turns out. A modified version passed the House in late March, by a vote of ninety-four to thirty-two, after several more rounds of conversation and debate, more references to Hindu suttee, speculations about secret ceremonies, and talk about railroads. A few alterations made it more palatable to erstwhile skeptics, in the end; provisions respecting military enforcement and the seizure or redistribution of polygamous men's assets were omitted, for instance, thereby lessening concerns about warfare and property destruction. But it was not the denuded and skeletal measure that some have imagined. It retained, among other clauses, basic evidentiary and enforcement measures, punishments for belief in as well as practices of polygamy, disfranchisement and disbarment clauses, denials of citizenship and civil office, and application to extant marriages. There were plenty of articles and limbs on which the Senate might build, in committees, chambers, and general floor debates.[67]

And build they did. Members rehashed arguments respecting scripture and schisms, citing exposés by Beadle and promises by Godbe. They generalized theories of proper religion and industry, too, even as they rendered specific their target of Mormon irreligion, for instance, by adding clauses mentioning Mormon bishops and reiterating the dangerous proximity of Mormon beliefs to Mormon practices. Lobbyists arranged themselves in the same cross-purposed and overlapping patterns as were evident during House debates. The Senate Committee of the Whole was inundated with information on all fronts, and the nation's newspapers narrated their every hope.[68]

When the bill finally died, then, it did so tabled amid the fallout of a prodigious discursive campaign, stalled less by cuttings-down than buildings-up and buildings-around. Godbeite considerations played a role, but so too did the peculiar circumstances of a postwar national politics, in which waning enthusiasms for Radical Reconstruction mixed with growing hopes for cohesion in industry. The Cullom provisions therefore lay dormant until another era of anti-Mormon and antipolygamy fervor, in the late 1870s and early 1880s, by which time Utah, Corinne, and Mormonism itself had all undergone further industrial changes of their own.

Godbeitism, as an oppositional movement and philosophy, was not long for this world, but its bureaucratic echoes were far-reaching. Played among various groups in Congress, Corinne, and elsewhere, the Godbeites lost social cohesion and territorial traction even as they gained discursive circulation and capital. Meanwhile they found their middle grounds reoccupied and reorganized by erstwhile opponents. Through their role in Cullom Bill conversation, especially, Godbeites cleared opposition to, bought time for, and allowed the advent of something else: orthodox, modern, corporate Mormonism.

Retrospect and Prospects

Perhaps the soundest argument to be made for the New Movement's significance is that it shows the constructive contentiousness of the railroad moment for Mormonism. The New Movement originated in response to Brigham Young's late 1860s industrial and mercantile programs, many of which were themselves catalyzed by the arrival of railroads and rail-riding Gentiles in Utah: the Zion's Cooperative Mercantile Institution, for example, as well as the expansion of priesthood authorities, ecclesiastical emphases on home manufactures, and the discouragement of mining. In turn Godbeites' peculiar arguments for economic, spiritual, and political 'liberalisms' earned them excommunication from a church that was forced, in contradistinction thereto, to defend the righteousness of its own peculiar, occasional institutions.

The Godbeite movement thus helped occasion the formation of Mormon orthodoxy, even as it pointed to its recent constructions and modern conditions. As we will see further in the following chapters, Godbeites evoked a language of antiquity, agriculturalism, and protectionism on the part of the LDS Church, even as they watched it develop through investments, corporations, and mechanics of modern industry. So too Godbeites' focus on personal religious experience arguably catalyzed the articulation—and indeed the promotion—of a particularly situated sense of Mormon religious ecstasy in Utah. In time LDS leaders learned, partly because of their own experience with the Godbeites, to effect a balance of openness and enclosure, modernity and preservation conducive to local strength and national incorporation.

Godbeites, though they did not succeed in making Godbeitism itself coequal with mainstream Mormonism, did situate themselves at the junction for many local and national trends, illuminating each in turn. They courted Saints, congressmen, and Corinnethians alike, all the while praising Protestantism, capitalism, mining, industry, and trade. That they were sometimes successful in harmonizing their voices with others' is evident from their positive evocations in national media and political debates. That they failed anyway—not unlike how the Corinnethians had failed—shows that rhetorical harmony needn't entail success. The Godbeite movement's rise and fall points to the persistence of differences within processes of nationalization, to the fickleness of alliance, and to the ubiquity of railroad concerns in and for religion.

THERE IS ANOTHER LESSON to be learned, finally, from the rise and fall of the New Movement amid the overlapping initiatives of lobbyists for and against industrial religion, one perhaps best traced from Cullom Bill conversations through subsequent evolutions of the tourism trade in Utah. The lesson is that even as secular government puts religion into discourse, trading too in the language of dissent—that is, while secular governance, its official stance of disinterest notwithstanding, speaks endlessly of its ostensible Other, incentivizing religious distinctions and capitalizing on interreligious critiques—tourism is the structure by which people may then navigate such discourse and dissent in place. Tourism is a mechanism by which interested parties observe religious groups themselves work to incorporate criticism in time and space.[69]

By way of transition to the next chapter and thence to an elaboration of this argument, consider the following description of the Cullom Bill. Titled "Cullom a Mormon Missionary," it appeared in the pro-LDS *Deseret News* in April 1870:

> Now, this is the actual result thus far of their scheme. Never was the subject of the "Mormons" and their religion so widely agitated as at present. Men cannot avoid thinking about it; politicians, editors, priests and lecturers all combine to make them do this. They will be far more likely now to inquire into the subject than if it had not been made prominent, and inquiry, is what the people of Utah want.... Had Mr. Cullom been a "Mormon" missionary he could not have given "Mormonism" one-hundredth part the fame he has bestowed upon it by introducing his Bill into Congress.[70]

It was an optimistic assessment, to be sure, one filled with sectarian hubris. But there was a logic to it. And it was not wrong. Cullom, the industrial lobby, and the rest had indeed helped put Mormonism into discourse, generating voluminous discussions about and new parties to the 'Mormon question' of acceptable and unacceptable religion in Utah. And LDS Church officials would spend the next decade attempting to manage such discourse through tourism.

CHAPTER FOUR

Steamboats and the Rise of Atrocity Tourism

✦

IN THE SPRING OF 1870—while the Cullom Bill drowned in congressional conversations and as the Mormons' Utah Central Railroad began regular operations between Salt Lake and Ogden—Corinne's boosters built a steamboat. More precisely they *rebuilt* one. The *Kate Connor*, named after General Patrick E. Connor's daughter, had been operational since late 1868, albeit in limited capacity and at irregular intervals. The anti-Mormon general launched the *Kate Connor* with hopes of transporting goods between southern and northern Utah over water—thereby bypassing the cities and roads of the Saints. But later Corinnethians imagined a greater future for the boat. By their plan it would be part of an "armada" that would capture not only the southern mining and lumber market but also the bourgeoning western tourism trade. If Corinne could not be Utah's political or railroad capital, it might yet become its steamboat capital: a haven for western travelers and traders, Gentile excursionists and excavators alike.

Beadle and his booster colleagues experimented with several plans for Corinnethian success in the era of transcontinental leisure travel, changing tack as necessary in response to shifting circumstances in and around Salt Lake City. The first of these, and the rationale for the *Kate Connor*'s relaunch in early 1870, was to steal the Utah Central Railroad's freighting and passenger business, by convincing its erstwhile clients that the Mormon line could never meet the demands of modern commerce and culture and by offering a genteel alternative for Salt Lake City–bound traffic. Later that year, after J. H. Beadle and company's aspirations were bolstered by initial returns from southern mines and overwater freighting, they spoke somewhat differently of Corinne as a stand-alone hub for tourists, health seekers, nature lovers, and businessmen, quite independent of Salt Lake City. This approach, however, did not last long either. Within a few more months, the Utah Central effectively cornered local transportation markets, and Corinne's first international visitors publicly declared themselves to be unimpressed by the town's alternative provisions. Bowing then to persistent public fascinations with Mormonism, and in hopes also of attracting new support from Central Pacific travel and settlement agents, Corinnethians retooled their tourism campaign and redirected their boats to Salt Lake City. By summer 1871 Beadle and others promised to escort interested Gentiles on atrocity tours of Utah's many Mormon hell-scapes there, and they offered new guidebooks and exposés for sale along the way.

EACH OF CORINNE'S freighting and tourism plans was doomed to failure. Within five years its flagship steamers were defunct, having run aground or—by increasingly ironic turns of history—being purchased by Mormon businessmen in order to promote contra-Corinnethian enterprises. Moreover, the modes of travel that *did* emerge in northern Utah and the greater West during the 1870s were crucial to the long-term sustenance and mainlining of Mormonism in America, rather than its destruction or marginalization. Such ends were surprising, from many vantages in the West—and so too were their mechanisms. Corinnethian transportation enterprises offer paradigmatic examples of the anti-Mormon efforts necessarily navigated both by Mormon apologists and by railroading middlemen, in the years to come.

"Novelty Enough": Ambivalent Plans for a Grand Tour

Three months before the christening of Corinne itself—named also for the daughter of a hopeful Gentile benefactor—the *Kate Connor* took its maiden voyage along Jordan River, south of the Great Salt Lake and Salt Lake City. It was December 1868, and leading Corinnethian J. H. Beadle, who was then still anxiously awaiting an official announcement respecting the transcontinentals' "great central city of the future," saw Connor's southern launch as both harbinger and buttress to Utah's northern Gentile capital. "For the present her work will consist in carrying ties and lumber to the Promontory," wrote Beadle, and soon he would speak similarly of carrying mining materials to Corinne. "But with the coming summer and further improvement, pleasure parties on Salt Lake will no doubt be in vogue with visitors, who can come from the new towns at the north end, spend several hours" in Salt Lake City or along the southeastern shores of the lake, "and return, all within two days."[1] Just think! Beadle rhapsodized, "of the day when the *Reporter* shall head its 'River Column' thus:"

HO FOR SALT LAKE!
The new and elegant steamer
KATE CONNOR
Will leave the wharf [near Salt Lake City],
Mondays, Wednesdays, and Saturdays
for all points North, and the landing at the new town of
GENTIL-ITY
Tuesdays, Thursdays, and Saturdays
making the through trip between these points in sixteen hours
PLEASURE PARTIES TAKEN AT REDUCED RATES.

Beadle invited readers to imagine a Gentile town through which all future commerce would flow and from which western excursionists might base round-trip pleasure tours to Salt Lake's islands, Salt Lake's beaches, and Salt Lake City itself. "How do you like the prospect?" he asked: of non-Mormons setting new routes and standards for Utahn industry, leisure, and elegance? "Hurrah for 'civilization' in Utah!"[2]

For all of his cheers and capital letters, though, Beadle felt ambivalent about the necessity or desirability of pleasure-boat tours to the Mormon capital of Salt Lake City. He could imagine easily, in late 1868 and early 1869—and he advertised publicly, as one reason to support Corinne—a scenario by which "a man steps off the [railroad] cars at Bear river [and] on the steamer, makes a tour of Salt Lake and is landed in the Jerusalem of the Mormons." But what would he then do, Beadle wondered, and what would be the appeal of so doing? Wrote Beadle, in a rare instance of literary ambiguity: "The trip overland has novelty enough without counting the strange people fixed in the Switzerland of America."[3]

Beadle's ambiguous phrase points to a number of contemporaneous motives for travel, many of them also ambivalent. The Continental Grand Tour—favored by eighteenth-century romantics and encompassing the monuments and metropoles of Italy and France, as well as the Swiss Alps—remained popular among European nobility in the nineteenth century, and improved roads and travel technologies also made the Grand Tour's cultured pleasures available to a growing middle class. These pleasures were, however, mixed. Some travelers relished feelings of superiority and progress relative to the Old World, while others bemoaned their cultural turns. Some gawked at the supposed "hedonism" of modern Italian life, while others coveted its colorful ways. And many relished the "agreeable kind of Horror" effected by encounter with the "sublime" Alps, whose gorgeousness consisted not in smoothness, delicacy, or other qualities traditionally associated with the Beautiful but rather in "roughness, darkness, vastness, power, solitude, and infinity—in short, the qualities in nature that had once terrified but gradually came to delight travelers."[4] Egyptian and Levantine loops grew more fashionable in the 1860s, and there too travelers thrilled in observing conditions deemed at once foreign and familiar, scary and sacred.[5]

Such mixed pleasures informed also the specifically American tours developed in the 1800s. The so-called American Grand Tour of the antebellum era covered the Hudson River Valley, the Catskill Mountains, and Niagara Falls in New York—each home to striking scenery and, in the case of the Hudson River Valley, namesake to a school of romantic landscape painting. Sometimes upper- and middle-class Americans also toured New England and the mid-Atlantic states, but it was mainly after the Civil War that they set their sights westward. Travel promoters encouraged people to "See America First." By eschewing a European Grand Tour in favor of an American one, especially one encompassing regions of the American West, Americans would be schooled both in the wonders of their country and the potential for its continued development. Such tours were imagined, still, as an act of leisure by the leisure class, but tourists did the important political and cultural *work* of national imagination, including the act of discerning similarity and difference among places and peoples of the greater West.[6]

Beadle's early 1869 phrase—that "the trip overland has novelty enough without counting the strange people fixed in the Switzerland of America"—indicated most clearly his recognition that Mormon encounters might be considered alternately appealing or unappealing, necessary or supplemental, depending upon travelers' perspectives and accommodations. Happily, Beadle then thought that he could control for these variables, if not control them directly. For, although he himself considered Mormons to be disturbing and dangerous specimens of misshapen humanity, he still thought them destined for destruction in the railroad age. Beadle hoped that he and his Gentile compatriots might teach their touristic clients how properly to look at Mormonism, during this era of Saints' presumptive sidetracking and subjugation. Like "the Dead Sea with its mystery and its mountain island" itself, they would show Mormonism to be one among other lifeless and "fixed" phenomena, a mysterious growth lacking egress as such. This was not to suggest that Mormons were harmless, just yet. Rather it was to propose that, from a safe distance—ideally after a ride on a Gentile boat via a Gentile capital—tourists could take pleasure—and take stock—in the reformations of Utahn culture.

Still Beadle wanted to cover as much ground and water as possible. He wanted to keep alive the notion of a persistent Mormon menace, even as he caricatured Mormonism itself as more stagnant than vibrant—and even while he portrayed Mormons' Salt Lake environs as intrinsically healthful for right-minded non-Mormons. Determined to deploy any and all motifs capable of capturing Gentile travelers' imagination, the result, in early 1869—some three months before the transcontinentals bypassed Corinne—was a mixed bag of mixed metaphors: "Taking the magnificence of the scenery, the salubrity of the summer climate, and the medicinal properties of these [thermal] springs, no doubt very valuable in many diseases, specially cutaneous, together with the Asiatic, religious and social notions of the people belonging and appertaining, and Utah must be the great watering place of the world, and that at no distant day."[7] By Beadle's account Utah was like unto both Switzerland and Jerusalem, with a Dead Sea and peoples like Asians. And it would be the sanitarium for the world's Christians.

"Worthy of Liberal Patronage": Corinne's Steamers

The 1869 visits of Schuyler Colfax and others confirmed that Utah would see many non-Mormon visitors in the transcontinental era, but they also confirmed that Ogden and Salt Lake City would receive more of their business than Beadle's "new town of Gentil-ity." In 1870 nearly 150,000 cross-country travelers necessarily stopped to change trains at Ogden, many of them leisure-class sightseers to whom railroad companies catered with comfortable seating, dining services, sleeping cars, and other amenities provided by contract with the famed Pullman Palace Car Company (along the Union Pacific line) or in Silver Palace Cars (along the Central Pacific). Although some of these were content seeing "this strange basin, with its stranger people" from car windows or at the Ogden station, visitors often wished to see the Mormon capital for themselves, and tour promoters and railroad officials alike were again happy to appease them. Package tours sometimes included a lengthy layover at Ogden precisely so that clients might take a side trip on the Mormons' Utah Central, which was by then running regular trains between Ogden and Salt Lake City with roundtrip fares around $2.50. This arrangement was lucrative for the Utah Central; the company earned approximately $3,000 in such passenger receipts in only its third month of operation, March 1870.[8]

Beadle and other Corinnethians accepted the fact of touristic interest in Salt Lake City, at first, but they thought they could reroute it through Corinne rather than Ogden. Practically speaking this was the first discernable phase and model of Corinnethian tourism. Anti-Mormon Gentiles focused that spring on maligning the Mormon branch railroad, promoting overwater transport from Corinne to points south instead. In June 1870 the *Daily Utah Reporter* announced substantial improvements to the *Kate Connor*, including a new engine and boiler, larger paddle wheels, a remodeled bar and dining room, and other additions "calculated to make her worthy of liberal patronage" by persons accustomed to Palace Car comforts. Soon afterward the paper ran general invitations "To Excursionists": "The side-wheel steamer KATE CONNOR . . . will be chartered to Excursion Parties by the day, week, or month." Riding high atop the Salt Lake, such a worthy vessel was sure to provide a comfortable and morally uncompromising vantage from which to observe the area's various wonders.[9]

As Corinnethians worked to renovate the *Kate Connor*, Beadle wrote a scathing and sarcastic review of a "Trip to Zion" on the "saintly" Utah Central Railroad, "by way of Gennesaret depot and Golgotha refreshment station":

> Our First Trip on Brigham's Railroad.
> Felt no particularly divine sensations, and hence conclude that this is very much like the railroads built by the world's people. The two passenger cars were crowded, principally with Eastern people, diverging from the overland excursion to visit this noted city of Saints.

Beadle concluded that "Zion is a Disappointment," since, in a West newly characterized by "well-built cit[ies] of magnificent size" like Omaha, Salt Lake City no longer "bursts upon the sight like Damascus upon the desert to the weary pilgrim of the Orient." It could be argued that Salt Lake City retained a certain charm, admitted the anti-Mormon author, but such was more naturalistic than cultural. "The brooks and the trees will always be beautiful, and the mountain scenery can never lose its sublimity," Beadle wrote, no matter how "common" the city might feel and how "weak," "illogical," "fanatical," and "barbaric" the Mormons might prove to be.[10]

Beadle thus recognized that many easterners—the likes of whom crowded his own car on the Utah Central—would persist in their desire to see the "noted city of Saints" even if they were destined to be "disappointed" or worse. But would that they could access Salt Lake City by means of a Gentile boat! hinted Beadle, instead of such cramped Mormon railcars! At least then they might enjoy more of the "sublime" Salt Lake environment without patronizing Mormon patriarchs! Such was the tenor of *Reporter* reports at that time, and exclamation points abounded. Meanwhile Beadle refused to acknowledge the possibility that the Utah Central's crowded and mixed-class conditions might actually satisfy the voyeuristic wants of many travelers who were determined to see Saints up close.

STEAMBOATS AND THE RISE OF ATROCITY TOURISM

PROSPECTS LOOKED GOOD, for a time, that Corinne's boats might indeed dominate Utah Central business in freighting if not also tourism. In August 1870 General Connor opened the Silveropolis mine, south of the Great Salt Lake, in partnership with the ex-Mormon Walker brothers; and it, along with Connor's nearby Silver King mine, proved lucrative in its first months of operation.[11] The Corinnethians were ecstatic, seeing anew in their city's future the fruition of Connor's early mining dreams and the possibility of a direct overwater route between Corinne and Lake Point, on the southern shore of the lake. Soon the *Reporter* featured regular pleas for investments in a larger fleet capable of capitalizing on Corinne's locative advantages. "With one or two steamers we at once open up the communication which is necessary to develop the vast resources directly in sight of Corinne. And it is only by this means" that Gentile mines in southern Utah "can be fully brought into the field of operation; for . . . [they are] separated from the railroad by a distance of some fifty miles of the worst roads in the Territory." "The next thing needed is the cash," they said, for "it alone can convert the iron and the timber and the coal into a thing of life upon the waves."[12] But once they had it, their steamers would pay dividends. Beadle and Toohy claimed that overwater transport to Corinne would cost half the time and money that it would take to go "around by railroad and wagons," over "long and crooked roads," through southern Utah and Salt Lake City to Ogden. Plus, Gentile traders would have the invaluable pleasure of knowing that they partook in the breakup of Mormon transportation monopolies and the boycott of the Utah Central.[13]

With such opportunities in mind—and thinking also that it might be possible to found a Gentile pleasure resort alongside the shipping wharfs at Lake Point—Corinnethians built a bigger, grander steamer in early 1871. Set to launch in May, the aptly named *City of Corinne* was approximately 150 feet long, having two engines, a large paddle wheel, three decks, elegant dining quarters, a bar, a dance hall, and eight state rooms—not to mention ample storage space for freight. Though principally owned by local coalman Fox Diefendorf, the *City of Corinne* was to be the embodiment of Beadle's recent commercial dreams: a genteel craft conducting a strictly Gentile clientele and trade, plying Salt Lake commodities independent of Mormon towns and trains. Likewise it was to be the (homologous) metonym for the city of Corinne itself, a blessed flagship of western capitalism and culture.[14]

Of course if local boosters spoke among themselves about capital gains, their outwardly facing advertisements stressed the cultured joys of Salt Lake steaming: "As a pleasure trip for travelers: the crossing of Great Salt Lake on this commodious and richly furnished steamer will at once become the

The *City of Corinne*, shown here after its rebranding as
the *General Garfield*, at Lake Point, Great Salt Lake, 1875.
(Photograph by Charles W. Carter; courtesy of the
Church History Library, The Church of Jesus Christ
of Latter-day Saints, Salt Lake City [PH 1300])

favorite resort of transcontinental tourists. The cool and healthful air of the mountains, the foam and spray of the ocean, apart from danger, the wildest and most beautiful scenery in America, will repay the visitor.... Those who have journeyed on the inland waters of Erie, Huron and Superior have yet to sail on the most romantic of all the lakes, for here it is in the heart of the continent."[15] Such articles contained little to no discussion of the 'curiosities' of Mormondom, in any case, for it was hoped that natural sublimity and environmental tourism were incentive enough for Corinnethian visitation and Salt Lake boating. Observing the references that it *did* include, the *Reporter* clearly wished that the *City of Corinne* might fare as well as steamships frequenting the Great Lakes—many of which were maintained by railroad companies, many of whose passenger receipts benefited from the rise of 'nature tours' and Hudson River aesthetics. Corinnethians hoped to deploy a discourse of natural sublimity with proven appeal to riders and promoters of the same railroads that framed salient distinctions between the pure and the profane in the first place.

Thus Beadle and company's plan in early 1871, bolstered by initial freighting receipts, was for Corinne's carriers to serve as sufficient motive and means to bypass the Mormon cities of Ogden and Salt Lake City entirely. They were arguably sufficient in several respects, for several sectors: businessmen or miners looking to connect southern Utahn goods with northern markets; overland travelers seeking temporary respite from railcar discomforts; swimmers and seekers of sanitariums; nature lovers and boating enthusiasts; and anyone anyhow invested in the rightful progress of science and patriotism in the West. Whereas Corinnethians were freshly concerned by Mormonism's vitality in the post-Cullom, post-Godbeite railroad era, they rebranded Corinne as Utah's premier hub of lakeside commerce, culture, and leisure.

CORINNETHIANS LAUNCHED their *City of Corinne* in an elaborate celebration, on May 23, 1871, promising an influx of patrons and "pilgrim[s]" wishing "to do their worship on the altar of science" rather than at the altars of Mormon barbarism. Thenceforth the *City of Corinne* would run thrice-weekly routes around the lake, at fares ranging from $5.50 to $10.00, offering tourists an "interesting and agreeable diversion in the somewhat tiresome experience of the long rail ride across the continent."[16]

Belying Toohy's expansive rhetoric, however—and perhaps forcing its focus on science and leisure—was the fact that the overwater mining trade was already stalling. Indeed it had never quite realized its lofty potential in the first place, even when Patrick E. Connor was running the *Kate Connor* from Lake Point and Silveropolis. By the spring of 1871 Connor had redirected some of his ore via Salt Lake City and the Utah Central, again, finding it a cheaper route north to the transcontinental trunk—and finding also that his specie concerns outweighed his sectarian ones.[17] He was not alone. The Utah Central dominated the regional ore trade for the next several years, and in 1872 alone it netted over $200,000 in profit, sometimes carting a hundred tons of coal and ore between Salt Lake City and Ogden per day.[18] Thus the grand *City of Corinne* was launched into uncertain economic waters, and the Corinnethian planning committee could only hope that their elegant appointments were well placed and attractive to excursionists.

Corinnethians' high hopes for the touristic function and appeal of the *City of Corinne* also masked another concern in the spring of 1871: that cultured visitors had deemed both Corinne and its boats disappointing. Consider, for instance, the impressions of Austrian diplomat Baron Alexander von Hübner. Arriving at Corinne in early June, only two weeks after the ceremonial launch of its steamer, Hübner found that the boat was already out of commission, with carpenters "hard at work fitting up her cabins" for the expected onslaught of tourists like himself. ("Everything was topsy turvy" then, agreed one Ophir-based miner, when characterizing Corinnethians' attempts to outfit themselves for every possible economic opportunity.)[19] Hübner described Corinne's finest hotel as a "wretched plank hut," and he registered also his amusement at how the "colossal ... chignons" of "the mistress of the house" and her daughter ill matched their rugged accommodations. These women may have intended to set themselves apart both from Mormon wives and end-of-track prostitutes by their "careful toilet," but Hübner read their efforts rather as an embarrassing embodiment of the town's pretensions overall.[20]

Local Attractions and Native Impressions

The town that Hübner visited was far from having the whitewashed walls and demographics that Beadle promised. Photographs, census reports, city council records, and letters from early visitors indicate a much more ramshackle and racially diverse town than that portrayed in the booster literature. There were indeed numerous sturdy buildings by then, including a grocery, a city hall, and the Presbyterian church, but most homes and stores were still sheltered by semipermanent or movable tents. Likewise, whereas there were several 're-spectable' businesses, such as a newspaper, hotel, banks, and outfitters for Montana-bound miners, Corinne also had a relatively large number of saloons, brothels, and gambling houses—as well as a persistent problem with loose hogs and gunfire in the main streets. And although most of the approximately eight hundred official residents were Anglo- or German American, at least one hundred were Chinese persons employed as merchants, railway laborers, cooks, launderers, or prostitutes.[21]

The presence of American Indians in and around Corinne constituted perhaps the greatest demographic disconnect between Corinnethian expectations and realities. Connor and Beadle had celebrated the displacement of Northern Shoshoni bands from Bear River Valley after the Bear River Massacre of 1863, as well as the Shoshonis' relocation to Fort Hall Reservation in Idaho around 1868, but neither resulted in complete removal. Granted many bands of Western Shoshonis (groups formerly based around Boise and the Snake River in Idaho), Eastern Shoshonis (formerly based near the Idaho-Wyoming border), and Bannocks *did* commit to living at Fort Hall or Wyoming's Wind River Reservation per terms of 1868 treaties. Numerous 'reservation Indians,' however, revisited former lands or new settlements to hunt, trade, or beg, driven there by food shortages and the failure of government agents to deliver promised protections. Moreover, some Northwestern Shoshonis were wholly uninvolved in and resistant to relocation treaties in the first place, and these so-called wandering bands continued to roam and live along the border of Utah and Idaho. These groups, which included survivors of Connor's 1863 military offensives, consistently wintered in the southern sections of Bear River Valley, not far from Corinne. They also met there with Utah Indian officials, generally in the fall and spring, to receive the small annuities promised them following the massacre in the 1863 Treaty of Box Elder.[22]

Beadle and his fellow boosters seldom publicly addressed the Shoshonis' presence in Bear River Valley, in 1868–71, except when listing persons and perils destined for replacement by white Gentiles upon Corinnethian ascent. Local papers, government, and commercial practices, however, belied this silence. Reporters and town officials often complained about Indians begging and "naked savages... in the suburbs," even as local businessmen banked on postannuity cycles of trade and whiskey sales.[23] Perhaps most irksome to leading Corinnethians was that the railroads themselves failed to drive Indians away. Quite the contrary, and notwithstanding a city council request to discontinue the practice, the Central Pacific allowed Indians to ride in freight cars for free.[24]

NOTABLY, BARON VON HÜBNER himself was neither offended nor disappointed by the presence of Indians around Corinne. In fact the opposite was true: he thought that Indian encounters stood substantially to improve his stay, by offering a kind of excitement that the town otherwise failed to deliver. "Some Indians of the Shoshone tribe have pitched their tents in a camp on the borders of the Bear River not far from the town," Hübner wrote. "Tomorrow the chiefs hold a *pow-wow*" and his Corinnethian hosts "propose to take me there."[25]

Like many of his Austrian and German contemporaries Hübner was fascinated by American Indians, and he longed to witness firsthand the types of savage-but-noble societies fictionalized and popularized by James Fenimore Cooper's *Leatherstocking Tales* and similar "American novels, those brilliant portraits of heroes whose ferocity was atoned for by acts of chivalry worthy of the Crusaders."[26] What he saw in the Bear River Valley, however, fell short of his romantic expectations. Gathered to receive governmental annuities, "the once powerful tribe of the Soshones" seemed "now degraded and miserable" to his eye. "Disease, brandy, and misery have degraded and debased features which in a few of them still bore the stamp of the manly savage virtues of their ancestors," thought Hübner, and even where he "could detect here and there movements of dignity and many pride," they were "mingled, however, with an expression of deep and indefinable melancholy." Hübner concluded, without attention to the murders or reservation policies that might have creased anyone's countenance, that "this race... has the presentiment if not the consciousness of its imminent ruin: it knows how it has sunk, and, what is worse, it equally well remembers what it has been." The diplomatic traveler did not begrudge the Corinnethians their unwillingness to embrace these sometimes neighboring bands, insofar as, from his perspective, the Shoshonis were "condemned to perish" anyway. He wished only that they could have managed a more festive performance of their former greatness.[27]

This Austrian tourist's conclusions—that once noble natives were doomed to die and that representations of past livelihood would be entertaining and edifying—encapsulates well general touristic models of Indian culture at the time. Imbibing the colonial notion that American Indians could not (or should not be allowed to) withstand the transformation of their erstwhile 'haunts' by white ranchers, farmers, and industrialists, many individuals and institutions partook in the practice of 'salvage ethnography': the museumization of artifacts representative of Indians' presumably doomed cultures, in order that members of a dominant group might look upon them and recall, with a mix of romantic nostalgia and racist disgust, a simpler way of life. Some people, acting according to a similar logic, enacted or employed others to enact 'Indianness' also in plays, cultural fairs, or, later, Wild West shows. Several towns in the American Southwest became famous, in the early twentieth century especially, both for preserving exempla of (usually) Pueblo architecture and artistry and for hosting performances of associated lifestyles and practices. For their part natives themselves were invariably though uncomfortably drawn into the economies of their own remembrance.[28]

Northwestern Shoshoni groups did think for a time about staging cultural performances, specifically for white observation, as part of their seasonal Bear River Valley and Cache Valley gatherings. The son of a prominent Mormon missionary recalled that, outside Franklin, Idaho, around 1874, "They gave out the word that they would put on an Indian dance and invited all the people of the town to come out and witness the performance free." A large number attended, and the Shoshonis indeed "put on the dance—free—but after it was over, they made the people pay 10 cents each to get out of the tents. It was taken as a huge joke, but the 10 cents was paid."[29] There is no evidence that anyone considered a similar scheme in 1871, when Baron von Hübner wished to attend the Shoshoni meeting outside Corinne, but undoubtedly he would have been interested. Regardless of any actual artificiality, Hübner may even have considered it more authentic and noteworthy than their honest and truly difficult proceedings. For their part the Corinnethians likely stood to make money from arranging tours of such Shoshoni gatherings, as well, their manifest lack of interest in raising consciousness about Shoshoni culture notwithstanding. However Beadle and his fellows were opposed to anything that might have affirmed—or given back—any foothold in the valley for Indians, no matter how small or seasonal. Theirs was an absolute frontier policy of exclusion, and it only grew more standoffish with time.[30]

Reconnecting to Salt Lake City

If Corinnethians refused to acknowledge the possible appeal of Indian cultures, they were forced to come to account with tourists' persistent desires to see something of Mormonism and Salt Lake City. In order to attract more passengers and fill more financial gaps left by recent mining failures, the *Daily Utah Reporter* eventually and begrudgingly reintroduced Mormon discussions, and it advertised anew a direct Salt Lake City steamer route. Corinnethians began thereby to institute a different model of tourism—this one a partial return to the first, when Beadle was most interested in tapping some of the Utah Central's trade.

Come late June 1871, Beadle, Toohy, and others spoke increasingly of one-way trips "for travelers across the continent, especially those with families accompanying them," between Corinne and Salt Lake City. "Either going West or coming East, the tourist will turn aside from the long land route to find rest and recreation on the waters of the lake and river," he proposed, and after landing at either the "Jerusalem of the Mormons" or the "town of Gentil-ity," the tourist could board a new train and continue onward. Such trips would presumably include a ride on the Mormon Utah Central—from Ogden to Salt Lake City or vice versa—but it would be one ride only.[31] And tourists would necessarily spend some of their time and money in Corinne.

With the renewal of focus on Salt Lake City came new support from the Central Pacific Railroad. Crucially: the company had never invested much in the town to that point, beyond building and maintaining a station there, even though it officially claimed responsibility for the tracks running through Corinne after May 1869. (Recall that the Central Pacific promised to reimburse the Union Pacific for the tracks and construction costs incurred between Promontory and Ogden, including around Corinne, when it agreed to fix its transcontinental hub at Ogden.) This is in part because ownership of area lands was never as sure as ownership of the line itself. The transcontinental companies debated for some time whether and how Utahn land grants and bonds would be transferred from the government to the Union Pacific and/or the Central Pacific once construction costs were reimbursed. Neither railroad seemed especially eager to resolve the land-title question in and around Corinne, in any case. Arid sections of northern and western Utah were considered of little value and low priority relative to urban or arable regions elsewhere along the line, and managers wished neither to incur Corinnethian taxes nor Mormon ire by claiming and improving plots in Corinne before their salability was confirmed. The resultant stalemate was frustrating to many Corinnethian settlers of would-be 'railroad lands' who—having no long-standing claims and no Mormonlike Modus Operandi of preemption—waited variously for the companies to resolve their disputes, open town lot departments, or quit claims. Some acquired patents while others refused to pay even when railroads were selling. Land agents and settlers traded doubts about when or whether the land would prove up.[32]

Central Pacific agents may have seen in the *City of Corinne*'s touristic charter an opportunity to capture part of the passenger traffic generally routed through Ogden and the Utah Central, thereby enticing travelers to spend more time along the Central Pacific and increasing the value of its land near Corinne. Whatever the motivation, on July 1, 1871, the *Reporter* proudly announced an "Important Arrangement" between the town, train, and steamboat: "The Central Pacific Railroad has just issued passenger tickets with coupons attached, for the steamboat route between Corinne and Salt Lake City." Admittedly this arrangement was flawed by Toohy's and Beadle's earlier standards. Based as it was on the presumptive appeal of Salt Lake City, the Central Pacific subsidy did little to ensure Corinne's economic self-sufficiency or the anti-Mormon terms of a *Corinne*-based tourism trade. Nevertheless town residents willingly forewent a small measure of control in return for railroad promotion and more traffic.[33]

A small measure, but not total control. For, Toohy and others decided that the first major postarrangement excursion to Salt Lake City would be for Independence Day, July 4. Setting the tone and template for subsequent trips, the Independence Day relaunch would establish forevermore Corinne's status as the Patriotic, Gentile, Protestant Hub of Utah. The *Reporter* encouraged all of Corinne's residents and neighbors—along with all transcontinental travelers in the area—to "turn out in large numbers for [a] Gentile demonstration in Salt Lake on the Fourth." All participants would be escorted by Gentiles through the streets of Salt Lake City, to the headquarters of the Liberal Institute, where leading Corinnethians would pledge allegiance to the nation and enmity to Mormonism.[34] (Nat Stein's "Ode on Independence Day," read at the event, included a resounding call to "Ne-er renounce fair Freedom's charter for some haughty lordling's cause" nor allow people to "intrench oppression's forces by uniting church and state.")[35] Inviting all patriots to travel to and from the demonstration via the *City of Corinne*, whether with or without subsidized tickets from the Central Pacific, Corinnethians guaranteed at least that they would enjoy the boat's "capacious stateroom, promenade deck, and sweet music" along with the invaluable pleasure of avoiding "a dusty trip in the church cars" of the Utah Central that surely would have "gratif[ied] the High Priest and annoy[ed] themselves."[36]

Thus, thought Toohy: if Gentiles *must* travel to Salt Lake City, and if the *City of Corinne* must run there itself, it was best that they cooperate, taking care to avoid the Utah Central or anything else that might "gratify the High Priest." The Fourth of July was the perfect symbolic opportunity to affirm the Corinnethian-Gentile identity, but forever thereafter Corinnethians would be available for charter, guiding Gentiles' tours and spouting anti-Mormon invectives as necessary.

The Corinnethian excursion model came back around, then, by July 1871, to a harsher version of Beadle's original vision: a Gentile-run tour through lands of Mormon degradation and danger, absent all references to railroads' inherent righteousness or the harmless whimsy of Asiatic customs. Beadle, Hollister, and others remade themselves as purveyors of anti-Mormon tourism in Salt Lake City itself.

The Theory and Politics of Tourism

Beadle's basic theories about tourism and its politics of perception were astute, even when his business ventures were not. For, he recognized that tourism was not merely the process of sightseeing in lands distant from one's home but that it also generated interest and structured observation among different groups in a pluralist world. As sociologist of tourism Dean MacCannell has written, "sightseeing is a ritual performed to the differentiations of society." I take this to mean—and Beadle seems to have understood—that, insofar as changes in demographics, economics, and territory (for instance) effect divisions of rank, labor, or place, sightseeing rituals attend to intercategorical spaces, allowing for their intellectual if not functional reduction. Tourist arrangements enable people to devise new theories of humanity capable of integrating new or newly posited difference, as travelers conceive of themselves relative to the peoples and lands they encounter along the way.[37] This process was comparable across European, Asian, and American Grand Tours, but the early American transcontinental tour differed in that it incorporated far-flung Utahn lands and therefore required the special theorizing of 'religion' there.

Western industrialists, sightseers, and Mormons all worked to that end, albeit with differing intentions and from different angles. Some seem to have been motivated by a combination of greed, prejudice, opportunism, and idealism, while others were less mercenary. In any case the literature, sites, and technologies of Utahn tourism inhabited the spaces between coarticulated forms of religion and irreligion in America; and they created new spaces in which people could think about the terms of articulation and the extents of their application. Tourism is a process *of* differentiation even as it enacted attention *to* differentiation. It is a ritual act of consciousness paid to, and paid within, processes of social distinction and expansion. And in this case tourism was component to the identification of religion in and around Utah.

Of course, this process could proceed in either positive or negative terms. Beadle and his colleagues knew as much, and their goal was to cast Salt Lake City tourism strictly in the key of atrocity tourism, or what MacCannell calls "negative sightseeing." Rendered the antitype against which tourists might appreciate their own rationality and religion, Mormonism, by this model, would "establish in consciousness the definition and boundary of modernity by rendering concrete and immediate that which modernity is not."[38] Properly Protestant and rightly republican persons alike would see in Mormonism's family structures, secret rituals, and theocratic governance the antithesis of their values, Beadle thought. Tourists would then recognize the corresponding wisdom of congressmen's anti-Mormon concerns, as well as those harbored more locally by the Corinnethians, and they would find ways to amplify them. Whether by supporting Mormonism's local antagonists, boycotting Mormon businesses, or convincing congressmen to commit to anti-Mormon action, negative sightseers in Salt Lake City would sound the death knell of Mormonism more loudly than other industries had to date.

Thus Beadle and company held out hope that tourists might complete railroads' would-be religious and political work, exposing Mormonism's persistent barbarity even when politicians failed to do so themselves. To that end Corinnethians closely tracked emergent patterns of Salt Lake City–based tourism well into the 1870s, and they continued to work there as guides when more local industries failed them.

Beadle as Tour Guide

When Schuyler Colfax visited Salt Lake City in 1869, LDS commentators complained that he was "run" around town by Corinnethian guides who shielded him from genuine Mormon encounters and thus slanted his opinion of Mormondom.[39] They were not wrong: O. J. Hollister had worked precisely thus, in an early instance of Corinnethian employment as tour guides to Salt Lake City. And J. H. Beadle played a similar role for other Gentile visitors at the time. Before the launch of Corinne's steamers and intermittently again after their failure, Beadle's business was pointing tourists in the direction of Mormon atrocities or, rather, the right direction for wrong religion. He is not always credited in their published travel narratives, but authors' diaries and drafts show Beadle to have been an influential stagehand in an increasingly verbose industry of observation and reporting.

Charles Carleton Coffin was among the tourists escorted by Beadle in late 1868, just before *Kate Connor*'s maiden journey at Corinne. Then conducting research for a book titled *Our New Way round the World*, Coffin spent five days in Salt Lake City. At least two of these were in Beadle's company, and according to corresponding sections of Coffin's diary, Beadle entertained him with stories about Brigham Young's fanaticism, Mormon violence, and "young girls" quietly longing for "Gentile husbands" like them. As Beadle explained to Coffin, such women were otherwise forced into plural marriages in the Endowment House—which Beadle elsewhere described as a deceptively innocent-looking and "unpretentious *adobe* building in the northwest corner of the [Temple] lot," where LDS leaders also ordered oaths of loyalty, murdered apostates, and barred entry to anyone outside the church. "The secret of B[righam]'s fame is the Endowment House—is sort of Masonic lodge," Coffin recorded. "Secret espionage." Finally Beadle directed Coffin to Brigham Young's home, recommended exposés of life in his personal "harem," and told riddles about polygamous family relations generally. Among his riddles was this: "A & B married sisters, then A married B's sister for second wife, & B married A's sister for second wife. . . . What will be the relationship of the children?" Beadle's atrocity tour combined horror with humor.[40]

Beadle was clearly an important source for Coffin. Notes from their meetings occupy some twenty-five of his sixty diary pages on Utah, and several of Coffin's published works (including a series of "Round the World Sketches" published in the *Boston Journal*) draw directly from them. Beadle had instructed Coffin to pay close attention to the telegraph wires running to Brigham Young's house, for instance, and to consider other mechanisms by which Young might have maintained constant surveillance over all Mormon settlements; and Coffin's report spent considerable time on the subject. So too Coffin took Beadle's advice about source material on Brigham Young's domestic life, reproducing at length the wife-by-wife and room-by-room account published elsewhere by author and activist Catherine Van Valkenburg Waite. Finally he echoed Beadle's and others' comparison of 'Oriental' and Mormon polygamy: "In the Orient there is one institution which has long been established,—concubinage. The modern Turk, the Arab, Hindoo, Feegian, and the King of Ashantee, all follow in the footsteps of their fathers. They keep concubines by the score. The harem never has flourished under the Christian civilization of Europe, but it has been

This Great Work Lifts the Veil From Mormonism

And we see it in all its Hideous Aspects. It deals fearlessly with the Heinous Doctrine of Plurality of Wives, and contains the full and Authentic history of the Mormons and their Outrageous Teachings.

SCENES IN THE ENDOWMENT OR
INITIATION CEREMONIES

"Scenes in the Endowment or Initiation Ceremonies," as J. H. Beadle imagined them. This advertisement for Beadle's *Mysteries and Crimes of Mormonism* was saved by LDS officials, who paid close attention to acts and genres of atrocity tourism. (Courtesy of the Church History Library, The Church of Jesus Christ of Latter-day Saints, Salt Lake City [Joseph F. Smith Papers, General Correspondence, Miscellaneous Items, 1904]) planted in Utah by the prophet and apostles of the church of the Latter-Day Saints, and is thriving with great vigor." Coffin was happy to add his voice to a chorus of outrage about 'Turks' in America.[41]

Beadle was not the only Corinnethian whom Coffin consulted during his brief stay in Salt Lake City. The Rev. George W. Foote, founder of the Episcopal Church in Corinne, also met with Coffin, and he seems to have amplified Beadle's predictions of an imminent crisis for Brighamite power: "Young men on R[ail] R[oad] will get new views," "disaffection is on the increase," and since "young women as a rule [are] all opposed to polygamy," it and other systems of restriction would surely end. Coffin repeated these and similar death knell presumptions in his formal reports, but—crucially—he also stressed the need for tourists, politicians, and others to support Utah's Gentile population in order to fulfill the railroads' schismatic potential. Coffin especially promoted Foote's efforts to establish a "Gentile School," which, he said, "is looked upon by the Mormons as one of Satan's agencies for undermining the church" and which "I heard ... severely denounced from the Tabernacle pulpit on Sunday."[42]

Coffin visited both the New and the Old Tabernacles, in Salt Lake City's Temple Block, and they seem to have been his most important sites of direct Mormon observation and encounter. Indeed they were and would remain central attractions for most Gentile tourists, then and in the wake of Coffin's visit. The New Tabernacle, completed in 1867, was surely the most eye-catching specimen of Mormon architecture at the time. Resembling from the outside (in Coffin's words) "a huge dish cover—oblong and oval, with rounded roof," it could seat several thousand people in an interior unmarred by visible support beams. Church leaders commissioned a massive pipe organ, to capitalize on the building's excellent acoustics, and they held important meetings and services there, including the October 1868 conference on "the railroad problem." Such meetings were generally open to the public, and Gentile visitors often aimed to attend Sunday services in the (New) Tabernacle during their stay. Coffin attended both morning and afternoon services himself—although these were held in the far less imposing setting of the Old Tabernacle, which was easier to heat in the winter months.[43]

Perhaps the most striking thing about the services that Coffin attended, given the general tenor and the particular guides of his tour, is the degree to which they show Mormon leaders to have been acutely aware of the outsiders and opponents in their midst. Indeed not only was the Reverend Foote denounced from the pulpit, but Apostle George Q. Cannon spent considerable time mocking the death knell thesis espoused by Coffin's Corinnethian escorts. Cannon "took up the railroad questions, predicted that it would be of incalculable benefit to the Saints; would not solve the Mormon problem, as the Gentiles hoped and predicted, but would strengthen the church."[44] Of course Beadle would come to fear as much too, in time, but for several years he remained positive that tourists like Coffin held the keys to Corinnethian victory.

For his part Coffin left it an open question to his readership: "How the opening of the road will work out the solution of the Mormon question, no one seems to know." The author predicted only that "a new element" will continue to "make its appearance in the territory," and that "one, if not two, towns will spring up on the line of the railroad, . . . peopled by men . . . who will be ready to 'pitch in and clean out' the Saints whenever they have an opportunity." In the meantime Coffin encouraged more Gentile tourists to visit Utah, especially after the transcontinentals were connected, to meet with the likes of Beadle and to write home about life in Mormondom. "A few months hence the public may have more light on the subject," Coffin concluded—and on that front at least he was right.[45]

"Whited Sepulchres": Genres of Exposure

It was indeed a few months thence, in June 1869, that Anna Dickinson spent four days in Salt Lake City, during a transcontinental tour on the newly completed railroad. Called "the most popular American orator" of the time by none other than Elizabeth Cady Stanton, Dickinson lectured regularly on the lyceum circuit in support of abolitionism and women's rights—and many people waited with anticipation to hear her thoughts on Mormondom.[46] O. J. Hollister was among them. Although Hollister seems not to have met her personally and there is no evidence of other Corinnethians having done so either, they reported on her visit from a distance, sure that it would have lasting effect on the terms and templates of tourism to come—and thus also their business.[47]

They were not disappointed. When Dickinson arrived in San Francisco that fall, she delivered what was to become one of her best-known lectures, a denunciation of Latter-day Saint practices alternately titled "Mormonism" or "Whited Sepulchres." The latter title derives from Dickinson's characterization of Salt Lake City: it may at first seem "pleasant to the contemplation of the traveler," she said, given its beautiful surroundings and orderly streets, but in reality its "inhabitants were in the depths of hell." Indeed anything superficially attractive about Salt Lake City life was truly rotten at the core. This included the practice of women's suffrage, always a puzzling aspect of Utahn life from the perspective of eastern suffragists who considered Mormon women oppressed despite their right to vote. According to Dickinson such freedom was in fact no freedom at all, because suffrage in Utah was regulated to ensure that no women could disobey the dictates of their patriarchal overseers.

With few exceptions, according to Dickinson, Mormon women were confused or exhausted enough to be contented with their state of polygamous slavery anyway. "The most ardent, enthusiastic, uncompromising advocates [of] this [marriage] system which degrades & violates them, body & soul, are the *women*," she wrote. However, so too "were the women of Turkey and Persia in favor of their system of selling females from the shambles," she reminded her audience, and so too did some Hindu women approve of suttee. This did not mean that others should stop fighting for their rights. Dickinson herself had peered into the dark doorways of otherwise attractive Mormon homes, she said, and—having spoken with some of the wives huddled within—she could attest to their desperate need of enlightenment and humanitarian aid. The great orator concluded that "the government at Washington" especially must recommit to erasing this foul blot from the middle of our beautiful country, this barbarous offense against "decency and Christianity alike."[48]

Although some of her contemporaries might not have considered Anna Dickinson a model Christian herself, given her sometimes radical views on feminism and race, her arguments about Mormonism exemplified American Protestant and secular distinctions between inner and outer, right and wrong religions. The by-then predictable nature of its cultural comparisons notwithstanding, however, Dickinson's lecture became an influential model for negative sightseeing in the emerging railroad era, promising as it did the possibility of—and providing also a metaphor for—short but penetrative peeks behind the tidy facades of Mormon life.

A NUMBER OF SOCIAL REFORMERS and sightseers shared Dickinson's abhorrence for multiple marriage, and they too traveled to Salt Lake City determined to find proofs of polygamous horrors and excesses. By 1872 there was a well-established but unofficial market for the revelation of such signs, capitalizing on the networks already promoted and patronized by the likes of Coffin and Dickinson. Some carriage drivers escorted tourists from train stations to downtown locations, told stories about the sexual exploits rumored to have transpired at, say, Brigham Young's multigabled home, and then introduced them to local anti-Mormons or Mormon hoteliers willing to tell more. However the *City of Corinne* never became a fixture of such atrocity tours, Beadle's efforts notwithstanding. Even with the brief backing of the Central Pacific, the competition from Mormon-backed branch lines and freighters proved too much for it. Other factors were at play too, as we will see, but, perhaps most important: Gentiles seemed to consider (what Beadle had once termed) a "dusty trip in the church cars" an edifying voyeuristic experience in its own right. Far from a deterrent, the Utah Central ride proved to be an attraction.

Helen Hunt, later to become famous under her married name (Helen Hunt Jackson) as a 'Friend of the Indian' and an opponent of American reservation policies, looked forward to a Utah Central trip in 1872.[49] This was not only because she considered the Utah Central a portal to the weird wonders of Salt Lake City but because she imagined the cars themselves to be somehow metonymic of Mormonism or imprinted by its institutions. "We expected to find 'Holiness to the Lord' inscribed on the panels, and portraits of Mormon elders above the doors," she wrote half-jokingly later, when recalling her surprise that "the cars of the Utah Central Railroad should be just like all other cars." Hunt and her companions were nevertheless determined to find evidence of otherness elsewhere, and they "scrutinize[ed] the face of every man and every woman about us, and search[ed] for some subtle token which might betray that they were not living as other men and women live." Finally they settled on one likely candidate for otherness and corruption: "Just as the cars moved out of Ogden, there entered in at the door of our car a big, burly man, perhaps fifty-five or sixty years old. His face was very red; he wore a red wig; and, as if determined to make the red of his face and the red of his wig both as hideous as possible, he wore about his neck a scarf of a third shade of fiery red. His eyes were small, light, and watery, but sharp and cruel. His face was bloated, coarse, sensual: I have never seen a more repulsive man. 'Oh! that is a Mormon.' we whispered, under our breaths. 'It must be.'" In this instance they were right. The man in question was Church Historian George A. Smith, a polygamous Mormon and church official of high rank indeed.[50]

Hunt's search for signs of polygamy continued in the Mormon capital, assisted at first by a driver who "turns around from time to time" to declare, "'That's a three-wife house.' 'That's a two-wife house,'" and so forth. However Hunt felt conflicted about some of the scenes that she encountered, and she struggled with the same sense of mixed mirth and sadness in Salt Lake City that Dickinson had observed before her. On the one hand she wrote that "the very air seemed heavy with hidden sadness. No stranger can walk the streets of Salt Lake City without a deepening sense of mystery and pain. We have been so long accustomed to the idea of polygamy as a recognized evil, we have seen the word so long and so often in print, that we are unprepared for the new sense of horror which is at once aroused by the actual presence of the thing. Each sunny doorway, each gay garden, is a centre of conjecture, of sympathy. Each woman's face, each baby's laugh, rouses thoughts hard to hear." But yet the doorways *were* sunny, the gardens *were* gay, and the babies *did* laugh. These were not idle observations but rather occasion for real reflection—"centers of conjecture," to use Hunt's term—regarding her own presumptions and expectations. By Hunt's description the women of Salt Lake City "are standing on doorsills, with laughing babies in their arms; they are talking gayly with each other on the sidewalk; they are leading little children; they are walking by the side of men; they are carrying burdens, or seeking pleasure, just as other women do— apparently. Their faces are not sad, as we looked to find them. If we did not know we were in Salt Lake City, we should" consider them "contented," "healthy," and "innocent."[51] What to think of their seeming cheer?

The future Indian reformer ultimately diffused her discomfort by recourse to religious comparison. Likening Mormonism in general to modern Catholicism— which, she thought, also had happy, intelligent, "credulous, simple, and devoted" people joined with a few "tyrannical and unscrupulous leaders"—Hunt concluded that, if only Americans eliminated the "great wrong of ecclesiastical domination in Salt Lake City," its homes could be truly happy places. As it was, though, "there is no escape from the shadow; there is no forgetting the wrong."[52] Least of all was there reason for defense or sympathetic romance.

If Hunt's reliance on motifs of sunshine and shadow echoed Dickinson's 'whited sepulchre' theme, her proposed resolution to the Mormon Problem was somewhat different. Granted she felt little reason to stay the hand of the government, should it choose a more active policy of anti-Mormon intervention. But she anticipated that the answer to polygamy would perhaps be less political—and certainly less millennial—than millinerial. Hunt concluded the account of her Salt Lake City tour thus: "A shrewd old man, who had lived in Salt Lake City for several years, said to me, one morning, pointing to the windows of a milliner's shop, before which we stood: 'They needn't trouble themselves to legislate about polygamy. This sort of stuff,'—waving his hand back and forth in front of the bonnets and ribbons,—'this sort of stuff will put an end to it. It's putting an end to monogamy, for that matter! It will very soon be here, as it is elsewhere, more than most men can do to support even one wife!'"[53] The fashion industry could render polygamy itself untenable.

HUNT'S SOURCE—the "shrewd old man"—is unnamed in her work, but his argument is recognizable, linked as it was to the logic of the death knell thesis. Corinnethians had long before predicted that railroads would bring eligible bachelors and enticing fashions to Utah, thereby destabilizing Mormon marriages and domestic economies; for their part, Mormon women had organized against them to "set [their] own fashions" and avoid "extravagance in dress."[54]

However Beadle and company since downplayed any sense of effortless inevitability entailed therein, having watched railroad-backed lobbyists deploy death knell notions in defense of governmental nonintervention against Mormonism. Indeed if anyone was espousing the transformative potential of modern fashions on Mormon marriage systems, at the time of Hunt's visit in 1872, it was not Corinnethians but rather the Godbeites on whose behalf such lobbyists had supposedly spoken—especially the Stenhouses.

Even before the official formation of the New Movement in 1869, T. B. H. Stenhouse and his first wife, Fanny Stenhouse, took pleasure in hosting Gentile visitors and representing a 'liberal' and cosmopolitan side to their community in Salt Lake City. During the Cullom Bill debates, the pair became much more vocal in their dissent from the LDS Church, and they soon surpassed other leading Godbeites in their efforts against Brigham Young. Indeed they went beyond them in the substance of their concern as well, by turning explicitly against polygamy—and by detailing their own difficult relationships with plural wives, from whom they had split by late 1869. Fanny especially introduced an antipolygamy component to her own ongoing work of hosting visitors in Salt Lake City, and at the urging of interested easterners, in 1872 she published a book titled *Exposé of Polygamy in Utah: A Lady's Life among the Mormons*.[55]

Fanny Stenhouse's book was an instant best seller in the East, promising as it did an intimate portrait of a cosmopolitan woman's marital misadventures in Utah, and thus also a firsthand account of life inside the 'whited' homes described elsewhere by Anna Dickinson. In it Fanny described the difficulty of coming to terms with the practice of polygamy, which was revealed after her conversion to Mormonism, and of convincing herself that it was God's will. She wrote briefly of the Endowment House ritual by which she agreed to "give proof of her faith in her religion by placing the hand of [a] new wife in that of her husband," consenting to their marriage "for time and for all eternity." ("I did so," she wrote. "But words can describe my feelings? The anguish of a whole lifetime was crowded into that one single moment. When it was done, I felt that I had laid every thing upon the altar, and that there was no more to sacrifice. I had given away my husband. What more could the Lord require of me that I could not do? Nothing!") At greater length, then, she described the arduous processes by which her husband came to recognize the tyranny of Brigham Young's economic rule in Utah, at the dawn of the New Movement, and by which they awakened each other to further corruptions of their faith. By Fanny's description polygamy was the ultimate such corruption, a betrayal of true religion and true love alike. Its inescapable ends were the estrangement of husband and wife, the mistreatment of secondary wives, and the death of "all that is worth calling love."⁵⁶

No doubt the most notable aspect of Stenhouse's exposé was its detailed descriptions of domestic life under polygamy: how wives divided tasks, where they lived, how they interacted with their husbands, and so forth. Such details satisfied many readers' desires for intimate revelations, even when Stenhouse herself demurred at the thought of invading Brigham Young's privacy ("His wives and children are as sacred to me as I would desire my own family to be with the public") or saying too much about Endowment House rituals ("In justice to the Mormons, I feel bound to state that the accounts which I have frequently read, professing to give a description of the 'Endowments' given in Salt Lake City, are almost entirely exaggerated," and "I myself saw nothing indelicate").⁵⁷ But it is Stenhouse's conclusion that stands quoting at length, given its familiar resonance with Dickinson's charges of wifely lifelessness and Hunt's plea for modern millinery in Salt Lake City:

> It is only after marriage that many [Mormon women] lose their elasticity of step, their joyous, happy looks, and that animation of countenance which makes even a homely face look beautiful at times. On some of their faces may be detected a deep melancholy; but, if they can be diverted from their sad thoughts for ever so short a time, they become animated, and even, it may be, beautiful. Add to this secret sorrow which casts a gloom upon their countenances, the little opportunity which they have of cultivating their taste for dress, and it will not be wondered at if the Mormon women are not always very beautiful to a man who is captivated by outward appearances. Many of these women are taught to be satisfied with simple clothing, and it is constantly drummed into their ears that love of dress is a sin in the sight of God. Thus this love of the beautiful, which is a part of woman's nature, has to be crushed out entirely, and that, too frequently, by her own husband.⁵⁸

Stenhouse granted that some Mormon women seemed miserable, but she considered their sadness to be a function of polygamous marriage and their inability to wear nice clothes.

Fanny Stenhouse offered a two-part salve for Mormon women's melancholy. The first, though it went unmentioned in her book, was a Salt Lake City dress shop under her direct management. The Emporium of Fashion (established 1871) offered "an excellent assortment of millinery goods of the Latest Style" and "the service of a first-class dressmaker."⁵⁹ Whether this was the milliner's shop to which a "shrewd old man" directed Helen Hunt's attention, we unfortunately do not know. In any case the second part of Stenhouse's solution harmonized well with the conclusion that Hunt reached outside that store. "The construction of the Pacific Railroad, the discovery of the great wealth in the mountains of Utah, and the free expression of the sentiments of thinking men who have outlived and abandoned Mormonism, have given the death-blow to Polygamy," Stenhouse wrote. "Were there none but Mormons in the Territory, it might have lived on so long as they were willing to remain in poverty; but with prosperity, and the changed circumstances which are ever certain to follow wealth, Polygamy is a doomed institution."[60] Thus railroads and mines brought wealth and, with it, an ability for women to satisfy their innate desire for beauty and fashion. Beauty and fashion in turn made Mormon women attractive to outside suitors, and—insofar as most Mormon men were disinclined to outfit multiple wives in expensive clothing—that presaged an era of exogamy and monogamy in Utah. In short order polygamy would go out of style.

FANNY STENHOUSE'S *Exposé* sold well. The New York–based publisher exhausted three editions in a few short months, and readers across America were exposed to her stylized version of the death knell thesis. Hoping to capitalize on its popularity, then, Stenhouse embarked on a national speaking tour in the fall of 1872, and she lectured in several marquee venues in major cities throughout the East.[61]

Stenhouse's inaugural lecture was held, however, in the much smaller venue of Corinne. From the town's perspective this marked a major scheduling accomplishment, and Corinnethians were proud to host her, notwithstanding Stenhouse's Godbeite pedigree and their own reticence to embrace any version of the death knell thesis that failed to culminate in Corinnethian calls to arms. A *Corinne Daily Reporter* article published the next day glowed in the memory of Stenhouse's "complete history of the horrors and suffering's [sic] experienced by women in that degrading institution" of polygamy, regretting only that she could not stay longer:

> She brought some startling facts to light, showing the teachings and workings of the Mormon Church, and relates incidents of the most heart-rending character. All this she knows by sad experience, having been for years the wife of a polygamist. She is a lady of high culture, the most refined feelings and possesses a fine education. . . . At the close of the lecture, by an unanimous expression of the wishes of the audience, Mrs. Stenhouse was solicited to remain and deliver her lecture on the Mormon

Reformation this evening, but prior engagements in the East, to the regret of all, prevented the lady from complying with the request. She left on the morning train to make a tour through the eastern States.[62]

Corinne may have been a small venue, but it was determined still to be the launching pad for all acts of anti-Mormon tourism. This fit the bill perfectly, and Corinnethians only hoped that Stenhouse's book and tour would reinvigorate their end of the market.

Beadle's Last Stand

J. H. Beadle was working hard to capitalize on the market for anti-Mormon literature and lectures as well around the time of Stenhouse's 1872 engagement. Indeed from 1871 through late 1872 Beadle collaborated with a publisher of popular western handbooks and travel guides to ensure that Salt Lake City tours became proper exercises in Christian pedagogy and anti-Mormon fervor, if not also direct Corinnethian promotion. At least these were Beadle's goals. The aims of his publisher, George A. Crofutt, were decidedly more complicated.[63]

Crofutt was already famous by then for having produced one of the first travel guides of the Pacific Railway era, a book credited with popularizing the term "transcontinental" itself. This was the cumbersomely but aptly titled *Crofutt's Trans-Continental Tourist's Guide: containing a full and authentic description of over five hundred cities, towns, villages, stations, . . . scenery, watering places, summer resorts; . . . to tell you what is worth seeing—where to see it—where to go—how to go—and whom to stop with while passing over the Union Pacific Railroad, Central Pacific Railroad . . . from the Atlantic to the Pacific Ocean*.[64] The nearly 250-page guidebook, updated and reprinted numerous times between 1869 and 1876, was sold usually for fifty cents on Central Pacific and Union Pacific railroad cars, as well as at railside newsstands, bookstores, and stations. In 1871 the 'transcontinental' companies circulated thousands of copies of this guide in Europe as advertisements for their lines. Known also for making famous and rendering ubiquitous John Gast's oil painting *American Progress*, which Crofutt offered cheaply to readers in chromolithographic form, *Crofutt's* was a wide-reaching and very influential publication.[65]

Not only was *Crofutt's Trans-Continental Tourist's Guide* well established by 1871, but its take on Utahn travel and culture was long before set in type. Granted, it was a somewhat multivocal and ambivalent position. On the one hand, among point-by-point mention of overland towns and attractions, it ran affirming descriptions of many Mormon settlements, and it specifically recommended side trips to Salt Lake City via the Utah Central, "owned and controlled by the citizens of Utah Territory." At the same time, however, Crofutt's book printed a positive report for Corinne and its Gentile charter. "The only Gentile town in Utah Territory" promised to be a place of "great importance in time," it said, and "the *Utah Reporter*, a Gentile paper," would be "a perfect thorn in the side of the Mormons."[66] It was unclear, from such descriptions, whether the publisher had any particular preference between pro- and anti-Mormon parties.

Crofutt's third narrative thread seemingly weighed in favor of the Corinnethians, but it too was ambiguous. Crofutt reprinted a three-page tale of Mormon depredations against American troops during the 1857–58 Utah Expedition, and beginning in 1871, he echoed Godbeite arguments about the "folly" of Brigham Young's previous antimining policies and anti-Gentile trade embargos. Crucially, however: in both cases his critiques remained retrospective in tense, and Crofutt implied consistently that railroads had already sounded death knells for Mormonism's chief martial and economic faults. "Thank God, and the Pacific Railroad," he said, that "a miner can now 'prospect,' a 'Gentile' can now engage in business without fear of being 'lost' by a [Mormon guard] or being warned out of the territory, simply because he is not a Mormon." To read Crofutt's full report was to learn that Utah was now completely safe for Gentile business and settlement—as at Corinne—and for Gentile travel and enjoyment—as through Salt Lake City—by virtue of the Pacific Railroad and its Utahn branch. Crofutt himself repeatedly underlined the message: "Again, thank God—and the Pacific Railroad—for such a glorious revolution in Utah."[67]

Beadle likely felt a mixture of appreciation and frustration upon reading Crofutt's tripartite Utah reports. Beadle's own advocacy of the death knell thesis was by then well known, of course, but so too was the frustration he felt when watching congressmen reframe it as a reason *not* to pursue anti-Mormon or pro-Corinnethian legislative action. Crufutt's evocation seemed similar, in that regard; whereas Beadle imagined unrelenting projects of unmitigated Gentility in Utah, Crofutt spoke of Mormon menaces mainly as a matter of the past, thereby, from Beadle's perspective, paying insufficient attention to railroads' inequalities of purpose or inconsistencies of action on behalf of liberal Christian republicanism. What is more, Crofutt had explicitly disavowed the task and tone of militant anti-Mormon exposé, at least for his popular *Trans-Continental Tourist's Guide*. The publisher maintained instead that "it is not the purpose of the writer of the GUIDE to indorse or condemn any man or his public acts," and he declared therefore that he would leave judgments respecting Mormons' contemporary religiosity to readers, visitors, lawyers, and politicians.[68]

Nevertheless Beadle hoped to budge Crofutt toward a more fully Corinnethian position. His efforts were somewhat successful, too, but—again—only somewhat so. For, while Crofutt did agree to help Beadle turn the "thorn in the side of the Mormons" by publishing some of his own anti-Mormon reports, thereby aiding Corinnethian efforts to reframe Salt Lake City tourism as an act of negative sightseeing, he also steadfastly refused to alter the tone of his own principal guidebook. Crofutt insisted on maintaining certain boundaries between his different publications and the touristic genres that they represented.

BEADLE AND CROFUTT'S collaborations began in earnest later in 1871, after Beadle obtained a written statement from William A. Hickman. "Wild Bill," as he was known, was Brigham Young's former bodyguard and a rumored leader of the Danites, an infamous and semimythical Mormon vigilante group.[69] Arrested on charges of murdering a Gentile trader during the 1857 Utah War, Wild Bill made a confession that detailed numerous other crimes—including a recent conspiracy to kill General Patrick E. Connor—which, Hickman claimed, were similarly ordered by Brigham Young or otherwise implicated church authorities.[70] Beadle planned to distribute this confession far and wide, thereby alerting travelers, traders, and politicians alike to the continuing threats of Mormon theocracy and violence. To that end he edited and organized it, revised sections, added appendixes and introductory matter, and offered it all to Crofutt for publication.

Hickman's exposé, which Beadle convinced Crofutt to publish in 1872 as *Brigham's Destroying Angel*, was a sensational tale of atrocities. Historians and relatives alike agree that Beadle modified content to optimal alarmist effect, but absent surviving originals it is difficult to know what, exactly, Beadle 'edited' versus what he fabricated wholesale.[71] The resultant 'confession' was in any case clear on several points. Brigham Young had "pursued . . . [a] damnable course," it said, and Hickman had followed him out of "fanatical belief." Together they committed grave errors in the name of religion, but Hickman had since recognized Young to be a fraudulent tyrant, and he was repentant.[72]

Meanwhile Beadle's introductory and concluding points—written in his own voice and under his own byline—were clearer still. Beadle argued that Mormonism, based as it was on the "sanctified selfishness" of "swindling" patriarchs and the physical or "mental slavery" of fanatics, "cannot exist under a republican government or in a civilized country without constant collision." "Our worst opinions of Brigham Young have fallen far short of the bloody reality," he said, and Mormon patriarchs had proven themselves less virtuous and less tractable than "marauding Arabs or wild Indians," tigers, bears, or hyenas.

Mormonism was barbarism and irreligion incarnate, and it must be destroyed. No compromise was possible, for only thus could the West be opened to right racial, religious, and republican settlement.[73]

This was a typical Beadle-esque argument, circa 1872, absent all hints of inevitable decline or innocuous diversion. And to reiterate: Crofutt published it. However Crofutt refrained from actively promoting *Brigham's Destroying Angel* in his mainstay *Trans-Continental Tourist's Guide*. Instead he advertised it in a supplemental work: *Crofutt's Western World*, a slim monthly magazine sold largely by subscription, featuring time-sensitive notices and serialized columns by roving reporters.[74] Save for brief reference to "Bill Hickman['s] . . . confession recently published," Beadle's book was kept beyond the bounds and off the pages of Crofutt's chief, railroad-backed guide.[75]

Generic distinctions should be as significant to us now as they were to Crofutt then. Although Beadle's books and similar exposés hovered always in the background of western tourism practices and publications—and although some promoters ensured their availability at Salt Lake termini—they did not generally set the tone of the main transcontinental guidebooks themselves. From the perspective of the mainline, they remained, rather, a form of niche literature, something available as a supplement or by subscription, but set apart from the niche of travel agents themselves. The railroads simply wouldn't have had it any other way, as we shall see. And neither would the Mormons with whom they partnered.

Ran Aground

By the time Beadle published *Brigham's Destroying Angel* and Corinnethians hosted Fanny Stenhouse in 1872, none were able to point audiences to their Gentile steamers, for they no longer existed. Despite brief support from the Central Pacific Railroad, they had proven economically unviable, especially as Mormon businessmen continued to corner Utah's mining traffic and capitalize on connections with the Union Pacific—and as tourists themselves continued to embrace the Utah Central as an important part of their visit. Brigham Young's son John W. Young moved specifically to commandeer Corinne's nascent bathing and boating trade, as well, and to neutralize or incorporate it within a growing network of Mormon leisure industries. Within a few short years of their launchings, both the *Kate Connor* and the *City of Corinne* were purchased and repurposed for Mormon resorts and pleasure parties, in an ironic twist that foretold the shape of Utahn tourism to come.

Respecting the *Kate Connor*: I have hinted already that it was not long for the ore trade, let alone a consistent or lucrative Corinne–Lake Point route.

Recognizing defeat, Patrick E. Connor sold the *Kate Connor* in March 1872. More than that, though: Connor sold his daughter's namesake to a Mormon bishop, who converted it into a sailboat and used the engine for his gristmill in Kaysville.[76] Parts of the *Kate Connor* thus remained along the southern shores of the lake, used for excursion parties by the bishop and his friends, while other parts supported church-sanctioned agricultural enterprises.

One month later, in April 1872, Fox Diefendorf sold the *City of Corinne*, after similarly declaring it a financial failure for himself and Corinne. The new owners used it for tours around Salt Lake and its islands, but the difference between their business model—soon to be lucrative—and the Corinnethians'—never lucrative—was location, lineage, and Latter-day Saint support. For, the old *City of Corinne* made its new home at 'Lake Side,' a Mormon-owned rival to the would-be (and never-was) Gentile bathing resort at Lake Point.

Located near Salt Lake City, along the line of the Utah Central, Lake Side grew also from the visions of John W. Young and from profits he made in transcontinental construction. Young imagined Lake Side as a stopover for railroad travelers and a day-trip destination for local Mormons both; and while appropriating the old Corinnethian steamship by proxy and in person (Young's ownership was fixed in 1875), he "monopolized the resort trade with a succession of Sunday school parties, reunions, ward parties and excursions in general" for several years.[77] Of Lake Side's new steamer era, historian Brigham Madsen writes: "During the summer of 1872, a number of sightseeing trips were chartered," and "the *Deseret News* . . . wrote glowing accounts of these salt-air refreshers now that the steamer was no longer a property of the citizens of Corinne."[78] Lake Side would have its own financial struggles and failings in time, but Mormon-friendly resorts were the wave of the future—and they were destined to dominate the Salt Lake sanitarium market by the end of the century.

John W. Young's resorts and railroads thus cornered Corinne from several directions. In short order LDS businessmen and their corporate benefactors laid out contra-Corinnethian routes of normative tourism and orthodox Mormonism alike, and both parties spent the 1870s and 1880s building durable platforms of Utahn cultural observation and religious practice.

CHAPTER FIVE

Patrons and the
Plays of Mormon Culture

✦

JOHN CODMAN, a wealthy and well-traveled Bostonian, wrote insightfully about what he took to be touristic familiarity with Mormonism during the early railroad era. "A maudlin curiosity induces many travelers to time their arrival at Ogden on Saturday," he wrote, "so that they may branch off and spend Sunday at Salt Lake City, take a drive of an hour or two there, go to the Tabernacle meeting, see Brigham Young's house, if not Brigham himself, peep into some dwelling where a man is supposed to have more than one wife, and return in time to take the Sunday evening train for the West." Such visitors often carried copies of Beadle's book *Brigham's Destroying Angel*, he said, along with "a small book by Mrs. Stenhouse." By supplementing these exposés with revelations from their own "extended visit of half a day," these tourists considered themselves "perfectly informed as to the character and social status of the Mormon people." Codman, however, thought that true religious comprehension demanded more than reading Beadle's and Stenhouse's publications or making a quick stop at the Salt Lake Tabernacle, regardless of whether people were motivated by romantic sentimentality or "maudlin curiosity." Knowledge demanded rather an extended stay, thorough investigations, and discerning analysis—the likes of which Codman offered to readers in his own book, following his own travels through Utah in 1873.[1]

If Codman intended to go beyond the trappings of an anti-Mormon atrocity tour, however, his writings were in many ways shaped by Mormon efforts to counteract them as well. This is not to say that Codman's reports were themselves overtly biased or that their counter-Corinnethian strain led always to acts of overcompensation and Mormon apology. (They weren't, and they didn't.) In retrospect, what they reveal best are not the iconoclastic or unscripted musings of a disinterested observer, but rather an entire mechanics of Mormon observation mobilized from the inside. Whether Codman was riding in LDS-owned railway cars, staying in church-approved hotels, visiting museums, attending Sunday services, watching plays at the theater, or indeed traveling to Corinne itself, Mormon officials served as Codman's functional if not physical tour guides. Their structures anticipated and supported his every turn away from Corinne.

MORMON LEADERS worked throughout the 1870s to acknowledge, incorporate, or bypass—and in any case to retrain—some of the touristic concerns addressed also by the Corinnethians. This entailed not only working to manage Codman's visit and others like it but also staging Mormon expressions and cultural encounters for Codman's fellow travelers. Suffragist Gail Hamilton, congressman and Speaker of the House James G. Blaine, Union Pacific executive Horace F. Clark, and palace-car promoter George M. Pullman all arrived in Utah on the same train as Codman, and—having bonded along the way—they shared a private railcar from Ogden to Salt Lake City.[2] This was an august if happenstance assembly representing powerful constituencies with interest in Mormon institutions: leisure-class tourists, social reformers, politicians, industrialists, and travel promoters.[3] It is no surprise therefore that Brigham Young, John W. Young, and others in their circle mobilized personally to meet it and, by guiding its members through the city, to represent those institutions in a positive light. Church leaders treated Codman's cohort to a VIP tour nevertheless representative of general Mormon representational efforts at the time.

For his part Codman benefited by being along for the tour, even when he did not recognize—as we might—the politics of the programs to which he was granted access and made party. Only by such recognition can we also see how the Youngs, while managing a tourist itinerary manifestly antithetical to the Corinnethians', worked meanwhile to broker and capitalize on businessmen's continuing investments in the safety and stability of Utahn travel, to ensure that future acts of touristic 'iconoclasm' or middle-ground synthesis would look something like Codman's.

A Southern Tour

John W. Young traveled to meet Codman's esteemed group in Ogden, in May 1873, with an illustrious company of his own: John Sharp, one of the principal Mormon subcontractors on the Union Pacific project; William H. Hooper, former territorial representative to Congress; and John Taylor, LDS Church apostle. It was quite the welcoming party, and its hospitality did not stop there.

Gail Hamilton wrote that Young and company "escorted us to Salt Lake City" in "a special engine" and that, after their "delightful" ride, "carriages were provided to take us to our hotel"—the Mormon-owned and church-approved Townsend House—where there was "good food and good service." After that "the freedom of the city was tendered" to them, but members of the Young family also checked in periodically with offers "to drive around town."[4] Hamilton agreed to one such drive with John W. Young's wife, while her group made plans to meet John and Brigham Young the next day for a tour of lands south of Salt Lake City.

The next day's trip was above all an opportunity for the Youngs to show off one of their latest railroad projects. The Utah Southern had been founded in 1871, and it was built mainly by Mormon laborers, from materials sourced by (in John Sharp's words) "our personal friends" at the Union Pacific Company in exchange for construction bonds. By May 1873 the railroad had reached as far as Utah Lake, some thirty miles south of Salt Lake City, and it connected numerous surrounding communities to the transcontinental line via the Utah Central.[5] Participants of this particular tour were, however, focused less on the lake or the residences around it than on the railroad's ability to transport ore from nearby mines. As Codman recalled, President Young was "unremitting in his attentions" to his group, eager especially to "show us some of the mining districts in the cañons," and to describe his sons' plans to construct more branches to other mines in the future.[6] Among these was a branch line designed to connect the Mormon capital with mines southwest of Salt Lake, for which construction had begun the month before the Codman tour and which would later be named the Utah Western. (The line was first conceived as a Gentile project, with Patrick E. Connor as one of its codirectors, but by April 1873 John W. Young had become vice president of the operation, and in 1874 he orchestrated its complete reorganization as "a primarily Mormon enterprise.")[7] For his part Codman was impressed, and he was sure that the lines would prove lucrative for everyone involved—not least the Union Pacific, which had invested in the Utah Southern and stood to benefit by freighting goods to and from it.

The corporate friendship of the LDS Church and the Union Pacific was both the occasion and subtext for this 1873 tour. If anything their relationship had only deepened since the opening of the first Mormon railroad, the Utah Central, for which the Union Pacific had provided much material, equipment, and professional training in the first place. In 1872 Young and company invited the Union Pacific to become a major official stockholder in the Utah Central, selling it nearly one-third of its shares; and they agreed further, then, to offer it stock and bonds in future lines like the Utah Southern. In these and other ventures Brigham Young assured subcontracting bishops that "the foreign capitalists in this enterprise do not seek the control" of it. That was not always true, but the Youngs did try to keep outsiders from commanding a controlling stake of Mormon railroading enterprises until they had committed to and invested in the social and political stability of Mormon Utah overall. For instance, only after a six-year tenure as official copartner did the church sell the Utah Central line outright to the Union Pacific, in 1878. In 1875 and 1881, respectively, the Union Pacific also acquired controlling stakes in the Utah Southern and Utah Western from the LDS Church and its agents. John W. Young was not always pleased with Union Pacific policies after transferring control to them, but for many years the company managed the formerly Mormon railroads as distinctively Mormon-friendly lines, and they tailored their tourist tracts and trade accordingly.[8]

A FEW THINGS seem to have gone unsaid, during this celebratory southern tour. The first is that the Utah Southern and Utah Western further ensured that Corinnethian boats would never transport many goods over the Great Salt Lake. Such fates were nearly sealed already in 1871, as Patrick E. Connor decided to freight mining materials via Salt Lake and the Utah Central Railroad rather than through Corinne, and as Corinnethians therefore launched the *City of Corinne* as a pleasure boat rather than a freighter. But this new wave of railroad building—including John W. Young's takeover of Connor's own would-be railroad project—guaranteed that Utah's southern mines would benefit Mormon trains rather than Gentile boats, forevermore.

Not that Corinnethian Gentiles now had any significant boats to their name, anyway. By the time of Codman's tour the Corinnethians had sold their *City of Corinne*, and Patrick E. Connor had sold his *Kate Connor*. John W. Young himself was by then docking the former at his Lake Side bathing resort, founded in 1870 on the eastern shores of the Great Salt Lake. It is unclear whether Young mentioned as much to Codman and his cohort, but Young hoped someday to construct a one-mile spur line from the Utah Central, thereby making it easier for him to bring people like them there as well. (The resort never did get its spur line, but its boat, bathhouses, picnic tables, and forty-square-foot dancefloor nevertheless saw considerable use by area residents and Sunday school classes.)[9] Young's imminent control of the Utah Western would in any case allow him to manage traffic to the docks and beaches at Lake Point—on the southern shores of the lake—that Corinnethians had hoped to run as exclusively Gentile affairs.[10]

If Young's recent projects to the south and east of the Great Salt Lake doomed certain Corinnethian business plans, the fact that his expanding railroad network also included a line running north of Ogden only made matters worse for Corinne. In 1871 John W. Young had chartered the Utah Northern to connect Ogden with towns in southern Idaho via Cache County, Utah, just east of Box Elder County and Corinne. This route would serve several purposes. It would provide Cache County Mormons with better means of intertown commerce and communication, as well as easier options for travel to Ogden and Salt Lake City, where thenceforth they might opt to sell their produce rather than in the closer town of Corinne. (Several surviving diaries from Cache County residents indicate that they did business in Corinne, the official antagonism of LDS officials and Corinne's boosters notwithstanding.) The line would also enable Brigham Young to build a health resort for Mormons and friendly outsiders at Soda Springs, Idaho, site of natural carbonated hot springs, where he sometimes vacationed with his family. Finally the Utah Northern would enable Saints to control the Montana and Idaho mining trades, whose agents then tended to cart wares to and from Corinne. In all of these ways John W. Young expected the LDS Church and its railroads to undermine and circumvent Corinne, routing freighting and passenger proceeds alike away from Corinnethian hands. "Church officials left no stone unturned in their effort to overthrow Corinne," writes Leonard Arrington.[11]

The last thing left unaddressed, while Brigham and John W. Young boasted of their railroad expansions in 1873, was the peculiarity of their excitement about mining returns. Mining remained a contentious issue for LDS leaders in the wake of the Godbeite schism, and—even though Mormons had long recognized the financial advantages of hauling precious metals, if not also prospecting—Brigham Young was not known to speak publicly in its favor. Quite the contrary. The elder Young usually left such speaking to his sons, if he allowed it at all, and he tasked them with taking the lead on any mining-related business that might benefit the church. Historian Robert Athearn explains the arrangement thus: "Brigham Young professed disinterest in the business of mining because of the type of people it attracted and the distractions it produced. Yet, since the industry promised to be an important contributor to railroads, he found his position increasingly difficult to defend. His sons, who also interested themselves in railroads, but who did not have to share the burden of their father's religious leadership, were free of any such strictures. While the elder Young chose not to participate personally in further [mining-related] railroad building, he not only permitted his sons to engage in it, but he encouraged them." The Youngs' plan was not only to profit from such projects but also to control them "as a counterpoise" to the Gentile mines and populations themselves.[12] Working to outflank their Corinnethian and Godbeite critics, LDS leaders simultaneously belied and underlaid their own pastoral position with industry.

Pastoral Lessons at the Tabernacle

The day after their railroad tour, the party of Codman, Hamilton, Blaine, Clark, and Pullman attended a Sunday service at the New Tabernacle in downtown Salt Lake City. As discussed in the previous chapter, this Tabernacle was the site at which transcontinental tourists were most likely to see Mormons engaged in religious practice—especially considering that Gentiles had no access to the Endowment House, where temple ordinances and plural marriages were solemnized until 1889. Its own open-door status was a subject of some debate among LDS elders who wished that "no unclean thing be permitted to enter into any part of this tabernacle," but such restrictions were generally considered both unpractical and undesirable in the railroad age. Indeed Mormon officials operated the dome-roofed Tabernacle specifically as a space of religious observation and cultural performance, and they and railroad officials both banked on its outside appeal. Railroad tours were scheduled so as to "enable passengers to spend a Sabbath at Salt Lake City"—either as part of a package tour or during a lengthy layover at Ogden—and accompanying travel guides encouraged travelers to visit the Tabernacle in the interest of architectural curiosity and ethnographic understanding alike.[13]

By Codman's account the service for this particular Sunday, in May 1873, was largely unremarkable. "The order of exercises was much the same as in a Congregational Church," he wrote, "with the exception that there was an economy of time in the administration of the sacrament while the preaching was going on, and a change in the substitution of water for wine. Nor did I notice in the hymns or prayers, or in the remarks of the first preacher, any peculiarity of doctrine which would have surprised me in one of our churches." Following the sermon, however, Brigham Young stood to offer "a few remarks of his own, evidently intended for Speaker Blaine," on the subject of polygamy as proper Christian practice. And it no longer felt like a Congregational service after that.[14]

There is no record of Blaine's reaction to Young's speech, in which—according to Codman's summary—Young "proved from the Bible conclusively to himself, if not to Mr. Blaine and the rest of us, that in the preaching the Mormons were in accordance with the teachings of Scripture, whereas he said all other denominations of Christians repudiated them." Codman for one was willing to accept Young's premise that the Bible contained positive portrayals of polygamous marriage, but he considered that insufficient proof of its continued legitimacy in the modern age. In reply to someone who asked Codman if it was not "all scriptural," he granted: "Yes, it was." However Young's examples and similar defenses were drawn only from "Old Testament Scripture," and while that was "good enough Scripture for those times," it "will not stand the test of modern civilization." Codman continued, with reference to the Hebrew Bible accounts of Abraham and Isaac, and of Jephthah sacrificing his daughter: "If Abraham lived in these days, and sharpened his knife to slay his son, we would put him in a lunatic asylum; and as to Jephtha, we would hang him—if the jury did not disagree, or find him guilty of forgery or petit larceny. Just so with your polygamy. The law of the land is against it. Anywhere else you would be convicted of bigamy. Only here, fortunately for you, no jury would bring in such a verdict."[15]

Codman did not print any rejoinder to his assertions of Christian biblical supersession and the legitimacy of the Anti-Bigamy Act, and he considered himself to have won the argument. However many Tabernacle services were designed for precisely such exchanges, and indeed also to entertain the logics of Codman's own suggestions, in public and at length. Codman came close to recognizing as much himself, when he noted that Brigham Young's speech seemed "intended for Speaker Blaine." But even after attending a Tabernacle address by Apostle Orson Pratt—in which Pratt compared the federal campaign against polygamy to an attack on infant baptism and other practices presumably protected by the First Amendment—Codman was blind to the ways in which tourist encounters constituted testing grounds for arguments made elsewhere and later, for instance, in the Supreme Court and other courts of public opinion. Like Coffin before him, Codman stopped short of recognizing or reflecting on the pastoral purpose of speaking directly to outside interest groups, in the Tabernacle, or of incorporating their concerns in (and as) the very substance of a sermon or Sunday speech.

FAR FROM AVOIDING THEIR SCRUTINY, the church welcomed visitors like Codman, Blaine, and Hamilton to view Mormonism on display at the Salt Lake Tabernacle. Moreover, LDS officials sometimes invited non-Mormon ministers to visit on trains and preach in the Tabernacle. Church members were encouraged to attend these events, and subsequent Sunday school sessions helped to explain and contextualize the visitors' words and to compare Mormonism with whatever sect they represented. Church Historian George A. Smith wrote in November 1869 that, since the construction of the transcontinental railroad, "we have had more clergymen of different denominations preach in our Tabernacle than for several years previous, and it has given our people an excellent chance to compare our religion with that of other denominations, as we have had Presbyterians, Congregational, Episcopal, Baptist & Methodist, luminaries, who have addressed audiences here varying from 3 to 8,000 people. Numbers of these divines have visited our Sunday Schools and addressed the children." Again, in 1871: "We know no better way to show our people the superiority of their faith than by having them see the contrast."[16] The church used the tourism industry for self-promotion, employing railroads as levers for strategic religious comparisons of their own. They invited visitors, and they shaped their stays.

Another 1871 visitor noted also Mormons' willingness to yield the Tabernacle pulpit to outsiders, but writing from an outsider's perspective, he expressed concern that such acts served Mormon interests far more than guests'. W. F. Rae argued that invitations to preach in the Salt Lake Tabernacle were in fact setups designed to benefit Mormonism alone. The whole thing was a "burlesque," he said. "The liberty of preaching in the Tabernacle means simply license to become a laughing-stock."[17]

While Rae's perception of one-sidedness is debatable, his references to burlesque and laughter were neither insignificant nor unfounded. Consider this story about an Episcopal priest who "accepted Brigham Young's invitation to preach": he "appeared in his surplice and Oxford hood," and "at the succeeding service, the President [Young] having taken a white table cover, placed it over his shoulders, and burlesqued the clergyman amid the hearty laughter of his flock."[18] Brigham Young intended to show, by this bit of mocking mimicry, that Mormonism was religion comparatively unadorned. Unlike the "long-faced deacons" who hoarded their grains as well as gospels (said Young, in a sermon on irrigation)—and unlike "an Episcopalian" who "appear[s] in a white surplice with a prayer book in his hand," offering little more than denominational jeremiads (said John Taylor, in a sermon on Mormon rituals)—Saints had "let [sectarianism] go entirely, hook and line," simply restoring basic biblical principles for all, and thus they "expect[ed] to receive certain ordinances revealed to us from God through His servants." It was a mixed message of cultic specificity and sectarian disdain, but in any case Brigham Young and his fellows used Tabernacle encounters as occasions for playful cultural comparisons, many of them emphasizing Mormonism's unique ability to address people's most basic concerns.[19]

A second example of Tabernacle assemblage as opportunity for staged religious comparison was the Newman-Pratt debate series of August 1870. Methodist minister John Philip Newman and LDS spokesman Orson Pratt took turns arguing the topic of polygamy in front of large local audiences at the Tabernacle; and they made national news, with both Salt Lake, Corinnethian, and nonlocal newspapers reporting variously the validity of their positions.[20] Unsurprisingly Methodist reporters and denominational authorities claimed absolute victory—credit for "the war" against polygamy "is due to the Methodists," said one—but Corinnethians Beadle and Toohy were not so sure. At least they expressed reservations concerning the terms of Methodist self-satisfaction and self-congratulation: "If the Methodists care to see polygamy worsted, and would assist in doing it, they must not give the public the impression that they are acting as Methodists. It is a contest between sense and nonsense, decency and indecency, republicanism and despotism, and we engage in it as citizens, not as sectarians. It began with Mormonism and will only end with it.... It would doubtless have been the same had there been no Methodists in the world."[21] Corinnethians wanted not only acknowledgment of their own religious establishments but also the broader articulation of anti-Mormon and antipolygamy interests in terms of Americanism, republicanism, true religion, or righteous modernization. The fact of Methodists' "sectarian" argumentation allowed the sectarianism of sects themselves to become the stuff of debate in Salt Lake City; and therefore Mormons were able to undermine pan-Protestant efforts at general Gentility, as at Corinne, by coopting nonsectarian or contrasectarian language. Corinnethians feared—rightly—that LDS apologists would articulate anew, in Relief Society meetings, Sunday schools, and in print, the 'fact' of their relatively simple biblicism, biblical restorationism, and progressive antiquity.

IF CODMAN WAS UNINCLINED to comment on the staging of comparative religions in the Salt Lake Tabernacle, he was very much interested in other aspects of Mormon representation and display there. Reflecting on the "splendid organ . . . entirely of domestic workmanship," Codman waxed poetic about Mormons' success in the realms of home manufacturing and agriculture. "Mills of every description abound in the territory, and almost every grain and fruit is indigenous to some part of the soil. All was to be of domestic production—food, clothing, and literature as well as religion, and so the organ was built here as an adjunct of the last."[22]

In allowing his mind to wander from pulpit aesthetics to domestic workmanship to agricultural production, Codman was not free-associating but rather following an anticipated line of sight and reflection. George A. Smith himself, when noting the "excellent chance to compare our religion" with those of Tabernacle guests, described precisely these conjoined advantages of downtown tourism: people regularly noticed the organ and learned about its provenance ("The organ in the new Tabernacle which is the largest and most beautiful ever built in the U. S. has attracted much attention," not least because it "was built entirely by Salt Lake Artists, and with the exception of about $1500.00 of furnishings purchased in the States is entirely of home material"), and they reflected more generally on Mormons' manufacturing and agricultural successes as well ("Many thousand eminent citizens of the U. S. and many from other countries have visited this city and universally expressed astonishment at the manner the desert has been made to blos[s]om as the rose by irrigation in a country almost destitute of rain, and so isolated").[23] Lest that associative script be too subtle, Mormon designers catalyzed consideration of agricultural accomplishments in other ways as well, for instance, with banners and displays placed in and around the Tabernacle.

Consider the 1874 visit of the Reverend W. W. Ross. Arriving from Canada by way of Minnesota and Nebraska, Ross was not treated to the same type of personal attention as was Codman's party; rather than being met by John W. Young at the train station, he was greeted by a "runner" from the Townsend House, who "thoroughly canvassed the passengers" aboard the Utah Central, trying to secure their business before they encountered any Gentile competitors at the Salt Lake terminal. However Ross did find a more elaborate and explicit display waiting for him at the Tabernacle, along these lines. "Within the Tabernacle," he wrote, "I saw two arches, remains of a recent celebration, symbolizing the productions of the soil at two different periods—viz., [18]47, when [Mormons] arrived, and '74, the present. The first was chiefly composed of sage brush and wild sunflower; the second, of branches of the trees adorning the streets, the various grains, including corn and sorghum—all prettily set off by various flowers common to European countries from which the emigrants had come." Among such symbols of agricultural accomplishment, Mormon dignitaries gave "resumes of the doings of the Saints in different parts of the Territory," then "pilloried" John Wesley, then sang hymns. It was a peculiar mode of sermon, Ross said, and he was surprised to have heard—and seen—so much about agricultural and economic affairs, crops and resources. For all of its mundane focus and content most attendees seemed to find it "almost as good as going to the theatre."[24]

Anticipating further discussion about theatrical aspects and venues of Mormon cultural displays below, two things about Ross's Tabernacle experience warrant stress here. The first is that, although Ross took from it the lesson that an ostensibly religious thing (a Sunday service) was really material and mundane in practice, this was not a judgment advanced by most railroad-backed guidebooks. As we will observe in the next chapter, these guidebooks were willing to let tourists decide for themselves whether such 'secular,' 'material' talk during ecclesiastical meetings constituted, belied, or coexisted with LDS religiosity. So too were many Mormons happy to force visitors, especially those expecting revelations exotic and esoteric, to grapple with the possibilities of overlapping ritual and regularity.

The second observation is more immediately significant. Even the most 'mundane' of Salt Lake Tabernacle demonstrations made the religious argument that the Great Basin was Mormonism's promised land: that its families had domesticated its wilderness, and that its farmers had made its deserts bloom like roses. This was an argument made for and among different generations of Mormons, at first. Whereas first-generation 'pioneers' commonly spoke of the lushness and fertility of Utah Valley, second-wave and second-generation Mormons in Utah remembered it rather as an arid wasteland, evoking Isaiah's prophesy ("The desert shall rejoice, and blossom as the rose") in order to celebrate their forebears' accomplishments and likenesses to biblical patriarchs.[25] Of course this was argued also with an eye to visitors like Ross, as in the Tabernacle decorations that he described, for the era of the second generation was the era of touristic articulation as well. But the most immediate meaning of such displays, for many Mormon attendees, was that pioneer Saints had accomplished feats of biblical proportions and that the LDS Church honored and protected their legacy, as against the Godbeites, by cultivating communal gardens and farms rather than digging in commercial mines.

Displays of domestic agricultural accomplishments between 1847 and 1874 claimed anew the values of Mormon communitarianism, agriculturalism, and nonindustrialization *precisely in the railroad era*, in any case, and they were staged both for in-group and out-group encounter. That Mormon leaders argued thus, while investing and incorporating themselves in industry, went unspoken. Likewise unmentioned was Brigham Young and his sons' own attention to mining. And ignored too was that some of the more memorable and pastoral church banners—such as one declaring "Utah's Best Crop" to be its children, in a humorous play on assumptions of Mormon fertility—were designed by congregants who had honed their graphic skills while working for the Union Pacific's photographic corps. Such corporate concerns were eclipsed by pastoral motifs, in the Tabernacle. Utah, they said, manifested a peculiar golden age in the Gilded Age.[26]

"An Adjunct to the Tabernacle":
The Salt Lake Theatre

"Next in importance to the Tabernacle, if it be not an adjunct to it," was the Salt Lake Theatre. So said W. F. Rae during his 1871 trip to Utah, and he was far from alone in perceiving a connection between the Tabernacle and the theater.

Tabernacle attendees considered services there "almost as good as going to the theatre," by the Reverend Ross's estimation, and there seemed to be an exhortatory or missionary dimension to plays at the theater. Both buildings were owned and operated by the LDS Church, and they were designed by the same architect, William H. Folson. Both structures afforded ample sightlines and opportunities for mutual observation between Mormon hosts and Gentile guests, as well as between LDS leaders and laity. Both framed encounters and comparisons between national and local ideals of worldliness and value, as a core aspect of their programming. Whereas the Tabernacle dealt in displays of pastoral care and cultivation, though, the theater was designed more for morality plays and the leisurely display of high culture.[27]

Latter-day Saints have always been a theatrical people. Joseph Smith supported a theater company for his people in the Nauvoo period, and Saints formed a Musical and Dramatic Association again a few short years after emigrating to Utah. In 1859, after the dust of the Utah War had settled, Brigham Young threw his weight behind the enterprise as well: "He gave it out in a meeting one Sunday, much to the gratification of his congregation, that he was going to build a big 'fun hall,' or theatre, where the people could go and forget their troubles occasionally, in a good, hearty laugh."[28] Such a theater would hold not only dramatic productions but also lectures and other forms of moral entertainment. Dancing, too, was a staple of Mormon life, with many settlements holding regular round dances under the supervision of their bishops. Brigham Young anticipated much supervised dancing at Salt Lake City's official "fun hall" as well.

Mormons' embrace of dance and theater was somewhat atypical among American Christian communities at the time, especially those with roots in the Northeast. As historian R. Laurence Moore has written, Joseph Smith and "Brigham Young had clearly developed what we might call an 'ideology' of play at a time when many other American clerics still thought of play as the devil's invention." By his account other denominations often considered amusements problematic in proportion to growing conditions of demographic dispersion, anonymity, privatization, and other circumstances that "weakened community surveillance" and threatened churches' ability "to exercise coercive moral discipline over the behavior of their members."[29] Harry S. Stout, writing of George Whitefield's eighteenth-century revivals, has described theater's perceived threat to church services as a matter also of formal proximity: "Both encouraged a suspension of belief in the experience of the everyday to introduce their viewers to different worlds," and "theater, in its capacity to combine the pageantry of art, the intensity of poetry, the enchantment of fiction, and the movement of dance, represented a religious-like amalgam of art and energy that, as one contemporary put it, had the power to 'get Possession of the heart.'"[30] Religious communities needed, in any case, to exert a measure of control over the stage and its powers, through mechanisms of either prohibition or incorporation. For their part Mormons chose incorporation, just as they would do elsewhere with different branches of touristic amusement cultures. This was not least because Brigham and his colleagues planned to operate the theater specifically as a site of both periodic emotional uplift and continuing community surveillance—indeed, as an adjunct to the Tabernacle.

Brigham's "ideology of play" theorized theatrics as an act and office of missionary work. Speaking at the opening of the Salt Lake Theatre in 1862, after a long prayer in which Daniel H. Wells dedicated to God everything from the building itself to its "footlights, and the oil and candles thereof," the church president asked that actors perform only virtuous works and that audiences hold them accountable to that task: "When the Saints come into this building and look on this stage to see our brethren and sisters perform to satisfy the sight, the ear, and the desires and minds of the people, I want you to pray for them that the Lord Almighty may preserve them from ever having one wicked thought in their bosoms, that our actors may be just as virtuous, truthful, and humble before God and each other as though they were on a mission to preach the gospel."[31] Again in 1864 Young advised actors that he considered them "missionaries as much as if they were called to go out into the world and preach the gospel, and the Lord would bless their efforts just as much if they performed their parts in the same spirit." Granted, on the latter occasion he was trying to resolve a dispute over wages, encouraging actors to work for free or payment in tithing scrip.[32] But the point was well taken: Young expected "the strictest virtue and decorum" from actors and audience alike, as well as in the substance of all productions, for the theater was an arm of the church. He wished to see no tragedies or "blood-curdling dramas," too, but only comedies and morality plays, where "good and its happy results and rewards" would be contrasted with "the weaknesses and follies of man," and where Saints would learn "a proper horror of the enormity of sin and a just dread of its consequences." Finally, actors should be church members in good standing.[33]

The would-be restriction of Gentile actors and tragic productions lasted only a short time, as theater managers soon wished to expand their offerings and showcase traveling thespians. By the time of Brigham Young's 1864 financial appeal to the house troupe, the Salt Lake Theatre regularly hosted visiting stars, who exposed local residents to national and international theatrical trends and for whose productions local actors would play supporting roles. Such engagements only became bigger and more frequent as the railroad approached Utah. Still, even when large troupes traveled to Utah on the train, the

Mormon stock company integrated their actors or introduced their productions with short plays of their own. Brigham Young continued to interject if anything seemed too violent or immoral, just as he would chastise members of his own flock if they became unruly in the pit. The house kept control over the frame.

RAILROADS WERE THE SUBJECT of considerable excitement and dramatic play in the Salt Lake Theatre. Not only were transcontinental connections anticipated because they would bring new acting talent to town, but LDS leaders and playwrights planned numerous railroad-themed events, dramatizing railroad progress and framing community expectations about accompanying social developments. During the October 1868 church conference on "the railroad problem"—indeed, on the same day that George Q. Cannon summarized the Corinnethian death knell thesis in the Tabernacle—the Salt Lake Theatre presented *Under the Gaslight*, a drama best known for a scene in which the heroine rescues a man tied to railroad tracks, seconds before he would have been crushed by an oncoming locomotive. "Produced With All Its Elaborate Scenery and Novel and Mechanical Effects! Including the intensely exciting RAILROAD SCENE!" *Under the Gaslight* represented, to its Mormon audience, the perils of life in modern New York, rife as it was with violence, social inequality, burglary, and mustachioed villains attempting to flatten innocent persons with otherwise promising tools of technology. But it also guaranteed rescue from such dystopian possibilities through acts of selfless nobility and mutual care. Together Mormons could shape a different future for Salt Lake City than the one prophesied by both local and federal antagonists, muffling would-be death knells and slipping all knots.[34]

Under the Gaslight ran again on May 8, 1869, two days before the completion of the transcontinental railroad at Promontory. On May 10 itself, the theater marked that momentous event with "a Grand Tableau representing the 'laying of the last rail,' of the U.P.R.R. and the passage of the first train, with a display of fireworks and a general illumination."[35] This was an affair outdone only by a formal ball and dance celebrating the completion of the Utah Central Railroad, in January 1870. Describing the latter event in a letter to his cousin, George A. Smith wrote glowingly that "twelve hundred persons were present, two hundred dancing at a time in twenty five cotillions. . . . At these parties strict temperance is observed, they are opened by prayer and dismissed by benediction, and the amusement consists in meeting friends, hearing music, dancing cotillions, County dances, Scotch reels, and double Cotillions where a man has two partners. . . . Each person behaves with the utmost propriety."[36]

The Salt Lake Theatre staged celebrations and dramatizations of railroad advances throughout the late nineteenth century. This photograph is from a performance of *Lightning Express* around 1900. (Courtesy of the Church History Library, The Church of Jesus Christ of Latter-day Saints, Salt Lake City [PH 1603])

Smith went on to praise the interior of the theater, which had been designed some years earlier by Elias L. T. Harrison. Such praise was deserved—it was an attractive space, boasting three galleries—but it was also tinged with irony, given the timing of Smith's writing: Harrison had recently been excommunicated precisely because of his 'Godbeite' disapproval of Brigham Young's railroad policies. Harrison was then forced to watch, in 1870 and for many years after that, as Brigham Young, George A. Smith, and other LDS leaders used his well-designed space to celebrate Mormon railroading successes and represent Mormon culture to tourists.

In December 1871 Salt Lake residents were treated to a performance of *Across the Continent; or, Scenes from New York Life and the Pacific Railroad*, which picked up where *Under the Gaslight* left off, but with added racist depictions of Indians, Chinese, and African Americans in the West. The highlight of Oliver Doud Byron's drama comes when "Black Cloud" and his band of Indian marauders attacks a California-bound party. Taking refuge in a railroad station with "Very Tart, a Chinaman," and "Caesar Augustus, called Coon because he is one," this otherwise white party is saved only when "an express train loaded down with United States Troops, making the unprecedented time of 12 miles in 11 minutes," arrives just in time to hold off their assailants. Following that display of technological progress and military power, the play ended, according to one favorable New York review, "when the American flag was brought to the footlights and waved over a hecatomb of fallen red-skins, and of living and happy, because virtuous, whites."[37] There is no record of how Mormon audiences responded to this final scene—if indeed Byron kept it intact for his Salt Lake showings—given their own antagonistic relationship with U.S. troops during the Utah War, or in light of the fact that several congressmen had supported the Pacific Railway Act because it would expedite military response to any *Mormon* disruptions of transcontinental emigration. In any case local reviewers thrilled in "the close of the performance, when the locomotive with its train of cars appear," and they spoke with pride of being able to produce such a "truly sensational drama" on "our boards." The success of *Across the Continent* proved the theater's capacity to host elaborate popular dramas while demonstrating also Mormons' willingness to embrace and partake in the motifs of manifest destiny and white racial purity.[38]

If the Salt Lake Theatre was willing to give space for certain national fantasies about railroading progress, Mormon playwrights also adapted the theme for local audiences. E. L. Sloan, editor of the church-friendly *Salt Lake Herald*, wrote a four-hour melodrama titled *Stage and Steam* that, according to friendly reviews, had "far less of the objectionable features of such pieces than many which have preceded it at the Salt Lake Theatre." Designed to contrast "the old stage coach with the locomotive methods and results" and thus dramatize "the march of civilization," Sloan's play featured a stagecoach robbery and a struggle on a railroad bridge, but its action was rather less bloody—and less military—than Byron's. Sloan also exchanged Byron's nonwhite and minstrel 'Others' for relatively proximate forms of racial diversity, scripting interactions between fast-talking 'Yankee' and backwoods-living 'Irish' comedic types as the backdrop to an expanding class of indigenous white 'Americans' in the West.[39] Such hybridic purity had of course been the racial vision of the Corinnethians as well, albeit with a distinctly anti-Mormon hue. (This is not to mention also Frederick Jackson Turner's later frontier thesis, which similarly posited that manly triumphs over western obstacles effected a different type of human being, the American, who drew upon the best features of Anglo-European life in order to forge from them something new.) It is unclear whether and how Sloan set his vision apart from theirs, except that he included a critique of mainstream Protestant ministers in the form of "Rev. Jerry Sniffle, an unworthy shepherd who gives substance to the wolves" and is "fleeced" by his fellow travelers. Sloan seems not to have identified any heroes as Saints, but his mainly Mormon audience was expected, nevertheless, to celebrate the civilizational advances that enabled them to shed eastern baggage and stagecoach inconveniences alike, in their new West.[40]

SLOAN'S *STAGE AND STEAM* had recently completed its run, in April 1873, when John Codman, James Blaine, and Gail Hamilton arrived in Salt Lake City. The theater was by then featuring a new star performer, Annette Ince, in a weeklong run of classical and European fare, and Codman and Hamilton attended a well-reviewed showing of *Madea* on May 24.[41] Such plays typified managers' efforts to stage highbrow moral dramas for the dual purpose of edifying local populations while demonstrating Mormons' refined cultural tastes—and their connections with topflight traveling artists—to outside guests like Codman and company. The Salt Lake Theatre had good reason to boast of its record, in this regard; in the 1872–73 season alone, it ran over two hundred total showings of more than one hundred plays, seventy of them featuring guest performers, from fantasies (*Rip Van Winkle*) to tragedies (*Macbeth*) to comedies (*That Rascal Pat*) to romances (*Romeo and Juliet*) to abolitionist melodramas (*Uncle Tom's Cabin*) to westerns (*Buffalo Bill*), as well as a handful of magic shows, dances, minstrel shows, and musical concerts. Salt Lake City was justifiably becoming known, in the words of theater historian John Lindsay, as "the best show town of its population in the United States."[42]

However this meant different things to its residents and visitors. Lindsay, a former member of the theater's stock company himself, meant clearly to celebrate the fact that a city of Salt Lake's size could support such a vibrant theater scene. But many audiences were interested in a different sense of Salt Lake City's being a "show town of its population." For them the city's best possible show was precisely *its population*, no matter the quality of its plays (which some admitted were very good).[43] These visitors went to the theater to look for and gaze at Mormons in the audience.

Gail Hamilton was one such visitor. Attending *Madea* with little interest in watching the play itself, she delighted rather in having identified "a row of Brigham's daughters, twelve strong," in the audience. These daughters would have been sitting in a section of the parquet reserved for members of the Young family, where indeed Brigham's many daughters and wives were known to attend plays regularly. (One of Brigham's daughters, Alice Clawson, was also an actress in the stock company, for a time.) As for Brigham himself, he had a special rocking chair next to his family section, which, in Charles Carleton

Coffin's words, he "sometimes occupies, when he wishes to be on a similar footing with the saints." More often, though, he sat in a reserved and elevated proscenium box, usually with "his favourite wife Amelia," and from it he "looks upon the audience most of the time" while the crowd also watched him. Sighting them was a common thrill among tourists, who were generally on the lookout for large families and multiple wives elsewhere in the theater as well.[44]

Indeed, nearly all of the aforementioned tourists had stories akin to Hamilton's and Coffin's. For instance, W. F. Rae, despite having "but little" to say about the play itself, was grateful to find Brigham and Amelia Young occupying their stage box, and he entertained himself by wondering whether Brigham's box was elevated precisely so that his other wives "could look up from the pit and envy their preferred rival." For her part, Anna Dickinson spent her time at the theater growing increasingly outraged by the fact and appearance of Mormon polygamy and then steeling her resolve against it: "I went to the theatre. I went expecting to be disgusted, but I was more than that. There were women all around me, and I would see one man here and another there, and each bending over ten or fifteen women, and I was told they were his wives and I looked around and saw these women and their degradation, such a sense and feeling of shame and despair came over me that I cried, 'Oh! God, let me die where I stand'; and then the second thought came, and I said, 'Oh no, let me not die, for that would be cowardly indeed, but give me strength to stand and do battle against this.'" Despite their varying senses of titillation and disgust, each of these tourists treated theater attendance as an opportunity for people-watching and Mormon-spotting more than an occasion to marvel at Saintly highbrow accomplishments. "We are not there to see the play," said Coffin, "but the people."[45]

"Blackened Sepulchres": Defenses on Stage

No matter how much Mormon hosts may have anticipated visitors' gaze at their plays, they were frustrated by Anna Dickinson's review in particular, as well as by her insistence on classing the Salt Lake Theatre as one among many "whited sepulchres" in Utah. "Anna went to the Salt Lake Theatre and expected to be disgusted, that is, she meant to be disgusted, and she was disgusted," wrote one English Saint, after reading an early review of Dickinson's anti-Mormon lecture. If "Anna was perfectly overcome" by the sight of polygamous families "decently enjoying the drama," it was likely because she was forced to compare their happiness with "her own loneliness and unproductiveness, and comparisons are peculiarly odious." Either that or Dickinson was motivated by a kind of mercenary greed, since "public lecturers, many of them, like lawyers, advocate or depreciate that which they are paid to advocate or depreciate." In any case, "Marriage is not a proper subject for disgust to pure-minded men and women," he said, for "scripture says it is honorable, and it is considered by the best men and women a holy estate.... We consider marriage an institution worthy of all respect and reverence, and therefore it is impossible for us to be disgusted at it, whether monogamous or polygamous." The author concluded that Mormons "could buy plenty of able and popular lecturers and preachers too," if they wanted. "But that is not the design. It is not desirable that Mormonism should be popular just yet." At least not until certain sightlines and tourist routes were better set in iron.[46]

Thankfully the LDS Church did not have far to look for powerful parties invested in the joint enterprise of defending Mormonism and stabilizing Utah's tourist trade. The aptly named George Francis Train, cofounder and promoter of the Union Pacific Railroad, was among them. In 1870 Train embarked on a lecture tour that included a segment titled "Blackened Sepulchres," in which he defended Latter-day Saints specifically against the charges leveled in Dickinson's talk. Brigham Young was an honorable man and a great promoter of progress in the West, according to Train, as was evident in Young's colonization work and his early support for the transcontinental railroad. ("Where would the Pacific Railway have been but for you?" Train asked Young privately. "The opening of the Railroads give the lie to your slanders. All said it would destroy you—it only strengthens your position.") Beyond that, Train's defense of Brigham Young and the Mormons differed somewhat depending on audience. In predominantly Irish locales, Train "remind[ed] my Irish Boys that twenty years ago, the same element that is now trying to steal [Mormons'] country and destroy [their] church, burnt Catholic Convents, destroyed Catholic Churches, [and] rode Catholic Priests upon rails."[47] Speaking to otherwise Gentile audiences in New York, San Francisco, and elsewhere, Train defended Mormon polygamists for "aknowledg[ing] their wives" and "not cast[ing] them off; whilst 'you,' he said with great emphasis 'have your mistresses by the score, and when you are tired of them you kick them out into the street to rot.'" No matter what Anna Dickinson may have told them, there was far less "rot" in Salt Lake City than in their own Gentile cities.[48]

Managers at the Salt Lake Theatre were thrilled to host Train in July 1870, during his "Blackened Sepulchres" tour, and the church newspaper encouraged local residents to "GO AND HEAR" "The irrepressible GEO. FRANCIS TRAIN" give his "DEFENSE OF BRIGHAM YOUNG!" and "REPLY TO ANNA DICKINSON."[49] Apparently Train's lecture at the theater included claims that he had personally thwarted the Cullom Bill. Though hyperbolic, that notion had some basis in fact, given the significant role played by railroad-backed lobbyists. The claim went over well, in any case, and so too did the dramatic conclusion to his lecture. Recounting the defense of Utah life that he had given in other cities, Train added a final flourish for the benefit of his Mormon audience: he "told the people that Utah was the only place in which he had found no gamblers, drunkards, jails, prostitutes, almshouses . . . ; the only place where a woman could traverse the streets at all hours of the day or night without fear of being insulted; where water was used at the sacrament instead of wine; the only place where men, women and children were dressed in home manufactured clothing, and he said: 'If you interfere with Brigham Young and the Mormons, so help me G–d, I'll tear down a Gentile church or two.'" Salt Lake Theatre attendees responded with "immense cheering."[50] Train proved to them the ready willingness of Union Pacific personnel to intervene on their behalf, and Mormons would find ample opportunity to call on them again in the future.[51]

An Indignation Meeting

Not long before George Francis Train's staged response to Anna Dickinson and the Cullom Bill, Mormon women staged their own show of indignation. More than three thousand women gathered at the Old Tabernacle on January 13, 1870, to speak out against the Cullom Bill and its underlying presumptions of women's entrapment in Utah, the likes of which had been fostered through anti-Mormon reports and tourist literature of the sepulchral sort. Tired of being stared at in the theater and at the thresholds of their own homes, Eliza R. Snow, Sarah N. Kimball, Bathsheba W. Smith, and other leaders among Salt Lake City women decided to speak for themselves, in a forum designed specifically for publicity and outside attention.[52]

The decision to speak out did not come easily. One woman joked about not being "an Anna Dickinson" and thus "feel[ing] some embarrassment in appearing before so large an assembly." (Of course she proceeded to speak eloquently and powerfully on her own terms.) Meanwhile Eliza R. Snow described her own decision to appear, thus:

> Heretofore, while detraction and ridicule have been poured forth in almost every form that malice could invent, while we have been misrepresented by speech and press, and exhibited in every shade but our true light, the ladies of Utah, as a general thing, have remained silent. Had nor our aims been of the most noble and exalted character, and had we not known that we occupied a stand-point far above our traducers, we might have returned volley for volley; but we have all the time realized that to contradict such egregious absurdities would be a great stoop of condescension, far beneath the dignity of those who profess to be saints of the

living God, and we very unassumingly applied to ourselves a saying of an ancient apostle in writing to the Corinthians, "Ye suffer fools, gladly, seeing that yourselves are wise."

But Snow and her compatriots refused to be silent any longer in an environment increasingly filled with 'Corinnethians' of another sort, especially while people like Dickinson toured the country claiming to know more about Mormon life and women's rights than they did.[53]

For these reasons they gathered, before a small group of reporters, to proclaim publicly their faith in polygamy and "the institutions of the Church of Jesus Christ of Latter-day Saints as the only reliable safeguard of female virtue and innocence, and the only sure protection against the fearful sin of prostitution and its attendant evils." Speaker after speaker echoed the sentiment. Far from crushing their independence or spirit, they said, Mormon civil, ecclesiastical, and familial systems granted women considerable freedoms and responsibilities, not least the right to vote and the ability to "dwell with [our husbands] and our children in the world to come, which guaranties unto us the greatest blessing for which we are created." Having been driven from their homes once already, in the Midwest, these women refused to let the U.S. government disrupt or demean the sanctity of their hard-won households and communities in the Great Basin.[54]

The organizers of the indignation meeting succeeded in attracting the attention of major newspapers throughout the nation—several of which reprinted lengthy quotations from or summaries of their speeches—and thereby exposing many readers to their own voices and arguments. They reached the homes and ears of the nation's most powerful advocates for women's suffrage, as well. Elizabeth Cady Stanton and Susan B. Anthony decided to stop in Utah during an 1871 cross-country lecture tour, in order to meet with Mormon women and understand better the terms of their enfranchisement. Granted, that trip was not entirely successful, from the perspective of Snow and her colleagues: Stanton and Anthony were met at the railroad station by members of the Godbeite New Movement, who then 'ran' them around town—just as they had done with countless visitors before them—and attempted to guide them to alternate visions of Mormon liberality and feminism. However the New Movement soon faded, and 'orthodox' Mormon women were able to forge an uneasy alliance with eastern suffragists that lasted for many years.[55]

Presidential Audiences

Recent literature on tourism talks of the "mutuality" of "gaze" struck between hosts and guests.[56] Accounts of Tabernacle and theater encounters provide ample evidence of this dynamic, but so too do stories about obtaining—or trying to obtain—a private audience with Brigham Young. Such stories demonstrate the church president's willingness to meet interested visitors, in order that he might personally explain Mormon religious practices and marital systems to them. (Indeed Young expressed frustration with Anna Dickinson for not having arranged a meeting with him and for therefore failing to take advantage of Salt Lake's full range of guest services, before critiquing LDS life.)[57] However they also show him to have staged such meetings in specific ways and specific places, the likes of which allowed him simultaneously to monitor his would-be monitors and cater only selectively to their interests in revelation.

Young's formal meeting with John Codman, Gail Hamilton, and the rest of their party aboard a train was far from unprecedented. In 1870, for instance, Young and several of his advisers met with principal members of the Boston Board of Trade in Ogden, for a meal in a specially appointed dining car. On both occasions Young spoke openly about his marriages and children, and according to the women's rights advocate Hamilton, they "had it out for a half hour or so." However on both occasions a director or president of the Pullman's Palace Car Company was present, as well, and his presence had something to do with Young's warm welcome. Albert B. Pullman was responsible for having invited Young to dine with the Boston party in 1870, and George M. Pullman (along with the Union Pacific's Horace F. Clark) was a featured guest for the Utah Southern tour in 1873. Young knew that he had the Pullmans and their ilk to thank for enticing tourists to Utah and thus delivering them to the doors of the Utah Central, Utah Southern, Tabernacle, and Salt Lake Theatre. He and his counselors usually had time for culture brokers such as these, and they were more than willing to meet them alongside and aboard the same machines that framed their friendship.[58]

More commonly, however, Brigham Young met visitors in his own Salt Lake City office. In those environs too, the president was known to answer questions about his multiple wives and defend the principles of polygamy, as well as to describe Mormons' success in the realms of agriculture and home manufacturing. Young met with a number of powerful dignitaries, editors, authors, lawyers, politicians, and businesspeople, but his visitors' registers from 1868 to 1871 contain also the names of general tourists and travelers of all stripes.[59] Some of these visitors came on official business, while others were drawn by curiosity and the proximity of Young's office and personal quarters, in the so-called Beehive House, to the 'Lion House,' where many of Young's wives and children resided. The two buildings were connected by a covered passage, but the Lion House was off-limits to visitors. Meetings in the Beehive House afforded tourists and travelers a decidedly curated glimpse of Young's private life: a position

A private audience with Brigham Young was a desirable part of a Salt Lake City tour, along with visits to Young's home, the Tabernacle, and the Salt Lake Theatre. The Salt Lake Temple was not completed until 1893, but sketches circulated well before then. (Photographs and montage by Charles W. Carter, ca. 1870; courtesy of the Church History Library, The Church of Jesus Christ of Latter-day Saints, Salt Lake City [PH 3442])

from which to wonder about conditions concealed behind Young's own formal antechambers, even as he spoke to them there in the key of disclosure.

In the two years following the completion of the transcontinental railroad, more than 1,700 traveling parties visited Young's office: approximately 615 in the first year and 1,100 in the second.[60] (Elizabeth Cady Stanton and Susan B. Anthony signed the guest book on June 23, 1871, but they were unable to meet with Young at that time.)[61] The church president admitted to feeling burdened sometimes by his heavy interview schedule, but he defended the practice as "too valuable a means of correcting false ideas and removing prejudice to be discontinued." "I am satisfied that such visits are, as a rule, productive of good results," Young said. "Many a one who comes to Utah filled with all kinds of outrageous ideas with regard to the Mormons in general and Brigham Young in particular, after having visited our City, seen its objects of interest and called at the office, go away with feelings greatly modified and often afterwards have a kind word for the people of Utah when they hear them assailed."[62] Office visits and personal interviews were, for Young as well as for many Gentile outsiders, a crucial component of a proper Mormon tour.

His own defense of the practice notwithstanding, Young did limit his private interviews over time. "Since the opening of the Pacific Railway, and [because], in consequence, the number of visitors has daily increased, Brigham Young has got tired of being stared at, examined, and commented upon, as an object of curiosity." Thus wrote our Austrian traveler Baron von Hübner in 1871, when he found it necessary to secure a letter of introduction in order to discourse directly with Young on matters of culture, commerce, family, or religion. (Thankfully the hotelier Mr. Townsend was willing to act as an intermediary between Hübner and the church president, vouching for the traveler's good character.) Even then, Hübner found that his meeting was structured as much as an opportunity for Young and company to stare at him as for him to observe them. Hübner was kept in conversation with Young's advisers for some twenty minutes, while Brigham Young listened and watched them from "a shadow behind [a] half-open door" in the parlor.[63] When at last Young emerged, Hübner was reminded that—railroad or no railroad, letter or no letter, invitation or no invitation—Young and the Mormons retained a measure of control over the moments and arenas of self-disclosure.

The purpose of Brigham Young's office discourses was less conversion than conversation, in any case. Many visitors commented on their surprise to find Young willing to discuss any number of topics, above and beyond the stuff of religious practice. Some found him overly willing in that regard, as if "demonstrat[ing] a firm desire *not* to engage in religious subjects," but time and again guests commented on his "polite," "entertaining," and down-to-earth mannerisms—and thus also on their need to remind themselves, despite themselves, that he was the head of a monstrous system.[64] (For his part, T. B. H. Stenhouse so feared that Brigham Young might charm a group of French travelers that he sought to "confine" and "dissuade us from all visits" with the church president.)[65] Young generally tasked office colleagues with giving testimony to the truth of the gospel and with arranging follow-up meetings between interested parties and the missionaries assigned to their home regions.[66] For the duration of their stays in Utah, then, Young knew that he could also rely on other structures and intermediaries—such as John W. Young and his businesses—to guide tourists to other important insights about Mormon life and religion in the West.

The Deseret Museum: Reframing Indigeneity

The final attraction on Codman and Hamilton's shared tour—in addition, that is, to their outing on the Utah Southern, trips to the Tabernacle and Salt Lake Theatre, and meeting with Brigham Young—was a visit to the Deseret

Museum. Housed near the LDS President's Office and the Tabernacle, the Deseret Museum was another of John W. Young's projects, and he specifically intended it to be a tourist attraction. As its chief curator explained, the museum was founded in anticipation of "a large influx of visitors to Salt Lake City" after "the opening of the Utah Central Railway in 1870," and it sought to "acquaint" them "with the mineral resources of Utah, our local animals & natural history." With a range of exhibits including also a "Church cabinet" and depictions of Indian life in the Great Basin, the museum served moreover to invite inquiry into Mormonism's own natural history and transcontinental journeys vis-à-vis those of area natives, foreign 'Others,' and American tourists.[67]

To such scientific and comparative ends, John W. Young and his collaborators collected several types of artifacts in different display areas. Prominent among them were "a large and varied collection of all kinds of Indian curiosities," including "war-weapons, scalps, ornaments, implements," "charms, arrow-heads, spears," "crania of red men, and relics of the past," housed in a row of cabinets identified as the "ethnological department." Such displays were meant to represent "ancient as well as modern races of 'Indians' or aborigines" and to "shew the implements still used" and "used formerly." They were phrased and staged predominantly in the past tense, however, and overall their ethnographic tone set up Mormons and LDS settlement schemes as an appealing alternative to Ute, Shoshoni, and Bannock life.[68]

It is noteworthy that Deseret Museum officials elected not to highlight the Mormon church's 'Indian farms' or similar missionary endeavors for Utahn natives, in their display cabinets. As described in chapter 2, these efforts—designed simultaneously to grow food for trade, train natives in particular agricultural techniques, expand Mormon settlements, restrict Indian movements, convert 'Lamanites' to Christ, foster cross-cultural understanding, and otherwise standardize Mormon-Indian relations—were an important component of LDS settlement plans and social programs in the 1850s, especially in southern Utah. Many such missions were deserted by the early 1870s, but the church then renewed and expanded its Indian programs in the north, precisely among some of the 'wandering bands' of Shoshonis that Baron von Hübner observed during his 1871 stay in Corinne. In the spring of 1873—less than three weeks before Codman and company looked upon the Indian exhibits at the Deseret Museum, in fact—missionary George Washington Hill claimed to have baptized one hundred Northwestern Shoshonis into the LDS Church, at a spot only twelve miles upriver from Corinne; and the following year Brigham Young authorized him to establish Indian farms in the upper Cache and Bear River Valleys, nearer the Idaho border. These too had mixed success, and by 1875 Hill had abandoned these sites in favor of another near Brigham City. Nevertheless

MUSEUM!

Opposite the Old Tabernacle Gate,

SALT LAKE CITY.

UTAH AT A GLANCE,

In Minerals, Ores, Etc., Home Products and Manufactures in Metals, Minerals, Silk, Cotton, Woolen, Dog's Hair, etc., Paper, Type, Paints and early Gold Coins and Currency.

UTAH ANIMALS, BIRDS & REPTILES.

Preserved specimens of Buffalo, Antelopes, Deer, Porcupines, Pelicans, Eagles, the Prairie-Dog, Ground Owls, Etc. Our Mountain Alligator and other Reptiles alive.

UTAH FOSSILS.

The Great American Fossil Elephant, Fossil Fishes, Plants, Shells, and Corals,

Utah Indian Relics and Curiosities,

Robes, Blankets, Weapons, Scalps, Ornaments, Ancient Mills, War-Clubs, Pottery and Stone-age Relics, Utah Works of early Art and Manufacture, Paintings, Sculpture, Photographs. The first Picture taken by the Action of Light, in this City, in 1849-50.

THE FIRST SEWING MACHINE MADE IN UTAH. THE FIRST WHITE MAN'S BOAT,

MADE BY KIT CARSON.

The Large and Varied Collections of the

Deseret Museum

Are being constantly added to from all parts of the earth.

Mr. Wm. D. JOHNSON, Jr.,

An assistant at this Institution, may visit our various Settlements to obtain specimens and complete our collections of Minerals, Fossils and Natural Curiosities of the Territory.

CHARTS, MAPS AND BOOKS OF REFERENCE FOR UTAH, WITH VIEWS OF LOCAL SCENERY. VIEWS OF THE YELLOW STONE, Etc.

Half a block West of "Deseret News Office". Open daily, except Sunday, from 9 a.m. to 6 p.m.
ADMISSION, TWENTY-FIVE CENTS, CHILDREN, HALF PRICE.
Private Arrangements for Schools.

News Steam Print.   **JOS. L. BARFOOT, Manager.**

Advertisement for the Deseret Museum, ca. 1875. (Courtesy of the Church History Library, The Church of Jesus Christ of Latter-day Saints, Salt Lake City [069 D451mg 187-])

it is clear—and significant—that church officials were interacting closely with contemporaneous Indian groups, using modern farming implements, at the same time that John W. Young was displaying mainly the trappings of primitivism in his museum.[69]

Church efforts to Christianize and resettle natives as farmers harmonized with federal Indian policy at the time, even as they complemented also the practice—pursued as much at the Smithsonian Institution as at the Deseret Museum—of salvage ethnography. Both 'acculturation' and 'museumification' assumed that traditional Native American practices were necessarily doomed to extinction and that natives themselves could avoid extinction only by abandoning them. (One must "kill the Indian in him" in order to "save the man," said Richard Henry Pratt of the Carlisle Indian School some years later, and John Wesley Powell, director of the Bureau of Ethnography at the Smithsonian Institution, basically agreed: "Only by giving to the Indians Anglo-Saxon civilization" might they "also have prosperity and happiness under the new civilization of the continent.")[70] John W. Young and the LDS Church's decision not to highlight Indian farming programs alongside their ethnographic displays is therefore noteworthy. The reason for this silence is not to be found in the mixed success of the settlements themselves, as if the Mormons were embarrassed to mention them. It is rather related to popular concerns about Mormon-Indian racial combination and mutual corruption—concerns shared in fact by John Wesley Powell himself.

Appointed special commissioner for the Office of Indian Affairs, Powell traveled to Utah in May 1873 to ascertain the welfare of Northwestern Shoshonis living outside Fort Hall Reservation. This was not coincidentally the same month as George Washington Hill's first mass baptism of Shoshonis in the Bear River; Powell's charge was precipitated by alarmed reports by George W. Dodge, the federal agent previously in charge of the 'wandering bands,' that they and the Mormons were growing too close for comfort. In particular Dodge had feared that Mormons, to whom some Indians turned for food and friendship when government annuities failed, were training them in treasonous opposition both to federal oversight and to proper Christianity. Referencing then a religious development in Nevada—wherein the Piute prophet Wodziwob promised the return of Indian ancestors and the retreat of American colonists—Dodge wrote in July 1872 of a "mysterious movement" spreading to the Fort Hall and Wind River Reservations, and he suggested that "Brigham Young and the Mormons were aiding and abetting the coming insurrection by preaching that the government agents were not providing for the wants of the Indians."[71] Thus Dodge amplified anew long-standing fears about Mormon-Indian coalition—as seen also in deliberations regarding the Anti-Bigamy and

Pacific Railway Acts in 1862—by predicting that Mormons would soon control Indians' hearts and minds and that together these communities would form a seditious and sectarian obstacle to American power.

Powell and his colleague G. W. Ingalls were persuaded by Dodge's assessments of resource scarcity if not also religious sedition, and they decided in 1873 that the Northwestern Shoshonis should be located finally at Fort Hall. This would enable government agents to care more closely for its Indian charges, they said, and to shelter them from depredations by crooked white traders accustomed to exchanging Shoshoni annuities for little of lasting value.[72] George Washington Hill rejected both premises as disingenuous, however. Commenting from his newly challenged Indian farm, this Mormon missionary argued instead that the commissioners were specifically setting up the Shoshonis for failure by removing them from the moral and temperate orbit of Latter-day Saints: "ingalls and powell are trying to turn all the Indians from us they can to give them their goods where they can sell them for whiskey." In any case Hill—whose notes on Indian vocabulary show that he was then learning phrases like "to baptise" and "to anoint with oil" as well as "do not waste anything" and "divide equal"—resigned himself to a lack of material support from the government, regardless of the possible complementarity of his own Shoshoni resettlement plan.[73]

Deseret Museum officials may also have resigned themselves to the possibility of misunderstanding, avoiding potentially controversial missions displays in favor of others awash in the aesthetic ideology of primitivism and salvage. Pertinent to this possibility is the fact that curators housed alongside their assorted Native American artifacts, in the ethnographic department, exempla of other 'primitive' societies, past and present alike. Young collected "stone-age relics from Europe, Asia, Africa, South America and the Islands of the Pacific," as well as a great number of "Oriental curiosities, Persian manuscripts, Hindoo shastens, Ivory & Bronze Dieties &c," many of them donated by Mormon elders from their travels "in foreign lands." These foreign items not only evidenced Mormonism's global reach. Perhaps more important, along with the remains of dead Indians, they provided literal data for Mormonism's sometimes nonspecific comparates—Islam, Hinduism, and primitive cultures—with which visitors might concretely compare the living, local, arguably modern stuff of Mormonism.[74]

THE DEBATABLE NATURE of *Mormon* modernity was an important premise and theme of the Deseret Museum, in a few respects. Consider, for instance, the temporal message of the so-called Church Cabinet. A collection of "relics" from "the early history of our various settlement[s], in Kirtland, Nauvoo, Carthage," this display contained also symbols of anti-Mormon violence and martyrdom in the Midwest: "the Carthage Pistol; the watch of David W. Patten; the cap of the martyred missionary Joseph Standing," and likenesses of Joseph and Hyrum Smith. Such artifacts mapped a virtual atrocity tour of early Mormon history. Unlike Beadle's atrocity tours of present-day Mormonism, however, this was a sympathetic and retrospective representation of Mormons themselves as a persecuted people, by which John W. Young invited visitors to view Saints' westward emigration as a tragic but necessary move. Culminating then in items pertaining to "the first [Mormon] settlement of these vallies" and, significantly, the "'last spike' of the Utah Central," the Church Cabinet implied that Mormonism generally had advanced beyond its midwestern beginnings, finding some measure of safety and fruition in the Great Basin.[75]

The Church Cabinet thus argued for continuity between Mormonisms or Mormon settlements in the Midwest and in Utah, even as it distinguished them, respectively, as provinces of persecution and promise. Midwestern 'Josephites' rejected the 'Brighamite' logic of such claims to presidential and geographical succession, but Brigham's son John found fairly ecumenical support among Utahns—Mormon and non-Mormon alike—for a key component of his display. This was its implication of a still-newer turn in Mormon and Utahn history, toward industry and technology. The Deseret Museum invited visitors to consider the nature of religiosity in the railroad age.

The last spike of the Utah Central pointed beyond the Church Cabinet, wherein it occupied a final position, in the direction of displays of Utahn natural resources. In addition to "wild animals indigenous to the Territory," these were of two sorts: agricultural products, including cotton and home-manufactured clothing, and specimens of Utahn quartz, silver, sulfur, and coal. The agricultural exhibits, acting in harmony with farming installations at the Tabernacle, presented Mormon settlers as agents of civilized order and domestic cultivation. By contrast, the minerals showcased an extractive industrial economy with which leading Mormons had long held a conflicted relationship, not least during the Godbeite debates. John W. Young and his colleagues staged these two displays side by side, seemingly without commentary about their relative propriety or sanction, but visitors found in them ample material for speculation and teleological imagination.[76]

Consider, for example, John Codman's impression of these displays. Codman took from his time at the museum the message that: whereas Utahn Mormons were capable of and poised for self-sufficiency in the prerailroad age, a fact demonstrated by the farming and home-manufacturing exhibit, the Union Pacific, Central Pacific, and Utah Central railways had opened Mormondom to the speculations and excavations of foreigners, the fruits of which were then displayed in the mineral cabinets. For him, although there was much to admire about the simplicity and communal nature of life in prerailroad Utah, the last spike in the Church Cabinet symbolized the last nail in the coffin of an early Mormonism and also the first prod by which to push Utahn markets and Mormons alike toward modernity. Admittedly there was little to this interpretation that strayed beyond the standard death knell thesis, save for Codman's sense that Mormonism could and would survive the transition. What is remarkable was that John W. Young seems not only to have anticipated and understood such readings but to have welcomed and staged them also on church property. There was little to lose in and through the positive appraisal of technological advance vis-à-vis religious retrenchment, after all. By then Young and his father both had laid ample groundwork by which to profit from John Codman–esque tourism *and* Patrick Connor–esque mining, dependent as they were on Utah Central connections with the transcontinentals.[77]

The Deseret Museum stood in a relation of synecdoche with Mormon Salt Lake City generally, during the early railroad tourism era. Its cabinets showcased a number of seemingly disparate and sometimes surprising cultural productions, and similar to Tabernacle performances of anti-Mormon argumentation, they incorporated ideas and items generally considered critical of or detrimental to Mormon lifestyles—precious metals, for instance—in a way that enabled selective comparison by Saints and Gentiles alike. Moreover the museum staged both Mormon and non-Mormon representations relative to other artifacts considered mutually foreign—Indian wares and 'primitive' icons—and at least one experience held in common: the transcontinental voyage. John W. Young's exhibits fostered among visitors the recognition of many Utahn Mormons' eastern origins and western trajectories and, thus, the fact that Mormons too once took overland trips—albeit arguably amid greater hardships. The museum's owner and directors therefore extended invitations "to every thoughtful visitor" capable of reflecting upon the environments, cultures, and trajectories of Mormons relative to those of foreigners, Indians, and themselves.[78]

Church members, railroad agents, Gentile miners, and even the Walker brothers contributed to various and overlapping sections of the Deseret Museum. All recognized it as a place where Mormon and non-Mormon visitors alike could reflect upon Utahn pasts and presents, reconsider the wealth of its natural resources, and compare LDS culture with that of distant foreigners or local primitives. It was, in other words, as 'ecumenical' a tourist site as Utah had, at that time, representing a common ground shared by some Gentiles and Mormons, at least insofar as they agreed to mutually exclude mention of live Indians.[79]

By late 1870, when the Smithsonian Institution in Washington, D.C., contacted John W. Young about the possibility of trading "duplicate specimens from the Institution" for any "vertebrate fossil remains," "ancient aboriginal relics of the West," or "articles illustrative of the modern Indians" of Utah, the status of the Deseret Museum was clear. Its founders, benefactors, and visitors had all bought the basic premise that the museum—and Utah generally—was an important site of scientific and ethnological investigation in and for America.[80]

There remained, however, a darker side to this sense that Utah and its Deseret Museum offered important data for human observation if not also humanistic understanding. Phineas T. Barnum, circus impresario and manager of the American Museum in New York City, wrote to John W. Young at the Deseret Museum in April 1871, offering to sell him some exhibits. "I can spare the life size moving [automatous] representation of 'The Last Supper.' It cost $2000. I will sell for $1200. What say you? It can be all packed in one or two boxes. I can also soon spare the living girl born without arms—cuts, writes, sews &c with her toes—also bearded girl 5 years old full whiskers & covered with hair. Would you like either or all of these?"[81] Whether Barnum assumed that the entire Deseret Museum would resemble a circus sideshow is unclear from his letter, and unfortunately we have no record of Young's reply. In any case Barnum would have been right to think that many tourists would hold such views themselves: they would persist in the assumption that Mormons were curiosities akin to bearded women and armless stenographers, and therefore they would come to Salt Lake City and the Deseret Museum expecting to see a freak show. Barnum's letter warned Young, implicitly if not explicitly, that Mormons would need to find different ways to publicly acknowledge, cater to, or capitalize on precisely that type of critical and salacious gaze, well into the future. Without capitulating to Corinnethian fantasies about Mormons being soulless or misshapen beings, that is, Mormon tourism promoters needed with one hand to extend the promise of exoticism and revelation while holding evidence of refinement and regularity in the other.

Thankfully Saints had some experience with this dynamic already at the Salt Lake Theatre, Tabernacle, and President's Office. Moreover they could call upon powerful allies when continuing and trademarking the work. Over the next two decades Mormon leaders and their railroading affiliates had ample opportunity to train public interests in combined projects of Mormon watching, ethnological inquiry, resource mining, and national apperception in Utah's many museums.

Many of these dynamics will be addressed in the next chapter. But we would do well to keep pace with Codman's own process, before going there ourselves. For, Codman had one more trip to make and a few more lessons to learn in Utah.

A Northern Tour: Codman's Last Leg

After their visits to the Deseret Museum and Tabernacle, Codman, Hamilton, Blaine, Clark, and Pullman bade good-bye to their Mormon hosts and returned to Ogden, where they boarded a Central Pacific train bound for California.[82] But Codman broke from this group there, and after one month's absence, he returned to Utah in late June 1873. This began the extended stay by virtue of which he would claim expertise beyond that of the typical tourist. John W. Young was once again Codman's guide, however, and once again Young took him along lines of strategic importance to the church. By the end of this last leg of his trip, Codman was brought under conviction of the benefits of Mormon business—as well as the atrocities of Corinnethian opposition.

"I left the city with Mr. John W. Young, at his invitation, for a tour to the North" on the Utah Northern Railroad, wrote Codman. The "pet scheme of my friend, John W. Young," the Utah Northern was by then completed as far north as Logan, and a bit beyond. Like all other Mormon railroads it was built mainly by Mormon laborers called to the task by church officials.[83] ("There was a requirement made from headquarters to build a narrow gauge railroad from Ogden to Soda Springs and . . . for the people to do a certain portion of labor to each man," wrote one such laborer who was paid in tithing credit, company stock, and "the railroad vouchers that circulated as money.")[84] For their part Corinnethians watched the construction and extension of the Utah Northern with increasing dread, sure that—if the line ever reached Idaho—it would sap their remaining freighting business from Montana mines.[85]

After a short stay in Logan and nearby settlements, John W. Young was called back to Salt Lake City, but he offered "one of his men" to escort Codman to Soda Springs, Idaho. This site, which Young intended someday to be the terminus for the Utah Northern, was favored by his family for its hot springs. Upon arrival Codman did in fact find "several members of Brigham Young's family . . . passing their summer here," but he reported little about the wives except that Amelia was "a very pleasant, agreeable, and rather pretty woman." Regarding the virtues of the site itself, he was far more effusive. Codman spoke at length about "the unquestionable virtues of the waters of Soda Springs," including their ability to soothe a "rebellious liver" and "rheumatic joints." "The really wonderful virtue of the waters, the pure, unadulterated air, the magnificent mountain scenery, the rides and drives, the hunting and fishing, all conduce to pleasant pastime and restoration of health." Codman returned to the site several times, and he predicted that—upon completion of the Utah Northern line—it would be a popular vacation spot and sanitarium among easterners as well as the Youngs.[86]

Codman was sold, converted to the merits of the environment if not also the faith of its residents. Before long he had bought land at Soda Springs, and as he began actively to promote it, he spoke increasingly in favor and defense of Mormonism as well. This was especially true after Brigham Young died in 1877. In an interview with the *New York Times* that year, Codman guaranteed that polygamy and other offensive practices would soon pass away too, and thus that Christians would have little reason to deny Mormons communion. In any case Codman refused to foreswear the virtues of Mormonism overall, to dismiss the corporate visions of the Young family, or to deploy anti-Mormonism as an incitement to touristic, industrial, or political investment in his new summertime home.[87] This is perhaps because of his early friendship with John W. Young and perhaps because of later relationships with other Mormons in the area. Or it may be because he had seen firsthand the failure of the Corinnethian project during that very first visit in 1873.

CODMAN STOPPED at Corinne on the way to and back from Soda Springs, in August 1873. For the first stop, he was escorted by John W. Young, whereas for the second he was not. Nevertheless Young's corporate hand was heavy there both times, in the form of a new spur line connecting Corinne to the Utah Northern.

Earlier that year, as they were watching the Utah Northern extend further toward Montana, Corinne's town officials had petitioned John W. Young for a truce and a compromise. By its terms Corinnethians gave the Utah Northern (and Young) two thousand dollars in cash, two thousand dollars in city warrants, one thousand dollars in goods, and a plot of land in return for a five-mile-long branch line to the Mormon railroad at Brigham City.[88] Corinnethians hoped that this connection would protect their northern freighting businesses from Mormon appropriation, at least until they devised a different method of Gentile economic independence or Mormon defeat. Meanwhile the branch line also eased commercial exchanges between Corinnethian Gentiles and Brigham City Mormons, the likes of which had been occurring—albeit often covertly—since 1869. In both respects, however, the new spur served as a painful reminder of John W. Young's ever-encroaching power and the present unsustainability of strict Gentility.

Young and his spur line transported Codman directly to the swirling center of these mixed feelings. There Codman encountered a number of other torn allegiances as well as raw nerves. To be sure, he found townsfolk still proud of their anti-Mormon charter: that Corinne was to be "a Christian landmark in [Mormonism's] midst, . . . throw[ing] its pure rays far and wide to scatter the darkness in which the 'twin relic of barbarism' had shrouded the land."[89] However several of Corinne's most stridently Gentile boosters had moved on. J. H. Beadle was one of these; Beadle had stopped living full-time in Corinne in 1872, splitting his time thereafter among far-flung western cities, Indiana, and Salt Lake City. In his absence emerged a new class of Corinnethian headmen like Alexander Toponce: a man who—although rumored to steal Mormon cattle and despite a stated preference to do business with "Gentiles, if possible"—had been trading railroad materials with Mormon businessmen for more than four years, even helping to construct the Utah Northern in the first place (much to Beadle's chagrin).[90]

Codman found little unity among even the longest residents of Corinne, though, or between their everyday lives and booster promises. Save for "grog shops" and dance houses there were few viable social institutions in Corinne, including religious ones. The three extant churches claimed only fourteen members among them, and—unlike those halcyon days when Presbyterians and Episcopalians shared facilities—they refused to cooperate.[91] (For his part the Episcopalian minister was pleased when nobody showed up for services, for he preferred to spend Sundays pounding quartz and panning for gold.)[92] Moreover, as with Toponce, neither these churchgoers nor the few hundred other residents of the town seemed consistently to forswear business or camaraderie with local Mormons, any rhetoric to the contrary notwithstanding.

Aside from ostensible anti-Mormonism and concerns about the lasting benefits of John W. Young's railroad connections, the one thing that did unite many Corinnethians at the time of Codman's tour was anti-Indianism. Indeed since Baron von Hübner's 1871 visit, leading Corinnethians had whipped themselves into a fresh fury of Shoshoni hating, and they believed, along with former Indian agent George W. Dodge, that Mormons were encouraging the Shoshonis to stay in the Bear River Valley and training them as an army. George Washington Hill's group baptism in May 1873—three short months before Codman's visit to Corinne—didn't help matters. Neither did Hill's ongoing settlement and missionizing efforts. Corinnethians howled—to Dodge, to John Wesley Powell and G. W. Ingalls, to anyone else who would listen, and thus presumably to Codman himself—that the Shoshonis and Mormons would surely join forces to attack Corinne and any other institutions of white Christianity in the West. Theirs was a local, frantic voicing of the same national fear about Mormon-Indian alliance that likely informed the nonspecific tenor of Indian exhibits in the Deseret Museum and perhaps also shaped Powell and Ingalls's decision to enforce Shoshoni settlement at Fort Hall.

Residents of Corinne had little real reason to worry, although they could point to instances of Indian-Mormon violent collaboration in the past. The

1857 Mountain Meadows Massacre, in which Mormon militiamen and Indian accomplices killed some 120 westward-bound emigrants in southern Utah, was a topic of renewed concern in the early 1870s; as pressure mounted to locate the perpetrators, a grand jury indicted several Mormon men in 1874. The subsequent trial of John D. Lee garnered national attention and—when it resulted in a hung jury on August 7, 1875—outrage. For their part the Corinnethians, while themselves caught up in that outrage, also tried to capitalize on it. Two days after the verdict the *Daily Mail* predicted that Brigham Young would soon arm his recombined and now-emboldened Mormon-Indian forces in an attack on Corinne. "Mormons Meddling with Indians! Mountain Meadows to be Repeated!" warned the editor, who claimed that one thousand Indian warriors had already gathered ten miles north of town. During the ensuing "Night of Terror!" August 10, Corinne's residents armed themselves in defense, huddled in fear, posted sentries at the outskirts of town, and fired shots at marauding Indians hiding in the shadows. At least that is what they claimed when petitioning government officials for support and a full military investigation.[93]

For his part, Hill was sure that the entire "Indian scare" had been invented. "It seems corinne was wanting some government patronage and did not know how to get it only by circulating lies of the blackest dye," he wrote, and he quoted "Indian John" as confirming that "Corinne has got up this excitement without any cause."[94] Indeed even the Corinnethian militiamen later expressed doubts that they had seen any Indians in the shadows, that night. But their reports had desired effects nonetheless: the governor authorized the dispatch of some fifty soldiers to the town from Camp Douglas, and these men drove the Indians from Hill's farm, forcing them to abandon their crops and demanding that they report to Fort Hall Reservation. Corinne's newspapers reveled in the attention, convinced that the government would grant them a permanent military station and finally help them secure the valley for Gentiles.[95]

If anything, however, the Indian scare had an opposite and ironic effect. Corinne's cry only persuaded Montana traders that the town was unsafe, and they shifted their business further in the direction of John W. Young's Utah Northern line and its neighboring Mormon settlements. The military company was recalled after only a month, too, and newspapers from Ogden to Sacramento ridiculed the entire "ruse on the part of certain bankrupt Corinneites to galvanize their town into life" as "The Corinne Farce." Corinnethians' only lasting success—if we can call it such—lay in a more permanent expulsion of Shoshonis from the Bear River Valley, thereby making them the true victims of the hysteria. But without any positive program for expanded settlement of its own, Corinne's anti-Indian campaign—inaugurated anew just before Codman's visit in the summer of 1873 and culminating two years later—merely hastened the fate that Codman himself predicted. "The people of Montana will dispense with Corinne," he wrote, "and its value as a trading mart will fall to zero."[96]

CODMAN THUS RAN UP AGAINST three lessons, during his guided tours of Corinne. The first was that rhetoric had never matched reality, even in the "Christian landmark" of Corinne—and that it certainly didn't by 1873, at the time of Codman's visit. The "Land of Gentility" was little more than a cluster of godless grogshops, aligned at the mercy of Mormon merchants and shuttered for fear of Indian ghosts. Meanwhile Corinne's predominantly exclusive, colonial, and violent settlement strategies continued to work against its boosters' vision of secular success. There were no beneficiaries of Corinne's appalling anti-Indian program, after all, excepting perhaps John W. Young. And indeed that is precisely the last lesson. Insofar as Young effectively cut across this terrain of continual disconnection and displacement, it was his brand of industrial Mormonism that would eventually emerge as the region's only powerhouse. Young cornered the mining and tourist trades in northern, central, and southern Utah as far as the Corinnethian opposition was concerned; and he established long-lasting and wide-ranging relationships with eastern capitalists and travelers, the likes of which would yield dividends for decades.

John Codman's tour thus became, for John W. Young, a victory lap of the entire enterprise. Young turned touristic tables on Corinne by making of it an excursion site demonstrating *not* a unified Gentile Protestantism but rather the shortfalls of modern western urbanity. Corinne, not Salt Lake City, had become the object of an atrocity tour.

A Middle Ground in the Making

Codman tried to forge unique meaning in the messy spaces between Beadle's and Stenhouse's books (on the one hand) and John W. Young's victory lap (on the other), their attempts to guide his authorial hand notwithstanding. In brief he made three moves respecting Mormonism and its interpretation, even before he invested in Soda Springs real estate and thus also the projects of Mormon translation and feeder-line extension. First he argued that Mormonism "was a harmless little beast in its infancy," and that, save for the notion of progressive revelation, its basic doctrines might have been unobjectionable to "even the Evangelical Alliance." But when midwestern bigots and persecutors "evoked the spirit of the devil wherewith to defend itself," Mormons used their "progressive revelation" clause to introduce "innovations" that were, in fact, problematic retrogressions and retrenchments. In short they reverted to a particularly tribal mode of Judaism (with aspects of "Mahometanism"), hiding behind outdated applications of theocracy and polygamy.[97]

Codman's third move was that of prescriptive modernization. Claiming that Mormonism's main atrocities were "things of the past" that "proceeded from a curious mixture of human passion and religious fanaticism, superinduced by remembrance of the persecutions which they themselves had suffered," he asserted that railroads, liberal markets, and renewed contact with New Testament–reading Christians would destroy polygamy, theocracy, and "Old Testament" literalism. Mormons would find their way (back, or anew) to a more peaceful Mormonism, one that might appeal to the Evangelical Alliance again. Referencing John W. Young's projects, and especially his success in "overcoming the senseless prejudices of Eastern capitalists against the safety of investment among the Mormons," Codman called railroads "peacemakers and civilizers" by virtue of their ability to force ecumenical alliances among Gentile and Mormon capitalists. The transcontinental railroad had placed Utah "on a line of 'distinct civilization' in religion," Codman said, and along that line Mormons would surely (re)make themselves into good American citizens, without need of additional governmental intervention.[98]

Codman's book thus transcended the Corinnethian tourism model and traversed John W. Young's terrain only to return to a modified death knell thesis—one usable by railroads, some Mormons, and friendly congressman at that time. This does not mean that Codman's book, *The Mormon Country*, was wholly a publicity piece for Mormonism or a celebration of John W. (or Brigham) Young. But it played well its generic role of guided cultural mediator, nevertheless; it seemed to moderate between pro- and anti-Mormon claims, and it promised that Utah would remain a special a site of rich cultural encounters, both on and off the railroad tracks.

IN DEFENSE OF the moderate tone of his book, Codman himself wrote that "my Mormon friends will say that their kindness is ill-requited by adverse criticism of their doctrines and practices," while "my Gentile readers will say that I have been so fascinated with the country and the people of Utah that I have given them unmerited praise. Both verdicts will be gratefully accepted as proofs of the impartiality claimed for the book."[99] More accurately we might conclude that the possibility of both readings—and the very fact that Codman kept alive debates about normative Mormonism and normative religion in the West, all the while plotting sites and routes by which to pursue it—classed Codman's guidebook with others of a type, all of them acts and agents of religious construction in Utah. Associated routes and symbols would change over time, as we shall see, but the commitments of mainline guides and railroad agents to maintaining the viability of the search itself seldom wavered.

It is no perhaps no wonder, therefore, that Leland Stanford—who grew increasingly committed, both personally and professionally, to the sustenance of industrial religion in Utah throughout the 1880s—kept a copy of Codman's guidebook in his collection.[100] For, transcontinental railroad officials were professionally concerned with maintaining precisely the infrastructure of such a middle-ground and mainline Mormonism.

CHAPTER SIX

Tourists and the Making of an American Mainline

✦

CHARLES FRANCIS ADAMS JR., president of the Union Pacific Railroad from 1884 to 1890, exerted—arguably as part of his job description—considerable editorial control over mainline tourism literature and its reporting on Mormonism. In 1888, for instance, he wrote to Edwards Roberts, a professional travel writer, regarding Roberts's forthcoming guidebook. *Shoshone, and Other Western Wonders*, published later that year, was due to contain a preface from Adams, who planned to sell it along his line. (Roberts's title references the Shoshone Falls in Idaho, newly accessible via an extension of the Union Pacific's Utah & Northern branch.) After receiving an advanced copy of the text, however, Adams expressed concerns about Roberts's depictions of Salt Lake City, Mormonism, and polygamy. He advised Roberts to omit critical and derogatory passages, for, as he said, "among our customers are the Mormons. A book brought out under the auspices of the Union Pacific should, therefore, in my opinion, contain nothing which is offensive to the Mormons. . . . No good tradesman has a right to offend any customer, no matter what his opinions may be, provided he is civil and pays his bills. To us the Mormons have always been civil, and they have always paid their bills." The resultant book thus spoke *not* of polygamy as a persistent "barbarism" in Salt Lake City or of the "treasonable and seditious" leadership of LDS Church authorities. Cutting such descriptions from previously composed sections on Utah, Roberts's published guidebook moderated also corresponding expectations among readers, cautioning them against the uncritical consumption of atrocity tales.[1]

Under Adams's direction, Roberts tempered his more hostile adjectives, and he encouraged his readers to do likewise. Instead—significantly—he instructed them to pay close attention to rocks and topography in the Mormon Great Basin, even while telling them, when gazing upon Mormon buildings, to "imagine what there is within."[2] Such directions, when coupled by railroad lobbyists' complementary work among national politicians and newspapermen, effected the mainlining of Utahn tourism and Mormonism alike in American minds and markets.

THE MAXIMIZING OF passenger traffic in Utah necessitated that its religious curiosities be rendered safely visible and visitable. Positioning itself between alarmist exposés of Mormonism and Mormon apologetics, most Utahn railroad literature endeavored to keep alive a rhetoric of curiosity and distinctiveness while taking care not to scare away potential non-Mormon tourists and settlers. This had been true since 1869, but it was especially so during the late 1870s and 1880s, as politicians unleashed a new barrage of anti-Mormon measures, railroad agents worked against them, and both parties put Mormonism again into discourse and public debate. Authors and agents found this to be a space of sensational imperative, in any case and in both eras. Religions—at least unusual religions—needed to be made objects of touristic visitation. And tourists needed to be enticed by opportunities to debate and discover the stuff of religion in situ. In order to justify the occupation and incorporation of Zion, not just its traversal, railroads necessarily partook in the construction and reconceptualization of Mormonism and religion generally in the West.[3]

Railroad literature worked to mediate and market Utahn religious claims by focusing strategically on the geographical, material, and sensory cultures of Mormonism, that is, by attending to what Adams would elsewhere describe as "the material side" of LDS religion. Meanwhile they engaged in a sort of domesticating comparison between Mormons and other religious groups. Railroad agents intentionally fashioned themselves 'ethnographers' as they fashioned—for themselves and others—'religion.' Railroad platforms, by their construction, became sites of religious reflection and definition. And Mormons, for their part, forged around them a terrain of mutual benefit.[4]

Thus, in the end: not only did railroad officials tread a middle route between anti-Mormon and pro-Mormon interests when selecting their point of juncture, but they went on to promote Great Basin travel through mediations of a differently productive and, from the Corinnethian perspective, especially frustrating sort. Such efforts were not unprecedented or unique to the Great Basin; railroad agents, having connected lands and markets throughout the West, worked also to delineate the geographies, peoples, and cultures encountered there and to promote tourism and settlement along train routes, between groups. Neither were their delineations ever selfless. In railroad media the historian consistently encounters a type of marketing language.[5] What is most interesting, in the present instance, is the effect of this marketing language in shaping both the popular and the political identification of Mormonism in America.

A Political Preface

Historians of Mormonism and nineteenth-century American religions are well acquainted with some of the legal and political disputes that surrounded Adams's and Roberts's 1888 correspondence and provided a context to its concerns. My aim here is not to retread these grounds but rather to trace railroads', tourists', and Mormons' interactions beneath—and influencings of—the canopy of congressional law. Scholars have paid insufficient attention to how railroads and corporate agents persistently framed such political affairs and their effects, from congressional boardrooms and national newspapers to more local spaces of touristic discernment. Only by recasting 1880s federal anti-Mormon policies in light of railroading concerns can we understand how Adams's preface was itself a profoundly political act. The first part of this chapter therefore attempts such a recasting. The following sections demonstrate how—even while Congress attacked and, in time, forced concessions from the LDS Church respecting institutions of polygamy and politics—Mormon material culture and geography were concurrently identified with Mormonism, by railroads and capitalists if not also by congressmen. Such identifications effectively permitted not only their retention or inhabitation by what J. Spencer Fluhman has termed "defanged" Mormons. They ensured also their lasting integration—as data and exempla of cultural pasts and possibilities—into American religious imaginaries.[6]

In 1887, the year before Adams's and Roberts's exchange, Congress passed the Edmunds-Tucker Act, which included many elements of the 1862 Anti-Bigamy Act and the 1870 Cullom Bill. It increased fines and prison sentences for polygamy and "unlawful cohabitation," disincorporated the LDS Church, permitted seizure of church properties beyond a total value of fifty thousand dollars, disenfranchised Utahn women, required antipolygamy oaths for prospective (male) voters and public officials, replaced local judges with federal appointees, and dispatched marshals and deputies to oversee related sentences. Aspects of the Edmunds-Tucker Act were based also on the 1882 Edmunds Act, the constitutionality of which was upheld by the Supreme Court in 1885. The entirety of the omnibus 1887 law was later ruled constitutional in 1890.[7]

Between 1885 and 1890, with politicians, judges, and marshals jointly backing antipolygamy laws as they had not before, "territorial officials commenced the systematic and intensive prosecution of Mormon leaders in Utah."[8] A so-called Raid sent numerous church leaders underground, while others served sentences at the Utah Penitentiary. (Then-president John Taylor died in hiding in 1887; and his successor, Wilford Woodruff, spent nine months in "the Pen.")[9] Meanwhile LDS authorities reallocated church properties and businesses in order to avoid seizure, placing some under the names of loyal churchmen and organizing nonprofit associations to hold and oversee others. Despite such efforts government agents confiscated some eight hundred thousand dollars in cash, properties, stock, and livestock from the church, but they returned most of that soon thereafter, in 1890. Restoration occurred when LDS Church president Wilford Woodruff, "acting for the temporal salvation of the church" (as he wrote in his journal), announced the end of sanctioned polygamy among Mormons via the so-called Woodruff Manifesto of fall 1890. The putative abandonment of polygamy removed the single largest obstacle to Utahn statehood—granted finally in 1896—and Mormon corporate success therein.[10]

Railroad agents were seldom public proponents of polygamy. But neither did they support the Edmunds or Edmunds-Tucker Act, let alone the Raid. To the contrary company officials and lobbyists had attempted to preempt and obviate these actions by intervening in preceding legislative conversations, just as they had for the Cullom Bill. In 1882, for instance, Sidney Dillon—then president of the Union Pacific—asked his lawyers to approach prorailroad congressmen, impressing upon them the fact that "the Mormons are our Friends" and requesting from them continuing lenience relative to "the Mormon Question." Charles Francis Adams Jr., who succeeded Dillon as president in 1884, added to his pleas a reiteration of the death knell logics that were partly responsible for having derailed Anti-Bigamy Act and Cullom Bill provisions until then. The Union Pacific had no interest in defending or interfering in the "moral and criminal side of the situation" in Utah, Adams wrote to President Grover Cleveland in 1885, but he wished *not* to disrupt the "material side" by unduly unsettling Mormon businessmen, politicians, and public works or by impeding traffic to and through Utah. "The railroads are preparing to carry into the territory a tide of immigration which would definitely settle the question of polygamy," he promised—again.[11]

By 1885 the Union Pacific controlled several railroads once owned by the LDS Church, including the Utah Central, Utah Southern, Utah Western, and Utah Northern; it was also working to extend and improve them under new names. Unsurprisingly Union Pacific directors feared capitalists' disinclination to invest in such projects during a period of political turmoil, along with any disruption of feeder-line traffic or discouragement to touristic visitation. For his part John W. Young shared their concerns. Therefore he traveled east in 1884 in hopes of convincing businessmen, lobbyists, and politicians to oppose new anti-Mormon legislation or, barring that, to place advocates on the committees responsible for implementing it. Meanwhile Young tried to persuade these same people to support a new railroad project of his own: the Salt Lake & Fort Douglas Railway. The two efforts were intimately linked, in his mind—or so he claimed when defending his efforts along the latter lines to members of the church hierarchy. "Business is merely the incidental part and only forms the veil to cover my real objects, which, if left too open, would scare away those to whom I now apply, and whose aid I fain would use for the benefit of our beloved cause," Young wrote in 1886. "And thus it is I plod along the path of business to the outer view, but truly and sacredly within am reaching every private avenue in my scope where I find a path to some party of influence whose kindly word assists us in resisting the horrible onslaughts of our enemies." An act in support of Utahn railroads was an act in support of the church.[12]

Even if Sidney Dillon, Charles Francis Adams Jr., and John W. Young agreed on this much in principle, Young sometimes thought railroad personnel could do more on Mormons' behalf. To that end he suggested that LDS leaders remind different companies of their reliance upon Mormon business, threatening to take it elsewhere if necessary. Seeing "opportunities to work *quid pro quos* in turning considerable immigrant transportation business to certain rail lines in return for influence on behalf of the Mormons," Young advised President John Taylor in 1885 to "divide our business between the U.P. and the [Denver & Rio Grande]," for instance, thereby spurring Union Pacific leaders to greater political action while rewarding other companies that were "interested in our welfare" but were previously "deprived of all of our business."[13] The Denver & Rio Grande had recently completed a line connecting Denver to Salt Lake City via eastern Utah and the Provo area, and company representatives indeed requested a share of Mormons' missionary and emigration business, offering to Taylor "a lower rate than the U.P." and a "choice of several routes" running to Kansas City, Missouri, Council Bluffs, Iowa, and Chicago. ("We are not selfish, and do not ask for *all* of the Business, but as the D.&R.G. are in Utah to do business, and the road and its employees are circulating considerable means throughout the territory, we would be pleased to have a fair proportion of the travel of those connected with the Church," wrote one agent in 1884.)[14] Agents of the Pennsylvania Railroad and the Chicago, Rock Island & Pacific Railroad made similar inquiries, and John W. Young thought Mormons would do well to grant favorable contracts in return for political support in Washington.[15]

Through these and other measures, including outright bribes to lobbyists and newspapermen, Young claimed some success in slowing the passage of the Edmunds-Tucker Act in 1887.[16] However their collective efforts were in vain, due in part, Young suggested, to the recent illness or demise of certain "friends" and at least one "railroad representative" in Washington and the East.[17] The fact of failure may also have been related to a more general weakening of the railroad lobby's congressional clout in the late 1870s and early 1880s, when several companies were embroiled in managerial controversies and implicated in financial collapses. The renewal of anti-Mormon legislation coincided with a rise in antirailroad sentiment and a lessening of railroad power.[18]

BUT THE 1880S WERE far from a total loss for the railroad lobby or the LDS Church, and neither did the passage of the Edmunds-Tucker Act jeopardize their friendship. Quite the contrary. In addition to their ongoing and mutual commitment to protect a "material side" of Mormon life erstwhile threatened by congressional offensives (more on this below), Edmunds era negotiations opened up important lines of inquiry between church and railroad officials respecting the requirements for Utah statehood. The first of these, broached by John W. Young with Democrats in the East, concerned the possibility of prohibiting polygamy. The second, pursued by different agents of the LDS Church with representatives of the Central Pacific in the West, yielded a broad influence campaign by which railroad agents swayed national newspapers and Republican politicians to the Mormon cause.

In the spring of 1887, as the Edmunds-Tucker Act neared its final vote and approval, John W. Young proposed "as a last resort" the so-called Scott amendment, named after the Democratic representative who agreed to introduce it on Young's behalf. The Scott amendment would have allowed a six-month delay of congressional action, during which time voters could elect a constitutional assembly in Utah Territory—and that assembly could then draft a state constitution, provided that it prohibited polygamy. If these conditions were met by the end of the grace period, the Edmunds-Tucker Act would be rendered void, and congressmen would consider a statehood act instead.[19] It was a bold play by Young to release Utahns from territorial oversight, and, as one historian recounts, "so quickly had they acted that their plan of action had not been approved by the Mormon leaders in Utah." The latter, including John Taylor, were displeased. (Indeed this displeasure, combined with concerns about the extravagant and unaccountable expense of Young's lifestyle in the East, led eventually to his falling out of favor with church leaders and his general omission from LDS histories.) Young assured the First Presidency that "the settlement of this issue was a political matter and that allowing a Utah constitution with an antipolygamy clause would in no way commit the church to abandoning its plural doctrine or practice" and, moreover, that practicing polygamists would benefit from "only hav[ing] to contend with Utah law and no longer with federal law." But Taylor resented Young for having publicly committed the church to considering formal monogamy in exchange for statehood. He perceived, rightly, that there was no going back from there.[20]

To say that church leaders were frustrated by the sudden and public nature of Young's proposition is not to say that they were wholly opposed to it. To the contrary, George Q. Cannon, Wilford Woodruff, and others had already discussed the idea of compromise among themselves—and also with Leland Stanford of the Central Pacific Railroad. As early as 1885, Stanford (by way of his agent Alex Badlam) had suggested to Cannon (by way of his agent H. B. Clawson) "a plan . . . by which we can get into the Union as a State" after suspending "the practice of plural marriage for the present." Cannon admitted to his journal that "probably I have had this method of becoming a State suggested to me scores and scores of times by leading politicians," including Thomas Fitch of Nevada, "but I never could see it."[21] Nevertheless he trusted Stanford's power and influence, and he was willing to consider his proposal and further conditions of support. In exchange for backing Utah statehood, Stanford then wanted the church to ensure "the casting of the electoral vote at the next presidential election in favor of Leland Stanford, present U.S. Senator, for President of the U.S. The latter desires this office."[22]

Stanford's presidential aspirations did not last long, however. By 1887, the year of Edmunds-Tucker, Stanford fixated on more general advantages of having Utah admitted to the union as a Republican state, as well as on LDS leaders' willingness to guarantee favorable taxation rates, the appointment of railroad-backed judges, and the continuation of positive corporate relations in the Great Basin. This was not to mention railroad officials' interest in securing the goodwill of church bureaucrats and bishops as a buffer against labor unrest, the likes of which had broken out along the Union Pacific and Missouri Pacific lines in 1886. If Mormons could guarantee these things, Central Pacific agents would work covertly to improve the church's public image, for instance, by pressuring Associated Press writers and major newspapers to place positive portrayals of Utahn culture and to refrain from running derogatory ones. Indeed railroad agents, working as intermediaries for the church, brokered payments as high as ten thousand dollars to several newspapers, promising additional monies if their opinion-swaying efforts yielded admission to the Union. The results were palpable. The tone of reports on Mormons in the *Chicago Times*, the *St. Louis Globe-Democrat*, the *New York Herald*, and other large papers shifted significantly in late 1887 and 1888—precisely the years when Charles Francis Adams Jr. demanded Mormon-friendly revisions to transcontinental guidebooks. As historian Edward Leo Lyman explains, "Never again prior to Utah's admission as a state would there be any appreciable barrage of anti-Mormon press coverage."[23]

The Central Pacific's influence campaign on behalf of Utah statehood was managed largely through the work of railroad lobbyist Isaac Trumbo, from the late 1880s through 1896. Brokering meetings between Stanford, Woodruff, and Cannon in April 1889, for instance, Trumbo revisited with them the idea of publicly committing to the discontinuance of plural marriage as a condition of Utah statehood. For his part Stanford said that he would be willing to go public with his support for the Saints by writing letters to the president and other Washington luminaries. Trumbo would work meanwhile to assure better public relations and political autonomy through multiple religious, literary, political, and corporate media.[24]

On the religious front, Trumbo reached out to Protestant and Catholic newspapers, and—through cash payments as well as political leverage—he secured editorial commitments to the idea that only polygamy stood substantially in the way of Christian fellowship and religious attribution for Mormons. Meanwhile he persuaded national secular periodicals to publish any official statement from the church on the subject of plural marriage and, along with it, a polygamy-free list of Mormon "Articles of Faith."[25] The latter, written in 1842 by Joseph Smith, was reproduced now with an eye to assuaging the concerns and capitalizing on the commitments not only of major Christian denominations but also of friendly tourists like John Codman. (In 1891 Codman lent his voice to the argument that "the original Articles of Faith of the Mormon Church, instead of being repulsive, were such as to meet with favor among the people," and only the subsequent addition of "other doctrines, such as baptism for the dead, and a plurality of wives," made Mormons repellant to most Christians.)[26] Trumbo requested that Joseph F. Smith "read the Articles of Faith out in the tabernacle" following announcement of the Woodruff Manifesto, and he made sure that the basic substance of both articles and manifesto were published in numerous venues throughout October and November 1890.[27]

While preparing key newspapers for the polygamy manifesto, then, and securing approval from them upon its eventual announcement, Trumbo approached also James S. Clarkson, chairman of the Republican National Committee, to win "first a larger tolerance in the Republican party, and finally the active friendship of that party in behalf of justice to [Mormon] people and Statehood for [their] Territory."[28] Together Trumbo and Clarkson convinced other leading Republicans to withdraw any support they may had voiced for the anti-Mormon Liberal Party in Utah and to welcome Mormons into the convention instead. Their condition for such embrace was that church officials work to have Utah enter the Union as a Republican state and therefore send

Republican congressmen to Washington. However, Republican backers were promised more than mere votes on partywide priorities. Trumbo and Clarkson offered key lobbyists, businessmen, and politicians stocks and subcontracts in Mormon railroad projects, which, they said, were sure to pay dividends once statehood and thus financial stability were granted to Utah and thus its church. As with John W. Young before them, Trumbo and Clarkson promoted railroads for statehood and statehood for railroads.[29]

THE LDS CHURCH'S CAMPAIGN FOR STATEHOOD and the alleviation of Edmunds-Tucker regulations was a multipronged affair, extending along several lines and enlisting the support of many. More often than not, these lines were railroad lines. And these supporters, when not outright lobbyists or railroad investors themselves, were people such as James G. Blaine who had been treated to personal tours of Utah's corporate landscape. As George Q. Cannon explained to a Tabernacle audience, Mormon political successes depended upon the backing of Blaine and other political tourists who had been shown firsthand the falsity of Corinnethian complaints and the strength of Mormon industry, when riding railways to and through Utah. "This great railroad that has been constructed across the continent, which has facilitated intercourse with the world, which has enabled hundreds and thousands of the people of the East and West to visit our Territory and see for themselves," has been "one of the best means of educating the public mind correctly in relation to Utah and its people that I know of; it has done more to dissipate this cloud of misrepresentation that has overshadowed us for so long a period than anything else I know of," Cannon said. "It is more difficult at the present time, in consequence of this, that is, this speedy means of intercourse, to circulate those falsehoods and have them receive credence than in past years. I am thankful that this is the case, I have done all in my power to urge public men to visit Utah," and when it came time to oppose anti-Mormon measures or support Utah statehood in Congress, "the men to whom I have gone in the Senate and in the House, have been men who have been in Utah Territory, have come down by the railroad to Salt Lake City, and have seen the city and the people."[30] Mormon statehood, achieved finally with the support of such men in 1896, was a matter of railroading politics throughout the nation.

Among historians, perhaps only Edward Leo Lyman has recognized the extent and importance of railroad lobbying for Utah statehood. Surveying especially Stanford's and Trumbo's work in this regard, Lyman's study of "The Mormon Quest for Statehood" concludes that railroad officials' "efforts to influence positive press treatment of the Mormons were at least impressive in extent and probably a necessary prerequisite to the attainment of the ultimate goal of Utah statehood." The analysis is excellent, and I disagree only with his calling the railroad officials "an unlikely lobby" for Mormonism.[31] They were a very likely lobby indeed, and their work extended well beyond Washington hallways and traditional press outlets. Railroad agents worked across aisles and across genres—in Utah and in Washington, in transcontinental guidebooks as well as in national newspapers—to mainline Mormonism in American politics and popular culture.

A Preface to Politics

Corporate collaboration between church and railroad officials may have delivered Utah statehood in time, but theirs was not an alliance of recent vintage or quick convenience. Rather it was an ongoing project extending some thirty years into the past and more into the future. Moreover even during the church-railroad lobby's moments of greatest perceived peril and failure, for instance, around the Edmunds-Tucker Act, agents from the Union Pacific and Central Pacific were successful—with the likes of author Edwards Roberts if not always Congress and Grover Cleveland—in maintaining a certain status quo of reportage relative to both the "material side" and the "moral side" of Mormondom. As railroad lobbyists worked to achieve Mormons' political autonomy in Utah, railroad reporters worked differently to secure Utah lands for Mormonism and acts of Mormon religious observation. The terms and tone of their writings were by then well honed, and their significance and utility to the LDS Church during such times of transition can hardly be overstated.

Railroad directors, passenger agents, and their approved guides did in the late 1880s what they had always done in Utah. Echoing George A. Crofutt's middling position in his 1870s *Trans-Continental Tourist's Guide*, they claimed to refrain from comment on the nonobvious beliefs, practices, or characters of the Mormons, or they phrased associated critiques in the past tense and subjunctive mood. Meanwhile they pointed visitors and readers instead to visible, material facts of Salt Lake life, such as its mountainous surroundings, urban planning schemes, irrigation systems, and architectural wonders—including some buildings confiscated by the government. Finally they charged them, their readers, with ascertaining the degrees to which such things were necessary to and constitutive of Mormonism, commensurate with or contradictory to religion, and (thus) capable of Mormon retention and/or American incorporation. In these ways railroads and railroad agents developed and retained a discourse whereby the physical environment, stuff, and trappings of Mormondom were evaluated in courts of public opinion, both before and after elements thereof were seized from and returned to the church. Meanwhile the LDS Church found new ways of existing in the spaces between visibility and invisibility, capitalism and communalism, sales and concessions.

In such paradoxical and promotional spaces Mormons successfully weathered the storms of governmental and Corinnethian intervention, transitioning themselves out of the polygamy age into statehood while educating tourists, politicians, and others—including friendly railroad agents—about the terms under which they could be acceptably embraced: as arguably contained, chastened, and cultured, and as arguably American, religious, and modern. Such attributes were exceedingly important, but so too was the fact of their ever-present, ever-available *argumentation* in Utah. Mormons, it was said, were peoples that safely raised questions regarding western cultural progress while securely preserving places for their debate.

Railroad Lenses and the Burtonian Frame

To make religion visible and visitable in Utah, railroad literature developed a distinctive line of sight. Distinctive, but not unprecedented: guidebook writers emulated and amplified a particular genre of prerailroad tourism and ethnography by repopularizing its tone, recasting its guidance, and extending its imagination to a larger traveling public. This genre was perhaps best exemplified by the writings of Sir Richard Francis Burton, who had tried in the 1860s to render intelligible distinctive features of Mormon life without making Mormons themselves seem monstrously 'other.' The new authors framed a similar touristic common ground in Utah by focusing on Mormon geography, Mormon comparability, and Mormon materiality.[32]

When Burton visited "The City of the Saints" in 1860, he was already famous for his covert expedition to Mecca—and soon he would become even more famous for his translation of *The Arabian Nights*.[33] Tourist, ethnographer, linguist, controversialist, and theorist of religion, Burton thought that he could ascertain cultural similarities and common influences across groups in time and space. With respect to Mormonism in Utah—by his account an especially fascinating case of mixed religious motifs—he wrote that

> we find syncretized [there] the Semitic Monotheism, the Persian Dualism, and the Triads and Trinities of the Egyptians and the Hindoos. . . . They are fetichists in their ghostly fancies, their *evestra*, which became souls and spirits. They are Jews in their theocracy, their ideas of angels, their hatred of Gentiles, and their utter segregation from the great brotherhood of mankind. They are Christians inasmuch as they base their faith upon

the Bible, and hold to the divinity of Christ, the fall of man, the atonement, and the regeneration. They are Arians inasmuch as they hold Christ to be "the first of God's creatures," a "perfect creature, but still a creature." They are Moslems in their views of the inferior status of womankind, in their polygamy, and in their resurrection of the material body: like the followers of the Arabian Prophet, they hardly fear death, because they have elaborated "continuation."[34]

Crucially: Burton was not concerned with establishing historical influence or direct transmission between Mormonism and such groups per se. Neither did he want to make Mormonism seem a Frankenstein of mismatched or unstably assembled religious limbs. Rather he wished to make Mormons seem *less* monstrous or, at least, more intelligible to easterners and westerners alike.[35] Burton insisted also that Mormonism's multiplicitous nature ensured its "general and no small importance"—as datum for study and relative self-understanding, if nothing else—to "the religionist . . . as much as the skeptic," as well as to "the philosophic observer," "the statist," and "the politician." Mormonism, said Burton, demanded careful consideration by anyone interested in the past or present of human nature.[36]

While Burton traded freely in the terms of contemporary Orientalism in his translations and travelogues, his was a decidedly complex version thereof. Orientalism itself consisted in a complicated combination of Western fears and fantasies about 'The East,' after all. But unlike most American congressmen at the time, for whom evocations of possible Muslim parallels fueled emphatically anti-Mormon theories and actions, Burton was inclined to a more sympathetic and romantic understanding of Islam, and (thus) also of Mormonism. In general Burton found that Islamiform 'otherness' provided a motif and aesthetic by which to critique and explore alternatives to Western culture's presumptively Victorian prudishness and Protestant antiritualism, not to mention also its celebrations of industrial progress, laissez-faire capitalism, and imperial expansion. In this he was not alone; amateur and professional Islamophiles started to swell the ranks and shape the directives of Masonic orders, home furnishings stores, theaters, and academic departments across Britain and the eastern United States in the late nineteenth century. (It is one of the great paradoxes of the era that their enthusiasm for Eastern languages, literature, dress, dance, architecture, and sexuality partook simultaneously in the exercise and critique of Western cultural and political domination.) Not all of these were as willing as Burton to consider Mormonism in a positive light. But Congress's drive to compare Muslims with Mormons was nevertheless laced with irony, as well as paradox, insofar as it fueled among many the desire to take interest in "the Islam of America."[37]

Just as Richard F. Burton eschewed a brand of anti-Mormon Orientalism elsewhere associated with Justin S. Morrill and his Anti-Bigamy Act, he did not share the predominantly Protestant fixation with the American West, as being a place of special promise and peril, that motivated Lyman Beecher's pleas and Sheldon Jackson's missions. Nevertheless Burton *was* particularly interested in the nature of the American West itself as it related—he thought—to Mormonism's own religious peculiarities and parallels. Frontier Orientalism, as practiced by Burton, was a materially attentive comparative practice concerned especially with the geographies of culture and the cultures of geography. Burton effectively popularized emergent 'environmentalist' theories of religion whereby people's beliefs, practices, and properties were considered intimately—sometimes dependently—related to topography and climate.[38]

To be clear about my own argumentative trajectory, by way of Burton: I do not doubt the direct proportionality of anti-Mormon hostility and Orientalist interpretation diagnosed elsewhere by historians such as J. Spencer Fluhman.[39] To the contrary, I recognize the importance of that relationship to the phenomena described especially in chapter 1. Nevertheless I am suggesting that frontier and touristic Orientalism—a mobile combination of imperialist exoticization and Enlightenment analysis—simultaneously offered interpretive possibilities less overtly or unidirectionally anti-Mormon, in part by participating in a trend similarly studied by Fluhman: the development of "less theological conceptualizations of religion" capable of giving Mormonism a "place at the table of American religions."[40] Tourism, including many Orientalist modes thereof, coincided with the retheorizing of materials and geographies in and around religion. And Burton was crucial to the development of *this* line of inquiry.[41]

Following Burton's lead in this respect, railroad guides commonly compared the Great Basin, and Mormonism, to lands of ancient religious significance and the cultures supposedly rooted there. They catered, moreover, to an audience eager to emulate Burton himself and excited by the fact that, in the words of one traveler, "the Trans-Continental Railroad has brought within easy reach a land as full of fascination as ever the scenes of Arabian Nights were to our youthful ears." Trains opened worlds ripe with sensory possibilities: of sights and sounds both modern and nostalgic, and of opportunities for the physical approximation (if not sensual embrace) of religious Others. It was a presumptively robust environment, this new 'West,' expectations for which remained high notwithstanding the variously subdued and exuberant articulations of the same travel writers. Railroads carried clients pleased by the notion that modern means had enabled modern people (in the previously cited traveler's words) to "see the curiosities" and observe "freaks of nature" for themselves.[42]

With regard to some questions implicit in such expectations, however, most guidebook authors catered to their audience obliquely and strategically. They did not say whether Mormons were themselves freaks of nature or whether religion was a freakish or natural thing to find in modernity. They did not dwell on Mormon polygamy, either, even though 'harems' and 'Asiatic sexualities' preoccupied youthful Orientalists and peripatetic comparativists alike. And they did not posit exact genealogical relations between peoples or places. But in all senses they hinted at analytical possibilities yielded through comparison of Utah's arid lands and salty waters to others in the Middle East. Railroads continually moved geography and environment to the forefront of religious consideration, circumscribing sensory expectations while connecting sites of excitement. And in this respect, too, they followed Burton.

RAILROAD AUTHORS' Burtonian inheritance was most obvious in their descriptions of Weber and Echo Canyons, the gorges through which trains entered Utah from the East. Indeed guidebook authors sometimes found occasion to cite their travel-writing predecessor directly and explicitly, then—especially when narrating the moments when the Great Salt Lake or its surrounding valleys came into view. Looking down on "the Holy Valley of the West" from Emigration Canyon in 1860, Burton had written that "the pilgrim emigrants, like the hajjis of Mecca and Jerusalem, give vent [there] to the emotions long pent up within their bosoms by sobs and tears, laughter and congratulations, psalms and hysterics. It is indeed no wonder that . . . the ignorant should fondly believe that the 'Spirit of God pervades the very atmosphere,' and that Zion on the tops of the mountains is nearer heaven than other parts of the earth."[43] A few train era guides reproduced this passage in its entirety, albeit relocating the occasion of its statement and sentiment from Emigration Canyon, where the railroads did not run, to Weber and Echo Canyons, where they did. Others also altered Burton's words slightly in order to raise the specter of Mormons' biblical literalism in the context of comprehensible religious experience. ("They give vent to their joy . . . firmly believing they had found . . . the 'Zion of the Mountains' predicted by ancient prophets," said one writer. "The Mormons are great on literal interpretation," but here at least "they had reasons for being enchanted," because "the view is simply magnificent.") Regardless, guidebooks retained Burton's topographical sentimentality and notion of taxonomic overlap—or similarity—between Mormonism, Islam, and Judaism.[44]

Railroad writers developed Burton's geographical sensibility by suggesting that religious response was a natural, if sometimes volatile and problematic, reaction to the peculiar beauty of Salt Lake Valley and the Wasatch Mountains. Consider further one guidebook's description of Weber Canyon. It feels like "the portal to some enchanted region," the author wrote. In this respect it was characteristic of a broader Rocky Mountain environment in which "everywhere there is something to arrest the eye, to strike the imagination, and to remind one of the wisdom and infinite power of the Architect who built up the mountain-crests and rent their sides with profoundest chasms."[45] But there was something especially impressive—and especially pedagogical—about Utahn valleys and canyons; they embodied, in paradigmatic and provocative form, a combination of awe, sublimity, and "curiosity."[46] Echo and Weber Canyons, in particular, were full of rocks jumbled, cracked, or eroded such that many assumed "a supernatural likeness to something not in the least heavenly." Among "towers and spires, turrets and domes," for example, there were the so-called Witches Rocks, which, "weird and wild-looking" as they were, bore "a fanciful resemblance to those dreaded and much-abused 'powers' of a dark age of ignorance and superstition."[47] Utah could be—or could be imagined to be—the natural home to religious sentiments both lofty and low, heavenly and superstitious.

With respect to religion and emotional response, Utahn topographies were considered to be predictably affective even if unpredictably effective. Railroads expected that some travelers, by focusing on the sublime, would reflect deeply upon divine wisdom, infinite power, grace, beauty, or the like, even as they imagined that others, by focusing on the curious, might have shallower experiences, perhaps investing rocks with more superstitious attributes.[48] In any case canyon encounters afforded modern travelers insights into the forms and functions of religious sentiment, as tourists were invited to imagine other people, in times near and far, having similar reactions in the same places.

Affirming Mormonism's relevance to global religious politics and projects of ethnographic comparison, trains taught tourists safely to 'play Mormon,' guiding them to precipices of supposed saintly significance, while also teaching them to 'play ethnographic,' recalling for them the importance of comparison amid pilgrimage and exploration. In both respects guidebook writers evoked Burton's lineage and legacy, but they also stretched its topographical foci in strategic ways—especially when it came time to narrate Mormons' 1847 trek through these and nearby Wasatch canyons in (what they claimed was) greater historical detail. Suggesting, with Burton, that it was 'only natural' that Mormons would have questionably religious experiences in such places, guidebook authors implied, moreover, that Brigham Young paused there to preach to his westward-bound followers. Indeed they pointed tourists to the precise place

Pulpit Rock, showing "mouth of Echo Canon where it is said Brigham Young preached his first Sermon in Utah." (Stereoview by William Henry Jackson, 1869; courtesy of Special Collections and Archives, Merrill-Cazier Library, Utah State University, Logan [Nineteenth-Century Western Stereo-View Collection, 1865–1899])

of that presumptive pause: Pulpit Rock, situated between Echo and Weber Canyons at Echo City, approximately thirty miles west of the Wyoming-Utah border.

There is no evidence whatsoever that Pulpit Rock, so named because of its shape, was the site of Brigham Young's "first Sermon in Utah" or that he "held forth to his flock from this rock during [Mormons'] pilgrimage hither." But that is precisely what railroad agents claimed, in reports and promotions dating as early as 1869 and extending through the 1890s.[49] There are several possible motives for suggesting this (see further below), but the simplest is that the re-signification of Pulpit Rock captured tourists' imagination and allowed for the better signposting of religion and religious expression in the West. Guidebook writers urged among travelers a refocusing on Mormonism itself there, in anticipation of Salt Lake arrivals. Moreover, they did so while planting particular and Burtonian seeds of inquiry. Were Brigham Young's words, imaginatively situated atop a fantastic rock amid an otherwise striking scenery, themselves lofty and divine or curious and superstitious? In Mormonism, did a godly but strange environment effect responses that were more godly than strange or more strange than godly?

No matter their inclination to respond along these lines, railroads built observation decks and pulled special observation cars from which tourists could

As early as 1870, Union Pacific overland trains attached special observation cars for the Echo and Weber Canyon portion of their journeys. In 1887 the company introduced special "Pullman Vestibuled" cars on its "Overland Flyer" passenger train, with advertisements highlighting Echo Canyon vistas and landmarks. Passengers not content with observing Pulpit Rock from inside their cars sometimes stood on the rear decks of their trains, as pictured in this postcard from ca. 1910. (Author's collection)

experience religion or conceive of experience, at Pulpit Rock. Porters even wakened slumbering passengers lest they miss it.[50] "Pulpit Rock . . . is on our right hand; we can almost touch it," exclaimed one 1888 Union Pacific guidebook, its first-person-plural narration stressing the shared nature of the experience of wondering about Mormon experience there.[51]

Stereographic Vision at Pulpit Rock

Just as overland travelers lingered over Pulpit Rock, so might we, in order better to see how railroad agents trained tourists to perceive of natural and technological sublimity there instead of the labor of their production. Pulpit Rock offers a paradigmatic example of the corporate mechanisms of Mormon imagination and religious placement in the railroad era West. Materialized through the stereoscopic observation, ritual activity, reading practices, and scrapbook making of everyday tourists in the West, Pulpit Rock both attracted and escaped their critical attention in ways that can help us recalibrate our own.

Among the most innovative accounts of temporal and spatial perception in the railroad age is Wolfgang Schivelbusch's *Railway Journey*. In it Schivelbusch claims that, not only did railways destroy nature, rearrange landforms, and divorce transportation from any organic relationship to topography, but they traveled so quickly over the spaces they destroyed that travelers paid little attention to the journey itself. Unlike when walking, horseback riding, wagoning, boating, or the like, traveling by rail necessitated neither real relationships nor real work; it consisted rather in 'time to kill' by reading, sleeping, or otherwise distracting oneself. Crucially, though: insofar as people *did* look out their train windows, they saw things only in a panoramic way, with a blurred foreground and an undifferentiated background. "The Panoramic," an increasingly pervasive mode and medium of perception in the nineteenth century, was characterized then not by discrete landforms but by their aggregate, and by "the tendency to see the discrete indiscriminately."[52]

I see railroads, in the United States, making selective efforts to complement or counteract the tendency to panoramic vision by finding new things to foreground—pictorially, discursively, and analytically—for their passengers. This is to say that Schivelbusch isn't quite right about panoramic perception as operative in the American context, or really about the time of travel as being a time of geographical inattention. Transcontinental journeys were lengthy affairs—in 1881 the trip from Omaha to Ogden took between fifty-four and ninety-two hours, depending on ticket class—and the productive occupation of people's time was a crucial object of concern. The mechanisms by which industrialists, travel agents, and guidebook writers then occupied it—and, arguably, by which they put travelers to work—might productively concern also modern historians and theorists of culture, insofar as they consisted in religion making. By this I mean not only to point to Sunday services and sermons being staged in Pullman cars across the country or to the fact that such cars aimed to replicate and express the aesthetics of bourgeois or upper-class domesticity.⁵³ I am more interested in how railroad agents selectively foregrounded arguably religious sites and sights from their surroundings and created new rituals around them.

Consider some of the principal media of perceptive occupation in and for the railroad age. The most popular books for sale along railroad routes in the Americas—not coincidentally also the ones railroads made most available—were railroad guides and travel narratives. Not only did this literature give travelers an opportunity to read about themselves and others like them, reading about themselves and others like them reading, but it asked travelers to pay attention to specific objects, in the foreground of their voyage, attaching to them special significance and weaving around them certain narratives.⁵⁴ Then, too, railroad companies sponsored and sold collections of stereoscope cards, designed to allow people to focus simultaneously at objects in the foreground and the background, in a virtual three-dimensional space, thus allowing them alternately to take surrogate tours from the comforts of their armchairs, to revisit scenes that they just sped past in real time, or to recall those scenes, along with the accompanying narratives from their guidebooks, well after the journey was complete.⁵⁵ Finally, rather than speeding indiscriminately over land or trapping travelers in the confines of their own tiny compartments, railroads built observation platforms for interested travelers to get a closer look at the things that they were told to be interested in.

Pulpit Rock is as good a place as any to linger and watch all of these dynamics and mechanisms—rails, guidebook accounts, stereographic representation, and observation-deck gatherings—converge around an object of supposed religious importance. Indeed it is a far better place than most, precisely because this stretch of land at the foot of Echo Canyon *was*, in fact, a very important locus in Mormon history—albeit for decidedly different reasons than the railroads claimed. Readers will recall that Echo City was one of the first worksites for Mormon laborers on the transcontinental railroad; some of their earliest graded beds weren't much more than a stone's throw from Pulpit Rock. This, then, was the very area at which the LDS Church and the Union Pacific christened a corporate relationship that would in time shape the entire West by frustrating secular aspirations, framing sectarian debates, catalyzing ecclesiastical initiatives, altering congressional actions, inciting public interest in Mormonism, and paving a path toward Utahn statehood.

Readers will also recall that Echo Canyon was where Mormon militiamen constructed rocky fortifications during the 1857–58 Utah War, some eleven years before Mormons shook hands there with a new class of men sent similarly by Congress to solve the Mormon problem. Though unkempt and eroded, some of these fortifications were still visible from the train line. Neither Mormon nor Gentile laborers had knocked them all down when working to ensure the gently sloped connection of Utah with the East.[56]

What was at stake in ignoring these particular pasts and places in favor of a story about a nearby rock formation? Not only did it hide the fact of mutual investment with a facade of technological neutrality, but it served overlapping interests among LDS churchmen, transcontinental companies, and experience-seeking tourists in associating Mormon religious experience with Utahn landforms and their premodern encounters. Meanwhile, by highlighting Pulpit Rock as the landform of primary concern in this respect, railroads pushed passengers to consider Echo Canyon and its surroundings less as places of anti-Mormon memory than as stages of the sublime. I do not mean to imply that the tale of Brigham Young's rocktop sermon was purposefully fabricated to obfuscating ends, necessarily. Its origins were likely more happenstance; Pulpit Rock, looking as it did, just happened to be there, along the railway route into Utah, at a place where the road grade necessitated that railroads slow down and where they often stopped to refuel.[57] All of this was reason enough for a story, and that story took hold in and through the photographic and descriptive work of railroad employees such as William Henry Jackson. Nevertheless its effects were clear: Mormon Utah was presented as a world before and beyond railroad time and space, a world to which—paradoxically—only right railroads would provide right access and proper perspective.

PULPIT ROCK WAS A FAVORITE subject of stereocard sets and guidebooks documenting the transcontinental train route, usually presented with the same basic storyline. This was where Mormons stopped, during their hard trek across the country; it is where Brigham Young, inspired by an environment simultaneously sublime and severe, godly and yet eerie, decided that Utah would be Mormonism's place of respite. In a sense this served as a railroading version of the also mythical story about Brigham Young having declared, "This is the Place!" at Emigration Canyon, some two days' walk from the railroad line. Emigration Canyon became a place of pilgrimage for some Mormons, whereas Pulpit Rock was promoted as a Mormon place of and for Gentile in-sight.

Tourists were consistently compelled to observation and commentary at Pulpit Rock, if not also acts of clear or innovative reflection. Overland travelers often clipped images of Pulpit Rock and Echo Canyon from transcontinental guidebooks, timetables, or advertisements for stereocard sets—overlapping genres of railroad literature, these—and pasted them into their diaries and scrapbooks. Yet some offered little by way of personal reflection to accompany such visuals. For instance, one 1874 diarist, though carefully cutting (from a Union and Central Pacific timetable) and rearranging images to match the order of his own encounter, offered no further commentary save for notes on the grade of the tracks; a different 1874 traveler wrote only that one Weber Canyon attraction "does not look much like the picture" in his guidebook.[58] A later tourist, having traveled to Utah in 1883, made copious notes next to clipped images of Echo and Weber Canyon scenes, but they were nearly verbatim transcriptions of accounts offered in three Union Pacific guidebooks. Indeed this last traveler, John G. Hunt of New York, seems to have composed his scrapbook well after his trip, and a vast majority of his sentences about Utah were derived directly from these books. As for Pulpit Rock, Hunt transcribed the promotional narrative in full: "Pulpit Rock [is] famous the world over," he wrote. "Brigham Young preached from it his first sermon in Utah, addressed to the pioneers then on their way to Salt Lake Valley in 1847." It "was on our right and we could almost touch it." This visitor made this railroad story his own, in retrospect if not also in the moment.[59]

Other travelers may have been more critical of Mormonism and Mormon religious experiences in Echo Canyon, but they frequently assumed the validity of railroad guidebooks' geographical focus and storylines as well. Consider William Cullen Bryant's 1874 travelogue *Picturesque America*. Reaching for iconoclastic critique, Bryant managed merely to alter the tone of guidebooks' own call to discern Mormon religious legitimacy in situ at Pulpit Rock. Meanwhile he strengthened popular associations of Mormonism with Utahn topographies and reinforced railroads' own importance as purveyors of unique religious vision in modernity.

"Brigham Young spoke to his deluded hundreds after their long pilgrimage, and pointed out to them that they approached their Canaan—preach[ing] the Mormons' first sermon in the 'Promised Land,'" Bryant wrote, in a relatively bleak but otherwise untroubled version of the then standard script. Inviting his readers to picture a "multitude of fanatics, stranger than all [the] strangeness" of the land itself, "standing on its varied floor and looking up at the speaking prophet," Bryant contrasted—and celebrated—his own ability to look upon that environment through the "window of a whirling railway-car." Railroad comforts protected tourists from the exhaustion and confusion likely felt by earlier migrants there, he suggested, and so too from their susceptibility to overwhelming emotions. Still: could not modern train riders visualize there a "weary multitude of half-excited, half-stolid faces turned toward the preacher," who issued "wild words" from "the long-silent rocks," thus calling out to them from an environment that had so intimately impressed itself upon his own soul? Why, Bryant asked wistfully, "has no one ever pictured for us all of the scene that could be pictured?"[60]

Railroad agents were of course already working to picture precisely that scene and to impress upon visitors the significance of the Pulpit Rock experience. This explains the ubiquity of the sermon story, the production of stereoviews, and the representation of Pulpit Rock on common timetables for overland travel. It explains, too, the invitation to people en route and at home to interact sensually with the terrain, whether by imagining the physical and emotional hardships of others traveling there without the benefit of the railroads, by immersing themselves in a virtual environment, by looking out from train windows or observation decks, or by testing whether "an outstretched arm from the car might touch" the now famous rock.[61]

The terms of Bryant's wistful excitement show that Pulpit Rock viewing was seldom a simple matter of landmark naming or touristic distraction, in any case. Rather it worked to construct and distinguish certain forms of natural sublimity and the technological sublime. Crediting elsewhere "the 'iron horse'" with setting "in motion a train of thought as swift as the locomotive," Bryant argued that railroads had opened people's eyes to the role of "natural scenery" in "developing the love of the beautiful, in refining the taste, and in cultivating the imagination" while (or perhaps better: because) simultaneously allowing them to alter and transform nature by developing its resources, cultivating it to ultimate aesthetic effect, and otherwise loosening its dependent hold on human emotions and economics. The American West was ripe with natural beauty, Bryant said, but the mountains and canyons of eastern Utah were not a prime example. To the contrary, "Nature's constructions" there were "at once weird, sublime, and grotesque," and more than one sight had "nothing sublime about it." Mormon emigrants, spiritually confused and physically fatigued as they were in 1847, failed always to distinguish among them and consequently found often a reflection and an amplification, especially in the aptly named Echo Canyon, of their own hybridic strangeness. Modern travelers by contrast possessed the appropriate frames—railcar windows, stereographs, comparative data, and hindsight—by which to differentiate the grotesque from the sublime in both nature and culture.[62]

Bryant may have dissented from guidebooks' appraisals of alpine beauty in Utah, but he nevertheless embraced railroads' accompanying claims to modern sensibility and industrial salvation from the strictures of premodern affect. For him too, then, Pulpit Rock became a site of and for religious reflection, even as he failed to recognize its thoroughgoing corporate construction to that end. Bryant stood there in judgment of Mormonism, without realizing that railroads had offered him precisely the platform of that possibility.

Sights, Scenes, and Scrapbooks

Guidebook writers directly backed by railroads, such as Edwards Roberts, avoided Bryant's dismissive tone respecting Utah's natural beauty and religious potential, tending instead toward positivity or ambivalence. Nevertheless they shared and shaped alike its sense of topographical sentimentality and the intimate relationship between western environments and Mormon expressions, and thus also its promotion of certain landmarks as sites for religious comparison and ethnographic consideration. Railroads effectively subcontracted the task of critique to their riders, even as they delimited its concerns. And thus railroads, in inventing Pulpit Rock and demanding acts of continuous industrial and humanistic investment there, anticipated and even desired reactions such as Bryant's.

What is more, though, railroad agents found ways to incorporate such reactions back into their own promotional narratives, even when they were overtly critical. The Union Pacific guidebook *Sights and Scenes in Utah for Tourists* (1888), for instance, reproduced an entire paragraph of Bryant's prose, without attribution, when touting the "really pastoral" beauty of the valley around Echo City, wherein travelers were likely to see their first Mormon homes dotting the land. About that valley, Bryant had written that "only the great outlines of the surrounding hills, and here and there the appearance on the horizon of some sharper, higher, more distant peaks, show the traveler his whereabouts, and take his mind from the quieter aspect of what lies about him. Near by, in valleys leading into this, are various Mormon settlements; for we are already in the country of the saints." Changing only the word "already" to "nearly" in the final clause—thereby retaining a sense of ongoing anticipation—*Sights and Scenes* also omitted Bryant's immediately preceding critique of Pulpit Rock's supposed sublimity. Similarly, the guidebook removed an accompanying suggestion that tourists look for the rocky remainders of Echo Canyon fortifications from the Utah War and that they recall thereby Mormons' former and perhaps ongoing threat to American safety. *Sights and Scenes* contained instead a short mention of the same fortifications in a different section, where it wouldn't distract from attention to Pulpit Rock, and it reassured readers that "since 1857 things have changed," thanks to the railroad, and "now we smile that we ever thought" Mormons were dangerous. The result of these omissions and removals was that Bryant's relatively affirming words could appear near the guidebooks' Echo Canyon and Pulpit Rock narrative, as a continuation of it. Bryant's prose read in that context as a positive appraisal of Mormon environments, as well as a commiserating text for railroads' erstwhile Burtonian echoes.[63] "It is no wonder that" Mormons "should fondly believe that the 'Spirit of God pervades the very atmosphere,'" after passing through Echo Canyon into valleys that Bryant himself described as stunning.⁶⁴ Right? Such was the sense left by railroad authors after they had cut Bryant's criticisms and pasted his adjacent writings back into the narrative that had inspired him to critique in the first place.

Sights and Scenes made Bryant ventriloquize anew the touristic invitation to keep appraising, in unresolved but resolute perpetuity, the connections between Mormon social patterns and the experiences that supposedly preceded and supported them. This was a decidedly strategic and indeed political editorial intervention, especially given the timing of its publication; *Sights and Scenes* circulated in 1888, in the immediate wake of the Edmunds-Tucker Act, the same year that Charles Francis Adams Jr. urged Edwards Roberts to soften his critical appraisal of Mormonism. Railroad agents wished to ensure that tourists continued their travels to Salt Lake City and that they did so in a state of sustained situational excitement, to seek further the nature of religion there.

JAMES G. HUNT, the aforementioned scrapbooker who reimagined his 1883 tour with help from later railroad publications, used *Sights and Scenes* as one of his principal sources. Thus *Sights and Scenes* became fodder for the clipping of later travelers, just as its writers had clipped components of preceding travel narratives for themselves. At each point citations were omitted, and storylines were rendered at once generically descriptive and yet amenable to acts of highly personal association or rereading. This was no doubt the design. But Hunt's archival remains show us that even the most individual of documentary acts—scrapbook making and diary writing, for instance—sometimes strayed little beyond the imaginary bounds and incorporative loops of the generic. Hunt did not push back in the direction of Bryant, let alone in any direction more antithetical to guidebook accounts. Rather he contented himself by clipping and transcribing things from *Sights and Scenes* and two other commiserating texts, and his improvisations were largely limited to occasions of omission or decisions to toggle among them. This is not surprising, even as it is significant. Guidebooks may have demanded from their readership certain reflections and judgments respecting Mormon experiential veracity or legitimacy in the Wasatch Mountains, but they structured simultaneously against innovation by continually delimiting its bounds.⁶⁵ By repeatedly resetting their own narratives through acts of critical incorporation or omission, guidebooks worked to ensure that few responses would stray far from their tracks or sound beyond their own echo chambers. By catalyzing but also reincorporating critiques such as Bryant's, guidebooks ensured and sourced scrapbooking actions also like Hunt's.

Hunt may have personified a strategically generic form, but his occasional strays from *Sights and Scenes*—moments where Hunt declined to transcribe particular sentences, for instance, or when he elected to paste parts of another guidebook instead—may be read for meaning. The fact that Hunt fully copied the paragraph that *Sights and Scenes* had itself copied from Bryant, without, however, copying the guidebook's further dismissal of Mormon hostilities in the Utah War, could indicate either a disinclination to defend the Saints or a disinterest in the entire matter. In any case it would be a mistake to consider such variations as the only occasions of authorial agency and power, in scrapbooks, or to read agency itself only in the key of resistance, as if scissor-handed acts always of railing against the machine. Hunt's scrapbooking and similar acts of touristic imagination were powerful in part *because* they reproduced and played with key aspects of railroad agents' structuring narrative and mythology.

Scrapbook keepers act as quintessential bricoleurs, in the sense described by Claude Lévi-Strauss, insofar as they save, reassemble, and reflect upon scraps of cultural argumentation, variously cutting with or against the grain of their own associations and differentiations. "Consider [a bricoleur] at work," writes Lévi-Strauss. "His first practical step is retrospective. He has to turn back to an already existent set made up of tools and materials, to consider or reconsider what it contains and, finally and above all, to engage in a sort of dialogue with it and, before choosing between them, to index the possible answers which the whole set can offer to his problem." Any such answer, however, will be constrained in part by "the particular history of each piece and by those of its features which are already determined by the use for which it was originally intended." Lévi-Strauss argues that, while bricolage is an act of playful world creation, only certain play is possible at any given time. Play happens in the scrapbooked spaces between images clipped from sources that have their own histories elsewhere.[66]

Railroad tourism is itself a matter of limited movement and structured improvisation, and scrapbooking—second only to guidebook reading or stereocard viewing among popular media of en route attention and post hoc recollection—is similar. Many scrapbook bricoleurs like Hunt managed, even after taking different guidebooks and promotional pamphlets under the knife, to reproduce key aspects of their structuring narrative and mythology. Nevertheless they did important work. Even as they were compelled to do so by cultural imperatives to discourse, (dis)placement, and travel—and even as their

A page from an 1874 railroad scrapbook, containing images clipped from a transcontinental timetable. These images associated Mormon religious expressions with Great Basin environments, and they framed Salt Lake City encounters relative to canyon perceptions as well. ([Unknown,] "Diary of a Voyage," 1874–75; courtesy of Beinecke Rare Book and Manuscript Library, Yale University, New Haven, Conn.)

clippings contained, still, the structural inertia of history and bureaucratic interests—many tourists created significant theories, artifacts, and continuations of religion. And in Hunt's case they strengthened by internalization guidebooks' interpretive associations between Great Basin environments and Mormon religion.[67]

In the City

Once travelers reached Salt Lake City—once they were more fully ensconced in the ostensibly natural environment of Mormonism, that is—they were guided through Mormonism's built environment. Here the search for religion assumed new urgency if not new direction, as tourists looked for additional expressions of a religiosity already associated with geography. Motivated by the notion that it could be everywhere or nowhere, with senses shaped by the guidebooks that they kept close at hand, visitors sought signs of religion in Mormon architecture, infrastructure, and urban planning.

Edwards Roberts's *Shoshone, and Other Western Wonders* is a valuable guide to late 1880s expectations and prescriptions for touristic interest in the Mormon capital, forged as it was in the crucible of Adams's railroading feedback. What is more, comparison between Roberts's early drafts and his approved copy yields unique insights into how railroad agents sought synthesis between anti-Mormon literature and Mormon apologetics by structuring expectations around particular structures, and by encouraging debate and speculation there about (in Roberts's words) the "strange commingling of the beautiful and the commonplace" along with the unappealing and the unknown.[68]

Roberts's own portrayal of this commingling seems to have shifted either as a condition or consequence of railroad patronage. Consider his original description of the Salt Lake Tabernacle. Every Sunday "the upholders of the Mormon church indulge in invective against all Gentiles and the Government to their heart's content," Roberts wrote, and "any newly-arrived Gentile" there inevitably "experiences a curious feeling, and he can hardly understand at first why all the treasonable and seditious talk is allowed by [the] Government." Such statements would have been at home in J. H. Beadle's writings or similar works of atrocity tourism. No doubt this was among the sections to which Adams objected, in his 1888 letter to Roberts, for fear that it would be "offensive to the Mormons" who had "always been civil" and "always paid their bills." The paragraph was consequently cut from the final, Union Pacific–backed publication, amid otherwise retained statements about Tabernacle design, seating capacity, and acoustics.[69] Other than its massive organ and fixed pulpits, *Shoshone* treated the Tabernacle as if a shell to be filled mainly with meaning by Mormon hosts or their scrapbooking Gentile guests.

In this respect *Shoshone* was typical of Union Pacific literature at the time. While some popular guides warned visitors that they, like W. W. Ross before them, were likely to encounter a mixture of mundane and lofty conversations in Tabernacle addresses ("Every possible thing, secular or spiritual, is discussed from the pulpit which the president thinks necessary for the instruction of the flock," said one),[70] others, like *Shoshone*, made no mention whatsoever of Mormon sermonic content. Writers of both types avoided judgments respecting the right relation of things 'mundane' and 'spiritual' in Mormonism and religion proper, in any case. But literature of the *Shoshone* sort especially ensured that, at the Tabernacle if not also Pulpit Rock, the loudest voices and clearest echoes would be generated by Mormons themselves.[71]

Railroads contracted directly with Mormon transportation companies and tour guides to guarantee as much, as well. In 1888 and 1889, Adams's Union Pacific and its rival, the Denver & Rio Grande, both struck deals with the recently established Grant Brothers Livery Company, whereby its carriage drivers

Visitors at the Salt Lake Temple construction site, ca. 1890, in carriages operated by the Grant Brothers Livery Company. (Photograph by Sainsbury and Johnson; courtesy of the Church History Library, The Church of Jesus Christ of Latter-day Saints, Salt Lake City [PH 3732])

received preferential treatment at railroad stations in Salt Lake City. Founded by a future LDS Church president and his siblings, Heber J. Grant's company competed against Gentile hackmen and their tendency to peddle Beadle-esque atrocity tours of Salt Lake's "whited sepulchres." Members of the First Presidency approved up to sixteen thousand dollars in seed money to the company in 1888, to that end: "The livery stable is one of the agencies that has been used against us to a great extent. Tourists have been stuffed with falsehood by carriage drivers and create a great deal of prejudice against us. It has been felt that this should be corrected and this appropriation was made with the hope that it would sustain this livery stable and that they might be able to get this business."[72] Grant Brothers Livery used its many carriages, including one capable of carrying forty persons, to carry tourists directly to the Tabernacle and Temple Block, where they might supplement *Shoshone*'s scant description with personal reflections.

In 1889 LDS officials placed Joseph C. Kingsbury at the east gate of the Temple Block, to greet such visitors and guide them through the Tabernacle.

According to Kingsbury's biographer, he "explained the doctrines of the Church and related the history of the Saints," but unfortunately there is little record of his principal talking points. The seventy-eight-year-old Kingsbury, having numbered among the original emigrants of 1847, seems mainly to have pointed to himself, relative to the built environment of Temple Block, as representative of Mormon history. Recounting Mormon pioneer experience in the Salt Lake Valley, Kingsbury taught tourists to wonder at all that Mormons had wrought in the supposedly once-barren lands around them. In the past fifty years Mormons had platted communities, planted trees, built tabernacles, and produced the material and agricultural yields on display there and at the Deseret Museum. Within a few years they would also finish construction of the Salt Lake Temple, and—while outsiders would not generally be granted access to its interior—one of Kingsbury's colleagues was willing to accompany them to the top of its scaffolding, for a bird's-eye view of Mormon civic order.[73]

Edwards Roberts included an image of the unfinished Temple, with scaffolding, in his *Western Wonders*, and many railroad-backed guides (including *Sights and Scenes*) printed sketches of its projected form as well. The analysis was primarily formal, in any case: guidebooks spoke mostly of the Temple's unique outer design, using architectural nouns familiar from preceding Weber Canyon descriptions. (Its "towers and turrets" are to be "of a very complex order," reported Crofutt in 1871, and "its architecture is purely Gothic," echoed Roberts in 1888.) But relative to canyon chapters they kept implications of witchcraft off the page, here. Guidebooks spoke of Temple matters external and observable, since non-Mormons couldn't get inside. And their discussions were short.[74]

So too respecting the Endowment House, from which outsiders were also excluded: guidebook writers were encouraged to leave interior speculations to their clients, perhaps in consultation with writings of a different sort, the likes of which they then framed skeptically. Roberts's descriptions are again representative. Before Adams's intervention, Roberts wrote that "so many" "polygamous marriages are performed" in the Endowment House, in ceremonies that "are generally regarded as mysterious" despite "several exposures, purporting to be absolutely true." After Adams's intervention, Roberts cut one reference to polygamy, phrased the other in the past tense, and exchanged mentions of "mystery" and "exposures" for a more general warning: "It is questionable how much reliance may be placed in the stories which from time to time have been given the believing public." Roberts still encouraged his readers to "stand outside and imagine what there is within," but he cautioned against considering someone like J. H. Beadle or even Fanny Stenhouse a credible guide.[75]

Lest the fact and function of Mormon buildings still seem scary, all Tabernacle assurances notwithstanding, the next stop on the guidebook-prescribed and Grant Brothers–assisted carriage tour stood to assuage certain concerns by giving space for others. This was Brigham Young's grave, situated on a hill overlooking Temple Block and the Beehive House, Lion House, and Gardo House (otherwise known as Amelia's Palace), a Victorian mansion used as presidential parsonage after Brigham Young's death in 1877. The Union Pacific allowed Edwards Roberts's criticisms to stand, here: "Brigham Young was a good deal of an autocrat in his day, and loved ease and comfort better, possibly, than he did his numerous wives," Roberts wrote. "Looking to-day at the home he occupied, with its large porch in front, its three stories, its dormer windows, suggestive of many rooms, one tries to imagine what his life at home was like, and what his power was. But there the 'palace' stands, with its windows all intact; and Brigham sleeps hard by, at rest at last, whether he was in life or not." Similarly reporting that "of the Mormon prophet himself nothing remains of his vast possessions but the lot wherein he lies buried," *Sights and Scenes* confirmed that, if ever there was an autocratic and power-hungry aspect to Mormon life, it had died with the pioneering church president. The buildings seen from Brigham's grave were inhabited either by a folksier remnant of the pioneer class, like Joseph Kingsbury, or by a different generation of Latter-day Saints entirely.[76]

Left unsaid by these and other railroad guides of the Edmunds-Tucker era was a related reason for looking upon the Temple Block and Gardo House, in particular, from the vantage of Brigham Young's grave. These properties had been confiscated by the government in late 1887, per terms of the Edmunds-Tucker Act, and they were returned to the church only after the Woodruff Manifesto of 1890. In the interim Saints retained full access—the church leased back the Temple Block and the Gardo House for one and seventy-five dollars per month, respectively—but they also stopped construction on the Temple, awaiting guarantees of long-term stability. Thus when the Grant Brothers and Union Pacific encouraged tourists to attend Tabernacle services, climb Temple scaffolding, and stand at Brigham Young's grave, they challenged them also to discern whether Mormons' supposed sedition was a thing of the past. Did modern Saints, changed and chastened as they were by the railroad era and now the Edmunds-Tucker Act, deserve to keep and keep building such supposedly religious structures? Heber J. Grant moved to protect other Mormon properties by other means, for instance, through stock sales or shifts in official ownership, but he rightly perceived that the fate of Temple Block was better tried in courts of touristic interest, in continuing collaboration with the Union Pacific. Here as elsewhere—in built environments as in natural ones—they asked: How and where did Mormonism rightly reside in Utah?[77]

The Exposition Car

If railroad guides refrained from public statements on the propriety of Mormon properties like the Gardo House, Temple, and Tabernacle—and if they encouraged tourists to attend Tabernacle services without classifying their sermonic content—company officials did, however, help Salt Lake City merchants preach a message of Utahn natural abundance and productive Mormon stewardship, on the road. In 1888 the Union Pacific donated a multiwindowed observation car to the Salt Lake City Chamber of Commerce—many of whose leading members, including John W. Young, had worked with and contributed to the Deseret Museum—to carry and stage museum-esque displays along railroad lines across the country. Chamber and LDS Church alike heralded the launch of the Utah Exposition Palace Car as a "mission" to the East, and the language was not misplaced. Whereas some denominations outfitted chapel cars for evangelism along the rails later in the 1890s, Mormons boasted a mineral- and produce-packed observation car and a gospel of Saintly nature.[78]

Taking charge of car decorations and promotions, H. L. A. Culmer commissioned paintings of Wasatch Mountain views and Salt Lake sunsets for its walls, and he outfitted the car with large display cases for specimens of Utahn mineral resources (marble, iron, gold, silver, lead, salt), agricultural yields (grains, grass, flour, fruit), and home manufactures (clothing, silk). Culmer also stocked it with thousands of copies of chamber of commerce publications including *The Western Wonderland!* (a thirty-two-page pamphlet bound between railroad advertisements), *Salt Lake City: A Sketch of Utah's Wonderful Resources* (a longer, illustrated version of the same), and editions of the *Salt Lake Journal of Commerce*. A key feature of the journal was an excerpt from Edwards Roberts's writings, approved by the railroads and now incorporated by Salt Lake City boosters. "The Scenery around Salt Lake City" was "full of attractions and curious bits of architecture," it said, along with "poetic chips of nature, with scenery full of strange contrasts to that found in Eastern States, and possessed of grandeur—almost sublime beauty."[79]

Transported freely across country by agreement with major railroad companies, the Utah Exposition Palace Car docked for several days at stations in Omaha, Council Bluffs, Milwaukee, Chicago, Buffalo, Troy, and other cities. Culmer's goal, at each stop, was to attract the attention of "leading men"— officers of city boards of trade, mayors, councilmen, professors, and other would-be travelers and investors in Utah—"for whom we send carriages and spare no effort to get them to the car." Such people, he found, were often familiar with Utah only as a land of curiosities and Mormon mischief. But after

The Utah Exposition Palace Car in 1888. (Photograph by Newcomb Studio; courtesy of the Church History Library, The Church of Jesus Christ of Latter-day Saints, Salt Lake City [PH 2826])

seeing the car's displays and listening to his encomiums, Culmer felt sure that he had secured among them "a different kind of notoriety" by making known "the wealth of our resources and climate to those who may hereafter visit us or who may be able to aid us by the investment of capital for the development of our resources."[80]

Culmer claimed great success in his mission on behalf of Utah and Utahn Mormonism's public image. But it was not without conflict or contention, and one review of Culmer's stay in Buffalo shows both the struggles and successes he encountered. "'Why is it,' asked [Culmer], 'that it is so difficult to impress upon the public that life and property are safe in Utah; that the Mormons are not heathens. I have talked and argued with hundreds of people during my trip, and have at times almost become angry at their dense ignorance concerning Utah and the Mormons.'" Culmer's conversation partner offered the following explanation: "To the majority of the people of the east, Utah and the Mormons are as distant and as little the subject of consideration as are the people of India. . . . The telegraph, upon which we rely for all our news, tells us blood-curdling tales of the Apaches and the Mormons, and we shudder as we think of either. Of course we know the Mormons are not Indians, but we think of both in one breath and we know as much of one as we do of the other. . . . We have no means of investigating the matter and we take it as it comes." This, he and other visitors concluded, was why the exposition car's work was so crucial. For those in the East inclined to consider Utah as "simply a curio hall without any natural resources," the car delivered them a different message of exceptional nature and American possibility. Containing "exhibits of the resources of the territory with no freaks nor fossils," it proved rather abundant raw materials by which to reimagine Mormons' place in the modern nation.[81]

REIMAGINATION TOOK PLACE along two primary lines, both of them informed and amplified by railroad promotions. The first, speaking to the aforementioned association of Mormons and American Indians, laid the groundwork—and pointed to the waterworks—by which to differentiate them. The second, speaking to the same writer's likening of Utah to the Indian subcontinent, stressed Utah's likeness to a nearer East instead: Palestine. Supported by the railroads, the Exposition Palace Car offered a vision of Utahn national incorporation premised on Mormons' success in simultaneously identifying, evoking, and transcending ancient landforms at home and abroad.

Among the Salt Lake Chamber of Commerce's publications was one describing Giant's Cave, a site of supposed Native American significance erstwhile popularized and promoted by the Union Pacific. (Giant's Cave was an adjunct attraction for Garfield Beach, a company-backed bathing resort to be described below.) In fact this handout drew most of its description directly from the Union Pacific's increasingly ubiquitous *Sights and Scenes in Utah for Tourists*, thus again demonstrating the influence of railroad literature on the terms of local promotion as well as outside perception. "When the cave was first entered, nearly thirty years ago," that guide claimed and the *Salt Lake Journal of Commerce* repeated, "it was found to contain a quantity of human skeletons."

> Whether the remains belonged to the present race of Indians in the Salt Lake Valley is not known, but probably they did. The skeletons are most likely those of warriors, slain in some Indian fight of long ago. Traditions of fierce combats are still preserved among the Ute tribe, and it was their custom to place the dead in hollow rocks or in caves such as the one we were describing. . . . Thus the cave was evidently a place of sepulcher. . . . Many Indian fights occurred in the neighborhood, if we are to judge from very strong evidence, and this one at the mouth of the cave may have been

the last of many, which resulted in the defeat and extinction of a tribe. . . . The idea of destroying their hiding foes in this awful manner, would be one very likely, indeed, to occur to the mind of the American Indian.[82]

The tone of the report was clear, if its implications for Mormon meaning were somewhat subtler. The supposed "defeat and extinction" of native Utahn tribes was attributed neither to Mormons nor Gentile warfare, here, but rather to ancient Indian infighting. Meanwhile the "present race of Indians in the Salt Lake Valley"—whose existence is seldom noted elsewhere in railroad guides like *Sights and Scenes*, except when commending on the "digger Indians" occasionally "begging" near Mormon settlements and Utahn train stations—is related to this extinct group.[83] More explicitly than the Deseret Museum displays that had preceded them, such writings suggested that Utah's native Ute and Shoshoni populations were dead, dying, or at best barely clinging to the lifelines of modernity, an era for which they were ill equipped at best.

Railroad promoters and Salt Lake boosters joined efforts to make places like Giant's Cave the sites and subjects of their own atrocity tours, focusing on lakeside Indian tombs rather than—to use Anna Dickinson's phrase—the "whited sepulchres" of Salt Lake City. The Union Pacific, the Salt Lake Chamber of Commerce, and their Utah Exposition Palace Car all offered cultured platforms from which to observe a rightly disappearing race: not Mormons, but Indians. Here we see how Mormon apologists aligned themselves and were aligned with white colonial projects, even as they have been made subjects of those same ventures.

All of this pertains closely to railroads' topographical and pastoral fixations and, in turn, to Orientalist alignments of Mormon era Utah with the Middle East. Touristic imaginations of American Indians and Mormonism were similar in certain respects, and yet they diverged in important ways along the rocks and waterways of Salt Lake. At the most basic level, Indians and Mormons were both said to have codependent or reflective relationships with western environments and topographies. Both were said to be less dangerous in an age of mass transportation and industry than before. Both, when visited, were said to provide rare insight into otherwise unimaginable states of raw humanity. And yet there were important differences, or so the railroads implied: differences not only of race, economics, and political stature but also of logical inherence in, constructive response to, and improvement of an environment known as often harsh and sometimes barbarous. Railway promotions claimed that Saints had found ways to domesticate and render productive the same environment that had shaped Mormon experiences, and their successes in this regard pointed to new horizons of cultural affiliation in America.

Outside of the Wasatch Mountains and Pulpit Rock, railroad guidebooks were most invested in mapping correspondences between Utahn topographies and Mormon religious expressions alongside Mormon waterworks and irrigation systems. By guidebooks' accounting Utahn canals were special sites of outdoor, extraecclesiastical, and thus easily observable correspondence between the natural and built environments of Mormonism. As such they were clear avenues for religious reflection and memory. A Rio Grande guide was typical in terms and order of reporting. It spoke of Utah's healthful climate, pointed tourists to the "turtle-roofed Tabernacle and white granite walls and towers of the Temple," and then ruminated on the grounds around them: "The gutters, or rather, the ditches, carry streams of pure, clear mountain water, which serves to irrigate the gardens, lawns and enclosures, and to these trenches is due the luxuriant growth of trees, flowers, plants and bushes which give Salt Lake City the appearance of one vast park and flower garden. The streets are beautifully clean, especially in the residence portion, and there is an oriental air about the city which carries one back to the banks of the Biblical Jordan, and is unlike that of any other city in the Union."[84] Observations of canals led to appreciations of public decorum and evocations of biblical topography.

Indeed it was with reference to Salt Lake City's irrigation canals and their agricultural yields that guidebooks again evoked biblical literalism as a hermeneutic for Mormon understanding. "Here, Isaiah's millennial rhapsody of prediction finds literal fulfillment," reported one. "The wilderness and the solitary place have been made glad, and the desert does rejoice and blossom as a rose."[85] Such claims amplified those made elsewhere by and about Mormons in Utah, for instance, in Salt Lake Tabernacle displays and early tourists' reflections on them. Transcontinental traveler Fitz Ludlow, for one, had written, while looking at an irrigation ditch near the Tabernacle, that "the associations of Palestine throng everywhere throughout Mormondom, and with special cogency they came upon me here. I remembered the declaration of the Psalmist, 'Thou turnest men's hearts as the rivers of water are turned.' . . . Nowhere on this side of the Holy Land could the preacher find such an illustration for [this] text." Ludlow considered irrigation a poetic metaphor by which to understand biblical poetry, just as he considered the act of irrigation, quite literally, to be occasion for religious comprehension.[86]

Perhaps Mormon religious culture was to be found somewhere in the gutters, streets, and flowers of Salt Lake City? Guidebooks raised the possibility with provocative intent, coupling there the implications of cultural geography with hints of geographical determination in Mormon life. Ignoring the prevalence of pre-Mormon irrigation practices as well as the fecundity of some

Utahn soils, Tabernacle and tourism promoters alike suggested that Great Basin lands had required water and that Mormons had effectively invented modern irrigation practices, even as they hybridized older social patterns complementary to the task, such as close-knit villages and communally oriented trade. Mormons were first and foremost an agricultural people, according to this refrain; they were industrious but not industrialized. Thus guidebooks described irrigation as a defining and enabling feature of Utahn settlement, and by their work canals became metonyms for Mormonism itself. Each was a cultural product of a peculiar environment, each sustaining questionably religious and arguably nonindustrial phenomena.[87]

This was not to say that Mormons were stuck in their own gutters. In adapting this argumentative line from Tabernacle to tourists and back, the chamber of commerce handouts clarified that Salt Lake City and Utah generally were happy to welcome other people and other modes of industry in the Mormon midst, now that its groundwork was set. Not only were Mormons "now well able to instruct the rest of America in the art of irrigation," but they had outgrown their early opposition to mining and Gentile trade. "Whatever differences prevail at present concerning other matters, there is little or none in regard to the advisability and necessity for diffusing information concerning our extraordinary resources, and inviting the home-seeker and capitalist to avail themselves of the rare opportunities here afforded. For the first time in the history of Utah the business men in the principal communities have agreed upon the necessity of inviting capital and population from other points."[88] Left unsaid here was that such agreement was generally brokered and pursued according to interests shared by the Union Pacific with chamber of commerce officer John W. Young. Likewise, neither party mentioned that celebrations of Mormon resource-development plans naturalized the mechanisms by which Brigham Young had controlled and gifted the very grounds from which railroad companies now contracted with his kin; but that was also true. If indeed certain things had changed, the fact of church-company collaboration had not.

The second of these points—that corporate naturalization resulted from affirmations of natural incorporation—stands elaboration. Railroads were not wrong to focus attention on resource distribution and settlement policies as key to understanding Mormon religiosity. How they did so, however, masked as much as it illuminated. To celebrate Utah's gridded settlements and canal culture as positively pastoral and basically biblical was, arguably, to naturalize Brigham Young's methods of 'placing Mormonism' without attending to the power dynamics thereof—how such distribution was maintained through a Modus Operandi, implemented by a highly organized priesthood system, to certain economic and political ends—or how such systems had been subject to debate among different Mormon factions about the proper focus and location of Sainthood. Certainly it did not acknowledge that such systems had been mobilized in pursuit of corporate connections with the same railroad barons who now dispatched delegates on behalf of the LDS Church. Likewise, to celebrate Mormons' increasing willingness to court outside investments in mineral extraction, without commentary on the Godbeite controversy, was to obscure the political processes by which railroad companies had themselves traded in the capital of Godbeite evocation just long enough to enable LDS agents like John W. Young to develop the infrastructure by which to benefit from such investments without disrupting the underlying Modus. But such was the tenor of the train.

In the end, perhaps the clearest message of what Culmer called "the worldly gospel we are now preaching to this worldly people" was that Utah itself was valuable grounds for religious discernment.[89] Pulpit Rock may have evoked sentiments reminiscent of "the hajjis of Mecca or Jerusalem," in Burton's terms, but Salt Lake Valley's waterways likened Mormons' "Promised Land" unto Jerusalem in the supposedly less ecstatic and more pastoral key of the Hebrew Bible. Mountain passes and manmade rivers thus complemented each other, in the touristic terms of religious emplotment, insofar as they witnessed to Mormons behaving variously like Muslims and Jews. Whereas both settings evoked notions of geographical determinism and cultural primitivism in Mormon life, too, the irrigation canals showed Mormons' early efforts to reshape the same nature that had supposedly shaped them. Meanwhile the smaller rocks and ores on display in the Utah Exposition Palace Car were said to evince Saints' more recent openness to ecumenical commerce, in the modern era, and thus also their willingness to dig still deeper beneath the surface of that environment.

If the Exposition Palace Car gospel naturalized Saints' presence in Utah through suggestions of topographical conquest as well as determinism in Mormon life, though, it did so consistently with contrast to American Indian experience. The complementary advertising of Pulpit Rock and Utahn resources, when triangulated by way of Giant's Cave, suggested that, whereas Mormons and Indians could both be imagined as having premodern or ecstatic experiences in Utahn places, only Mormons escaped being fully entrapped and entombed by them. Mormons, unlike Indians, were said to have dominated and domesticated the same geography that constrained and constructed them, especially through their irrigation systems. Moreover, Mormons, unlike Indians, were said to have made, and to have made available, particularly tangible materials by which to theorize different modes of religious expression, as at Pulpit Rock and Temple Block, and to reconsider the materiality of religion itself, from train stations to Tabernacle seats. Thus railroads helped Americans to see Mormons themselves as a colonial resource, whose capacity to displace Indians and anchor modern religious concerns was equally if not more valuable than their mineral deposits.

Therefore while modes of Indianness and Mormonism were sometimes similarly considered to be 'vanishing' or 'disappearing' in the late nineteenth century—and while representative examples were preserved, for the sake of pedagogy, in fact and discourse—Mormons were said to have different (and differently religious) lessons for Americans, on the whole, and to have different (and generally better) chances of becoming whole Americans themselves, by virtue of their particular places of settlement, geographical adaptations, built environment, and phenomenological likenesses to Middle Eastern groups. Whereas modern Indians offered negative examples of culture, contemporaneousness, and civilization, modern Mormons offered more questionable and ambiguous examples, if not more certainly positive ones.

Mapping Material Religion

Perhaps more than any other group—Mormons, amateur ethnographers, Salt Lake Chamber of Commerce members, and scholars included—railroad boosters were persistent and powerful promoters of Utah's Palestinian likeness, and they spoke frequently of the Great Salt Lake as "America's Dead Sea" and of the "oriental air" breathed throughout Salt Lake Valley settlements. Boosters amplified such rhetoric beyond the walls of the Tabernacle and the circles of intra-Mormon address, but that is not all. In the wake of the Utah Exposition Palace Car's tour, the Rio Grande Western Railway took additional steps to render visual railroads' thoroughgoing implications of religious parallelism and the significance of topography, and to invite reflection on the likeness of groups gathered in comparable atmospheres, all the while further displacing native cultures in the act of oriental-occidental morphology. The "Promised Land" map—published in 1891, reproduced frequently after that, and soon to become a ubiquitous feature of Utahn publicity—showed geographical similarities between Canaan and 'Deseret,' or the Mormon Great Basin area.[90]

Maps are oftentimes more fictive than descriptive, but the visual lie of this particular map—the cartographic similarity created by inverting and exaggerating aspects of Palestinian topography—was a lie in the direction of a certain type of comparison and material consideration. Here epitomizing the railroad era trend of evocative cultural geography, the Rio Grande's map stood in for

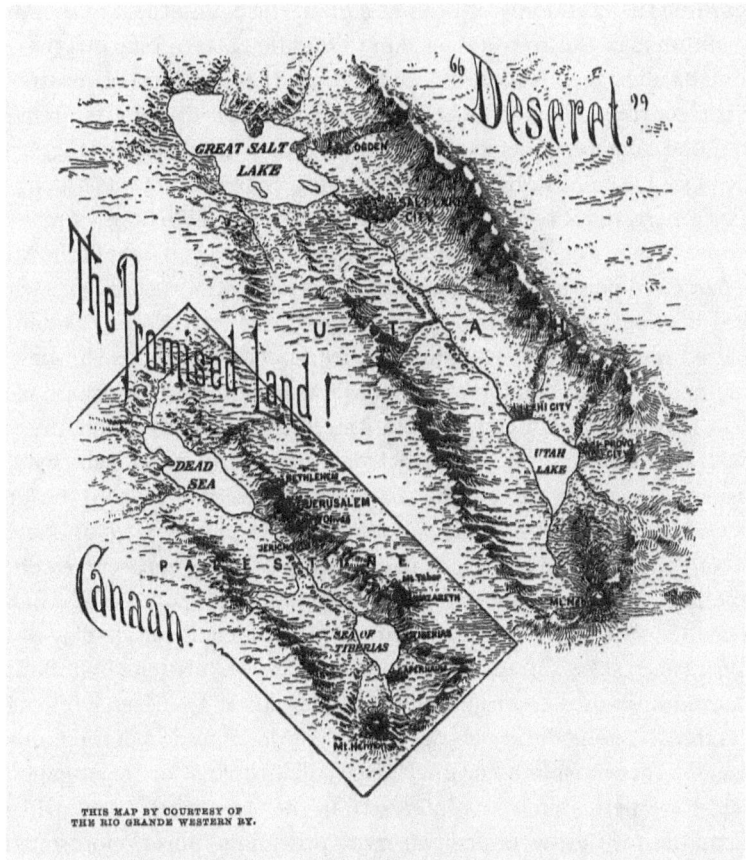

"The Promised Land!," a map published by the Rio Grande Western Railway, 1891. (Author's collection)

textual assertions of religious heritage, Semitic or otherwise, making space for the public play of (semi-)scholarly environmentalism and (semi-)sympathetic entertainment both. To describe this as a matter of play is not, however, to ignore the imperial premises or effects of such acts of cartographic imposture. In this case, mapmakers' seemingly documentary observations of the "striking comparison" and "compar[able] cut" between "the Holy Land and Utah" enticed readers to explorations and empirical discoveries of their own, on a domestic counterpart to Middle Eastern pilgrimage that served simultaneously to overlook Indian landmarks and naturalize Mormon claims to western indigeneity.[91]

Regarding the marketing of Utah as a domestic counterpart to the Middle East—and thus of Utahn travel as akin to Middle Eastern pilgrimage—a few phenomena merit recollection and recognition. First and most obviously: early American tourists to the Holy Land, often Protestant Christians, frequently disliked the socioreligious cultures and peoples encountered there, their mythic place-based nostalgia notwithstanding. Indeed there was much cross-criticism among those seeing themselves or others as 'indigenous,' 'foreigners,' 'interlopers,' 'pilgrims,' 'travelers,' and 'tourists.' Second: in light of the Middle East's perceived political, racial, and religious stagnations, combined with its physical distance, Americans often presented American places "as heir[s] to [its] sacred topography."[92] Heirship was expressed sometimes through site-naming and political metaphor—both Mormons and non-Mormons participated in this practice, of course—but Americans found other means of domesticating the Holy Land. These included circulating maps, paintings, and photographs; building three-dimensional dioramas; and touring the United States and territories with giant panoramas, all depicting sites of (generally Christian) religious interest.[93] Such panoramic presentations occurred often in conjunction with celebrations of American westward expansion and cultural progress. Thus we find instances not only of the concurrent display of western and eastern scenes in museums and catalogs, but also the installation of Holy Land miniatures and full-scale reproductions at American world's fairs, such as the St. Louis World's Fair of 1904, a commemoration of the Louisiana Purchase.[94] These displays became "place substitutions" or "surrogate destinations" for American tourists interested in the Holy Land.[95] And, whenever American 'curiosities' were deemed more proximate, purer, more religious, more marketable, or more anthropologically rich than 'old world' ones, surrogates could become superseders.

This was the moment of Utahn touristic development, and it was in light of such concerns that railroads promoted Utah as an especially appealing self-originating and self-contained destination. Railroads implied that Utah contained landforms reminiscent of the Holy Land, with peoples likewise questionably religious, and they were more easily approximated and incorporated—both theoretically, physically, and materially—by a westward-expanding American culture. As historian Jared Farmer has noted, "Publicists encouraged tourists to see Mormons as latter-day Hebrews or as latter-day Sodomites"—not to mention Burton's other Middle Eastern options—in a land nevertheless pitched as "an American Canaan."[96] Railroads' graphic rendering of Mormondom's Semitic contours did not necessarily constitute a positive defense of Mormon religious legitimacy, in any case, so much as a commensurate strategy for evoking touristic investments premised on a combination of genealogical curiosity, sentimental ambivalence, and national pride.

RAILROAD MAPS AFFIRMED the methodological boundaries that guidebook writers set for themselves when discussing the stuff of religion, for instance, when announcing their intention to avoid judgment regarding the content and veracity of specific theological claims, focusing instead on environment and material culture.[97] The fact of theological avoidance can be read as an instance of argumentative temerity on agents' part, or as an attempt to maintain boundaries between discussions of religion and, say, culture. It may have been both those things, but it was also—and most immediately—a suggestion of the proper analytical grounds and foci of ethnographic discussion and religious tourism.

But did guidebooks' focus on Mormon geography and material culture imply its 'baseness' or insufficient religiosity relative to a more 'immaterial,' worldly Protestantism? Did it in fact enact Sheldon Jackson's (ostensibly) antimaterialist mission and/or J. H. Beadle's dream to make Mormon matters the stuff of negative sightseeing? The idea is commensurate with many modern theories of religion in modernity, based as they are in scholars' recognition of both Protestantism's and modernity's denials of the persistent materiality of religion. In Sally M. Promey's words, "Part of the narrative and theoretical/theological work of both modernization and the Reformation concerned a process of disenchantment of the material universe in favor of 'spiritual' transformation." The "weight" of secularization theory "settled disproportionately on the material practice of religion," just as Protestantism sought to sink 'Catholic' or 'fetishistic' iconolatry. Therefore, "If Western modernity's narration left any space for religion, its developmental trajectory had to progress from fetishistic engagement to abstract thought, from material involvements and practices to 'belief.'"[98] Such narrative denials would seem to have space for Mormon spaces, if at all, only as sites of iconolatrous irreligion. Then again narration is one thing and practice quite another. Continues Promey: "From the start these narratives have been insufficient to contain the ways people *actually*" practice religion, including modern Protestants: materially and persistently. Iconoclasm and secularization theories tried to make certain practices seem more-than-material while making others appear less-than-spiritual or less-than-rational. For, through such balancing equations Protestants and modernists sought the enchantments of disenchantment and the material comforts of abstraction.[99]

Railroad tourism is a complicating instance of religion making, from the perspective of Reformed theories, or for those maintaining inverse proportionalities between modern industry and religious practice. But it challenges even their critics to explore new loci for the theoretical and material constructions of modern religion. After all, the question that occupied nineteenth-century tourists, capitalists, and Mormons remains germane: What is to be made of an industry that promotes religious observation in the world and that maintains a space for religion—or for peculiar religion—precisely on the grounds of its manifold materiality and visitability?

Again, one argument would be that this was an instance of antitype manufacturing in America: that, by presenting Mormonism *in site* and *in stuff*, the tourist industry set up an 'Other' for many Americans, thus forging an opponent for the type of binaries necessary to sustain modernist ruptures from premodern things. Dean MacCannell's observation that tourist sites have the ability to organize positive and negative social sentiments and that they can "establish in consciousness the definition and boundary of modernity by rendering concrete and immediate that which modernity is not" is relevant here again. Like something set in amber or a museum unto itself—the "mountain walled treasury of the Gods" was how one railroad company consistently referred to Utah—Mormonism, by this model, might have been the materialistic antitype against which tourists reconceived their own modernity, progress, and religion. This was the guiding hope behind J. H. Beadle's atrocity tours, after all.[100]

Although there is considerable truth to this argument—railroads did mobilize an antiquarian market, with all attendant disgusts and desires—I want also to stress the messiness of the process, on the ground, and the productivity of that messiness. Beadle's vision did not come to pass, in the end. This was because in the rituals of railroading tourism we see the necessary flipside of a phenomenon described elsewhere by Frits Staal, in his studies of Vedic practice. Rather than "meaninglessness" or an absence of semantic content, that is, there was in tourism an overabundance of meaning—an excess of meaning produced through the proliferation of semantic opportunities and the multiplication of possible decisions. I have suggested already that politicians and railroads both 'put Mormonism into discourse,' but railroads did so in particularly spatial, particularly invitational ways: by compiling and distributing data on Mormonism, by highlighting Mormon sites and artifacts, by celebrating the context (if not necessarily content) of religious distinction, by encouraging ethnographic encounters, and by applauding debates and speculations. Meanings and determinations were neither fixed nor absent, in this system;

nor were they unidirectional, the net gain of 'The Mormon' as discursive object notwithstanding. Tourism literature guided readers to the material culture and geography of Mormonism, true, but it struck a less prescriptive pose when asking about Mormon religiousness, inviting tourists to render their own judgment. And dotted parameters proved variously productive places, for positive and negative sightseers as well as the guides and guidebooks that structured oscillations of ambivalence between them.[101]

As a structure, tourism established spaces and languages through which people debated the wobbling pivots of religion relative to the fixed materials of Mormonism. The conversations were guided, but the determinations were multiple. Some tourists, like Fitz Ludlow and John Codman, bought into the narrative of Mormon religious legitimacy and righteous placement in the West. Others, like William Cullen Bryant, Anna Dickinson, and W. F. Rae, did not.[102] Latter-day Saint hosts met all of them, anyway, in the Salt Lake City spaces framed by railroading questions, with hopes of guiding conversations to the church's own benefit—for instance, by working further to advance Utah–Holy Land parallels and their industries of observation. Meanwhile and above all, railroad writers like Edwards Roberts worked to keep the debate alive, inviting ever more communicants into the fray, if only to recast their reflections after the fact.

TRAVEL GUIDES POINTED TO material factors from which readers might draw their own conclusions about religious culture and cultivation in America. Thus reported one Rio Grande guide: "On an eminence overlooking the picturesque valley of the Jordan, the modern metropolis, Salt Lake City, has been built, with its broad streets, its odd shaped Tabernacle, its great Temple ... and its quaint buildings and edifices." All of this "furnishes profitable speculation in the odd and mysterious," it said, just as (according to a different Rio Grande writer) the "striking similarity in the topography [between] this region and the 'Promised Land of Canaan' ... furnishes much food for thought." Salt Lake City "has the breath of age, commingled with an atmosphere of comfort and modern amelioration."[103]

There is indeed "food for thought" here: Utah was presented as a site of comfort with a "breath of age" or, alternately, as a site of age with modern updates. It was a place of oddness within similarity, in any case, and of abundant opportunity for "profitable speculation." These were speculations, not just of the economic and mineral sort, but of the humanistic variety as well. Railroad agents prompted Americans to become mobile students of culture, with culture—and with religion—located somewhere in the space between Utah's mountains and its "broad streets."[104] And many leisure-class travelers took their lead, with scrapbooks and guidebooks in hand.

Resorting to Curiosity

For his part, scrapbooker James Hunt—who derived most of his personal narrative from railroad guidebooks—diverged significantly from their script only once. This was at Garfield Beach, where Hunt recalled "having a great flirtation with the Mormon girls, who had a picnic at the beach that day."[105] Even that unscripted flirtation, however, was predictable, and it illustrates how railroad companies managed lakeside resorts so as to cater to travelers whose desires for exotic experience and sensual encounter were left unsatisfied after visiting Pulpit Rock, Temple Block, and Brigham Young's grave—let alone also the Deseret Museum and Utah Exposition Palace Car. Indeed Garfield Beach was in many ways designed for that moment.

The Garfield Beach bathing resort was built in 1881, due west of Salt Lake City. Accessible via one of John W. Young's former railroads (the Utah Western, purchased by the Union Pacific in 1881 and renamed the Utah & Nevada), Garfield Beach was home to a rebranded relic of Corinnethian tourist efforts, as well: the former ship *City of Corinne*, now renamed the *General Garfield*. Backed by the Union Pacific, Garfield Beach also incorporated aspects of both Corinne's and John W. Young's business models for bathing resorts, at Lake Point and Lake Side, and it flourished for many years in the physical and promotional space between them.[106]

On the one hand, Garfield Beach catered to its local clientele by employing a Mormon band for its dance hall and by avoiding raucous parties and liquor sales on Sundays. (It was in fact illegal to sell spirits on Sunday, but the law often went unenforced.) Meanwhile, by using the *General Garfield* to escort visitors to Giant's Cave, resort managers retained the boat's original purpose but altered its focus. The former *City of Corinne* now guided tourists on an LDS-friendly atrocity tour of a supposed Indian gravesite, rather than an atrocity tour of living Mormon curiosities.[107]

On the other hand, Garfield Beach sold sensuality, of a sort. *Sights and Scenes* and other Union Pacific pamphlets promoted the resort with an image of a single young woman in her bathing costume, fixing her hair for a swim, staring forward as if to invite the viewer to join her. Meanwhile Utah & Nevada Railway guides featured a statement by John Muir wherein he happily recalled stripping and consummating a "lusty relationship with the brave old lake" itself.[108] On offer at Garfield was not just the peculiar sense of tingling buoyancy

"On the Beach at Garfield," advertisement by the Union Pacific Railway. (In *Souvenir and Views of Union Pacific*, ca. 1898; courtesy of History Colorado Center, Denver [MSS #907, 3000339.1])

in highly salty waters but also the titillating possibility of beholding Utahn 'natives' and Utahn nature in a state of undress.

The design of Garfield Beach's chief competitor suggests that tourists' interest in exposure applied not only to individual bodies but also to group marriages. Lake Park, founded by the Denver & Rio Grande Western Railroad in 1886, featured an elaborate pavilion adorned with delicate latticework,

Lake Park Bathing Resort pavilion and Denver & Rio Grande Western train, ca. 1887. (Photograph by C. R. Savage; courtesy of the Church History Library, The Church of Jesus Christ of Latter-day Saints, Salt Lake City [PH 500])

archways, and other Orientalist architectural motifs. Such motifs were increasingly common at seaside resorts in America and Europe in the late nineteenth century, but their deployment on the Great Salt Lake in the Edmunds-Tucker era predictably evoked the primary social grounds for likening Mormons to Muslims, polygamy. Lake Park's design invited tourists again to play the role of a Richard Francis Burton in Utah, breathing deep the "oriental air" of America's own "Promised Land," and wondering anew about the nature, appearance, and appeal of practices sought also by U.S. marshals for prosecution.

Flirting with Mormon girls as well as Orientalist aesthetics, travelers like James Hunt proved P. T. Barnum's point, as expressed in his exchange with John W. Young at the Deseret Museum: some tourists were determined to look upon Mormondom with a critical and salacious eye, and therefore boosters would do well to acknowledge, cater to, or capitalize on their gaze. Thus while railroad agents supported Mormon displays of refinement and regularity with one hand—for instance, at the Tabernacle, the Exposition Palace Car, and certain resort policies—they extended the promise of exoticism and revelation with the other—through Union Pacific-backed experiences at Pulpit Rock and

Garfield Beach, and through Denver & Rio Grande–promoted attention to Palestinian environments and Moorish aesthetics.

The goal, in any case, was never to collapse the distance between these hands, let alone crush Mormons in the clap, but to hold them ever and always in tension—and then to invite tourists into the interstitial space of discernment. In this respect too railroad promoters demonstrated affinity and aptitude for Barnum's own methods of voyeuristic incitement, as implemented, for instance, in his advertising of Joice Heth (supposedly the centuries-old former nurse of George Washington) and the Feejee Mermaid (a creature with the tail of a fish and the head of a monkey). Whereas Barnum simultaneously asserted authenticity and yet suggested duplicity surrounding these figures, thereby inviting but also establishing boundaries and terms for debate, railroad agents in Utah avoided discussion of polygamy and sedition in certain places (as at the Tabernacle), all the while evoking the possibility of sexual impropriety, domestic disorder, and past offenses elsewhere (as at lakeside resorts and Brigham Young's grave); and they pushed various comparative possibilities within the shared frame of 'Palestinian Parallelism,' for instance, in the Denver & Rio Grande's different promotional maps and architectural motifs.[109] From Pulpit Rock to Garfield Beach, though, and from Tabernacle seats to Temple spires, the questions posed and the discernments invited were essentially the same: whether or not these places were religious; whether or not they were crucial to Mormonism; whether or not Mormonism was crucial to Utah; and whether or not Utah was crucial to the Union.

Railroads mapped a path by which to respond affirmatively to the last three questions, at least. Certainly the clearest message of railroad-sponsored tourism literature was that Mormons were *who* they were because of *where* they were. According to these guidebooks, Mormonism happened within a geography, it imagined a geography, and it could be understood in terms of that geography. By positing mutually determining relations between Utahn locations and Mormon behavior—and, moreover, by highlighting the agricultural lessons and mineral resources wrought under conditions of Mormon stewardship—railroad agents suggested that such locations, lessons, and resources (if not also behaviors) could be usefully integrated into the American state, for purposes of play as well as profit.

But what of the first question: Are they religious? Railroads tracked passengers to the heart of the matter, but agents hesitated to provide direct answers themselves. As one guidebook author declared to his readers, it was still a matter of open inquiry "whether Mormonism be a religion or not." Rather than "express opinions of the religious aspect of Mormonism" himself, he and like authors invited tourists to decide whether that "aspect" was best identified in moral philosophy, articles of faith, domestic arrangements, physical geography, or material culture. Nevertheless the railroads would tell them where to find these things; they would help them see them; and they would give them the platforms, itineraries, opportunities, and words with which to get there and decide for themselves.[110] Railroad agents' job was to get outsiders on site, bringing them to a land of promised religion and religious promise, in order that they might think hard about where the 'religion' was and what its 'promise' would be. For them, the fact of the religious question in Utah—its asking, its appeal, its debate—was always more important than its answer.

RAILROADS MAPPED UTAH as necessary grounds of religious debate in America, and they took steps to preserve it always as such. Indeed if there was an overall structural imperative at work in railroad promotions of Utahn travel, it was the steadfast insistence that Utah—and Mormonism—be maintained as component and elemental to Americans' religious—and therefore also secular—self-understandings. True, P. T. Barnum, John Codman, William Cullen Bryant, the Youngs, Charles Francis Adams Jr., and others may have had different ideas about the stuff of true religion in the world, but they all agreed that the "material side" of Mormonism was crucial to its recognition, in positive and negative valences alike. Their common project was the imperative to place discourses about religion in and around Utahn cultural heritage sites.

Railroading Termini

Securing Utahn lands and locations for acts of Mormon observation was not the same as securing them for Mormonism, per se, but these were commensurate ends. As transcontinental railroad companies and the LDS Church both sought stability, in the 1880s, they found it in each other and in joint projects of political aspiration and product placement. For their part, railroad companies sought LDS institutional support in electoral politics and labor relations, through emigration contracts, and in the form of shipping and stockholding proceeds from Mormon-owned businesses. Meanwhile they invested heavily in resorts and observation platforms for which they knew the chief clientele, if not locals themselves, were tourists interested in observing Saints in a supposed state of nature. Editorial intervention in national newspapers and transcontinental guidebooks collaborated to cultivate public interest in Mormon culture while assuaging concerns about church power and polygamy, or else to acknowledge such concerns in Utahn environments devised specifically for the high drama of modern discernment. There hosts and guests worked side by side to determine the structures and institutions of importance for Mormon sustenance, statehood, and religious identity itself in the West, while travel agents advocated for both the touristic and political mainlining of Mormon Utah in light of—rather than despite—its manifest and debatable differences.

From 1890 to 1896, after the Woodruff Manifesto and through the transition to Utah statehood, railroad guides increasingly encouraged readers to visit Salt Lake City not with a fearful eye for Mormon curiosities but with a hopeful eye for Mormons' contributions to, and absorption within, a common American culture. They invited visitors not to consider Salt Lake City a distant hothouse of curios but to come to Utah with an eye for architectural and material curiosity nevertheless. In short, they encouraged readers to appreciate the material culture of Mormonism. And they encouraged readers to appreciate the material accomplishments through which Mormons had dominated and shaped the same topography that arguably informed their religiosity. Mormonism retained hints and reminders of a primitive naturism, they suggested, but it also manifested modes of natural subjugation necessary to modern national growth.

Guidebooks dwelled at length on accomplishments in the realms of architecture and urban planning. The Tabernacle was one of the world's great wonders, they said, and so was (or so would be) the Temple. The streets were lined with trees and irrigation ditches, and Brigham Young's houses were worth seeing. These things had all been the sites of theocratic practice in the olden days of geographical isolation, but no longer. Now they were relics, of a sort, of an older Mormonism: the Mormonism of Utah's pioneers, a class now fading from view.[111] Railroads, by their own accounts, had helped open the geography and material culture of Mormonism to widespread enjoyment and visitation. And now they invited a kind of retrospective appreciation of Mormon pioneers through their maps and materials.

Thanks to the intervention of the railroads, said their guides, the Mormon Promised Land would persist more as a cartographic and promotional fact than as a political one. Salt Lake City could be safely packaged as a curious but harmless model of alternative social formation, one arguably premodern but now situated within modernity, all the while holding a mirror back at it; one formerly isolated and unknown but now open to transportation and comparison; and one inviting the development of shared space and shared American identity. This was an effort in which many Mormons participated, too. LDS Church members performed harmonious myths of origin and identity, designing new material platforms for mutual Mormon-tourist observation, and inviting tourists to look kindly upon structures that Saints themselves reclaimed in 1890.

Thus did the focus on the material culture of Mormonism support a variety of social, political, and definitional moves made around the wobbling pivot of religion. The structures of tourism were fairly stable, and so were its terms. So what was under debate was the degree to which the materiality of Mormonism constituted or precluded its religiosity. Some clearly intended the 'move to material' and the 'focus on geography' as a mode of containment. Some intended it as a mode of eulogy or posthumous appreciation. Some used it as a lever to posit multiple Mormonisms. And others used the occasion to retheologize and expand material holdings. The point is that none of it was automatic, immediate, or given. None of it was innocent or neutral, either. What *was* clear was that railroad platforms were platforms of religious definition, of religious theory making, and of religion making. Tourism, then, was an industry of religion.

CONCLUSION

The Recreation and State of Religion in 1893

✦

ATTENDEES OF THE Chicago World's Fair in 1893 encountered, at center of the Utah section of the Agricultural Pavilion, a scale model representing a new plan for Gentile settlement in Utah's Bear River Valley. Featuring mountains, foliage, and running water, this large relief map announced the progress—real and imagined—of the Bear Lake and River Water Works and Irrigation Company. Chartered in 1889 to dam the Bear River at the Cache Divide (between Cache Valley and Bear River Valley) and extend two canals thence to the Great Salt Lake, the project was designed to embrace some 150,000 newly arable acres, including Corinne. The company, headed by eastern promoter John R. Bothwell, covered lands previously managed by Alexander Toponce; and it retained Toponce's corporate priority—like J. H. Beadle's before him—of selling parcels to "Gentiles, if possible." To that end Bothwell commissioned elaborate promotional materials addressed (mainly) to British and (secondarily) to midwestern investors, wherein he triumphantly announced that they were "open[ing] the lands" to non-Mormons "ready to 'Possess the promised land.'"[1] The World's Fair relief map was to be the crowning achievement of Bothwell's advertising drive.[2]

The Bear Lake and River Company's relief map garnered much positive press at the fair, where it won an award for best irrigation display. These accolades, however, were not accompanied by the success of Bothwell's company itself—or its message. Quite the contrary, the Bear River corporate model was belied by considerable financial struggle and managerial distress in Utah, just as its Protestant prescriptions were undercut by the grounds of reception in Chicago. It seems that Mormons had so owned the language of irrigation in the West that, for many Chicagoan visitors, the Bear River corporate display offered proof of Mormons' fortitude: evidence *not* of Mormons' superfluity or supersession, that is, but of their cultural and locative righteousness. For Hubert Howe Bancroft the Bear River model occasioned reflection on the "worth[iness] of the [Mormon] community." Others "inquir[ing] for the Utah exhibition . . . on account of the irrigation map" saw it likewise. Churchmen and conference-goers from the Great Basin similarly recalled the display as an "addition" to the many "attractions" of Mormon Utah and proof that Mormons were "the beginners of American Irrigation."[3]

Meanwhile the Bear River Company struggled in Utah. It had no broad base of operations, no clear assets, no extensive bureaucratic network, no powerful lobbyists, no motivated emigrant class, and no established systems of public-private trusteeship or codependency. In these respects it was quite unlike the LDS Church and the railroads that bolstered its pastoral posture. Therefore when miscalculations resulted in nonpayments to workers along would-be canals—as they did soon after the company's incorporation—workers sued subcontractors, subcontractors sued contractors, and contractors sued owners. Bothwell was unable to collect sufficient funds from current or prospective residents, and having sold water and land titles to only 12,000 acres, his business entered receivership in 1893.[4] The Bear River Company folded that May, the same month when its expensive scale model was erected at the World's Fair.

Thus the Corinnethian enterprise finally bankrupted itself to produce something of greatest utility to its Mormon antagonists, capable as it was of being selectively and strategically misread according to a hard-won railroading paradigm. The irrigation display broke the Bear River Company's bank, and the opening bells of the World's Fair sounded nobody's death knell more than its own.

THE FAILURE AND FUTURE of the Bear River Irrigation Company parallel the trajectories of other Corinnethian enterprises. In short order the company's resources were subsumed and reorganized by Mormon businessmen, and its messaging was harmonized with a more church-friendly promotional aesthetic—an aesthetic tested and triumphant in other venues at the World's Fair, as well.

Scholars of Mormonism have argued elsewhere for the importance of the 1893 World's Fair as a mainstreaming moment for the church. Reid L. Neilson especially has shown that, despite their indignation at having been barred from participating in the World's Parliament of Religions, Mormons effectively promoted the LDS Church in other venues at the World's Fair. In the Utah Territory Building, the Congress of Representative Women, and especially during performances of the recently revamped Mormon Tabernacle Choir, Saints showcased home manufactures and performed a wholesome patriotism; and their winning displays (the choir won second place in a close competition) primed an otherwise reticent public to accept Utah statehood in 1896.[5] The example of the Bear River display both confirms and complements these findings. However it points also to a shared corporate heritage: public perception and church policy alike manifested methods honed through three decades of railroading interactions. Utah's exhibits staged exempla of material culture and geographical specificity, inviting onlookers to debate the degree to which it proved or precluded religion. The case of the Bear River display showed popular willingness to conflate Utah, irrigation, and Mormonism; and it demonstrated also a willingness to admit—yea, even to elevate—Mormon forms in national forums. Mormonism had value for people talking about western settlement and expansion, as well as the right relative terrains of 'religion' and 'culture.' And that fact had value for the church.

The fate of the Bear River Company after the fair proves further this heritage. Purchased and reorganized in 1894 as the Bear River Irrigation and Ogden Water Works Company, its new directors included William H. Rowe, an officer of the Zion's Cooperative Mercantile Institution. For reasons both personal and promotional they abandoned Bothwell's anti-LDS tone, and they worked instead to harmonize their corporate brand with that of the church generally and its specifically railroading imagination. Thus the company's inaugural prospectus included, among other images, the Rio Grande Western's "Promised Land" map—showing the ostensible parallelism of Utahn and Palestinian environments—and other railroad publicity shots then growing in popularity among Mormons. Meanwhile it contained several visuals with specifically LDS provenance, such as C. R. Savage's "Utah's Best Crop" collage depicting a field of baby heads—a riff on an 1870s Tabernacle display. Finally, to accompany its proclamation that "the Company will particularly encourage ... settlement" on a modified Plat of Zion model, the prospectus reproduced three photographs from a new initiative by the Utah Irrigation Commission (of which Rowe was an executive committee member) to document the harvests of Mormon settlements throughout Utah.[6] Among other publications drawing images from this initiative were *The Resources and Attractions of Utah, as They Exist Today*, a booklet prepared by H. L. A. Culmer for distribution at the California Midwinter Fair in 1894, and the Utah Irrigation Commission's own *Irrigation in Utah*, designed for the Third National Irrigation Congress in Denver later that year.⁷ Together these 1894 publications demonstrate the polishing of an image honed at the 1893 World's Fair as well as its origins in railroading promotions and economic exchange.

As they had done with and through railroads, then, Mormon captains of industry took charge of their corporate image—in Bear River Valley as elsewhere in Utah—and showed themselves no strangers to the practice of inhabiting aggressively modern capitalistic forms while leveraging through them the myths and motifs of a nonindustrialized, pacific, Israelite-ish community.

A Complementary Route

If the fate of the Bear River Canal points to promotional alliances between LDS Churchmen and transcontinental businessmen, so too does the experience of George Q. Cannon and other Mormon officials before, during, and after the World's Fair. Transported to Chicago in specially outfitted cars "gratuitously tendered for our use by the Pullman Company," First Counselor Cannon, President Wilford Woodruff, and the full Tabernacle Choir stopped along the way in Independence, Missouri. Whether or not their visit was meant as a show of strength and industry-backed success relative to the rival 'Josephite Church' centered there, the fact was that railroad support had underwritten the thoroughgoing association of Mormonism with Utah, and vice versa, and furthermore that it had helped 'Brighamite' Saints articulate Mormon orthodoxy relative to 'Godbeite' disputants there as well. It was only fitting, therefore, that the First Presidency would return to Independence in the comfort of a custom Pullman Palace Car, as part of its railroad-backed tour to promote Utah and Utahns alike as resources for national enrichment.⁸

Upon arrival in Chicago, Cannon and company "called upon Mr. Pullman and paid our respects to him for his kindness in sending us a private car," and they also met with—and were escorted around town by—agents from several railroads.⁹ All of these people welcomed them warmly and admitted them freely to events. Indeed so too did other influential promoters and performers. William "Buffalo Bill" Cody, for one, "arranged to have our party admitted free" to his Wild West show, which was running a short distance from the exposition fairgrounds. "Enjoyed the performance," Cannon wrote, in an understated appraisal of a production known for its sensational excess and sensory overload, not to mention its violent representation of Indian conquest.¹⁰ Cannon preferred to save his most glowing adjectives for performances by the Mormon Tabernacle Choir, which "did splendidly and made a fine appearance." This was true, he said, even when "the audience appeared cold and unsympathetic," or when audience members were distracted by installations with more "ornamentation."[11]

Whether Cannon and his fellow church officials learned anything about how to 'warm up' an audience from Buffalo Bill or other 'ornamented' installations at the World's Fair, we unfortunately do not know.[12] What we do know is that LDS officials had learned much along these lines from the railroad companies themselves and from the same agents who had helped them get to—and around—Chicago in the first place. And while this book has presented multiple occasions and locations for such knowing, among the most striking—and certainly the most contemporaneous—was that which awaited Cannon's return: Saltair.

The Play and Politics of Saltair

Saltair was a bathing pavilion, water park, retreat center, and dance hall situated on the Great Salt Lake, a short train ride from the Mormon city center. It was an expensive affair, but Saltair's value to the LDS Church far exceeded the costs of its construction and operation. Speaking in terms of analogy, Saltair was to the Utah exhibits at the World's Fair what Garfield Beach and Pulpit Rock were to the agricultural demonstrations of the Tabernacle, Deseret Museum, and Utah Exposition Palace Car. That is to say: Saltair manifested and operationalized Brigham Young's "ideology of play" for a modern generation of Mormons—more so, even, than the Salt Lake Theatre had done before it—by winking at, giving space for, and incorporating the determinedly critical and salacious gaze of Gentile tourists to Utah, and by complementing thereby the relatively subdued demonstrations of refinement staged elsewhere or adjacently. And Saltair's "ornamentation" was at least as important to Mormon cultural and political mainlining as those were.[13]

Built with great anticipation by high-ranking LDS officers (including Cannon and other members of the First Presidency) and by the church itself (which held half of the company's stock), Saltair opened for business in 1893, that banner year for Mormon self-promotion and cultural mainstreaming, just before Cannon's trip to the World's Fair in Chicago. In several respects Saltair also served as the capstone for these long-running and contemporaneous campaigns. Not only did Saltair become a must-see for Utahn tourists generally, but Cannon returned from his Chicago trip with a renewed commitment to Saltair's success premised upon a heightened sense of its economic, political, and promotional utility for the LDS Church itself.[14]

Like the resorts of John W. Young before it, Saltair was a two-pronged project

Saltair Bathing Resort, 1893. (Photograph by Frank King; courtesy of Beinecke Rare Book and Manuscript Library, Yale University, New Haven, Conn.)

of industry and promotion. LDS businessmen constructed the Saltair Railway (later, the Salt Lake & Los Angeles Railway) to connect their resort to the city, so that they might more easily transport Mormon and Gentile tourists between them. Indeed when they were unable to see the inside of the Salt Lake Temple, which also opened in 1893, Gentiles were encouraged to make a day-trip to Saltair, where they could interact and enjoy the healthful climate with Utahn locals. Company board members and LDS officials similarly imagined Saltair to be an "advertising agent" for the territory's "name and fame"; it was to be the "Coney Island of the West," they said, albeit with a more family-centered and wholesome aesthetic. Their promotional language generally stressed familiarity and fun over strangeness, therefore, and in contrast to travel guides, it reserved adjectives of curiosity for conditions of salinity.[15]

But architectural decisions belied the message of wholesome, American normality with implications of a broader, cultural exoticism. The Saltair Group hired Richard K. A. Kletting, who had designed the arabesque pavilion at the Denver & Rio Grande's Lake Park resort in the late 1880s, to develop a similar aesthetic at Saltair, and indeed to adorn its (much larger) pavilion with (many more) minarets, domes, and arabesque towers. Cannon and other members of the First Presidency loved the "magnificent" design, not least because, in the words of one *Deseret News* reporter, Kletting's "semi-Moorish architectural

"Pavilion, Saltair Beach, Salt Lake, Utah," showing train tracks. This seems to have been a proof for an Underwood & Underwood stereoview set later published as "The Latter-day Saints' Tour," with commentary by Brigham H. Roberts (Ottawa, Kans.: Underwood and Underwood and Republican Print, 1904). (Detail of WA Photos Folio 18, Beinecke Rare Book and Manuscript Library, Yale University, New Haven, Conn.)

lines" evoked "a delightful oriental dream." Railroad guides often echoed this evocation, agreeing that there existed few better places to consider the curious splendors of Utah than a sparkling "Moorish" theme park on "the Dead Sea of America."[16] Thus while the church's "Coney Island" evinced a larger, prestatehood, and postpolygamy climate of Mormon accommodation to American culture, accommodation occurred via the strategic deployment of extant touristic modes, means, and motifs: resorts, railroads, Moorish design, and implied

Orientalism. The church accepted and incorporated a particular, touristic type of Mormon imagination.

It was no coincidence that the LDS Church most actively embraced Moorish architectural themes at the same time that it was reconsidering and phasing out polygamy. And it was no coincidence that the church did so mainly at areas designed to be tourist attractions—in this case an amusement park and sanitarium. Thanks in large part to prior acts by Richard Francis Burton and his railroading followers, the 'open secret' of polygamy could be framed there in a way that seemed, if not altogether less dangerous, local and approachable. Saltair's design was a winkingly self-conscious affair; it catered to certain imaginations while also memorializing, historicizing, and re-placing them. Aware of questions about Mormons' proper whiteness in and for the West, Mormons owned that status by distancing themselves from Indians while flirting still with the titillating difference of Islamiform otherness. Attentive to expectations that 'modernity' would 'liberalize' and 'domesticate' Utah, Mormon promoters encouraged intergroup observation and approximation, and they demanded of their visitors speculation in the nature and industry of American religion.

THREE MONTHS AFTER Cannon's return to Salt Lake City and Saltair from Chicago, he embarked upon another eastern tour, this time "to raise money to build the Salt Lake and Los Angeles Railway"—or, rather, to extend its line from the city and resort to the mines at Coalville. By his account, "Capitalists in the East must have the church endorse the bonds if they buy them," for they trusted its economic responsibility in the post–Edmunds Act and post–Woodruff Manifesto era of financial restitution.[17] But Cannon was not the only person working to sell easterners on either LDS railroad bonds or financial stability, at the time. To the contrary, this was the project boosted and leveraged also by the political lobbyists Isaac Trumbo and James S. Clarkson, who offered stocks and subcontracts to Washington powerbrokers in exchange for supporting Utahn statehood. Trumbo and Clarkson assured would-be backers that the transcontinental railroads supported the Saints, that Saints supported railroads, and that investors could bank on the lucrative yield of *both* natural resource extraction, as at Coalville, and cultural tourism, as at Saltair—provided, that is, that the LDS Church remained in a particular position of power. The profitable incorporation of Utah depended not on the destruction of Mormonism but rather on its political coherence and capacity for mobilization. And that in turn depended on Mormonism's selective public framing as one among Utah's unique natural resources, on the one hand, along with continuing church patronage and partnership in the industries that connected them, on the other.[18]

The Stuff of Tourism

Utahn Railroads and Utahn (orthodox) Mormonism grew increasingly interdependent with time, from 1869 through 1896. Latter-day Saints reworked and rebranded aspects of their history, settlement policies, material culture, and managerial order so as better to interface with railroading infrastructure, all the while raising financial and social capital for new projects concerned simultaneously with internal improvement, sectarian regulation, and external display. Meanwhile transcontinental businessmen and federal bureaucrats did likewise, variously intertwining their own infrastructural and representational interests with Mormons', and in any case preserving for them a place at the center of national observation. In the center too were the tourists, riding the rails of multiple concerns and tying them together for posterity.

It was not long before railroad and church officials joined in the development of package tours in and around Salt Lake City. Railroad agents provided cheap transportation and lodging, while church groups led tours of Mormonism's sights, and each used the literature and the infrastructure of the other. Both agreed on a baseline for cultural promotion and the objects of religious consideration: material culture and geography. Both agreed tacitly, also, that the enticement to Utahn visitation was foremost among tasks, with on-site decisions and on-site promotions being a separate, more open field of possibility.

Tourists encountered modes and motifs of Mormon life safely incorporated within the frame of capital development. By way of final representation, consider an 1894 tour of Utah and Salt Lake City undertaken by members of the International Association of Ticket Agents, wherein they were guided to and through various tourist attractions and exhibitions in order that they might better sell western travel to others. Consider, more specifically, the scrapbook kept by one member, Isaac Hoffman, featuring images and clippings from the trip. At the center of one representative page is an article, titled "A Host Enraptured: The City's Guests Entertained in Splendid Style," which described the ticket agents' tour around Salt Lake City and afternoon excursion to Saltair. Around that article Hoffman pasted six other items: an image of the Salt Lake Temple, completed in 1893; a headshot of Brigham Young, who died in 1877; a Rio Grande Western Railway timetable; a collage depicting Ogden buildings

A page from Isaac W. Hoffman's railroad scrapbook, 1894.
(Courtesy of the Church History Library, The Church of Jesus Christ of Latter-day Saints, Salt Lake City [MS 12798])

and railroad junctions; and two pictures of irrigated agricultural fields. The last three items were clipped from the 1894 booklet *The Resources and Attractions of Utah*, and it, in turn, had derived one of them—the Ogden collage—from a Denver & Rio Grande promotion.[19]

This was not a happenstance assembly of items and images, articles and attractions. To the contrary, together these embodied a basic public relations script in the railroad age: a cohesive, even if (or perhaps partly because) hodgepodge representation of Mormonism and its encounter, emphasizing the architects and venues of religious work. Indeed, it was more than that. Train trips, memorials, standings-outside-the-Temple, wadings-inside-the-lake, and celebrations of Mormons' agricultural prowess constituted not only a particular touristic imaginary relative to Mormonism. Considered in concert with their industries of observation—not least of them being scrapbooking, an act of structured improvisation among images freighted by institutional interests—such acts and assemblages also constituted Mormonism itself.

The Iron Cage

If scrapbooking is an analog for religious creation and theory-making, railroad networks themselves—particularly in the American West and the Great Basin—might usefully be considered through a different metaphor, namely Max Weber's "iron cage." This is not simply because of the structural similarity of steel rails and iron bars but because both railroads and Weber's cage represent particularly constraining modes of religious production and bureaucratic regulation in and for modernity.[20]

In the "iron cage" passage of *The Protestant Ethic and the Spirit of Capitalism,* Weber claims (by Talcott Parson's influential translation) that, notwithstanding the ascetic impulse to eschew ornamentation, the cloak of "external goods" and the pull of the proscribed eventually became "an iron cage." This passage is among the more opaque sections of a work that is otherwise assumed to be relatively straightforward in its thesis. But much of this classic text is complicated, and various claims there and elsewhere in Weber's oeuvre seem sometimes to conflict, not least on the subject of religion in secular modernity. Granted, there are moments when Weber suggests that Protestantism shapes capitalism, capitalism creates industry, and technology makes societies more rational, calculating, and secular. This is the 'secularization thesis' as commonly understood by many students and historians—not to mention also the Corinnethians, whose death knell thesis anticipated it by a generation. But at other times Weber suggests that Protestant modernity had in fact begotten new forms and locations of religion, even as it seemed simultaneously to regulate them as part of a "new form of control, penetrating to all departments of private and public life, that was infinitely burdensome and earnestly enforced."[21] Religion, in this reading, did not retreat from the public sphere, so much as it became reinvented and reinvested therein—for instance, in and among America's ever separating and recombining sects and its sectlike businesses, fraternal orders, and schools. If not the precise stuff of the iron cage itself, as Weber conceived it, this dynamic was definitely ironic: modern Americans were incited to the hard work of rational calculation and religious competition, on the one hand, even as their outputs were systematically constrained and commodified, on the other.

Corinnethians articulated a proto-Weberian secularization thesis without recognizing the deeper, more elusive, and indeed cagier insights of Weber himself. That is to say: their death knell thesis failed to account for how 'religion' reproduced itself—or how secularizing efforts reproduced religion—in the debates, discourses, and disciplines of 'righteous capitalism.' Corinnethians talked a great deal about religion, and so did politicians; and they both outsourced to lawyers, ministers, philanthropists, businessmen, travelers, and others the projects of sectarian regulation. The result was thoroughgoing public interest in religion, again: in its discussion, adjudication, location, projection, and performance. But not only that. Capitalists and congressmen alike found themselves dependent not merely on religious discussion (whether prescriptive or proscriptive) but also on religious groups themselves. Administrators placed and pitted groups against each other in positions of relative power, and Mormons found themselves well suited to compete—among themselves and against others—for contacts and contracts with bureaucrats and businessmen.

If railroads built an iron cage around Mormonism, it was intended neither to destroy Mormonism nor to render it flatly Protestant. Neither did it seek to displace Mormon systems of economic regulation and mobilization with laissez-faire substitutes. Railroads were rather more interested in maintaining a productive corporate relationship with the Mormon Church. This relationship was premised on an appreciation of the church's bureaucratic acumen in the quasi-mercantilist regulation of land, markets, and labor forces. It was also premised on the knowledge that there was a touristic benefit to maintaining Utah itself as a place of infinite religious interest, discussion, and debate. Mormon Utah was in both senses a place of modern difference protected as such by the iron fabric of the railroads themselves.

This dynamic does not necessarily contradict the insights of recent scholars of the secular, as outlined in chapter 1. I see them instead as complementary and commensurate insofar as we recall that the secular—or Protestant technologies of the secular—consisted and remained always at the level of process more than product, act and enactment rather than accomplishment. Neither does this depart necessarily from Weberian theory, provided again that we prove willing to think creatively with(in) Weber's iron cage. And to that end, we would do well to recall the precise moment of that analogy's articulation.

Max Weber undertook a railroad tour of the United States in 1904. The principal purpose of his trip was the delivery of a paper on agrarian economics at the St. Louis World's Fair. But he was also composing the second half of *The Protestant Ethic* at the time—including the concluding section about the iron cage. The thought of Weber using a railroad tour as an opportunity to theorize religion in modernity is intriguing. How might his traversal of the steel webs of American industry have informed—or even inspired—his conception of the iron cage? Unfortunately, limited archival remains may not permit much more than speculation about the answer to this question. Nevertheless, *The Protestant Ethic* carries with it the traces of his encounters on that trip, and I consider it significant that Weber's account became somewhat less linear and rather more conflicted at the end. The railroad may well have been the immanent frame of Weber's most insightful, albeit (or rather *because*) confusing, insights into the secular.[22]

By my reading there is less fault in Weber's supposed prophesies about the disappearance or alteration of religion in modernity than there is in his assumptions about the 'rationality'—efficiency, scientificity, singularity—of bureaucracy itself. This was decidedly *not* the nature of modern bureaucracies in America, neither those propagated through Congress nor those created by railroads. Rather these were riddled with the inefficiencies of cross-purposed action, overlapping job descriptions, duplication of tasks, wasteful expenditure, contradictory subcontracting, infighting, outfighting, opacity, and confusion. Such environments proved highly productive and hospitable to religious discourses and forms—and *not* because those discourses and forms were necessarily or similarly 'irrational.' For its part Mormonism, which had more effectively implemented systems of state capitalism than had most railroads (let alone the U.S. government), stepped into the bureaucratic environs of modern governance ready to mobilize labor and materials in the direction of certain leaders' ideals. If railroad tracks constituted an iron cage in and for modern American life, Mormons found within it ample space—if not also systemic demand—for spirited debate and religious articulation.

The End of the Tour

In 1869 J. H. Beadle argued that modern industry would destroy Mormonism and that western travelers and would-be settlers might be attracted to Utahn landscapes without reference or resort to 'America's Islam.' Little did he know that, over the next twenty-five years, LDS officials and businessmen would flip his secular script entirely, repeatedly finding ways either to bend railroads to their benefit or to reshape Mormon institutions themselves in order to flourish in their increasingly networked world. Meanwhile railroad barons, seeking favorable contracts and uninterrupted freighting—not to mention also the lucrative receipts of transcontinental tourism—cultivated friendships with Mormon businessmen in Utah, intervened on their behalf in Congress, and worked elsewhere also to ensure the commensurability of their bureaucratic and social interests. The result of their efforts was the combined naturalizing (in Utah) and mainlining (in America) of Mormonism, as tourists especially were convinced that Mormons were a spectacularly geographical people, from whom they might learn to conquer and cultivate western lands, and that they evoked, safely, an Oriental 'otherness' around which Americans might learn to locate and define religion in the modern West. By 1893 Mormonism's status was secure. It was as a religion of and for the railroad era.

ACKNOWLEDGMENTS

The Howard R. Lamar Center for the Study of Frontiers and Borders, the Autry Institute for the Study of the American West, and the Charles Redd Center for Western Studies have supported my research. At the University of California, a Hellman Family Fellowship and a Regents Junior Faculty Fellowship provided time and resources to complete my writing. I am also grateful to the Center for the Study of Material and Visual Cultures of Religion at Yale, with whose support I first developed several arguments in this book. Other ideas and materials were presented at meetings of the American Academy of Religion, American Studies Association, John Whitmer Historical Association, and Mormon History Association. I benefited from the feedback that I received in these forums, and especially from responses and questions by Lisle Dalton, J. Spencer Fluhman, David Howlett, Pamela Klassen, Nancy Levene, Laurie Maffly-Kipp, Colleen McDannell, John Modern, Max Mueller, Barbara Mundy, Reid L. Neilson, Margaret Olin, Benjamin Park, and Judith Weisenfeld. Earlier versions of parts of chapter 6 appeared in "Transporting Mormonism: Railroads and Religious Sensation in the American West," in *Sensational Religion: Sensory Cultures in Material Practice*, edited by Sally M. Promey (New Haven, Conn.: Yale University Press, 2014); and "Railroading Independence: Pulpit Rock and the Work of Mormon Imagination," *John Whitmer Historical Association Journal* (Spring–Summer 2017).

All researchers owe special debts to administrators, scholars, and staff at the libraries they frequent most. For me, these have been the Beinecke Rare Book and Manuscript Library (Yale University), Huntington Library, J. Williard Marriott Library Special Collections (University of Utah), L. Tom Perry Special Collections (Brigham Young University), Merrill-Cazier Library Special Collections and Archives (Utah State University), Nebraska State Historical Society, Stephen A. Hart Library (History Colorado Center), U.S. National Archives, and Utah State Archives and Historical Society. Above all I am grateful to Anne Berryhill and others at the LDS Church History Library in Salt Lake City. It is an understatement to say that my job would be impossible without them. More accurate is to say that I am inspired always by their knowledge and commitment to the work of history. Thanks also to Edward Leo Lyman, who shared archival gems from his personal collection.

I am lucky to have had extraordinary mentors and teachers at Yale University and Wesleyan University. Together they informed the questions that I ask and the methods that I deploy in this book. Jon Butler and Harry S. Stout trained me to think of American religious history as consisting in and through historiography, and thus to embrace the productive possibility of historiographical heresy. John Mack Faragher and Tisa Wenger inspired me to pursue case studies and archives in the American West, and to track closely with the many voices evidenced and obscured there. Meanwhile, Kathryn Lofton and Sally M. Promey pushed me to think broadly about the nature and location of data itself in the history of religion, and to consider also the material and ritual economies of frontier sensationalism. And I never would have decided to pursue a vocation in this field, in the first place, if it were not for the models set by Ron Cameron and Peter Gottschalk.

Fellow students of American religions at Yale were and have remained inspirations to me: Alison Greene, Sarah Hammond, Emily Johnson, Alexandra Kaloyanides, Kathryn Gin Lum, Michelle Morgan, Shari Rabin, and Molly Worthen. I am particularly grateful to have studied closely alongside Kati Curts and Sarah Koenig, with whom I had (and continue to have) countless productive conversations about technology, corporate culture, and settler colonialism in the American West.

Colleagues in the Young Scholars in American Religion Program at IUPUI challenged and supported me when preparing this manuscript for publication, encouraging me to explore new directions while strengthening my faith in the field. I am lucky to have been in a cohort with Kate Bowler, Heath Carter, Joshua Guthman, Brett Hendrickson, Kathryn Gin Lum, Lerone Martin, Kate Moran, Angela Tarango, Stephen Taysom, T. J. Tomlin, and Grace Yukich, under the true mentorship of Laurie Maffly-Kipp and Douglas Winiarski.

Meanwhile, I could not have asked for a better working environment than the University of California, Santa Barbara. Catherine L. Albanese, Rudy Busto, Kathleen Moore, Elizabeth Pérez, Wade Clark Roof, Inés Talamantez, and Ann Taves have all challenged me to think differently, and so too has Joseph Blankholm, with whom regular lunchtime talks have also become reliably motivating affairs, for me, over the past several years. And this is to name only the Americanists! I am also thankful for collegiality and conversation with Aryeh Amihay, Ofra Amihay, José Cabezón, Juan Campo, Thomas Carlson, William Elison, W. Randall Garr, Dominic Steavu, and other members of the religious studies and history faculty here. Meanwhile, Philip Deslippe, Matthew Harris, Samantha Kang, Shelby King, Kolby Knight, and Sasha Coles have engaged in numerous discussions of book-related materials, and so too have students in different courses on tourism and corporate culture(s) in the Gilded Age. Alec Adams and Bhavi Bhagat have undertaken research assignments and formatting tasks, as well. It has been an honor to teach and learn among them.

Elaine Maisner at UNC Press saw merit in this project early on, and she always engaged my endnotes—even while pushing me to greater narrative economy. I am indebted to her for her confidence and foresight. I am also grateful to the Press's external readers, whose comments and concerns similarly urged me in positive directions. Richard Callahan Jr., Kati Curts, J. Spencer Fluhman, Marko Geslani, Pamela Klassen, Kathryn Lofton, JoAnne Mancini, Joshua Rubin, John G. Turner, and Douglas Winiarski also offered insightful feedback on chapter drafts. This book is better as a result of their readings. Of course all remaining shortcomings accrue to me.

Although I am excited to celebrate this publication with many of the above-named friends and colleagues, I wish to mention again a few who have been with me at every stage along the way. One is Joshua Rubin, who has been among my closest confidants and most challenging readers since graduate school. The others are Kathryn Lofton and Marko Geslani, with whom it is also an extraordinary pleasure to live in dialogue. They know most all my footnotes, both academic and personal, and I have written this book with their reading-voices in mind. This year, I look forward to sounding those voices in Corinne.

Finally: to my parents, and to Nonie Hamilton and Isla Walker, I owe debts of the highest order. For keeping all things in perspective, and for everything else: thanks are not enough. Moreover, for these, my Reasons: much love.

NOTES

Abbreviations

BYOF   Brigham Young Office Files, 1832–78, CR 1234 1, Church History Library, The Church of Jesus Christ of Latter-day Saints, Salt Lake City
CG   *Congressional Globe*
CHL   Church History Library, The Church of Jesus Christ of Latter-day Saints, Salt Lake City
CP   Central Pacific Railroad
DCR   *Daily Corinne Reporter*
DN   *Deseret News* (Salt Lake City)
DUR   *Daily Utah Reporter* (Corinne)
HOLC   Historians Office Letterpress Copybooks, 1854–1879, MS 2737, Church History Library, The Church of Jesus Christ of Latter-day Saints, Salt Lake City
GBK   Leonard J. Arrington, *Great Basin Kingdom: An Economic History of the Latter-day Saints, 1830–1900* (Cambridge, Mass.: Harvard University Press, 1958)
GQCJ   Journal of George Q. Cannon, Church Historian's Press, online at www.churchhistorianspress.org/george-q-cannon
JD   G. D. Watt, ed., *Journal of Discourses*, 26 vols. (London: Latter Day Saints' Book Depot, 1854–86)
JH   Journal History of the Church of Jesus Christ of Latter-day Saints, Church History Library, The Church of Jesus Christ of Latter-day Saints, Salt Lake City
JHBS   John Hanson Beadle, "Scrapbook containing editorials and dispatches from the Salt Lake Daily Reporter and the Salt Lake Weekly Reporter, October, 1868–August, 1869," MIC A12, Utah State Historical Society, Salt Lake City
SJP   Sheldon Jackson Papers, RG 239, Presbyterian Historical Society, Philadelphia
SLH   *Salt Lake Herald*
UM   *Utah Magazine* (Salt Lake City)
UP   Union Pacific Railroad
UPRC   Union Pacific Railroad Collection, RG3761.AM, Nebraska State Historical Society, Lincoln

Introduction

1. The 1863 massacre and removal of Bear River Valley's Shoshoni populations are described in (among other sources) Blackhawk, *Violence over the Land*, and Brigham D. Madsen's books *The Northern Shoshoni*, *Glory Hunter*, and *The Shoshoni Frontier*. *Railroading Religion* describes subsequent but related battles over the nature of true religion, civilization, and whiteness in the West.

2. Respecting the quotation marks placed around 'Mormonism' here, a note on terms (and on quotes) is in order. In keeping with common contemporaneous identifications, both emic and etic, I generally use 'Mormonism,' 'Mormon,' and 'Saints' descriptively to refer to the Utah-based Church of Jesus Christ of Latter-day Saints (LDS Church) and members thereof. There are exceptions to this rule, however, and I sometimes speak of different 'Mormonisms.' These include the so-called Josephite or Godbeite factions that refused to recognize the LDS Church (which they called the 'Brighamite' church) as the rightful inheritor of Joseph Smith's prophetic legacy and thus as Mormonism proper. As described in later chapters, politicians and railroad agents intervened in that intra-Mormon debate in ways that (sometimes purposefully, other times ironically) affirmed and secured the thoroughgoing association of Mormonism with Utah and its LDS Church. Throughout this book, I use double quotation marks when quoting directly from a source, and I use single marks when introducing or flagging a significant term under (or for) general debate.

3. On the 1856 Republican presidential platform, the 1857 Utah War, and the Republican and Democratic politics of antipolygamy before and during the Civil War era, see Rogers, *Unpopular Sovereignty*; Furniss, *Mormon Conflict*; and Gordon, *Mormon Question*, 55–63.

4. The name 'Corinnethians' was a cheeky reference to the Christian congregations addressed in Paul's biblical epistles (1 Corinthians and 2 Corinthians). Elsewhere, as we shall soon see, Corinne's founders also referred to themselves as model 'Gentiles.' This is a term that Mormons themselves derived from Judaism (where it meant non-Jews) to refer to people and policies outside of the Mormon faith. However, it was also adopted as a badge of honor by certain non-Mormons who spoke of 'Gentility' as the proper admixture of religious (usually Protestant) and secular sentiments of and for Western modernity. By thus deploying these two terms, Corinne's 'Corinnethian' 'Gentiles' laid claim to a subject position of simultaneously ancient and modern significance that was at once majoritarian and powerful (in the United States generally) and yet marginal and threatened (in Utah if not also elsewhere).

5. J. H. Beadle, "Editorial," *Utah Reporter*, July 2, 1870; *Cincinnati Commercial*, October 17, 1868. On the term 'Gentile,' see note 4, above.

6. Corinne and Bear River Valley appear infrequently in the historiography of the American West. Leonard J. Arrington offers one of the few references to the area in his *Great Basin Kingdom*, when he reports that the arrival of the transcontinental railroad in 1869 included some controversy about whether to locate the main junction in Ogden or Corinne. "Corinne was the last of the 'Hell on Wheels' transcontinental railroad camps," Arrington writes, and "Gentile speculators had invested in its real estate." But LDS Church officials ultimately "tipped the scales" in favor of

Ogden, and by 1880, "the budding Gentile capital of Corinne was virtually a ghost town" (*GBK*, 264–65; see also Morgan, *Great Salt Lake*, 297–302). There exists also an excellent local history of Corinne: Brigham D. Madsen, *Corinne*. Madsen's book focuses on the founders' railroad advocacy, mining trade, canal development, and newspaper wars, and it has proven an excellent guide to early Bear River Valley personnel and their business ventures. However Madsen, like Arrington, ends his story early, in the 1870s, and in this way and others, he misses opportunities to connect Corinnethian histories with broader national trends and theoretical concerns. Locating Corinne and its various interlocutors vis-à-vis histories and historiographies of land-granting, industrial development, tourism, secularity, and bureaucratization, this book takes this 1869 footnote and local story and expands it into a signifying moment in the history of Western settlement and religious development.

7. On shifts in nationwide anti-Mormon rhetoric in the nineteenth century, see Fluhman, *"Peculiar People."* Corinne's history shows how some of these shifts played out at a local level. Reed Smoot first took his seat as U.S. senator from Utah in 1903, but congressmen formally debated his fitness for office until 1907. On the Smoot trial and related debates of Mormon 'national values,' see Flake, *Politics of American Religious Identity*.

8. *JD* 12:54.

9. Rae, *Westward by Rail*, iv; Bowles, *Our New West*, 260. Recognizing Young's efforts to build railroad connections throughout Utah, Leonard J. Arrington has led the way in new studies of the Mormon railroading era; see his *Great Basin Kingdom*, esp. part 3. My hope here is to go beyond a basic recognition of LDS projects in railroad building to an appreciation of railroads' role in the creation of Mormonism itself. This entails study of a different sort of promotional effort than that highlighted by Arrington: not only the 1870s LDS efforts to promote the expansion of railroad infrastructure (see *GBK*, 292) but also the efforts, by churchmen and railroad agents alike, from the 1870s through the 1890s, to promote and repackage the infrastructure of Mormonism. For present purposes, *this* was the aspect and era of Mormonism's most significant transportations.

Chapter One

1. Boller, *Among the Indians*, 406.

2. As quoted in "Discourse of George Q. Cannon, October 7th, 1868," *JD* 12:289–97, at 293.

3. *Decatur (Ill.) Republican*, May 20, 1869.

4. Ibid.; Thomas Fitch, commentary on H.R. 1089, February 23, 1870, *CG*, 41st Cong., 2nd Sess., 1518; Mrs. T. B. H. [Fanny] Stenhouse, *Exposé of Polygamy*, 205.

5. Justin S. Morrill, "Utah Territory and Its Laws—Polygamy and Its License: Speech of Hon. J. S. Morrill, of Vermont, in the House of Representatives, February 23, 1857," *CG*, 34th Cong., 3rd Sess., app., 284–90, 285, 288.

6. Ibid., 286. On legal systems in Mormon communities, see Firmage and Mangrum, *Zion in the Courts*. On the Nauvoo Legion (chartered 1840–45, reinstituted 1849, suspended 1870, and disbanded 1887) and the Danites, see Gardner, "Nauvoo Legion"; Rebecca Foster Cornwall and Arrington, "Perpetuation of a Myth"; Gentry,

"Danite Band of 1838"; and Ronald W. Walker, Turley, and Leonard, *Massacre at Mountain Meadows*.

7. On the Utah Expedition of 1857–58 and its political effects, see Furniss, *Mormon Conflict*; and Rogers, *Unpopular Sovereignty*.

8. Noteworthy here is the winking, masculinist humor with which antibigamy measures were sometimes discussed in Congress. Some congressmen joked that multiple marriage was most common among naval officers and thus that politicians would need to find language by which to exempt them from legislative strictures targeted at Mormons. Others added that they would need to exempt D.C. residents as well, since U.S. congressmen were known to keep multiple houses, concubines, and the like. See January 4, 1858, *CG*, H.R., 35th Cong., 1st Sess., 184; and March 23, *CG*, H.R., 41st Cong., 2nd Sess., 2180. Rosenberg, "Rescuing Women and Children" usefully explores how some critiques of 'patriarchy' actually elide and strengthen the patriarchy of its supposed critics.

9. Morrill, "Utah Territory and Its Laws," 285. On rhetorics of separate spheres and feminine virtue, see, e.g., Welter, "Cult of True Womanhood"; and Kerber, *Toward an Intellectual History of Women*, 159–99. On systems of honor and assumptions of domestic virtue in southern anti-Mormonism, see Mason, *Mormon Menace*.

10. Helpful introductions to Mormon Christology and relations to the Hebrew and Christian Bibles include Barlow, *Mormons and the Bible*; Richard L. Bushman, *Joseph Smith*, chapter 4; Shipps, *Mormonism*, chapters 2–3; John Turner, *Mormon Jesus*; and Bowman, "Crisis of Mormon Christology."

11. Catholicism was compared to Mormonism in various newspaper reports, atrocity novels, and Protestant apologia. But Morrill and other congressmen tended to avoid the comparison—or, rather, to acknowledge it in ways precisely designed to dismiss its legal significance and to ensure the protection of Catholicism from anti-Mormon legislation. Morrill said in 1857: "It is clear that an ecclesiastical hierarchy exists in Utah, with a plenitude of power greater than that which can today be exercised by the Pope of Rome. . . . Whatever of similitude may exist in many respects, it would be libelous upon Catholicism to charge that Catholics claim the prerogatives for their church which are claimed by the Latter Day Saints for the Mormon church" ("Utah Territory and Its Laws," 289). Later, too, while discussing the possibility of imposing property limitations on the LDS Church, Morrill assured colleagues that the Catholic Church would not be adversely affected (June 24, 1862, *CG*, H.R., 37th Cong., 2nd Sess., 2906). Morrill and his congressional colleagues also avoided claims of a shared Mormon-Jewish legalism and cultural exclusivity (two other common tropes), their studied references to "literal interpretation" of prophecy and revelation notwithstanding (Morrill, "Utah Territory and Its Laws," 289). Of course the Mormon-Muslim comparison allowed for the residence of subtle anti-Judaism—if not also anti-Catholicism—by conceding to Mormonism a different Semitism, an affinal spot in a Semitic world far from America and from western Christianity. On distinctions made between 'Semitic' races, religions, and languages and Indo-European or Aryan races, religions, and languages, see Masuzawa, *Invention of World Religions*.

12. Morrill, "Utah Territory and Its Laws," 289, 285.

13. Marr, *Cultural Roots of American Islamicism*, 186. See also Fluhman, *"Peculiar*

People," 29–39; and Givens, *Viper on the Hearth,* 130–33. Givens notes that the character of the demonic Asiatic Muslim was developed already by the time of Mormonism's ascendancy and that "exploiting that ready-made category was easier than constituting an alien identity from scratch." Such categorical exploitation enabled anti-Mormons to "dehumanize" Mormons without claiming "actual ethnic identification" between peoples and cases (133). But "ready-made" and "easy" do not mean uncomplicated or final. Comparison is work, and—in Congress as elsewhere—the Mormon-to-Muslim comparison may have been designed to eschew certain topics and stop certain conversations, but it invariably repositioned and inaugurated others. On the "problem of Mormon whiteness" and shifting perceptions of Mormon racial identity, see Fluhman, *"Peculiar People,"* 110–17; and Reeve, *Religion of a Different Color.* On American Muslim practices and populations, see GhaneaBassiri, *History of Islam in America.*

14. Morrill, "Utah Territory and Its Laws," 288. Morrill here anticipated arguments made in 1878–79, in the case of *Reynolds v. U.S.* (a trial of the legitimacy of the Anti-Bigamy Act): that there existed a distinct difference between beliefs and acts, which are susceptible to legal intervention, having no rights to protection from laws of general applicability by virtue of religious association. See Gordon, *Mormon Question,* 119–45.

15. Morrill, "Utah Territory and Its Laws," 287. The First Amendment's religion clauses and jurisdictional limitations applied only to Congress—and states were left to determine and manage their own government-church relations—until the 1940s. Congress had more control over territories, but the rights and purviews of their religious regulation were the stuff of debate throughout the nineteenth century.

16. On the Christian precedents and presumptions of common law, see Gordon, *Mormon Question,* 65–77; and Jakobsen and Pellegrini, *Love the Sin.* Compare Green, *Second Disestablishment,* 149–247.

17. Morrill, "Utah Territory and Its Laws," 289.

18. *CG,* H.R., 35th Cong., 1st Sess., March 11, 1858, 1084, 1085.

19. Ibid., 1086.

20. Ibid.

21. H.R. 391, 37th Cong., 2nd Sess., 1862.

22. The interview story is recounted in Nibley, *Brigham Young,* 369. Compare T. B. H. Stenhouse to Brigham Young, June 7, 1863, in BYOF, Incoming Correspondence. Stenhouse was at that time the assistant editor of the LDS Church–owned newspaper the *Deseret News.*

23. Speech of Hon. S. R. Curtis, of Iowa, H.R., February 24, 1859, 35th Cong., 2nd Sess., *CG,* app., 250–55, at 250.

24. The construction of schools, roads, canals, and even railroads had been funded by land grants in the past. The Land Ordinance of 1875 laid aside sections of land to support public schools, for example, and the Illinois Central Railroad became the first land grant railroad in 1850. But the scale of those projects and the public resources allocated for them paled in comparison to that of and for the transcontinental railroad. On the politics, economics, and management of transcontinental construction, see White, *Railroaded*; Klein, *Union Pacific*; Athearn, *Union Pacific*

Country; and Orsi, *Sunset Limited*, esp. 65–91. On land grants and land policy more generally, see Decker, *Railroads, Lands, and Politics*; Robbins, *Our Landed Heritage*; and Paul W. Gates, *Illinois Central Railroad* and *Jeffersonian Dream*.

25. White, *"It's Your Misfortune,"* 140.

26. On the economic philosophies and programs of the Civil War era Congress, see Richardson, *Greatest Nation on Earth*. Classic works on manifest destiny include Weinberg, *Manifest Destiny*; Merk, *Manifest Destiny and Mission*; Horsman, *Race and Manifest Destiny*; and, more recently, Stephanson, *Manifest Destiny*; and Greenberg, *Manifest Manhood*.

27. On yeoman utopianism and Jeffersonian agrarianism vis-à-vis the Homestead Act, see, influentially, Henry Nash Smith, *Virgin Land*, esp. chapter 15. On religious debates respecting nonsectarian education, and on the discourse of nonsectarianism itself, see Hamburger, *Separation of Church and State*, esp. 219–29; and Marsden, *Soul of the American University*, part 1. Most studies of nineteenth-century anti-Indian railroading action have focused on the northern plains (and thus the Northern Pacific) or the Indian Territory (and thus the Atlantic & Pacific). See Lubetkin, *Jay Cooke's Gamble*; Dee Brown, *Hear That Lonesome Whistle Blow*, chapter 10; Clark, "Railroads and Tribal Lands"; Hoxie, *Final Promise*, 45–48 (itself in conversation with another important work on the topic: Miner, *Corporation and Indian*); White, *Railroaded*, 134–39; and Voss, "Railroads and Coal." See also Deloria and DeMallie, *Documents of American Indian Diplomacy*, chapter 8. Attending to Mormon connections, the current project adds to a historiography on railroads and land grants a refocusing on their investments in religion and religion's investments in them.

28. The Pacific Railroad Survey (authorized by Congress in 1853) reported that there were several viable transcontinental routes running through southern, northern, and central portions of the American West. Politicians debated the merits of these routes through the Civil War, when Congress settled on a central line favorable to northern industry. This was the route along the 42nd parallel—the modified Overland Trail route—ultimately followed by the CP and UP. On John W. Gunnison's 1853 railway survey and its connections to sectional and specifically anti-Mormon politics, see Rogers, *Unpopular Sovereignty*, 65–70.

29. Speech of Hon. F. P. Blair Jr., of Missouri, H.R., May 25, 1858, 35th Cong., 1st Sess., *CG*, app., 421; Curtis speech, February 24, 1859, 252.

30. Speech of Hon. J. R. Barret, of Missouri, H.R., May 29, 1860, 36th Cong., 1st Sess., *CG*, app., 362–65, at 363. Barret estimated this expense at "more than eight million dollars per annum."

31. *CG*, 36th Cong., 2nd Sess., January 17, 1861, 433.

32. Speech of Hon. Jeff. Davis, of Mississippi, S., January 20, 1859, 35th Cong., 2nd Sess., *CG*, app., 277–87, at 279, emphasis added.

33. "The Pacific Railroad and the Mormons," *Baltimore Sun*, July 19, 1869.

34. *CG*, 36th Cong., 2nd Sess., January 5, 1861, 250; Barret speech, May 29, 1860, 364; *CG*, S., 36th Cong., 2nd Sess., January 5, 1861, 254.

35. *Senatorial Excursion Party*, 50, 54.

36. Curtis speech, February 24, 1859, app., 250–55, at 254.

37. "The Mormon Troubles," *New York Herald*, September 4, 1869. Brent M. Rogers has also recognized that the Pacific Railway Act and the Morrill Anti-Bigamy Act were

linked by anti-Mormon animus by way of a shared desire to expand federal powers in the Great Basin and the greater West (*Unpopular Sovereignty*, 285–86). However, Rogers suggests that these laws were also coherent in application and effect, serving together to limit and/or end Mormon power and sovereignty in the West, whereas I argue that they worked more often at cross-purposes. This was not least because (as I suggest here) politicians pointed to the Railway Act as justification for not enforcing the Anti-Bigamy Act. Furthermore, the transcontinental companies themselves inaugurated a new era of Mormon power when and insofar as they purposefully moderated anti-Mormon legislative efforts like the Anti-Bigamy Act over time.

38. Marx, *Machine in the Garden*, 198; Stolow, "Salvation by Electricity" and "Wired Religion." See also Porterfield, *Corporate Spirit*, 119–20.

39. *Latter Days*; Louisa Sanger to Eliza Ann Graves Rich, April 15, 1858, in Eliza Ann Graves Rich Correspondence. See also the Rev. I. E. Dwinell's May 1869 sermon, *Higher Reaches of the Great Continental Railroad*, which (typically) cited Isaiah 40:3–5 and (less predictably) Nahum 2:3–4 in praise of the newly completed "Highway for our God."

40. Asad, *Formations of the Secular*; Fessenden, *Culture and Redemption*; Klassen, "Fantasies of Sovereignty"; Modern, *Secularism in Antebellum America*; Sullivan, *Impossibility of Religious Freedom*. *Railroading Religion* interfaces with this historical and historiographical terrain in several ways. At one level, I question somewhat the ubiquity of the American Protestant secular thus described, or, better, the degree to which a certain discursive ubiquity constituted ubiquity in fact. After all, the Corinnethians were ultimately unable to enact (in the heart of the West, no less) precisely the type of functionally pro-Protestant public and private purifications described above, thereby showing the limits of any putative civil religion and Protestant secularity even while highlighting again its presumptive operations. That said, I do understand both the broader discursive milieu of the Corinne versus Salt Lake debates and also the Utahn Mormonism that emerged from them, in the railroad age, to have played a role crucial to the secular *as* practice rather than achievement. The following chapters develop this argument.

41. Committee of Correspondence, circular, December 19, 1838, reprinted in "Western Railroad," *Haverhill (Mass.) Gazette*, January 18, 1839; "The Western Railroad," *Boston Courier*, January 21, 1839 (including coverage from *Worcester (Mass.) Aegis*, January 16, 1839). See also coverage in the *Daily National Intelligencer* (Washington, D.C.), January 24, 1839, and *Virginia Free Press* (Charlestown, W.Va.), February 7, 1839, both citing the *Boston Transcript*; Adams Jr., *Railroads*, 65; and Winsor, *Memorial History of Boston*, 130–39. Compare the treatment of this incident in Nye, *American Technological Sublime*, 56. I acknowledge that, because Massachusetts officially disestablished in 1833, this ministerial reticence might be read as an articulation of freshly felt rights to critique and thus that the railroad overture might be better described as 'no longer palatable' than as 'not yet palatable,' but a similar reticence may also be found before 1833, and the point remains that palatability pushes were always strategic, regional, corporate, and contested. Consider also another example of complexity belying apparent consensus: one often-cited article—"The Moral Influence of Steam," a 1846 source common to Leo Marx's, David Nye's, and John Lardas Modern's arguments—reveals not really a descriptive (and thus evidentiary)

accounting of Protestant technological excitement but, rather, the fractured grounds of its prescriptive articulation; it is an anxious piece of sectional politics, a reflection on the relative merits and regional possibilities of railway and steamboat travel in the Old Southwest, pending approval of a more northerly railroad route across the nation. Charles Fraser, "The Moral Influence of Steam," *Hunt's Merchant's Magazine* 14, no. 6 (June 1846): 499–515. Compare Marx, *Machine in the Garden*, 198–99; Nye, *American Technological Sublime*, 57; and Modern, *Secularism in Antebellum America*, 32n79. To his credit Nye recognizes the sectional specificity of certain prorailroad arguments—as well as antirailroad "counter-narratives"—in his later study, *America as Second Creation*, chapter 8.

42. Miller, *Life of the Mind in America*, 295–306; Marx, *Machine in the Garden*; Kasson, *Civilizing the Machine*; Nye, *American Technological Sublime*; Otto, *Idea of the Holy*. Henry Nash Smith never used the term "technological sublime," but his work and method loom large in this literature; see *Virgin Land*. John Lardas Modern's fascinating study of technological secularity, *Secularism in Antebellum America*, shares some sources with scholar-proponents of technological sublimity (see preceding note). Modern explains friction in the Protestant-secular-interface by positing that, although Protestants and republicans—and a diverse group of social actors and institutions influenced by them—secured codependent senses of self as centered in legible systems of feedback and automation, they nevertheless felt 'haunted' by perceptions of de facto opacity, tyranny, restrictions of choice, and things unknown (even unknowable) in their society of promised transparency and republicanism. (Nevertheless, he goes on to argue, these people generally assured themselves that no real data ever *truly* slipped the gears of their secular public-private differentiation machines and, thus, that all would become legible again through commonsense reasoning and the systemic analysis of perception itself.) Modern's analysis is in many respects compelling and often likely right. Nevertheless I worry about the degree to which the historical and historiographical rhetoric of the technological sublime has entered into the literature on the secular, *not* as evidence of a certain prescriptive rhetoric respecting the righteousness of secular subjectivity, but as evidentiary, descriptive proof of modernity's sentimental or affective hauntings. To my mind the managerial language of the technological sublime may be understood, as such, to do the work of the modern without affective reification.

43. Hawthorne, *American Notebooks*, 102–5, and "Celestial Railroad"; Twain and Warner, *Gilded Age*, chapter 3; Whitman, "Passage to India." On Ralph Waldo Emerson's mixed opinion about railroads' capacity to effect religious awakening, see Kasson, *Civilizing the Machine*, chapter 3.

44. Freed, *Railroad Passenger Fares*, 233–38; H. Roger Grant, *Railroads and the American People*, 36.

45. This sense of the secular as practice resonates with Walter Benjamin's conception of the secular as described by Talal Asad in *Formations of the Secular*, 63. Respecting religion and modern industry, I am influenced by Callahan, Lofton, and Seales's argument that "religion and industry," being "codependent as institutional bodies, as social organizers, and as moral vantages for national life," work together to "regulate bodies—geological, demographic, and biological—and fit them into

the requisite disciplines of modern labor and consumption"; see their "Allegories of Progress," 3–4.

46. "Discourse of George Q. Cannon," 293.

47. Beecher, *Plea for the West*; Strong, *Our Country*, chapter 6.

48. 'Mainline' is undoubtedly a railroading term: its American, colloquial, adjectival designation of power and influence derives from twentieth-century descriptions of wealthy communities located along the Main Line of the Pennsylvania Railroad outside Philadelphia. The history of its synonymy with 'orthodox' and 'mainstream,' in reference to Protestantism, is unclear but seemingly dates to the mid-twentieth century (Coffman, *Christian Century*, 9). I deploy the term 'mainline' in a purposefully anachronistic way—in application to the makings of mainstream Protestantism along the main line of the nineteenth-century transcontinental railroad—to highlight the industrial histories that simultaneously undergird and belie its twentieth-century adoption, ubiquity, and common-sense status as synonym for Protestant orthodoxy. On Methodism's identification as "railroad religion" in Appalachia, see Callahan, *Work and Faith*, 60–63.

49. Bender, *Winning the West for Christ*, 3; Sheldon Jackson, "Pioneer Presbyterianism in the Rocky Mountain Territories, 1869–1876, Historical Sermon Prepared and Preached at the Request of the Presbytery of Colorado," November 1876, in SJP, box 27, folder 2; "The Union Pacific Railroad Occupied for Presbyterianism," *Presbyterian* [n.d.], in SJP, Scrapbook 59, 1; Sheldon Jackson, "Home Missions," in SJP, Scrapbook 59, 45.

50. R. P., "The Church on the Pacific Railroad," in SJP, Scrapbook 59, 18–20; "A Home Mission Work," in SJP, Scrapbook 59, 11–12.

51. Bowles, *Our New West*, 56.

52. On Presbyterian missions in the Southwest and the conception of "exceptional populations," see Banker, *Presbyterian Missions and Cultural Interaction*.

53. R. P., "Church on the Pacific Railroad"; Melancthon Hughes to Sheldon Jackson, June 28, 1869, and H. R. Wilson to Jackson, July 9, 1869, in SJP, box 1, folder 3. There are several clergy passes from 1869 to 1871—some for complimentary trips, others for half-price fares—in SJP, box 27, folder 2.

54. R. P., "Church on the Pacific Railroad." See also Jackson, "Pioneer Presbyterianism."

55. "Union Pacific Railroad Occupied for Presbyterianism"; Jackson, "Pioneer Presbyterianism"; Sheldon Jackson, "Cheyenne, the Magic City of the Plains," *Presbyterian*, July 18, 1869, in SJP, Scrapbook 59, 13. On Jackson's novel and wide-reaching appointment, see Bender, *Winning the West for Christ*, 15–17, 19–20; Murray, *Skyline Synod*, 54; and Stewart, *Sheldon Jackson*, 100–106.

56. Bender, *Winning the West for Christ*, 19, 25, 29; see also Jackson, "Pioneer Presbyterianism," for discussion. The Presbyterian Church in America had been divided into Old School and New School factions since 1837. After 1885 Jackson's work focused on, and was based in, Alaska.

57. Stewart, *Sheldon Jackson*, 103; Jackson, "Pioneer Presbyterianism"; Bender, *Winning the West for Christ*, 16, 20; Murray, *Skyline Synod*, 54; M. H. Bristol to Jackson, February 1, 1870, SJP, box 1, folder 11.

58. Frank F. Ellinwood, "Utah and the Next Vexed Question," in SJP, Scrapbook 59,

83–86, citations at 83 and 86; Ellinwood, "Among the Mormons," in SJP, Scrapbook 59, 86–88. Ellinwood was later the secretary of the Presbyterian Board of Foreign Missions, and he also was an author of books and lectures comparing 'Oriental' religions with Christianity. Jackson kept close tabs on Corinnethian developments, and he pasted one of Beadle's larger booster pamphlets—the four-sided "Corinne: Its Past, Present and Future" [August 2, 1869]—into his scrapbook, a mere page away from Ellinwood's articles on the Mormon question (SJP, Scrapbook 59, 78–81).

59. [J. H. Beadle], "Arrived," *Salt Lake Daily Reporter*, December 8, 1868, in JHBS. There are no lists of Corinnethian residents in 1869, for the months before and after the transcontinental railroad connection. U.S. Census data for Corinne City, Box Elder County, Utah Territory, in June 1870 (more than one year after railroad completion) show approximately 783 residents at that time, including people staying at hotels and boardinghouses. Six hundred and ninety-nine of these were listed as "white," including 107 born in Great Britain, 65 in Mainland Europe (more than 40 in 'Germany' and 5 in France), 28 in Canada, and 17 in Scandinavia. Four were listed as "mulatto," with birthplaces in Kentucky, Missouri, and Ohio. Eighty were considered to be "black," including 68 people born in China, most of whom worked on the railroads and in laundry. The 12 non-Chinese blacks were born in Virginia (3), Ohio (2), Utah (2), D.C. (1), Kentucky (1), Missouri (1), and New York (1). Not counted here are Ute and Shoshoni groups sometimes residing within Corinne's borders. A letter from a Presbyterian missionary in Corinne, dated May 17, 1870, states that there were "in and around the city some five hundred Indians (Shoshones and Utes)"—and he also estimated the Chinese population considerably higher than the above census numbers, around 200 or 300 (E. Bayliss to Jackson, May 17, 1870, SJP, box 1, folder 13). Corinnethian boosters did not often acknowledge these populations, preferring to characterize their city as white and their contest with Mormonism as being one over the future of western whiteness. The best local history of Corinne and its founders is Brigham D. Madsen, *Corinne*. See also personnel lists in "Brigham Correspondence," dated March 11, 1869 [*Salt Lake Weekly Reporter*, ca. March 13, 1869], in JHBS; and Toponce, *Reminiscences*, 195–96.

60. Beadle, *Life in Utah*. The book appeared in seven editions, one in German, between 1870 and 1904.

61. Ibid., 327–28, 312.

62. Ibid., 5–6, 120.

63. Ibid., 8–9, 67, 250–51.

64. Ibid., 508–9, 202; *Corinne Journal*, May 25, 1871; "Editorial Correspondence," dated February 18, 1869 [*Salt Lake Weekly Reporter*, ca. February 20, 1869], in JHBS. Also Tullidge, *Tullidge's Histories*, 241. Beadle spoke more of Connor's Corinnethian support in his 1869 publications than in the 1870 *Life in Utah*, perhaps because Connor had by then abandoned the region for lands south of Salt Lake. On the Northern Shoshoni, Connor, and the Bear River Massacre, see, respectively, Brigham D. Madsen, *Northern Shoshoni*, *Glory Hunter*, and *Shoshoni Frontier*. On the prehistory of the massacre, see Blackhawk, *Violence over the Land*.

65. Beadle, *Life in Utah*, 508–9.

66. Ibid., 8, 532, 507–10.

67. Ibid., 118–21, emphasis in original.

68. Hughes to Brother Cleland, June 14, 1869, in SJP, box 1, folder 3. The Episcopal Church came to Corinne primarily through the initiative of Daniel S. Tuttle, missionary bishop of Montana, and the Reverend George W. Foote, his brother-in-law. The two men had been active in Salt Lake City since 1867, working among its small non-Mormon community to sustain weekly services and support a Sunday school. Corinne was a secondary stop for Tuttle and Foote, but they lost little time establishing inroads at Corinne after learning of boosters' plan to make it (by Tuttle's recollection) "the commercial centre" that would "speedily absorb into itself all the non-Mormon population and business of the Territory." Tuttle wrote: "It was a town of tents" in early 1869, but a "belief prevailed that it would become the . . . great town of Utah." In order to be on the ground floor of development, therefore, "Our Rev. Mr. Foote, ever on the alert, had secured a lot there." Tuttle, *Reminiscences*, citations at 106, 242–43. On Utahn Episcopalianism and the missions of Bishop Tuttle, see also Frederick Quinn, "Daniel S. Tuttle."

69. Hughes to Jackson, June 28, 1869. See Brigham D. Madsen, *Corinne*, 5–11, for descriptions and numbers of early residences in Corinne, and see Spude, *Promontory Summit*, for a description of the arrangement, construction, and content of tents in Promontory, Corinne, and other end-of-the-track towns. The gambling tent measured some fifty feet by one hundred feet.

70. Sheldon Jackson, "Domestic Missions: Corinne, Utah," *Presbyterian*, September 4, 1869; also SJP, Scrapbook 59, 82–83. The Corinnethian pamphlet cited and summarized by Jackson—and pasted in his personal scrapbook—was "Corinne: Its Past, Present and Future."

71. Jackson, "Domestic Missions"; also SJP, Scrapbook 59, 82–83.

72. "A Voice beyond the Mountains," in SJP, Scrapbook 59, 91–92; Stewart, *Sheldon Jackson*, 100. Compare Acts 16:9.

73. *Salt Lake Daily Reporter* [ca. October 30, 1868], in JHBS; *Cincinnati Commercial*, October 17, 1868.

74. "Corinne," *Salt Lake Weekly Reporter* [ca. March 20, 1869], in JHBS.

75. "Brigham Correspondence," dated February 21, 1869 [*Salt Lake Weekly Reporter*, February 27, 1869], in JHBS. We see, in these statements, an expression of tensions subsequently central to Utahn railroading promotions: whether to eradicate Mormonism or to preserve it somehow as an attraction, and whether to consider Mormon encounters necessary, unnecessary, or supplemental components to overland excursions. Beadle generally sided with camps arguing for eradication and unnecessity. The West had enough novelty without them, he said.

76. Ibid.

77. Ibid.; Hughes to Jackson, June 28, 1869; Brigham D. Madsen, *Corinne*, 7–9. Williamson seems to have issued only quitclaim deeds when first auctioning town lots and also to have paid "little regard . . . to whether or not the lots were situated on railroad lands granted under the Pacific Railroad Act or on alternate sections of government land that would become open to homesteading and the award of patents of ownership." Both facts rendered titles insecure and subject to subsequent contestation. Brigham D. Madsen, *Corinne*, 55–56; H. D. Moon to Willis Drummond, November 15, 1871, Old Townsites, docket 1, box 28, U.S. National Archives, copy in Brigham D. Madsen Papers, box 51, folder 19. Williamson acted as provisional mayor

of Corinne's temporary city government until 1870, and from 1876 to 1881 he served as commissioner of the General Land Office.

78. Hughes to Jackson, June 28, 1869.

79. "Bear River Correspondence," dated March 15, 1869 [*Salt Lake Weekly Reporter*, ca. March 20, 1869], in JHBS; "The City of the Future" [*Salt Lake Weekly Reporter*, ca. March 27, 1869], in JHBS, emphasis in original. The town also seemed to have the support of Williamson and O'Neil's colleague, land agent and townsite adjutant J. E. House.

80. "Brigham Correspondence," dated February 21, 1869.

81. Klein, *Union Pacific*, 207–9; Spude, *Promontory Summit*, 12–13; Ames, *Pioneering the Union Pacific*, 317–18; "The Pacific Railroad Bill," *DN*, April 28, 1869.

82. "A Grand 'Skedaddle,'" dated March 25, 1869 [*Salt Lake Weekly Reporter*, ca. March 27, 1869], in JHBS.

Chapter Two

1. JH, January 1, 4, 1869; Arrington, *GBK*, 265. See also S. S. Wadsworth to Brigham Young, December 1, 1869, in BYOF, Incoming Correspondence. Wadsworth owned a forty-acre lot along the Ogden River—"a good place for building purposes or machine works"—for which he had been offered "$100.00 per acre by Gentiles," but "the [Mormon] orthorities" convinced him to "give the Church the first chance."

2. "Part of Ogden City Weber Co. Utah . . . Showing the boundaries of land proposed to be donated by Brigham Young . . ." (blueprint), UPRC, subgroup 164, box 650; Durant, as quoted in Arrington, *GBK*, 265, 486n25. Acreage estimates vary; compare Spude, *Promontory Summit*, 12.

3. Fox, "Mormon Land System," 13–14. On Mormon millennialism, see Underwood, *Millenarian World of Early Mormonism*.

4. See Fox, "Mormon Land System," esp. 3, 7–25; and Jackson, "Mormon Village" and "Sacred Space and City Planning." Thomas Carter describes how the plat was effectively ignored during the Nauvoo era—but also how it was picked up again, in sense if not specifics, by Brigham Young after 1847—in *Building Zion*, esp. 11–15, 32–36. Stephen C. Taysom also describes the early development and shifting deployment of the plat in *Shakers, Mormons, and Religious Worlds*, esp. at 55–61, arguing that Great Basin Mormonism imagined Zion and its blueprint in a more metaphorical and individual way than had midwestern Mormonism(s). This is surely correct, even as—as I will argue here—LDS Mormonism remained a matter of geographical imagination and land management in the Great Basin, mechanisms that in time both enabled railroad connections and were enabled by them.

5. Fox, "Mormon Land System," 13, 8. See also Thomas Carter, *Building Zion*, 33.

6. On the Law of Consecration (revealed February 1831) and the First United Order (as distinguished from later applications of United Order principles in Utah), see Arrington, Fox, and May, *Building the City of God*, esp. chapter 2. On later, Utahn efforts at communalist economics and United Order reinstantiations, see further ibid., chapters 4–12.

7. Jackson, "Mormon Village," 2–3; Fox, "Mormon Land System," 15. Such paradox was not unusual for communalist settlements, but Mormonism was especially

characterized by its hierarchical organizational structure. See Pitzer, *America's Communal Utopias*.

8. On the priesthood orders of marriage and (arguably) the Female Relief Society, see Flake, "Development of Early Latter-day Saint Marriage Rites"; and Ulrich, *House Full of Females*, chapters 3–5. Brigham Young reconstituted the Relief Society in 1867.

9. See Flake, "Ordering Antinomy," for an analysis of Joseph Smith's organization and management of authority across categories of priesthood, council, and kinship.

10. Mason, "God and the People," 350, 357–58.

11. For a chronological accounting of Joseph Smith's institutional and political efforts (and resistance thereto), see Richard L. Bushman, *Joseph Smith*.

12. Jonathan Z. Smith notes that religious distinctions "are found to be drawn most sharply"—and sometimes most violently—"between 'near neighbors,' with respect to what has been termed the 'proximate other'" (*Relating Religion*, 258).

13. Beyond the scope of this study are many important groups who refused Brigham Young's prescriptions for theodemocratic removal (and the functional if not factual relocation of Zion City) to Utah, groups like the so-called Strangites (who focused on Wisconsin and Michigan), Rigdonites (Pennsylvania), and Wightites (Texas). On these groups and their divergent claims about the rightful authority of certain ecclesiastical offices, see D. Michael Quinn, "Mormon Succession Crisis of 1844." On the so-called Josephites—advocates of continued Mormon focus on Illinois, Missouri, and the greater Midwest, led by relatives of Joseph Smith—see also chapter 3 of the present work. Brigham Young's dissolution of the Female Relief Society was a point of contention between so-called Brighamites and Josephites for many years after 1845, even as Utahn women found other venues for the continuation of their work. See Ulrich, *House Full of Females*, 127–28, 179–83, and chapters 12, 14, and 15.

14. The Deseret General Assembly first met officially in the spring of 1849, and the body was officially dissolved two years later. Leonard Arrington writes that the Mormon Council of Fifty, which constructed this assembly, "continued to function as a 'ghost government' until the 1870's" (*GBK*, 50). The territorial assembly of Utah, by means of a joint resolution in 1851, adopted many laws enacted by the provisional government of Deseret. On Mormon plans for Deseret, see Arrington, *Brigham Young*, 223–29; Leonard, "Mormon Boundary Question"; and Rogers, *Unpopular Sovereignty*, 40–44.

15. Jackson, "Sacred Space and City Planning," 252. See also Fox, "Mormon Land System," 37. Although Thomas Carter downplays the importance of the blueprint to Brigham Young himself, noting that Young "never felt obligated to speak of it or supply a replacement document," he agrees that "in spirit, Young adhered to Smith's basic plan in laying out Salt Lake City," and thus that the early Utahn "period in Latter-day Saint landscape history . . . represents a throwback to the older, millenarian Zion visualized for Missouri and comes closest to achieving Joseph Smith's plan for the ideal Zion" (*Building Zion*, xxii, 33, 14).

16. See below for further discussion of Mormon-Indian relations. As Leonard Arrington has written, "Brigham's decision to settle near the Great Salt Lake was based in part on information he had learned about the Indians in the area," and he "hoped to avoid crowding either the Shoshonis in the north or the Utes in Utah Valley" by settling between them. Intergroup hostility and violence grew, however, especially as

Mormon groups spread southward into Ute territory. See Arrington, *Brigham Young*, chapter 13 (citation at 212); Farmer, *On Zion's Mount*, chapters 1, 2 (the term "mixed-bloods" is his; see 50); and Blackhawk, *Violence over the Land*, chapter 7.

17. Brigham Young, "Epistle to Orson Hyde," JH, October 9, 1848. See Arrington, *GBK*, 52; and Fox, "Mormon Land System," 48.

18. Wilford Woodruff, as cited by Fox, "Mormon Land System," 98, and Larson, "Land Contest in Early Utah," 310; Wilford Woodruff, William Clayton, and Norton Jacob, as cited by Arrington, *Brigham Young*, 169, 462n6. There were a few ways in which private citizens might purchase acreage (officially) at costs less than one dollar per acre: via large wholesale deals, for instance, and via the Donation Land Claim Act (1850), by which people received free land in the Oregon Territory in exchange for promised settlement and cultivation. (The Homestead Act, passed later in 1862, also granted free land to long-term settlers.) Mormons attempted to have Oregon-esque land laws applied also to Utah Territory in the 1850s, but their efforts met with resistance by congressmen who recognized and feared Mormons' self-generated drive to settlement. On Utahn petitions and memorials to Congress, see Fox, "Mormon Land System," 108.

19. On the origin of this peculiar (and uniquely Mormon) circumlocution for Trustee, see Arrington, *GBK*, 431n103.

20. Linford, "Establishing and Maintaining Land Ownership," 130–31; *Acts, Resolutions and Memorials*, 61–62. Leonard Arrington notes that the delay in confirming land titles in Utah "was undoubtedly purposeful, being based on the hope of forcing the Mormons to change their social institutions, but actually made it easier for the Mormons to establish and maintain their own somewhat unique property institutions" (*GBK*, 249). I am making a similar claim here.

21. Justin S. Morrill, "Utah Territory and Its Laws—Polygamy and Its License: Speech of Hon. J. S. Morrill, of Vermont, in the House of Representatives, February 23, 1857," *CG*, 34th Cong., 3rd Sess., app., 284–90, at 286. See chapter 1 for discussion.

22. Fox, "Mormon Land System," 113–17; Linford, "Establishing and Maintaining Land Ownership," 133; Morrill, "Utah Territory and Its Laws," 286, emphasis in original. On such "mixed" enterprises—businesses that were "partly public and partly private"—see Arrington, *GBK*, 54–55.

23. Morrill, "Utah Territory and Its Laws," 286; Larson, "Land Contest in Early Utah," 313; Fox, "Mormon Land System," 113.

24. Linford, "Establishing and Maintaining Land Ownership," 133–34; Fox, "Mormon Land System," 113.

25. Arrington, *GBK*, 52.

26. For definitions and descriptions of 'The West' west of the 98th or 100th meridian, see Nugent, "Where Is the American West?"; and White, *"It's Your Misfortune."* For regional approaches to the study of religion in the United States, see, e.g., Shipps and Silk, *Religion and Public Life in the Mountain West*. Jan Shipps's introduction to this last volume, subtitled "Religion in the Mountain West: Geography as Destiny," notes that certain features and concerns are common to the American West, among them a "paucity of water," the "issue of tourism," and the fact that "the federal government owns huge portions of land." Given the chapter subtitle, problematic though it may be, the reader might reasonably infer that such features and concerns

influenced social formations and concerns, particularly religious ones, in the West. Such inference is welcome and potentially constructive—we might well investigate the ways in which such facts influenced articulations of religiosity in the West—but there is no follow-through in that regard there, neither in Shipps's article nor in the others contained in the volume.

27. According to Mircea Eliade's model, 'The Sacred,' by manifesting itself in topographical or symbolic hierophanies, may create 'center spaces' for particular groups and peoples. The inner experience of religion is one of attempted and cyclical re-experience, reinhabitance, and reinscription of the sacred space and its underlying power, while its external appearance is one of topographically focused and regionally bounded peoples, in historical places and circumstances, reenacting ahistorical and transcendent phenomena. See Eliade, *Patterns in Comparative Religion*. Such language is far from alien to accounts of Latter-day Saints' encounter with the Great Basin and periodic reenactments thereof. See, e.g., Shipps, *Mormonism*, chapter 6; and Francaviglia, *Believing in Place*. But the proposal here will be that, contra Eliade, the foremost task of the scholar is to historicize the language of nonhuman social determination and to explore the empirical conditions of discussions about nonempirical forces.

28. See Jonathan Z. Smith, *To Take Place*. See also Chidester and Linenthal, "Introduction," for a similar framing of the problem. Other studies of religious placement and cultural geography include Tweed, *Crossing and Dwelling*; Gill, "Territory"; and Knott, *Location of Religion*.

29. In part I am calling here for a return to an often overlooked aspect of Émile Durkheim's particular 'Sacred': the fact that it is and was—as datum and analytic—intimately related to notions of property rights and ownership. See Durkheim, "Rule Prohibiting Attacks on Property" and "Right of Property" (3 parts), in *Professional Ethics and Civic Morals*; and see discussion in Jonathan Z. Smith, *Relating Religion*, 101–5. From a different angle, this approach—and this return to place rather than space—is commensurate with scholarship in indigenous religions that resists the abstractions of "Land Religion"; see, e.g., Denison, *Ute Land Religion in the American West*.

30. Shipps, *Mormonism*, 122.

31. Arrington, *Brigham Young*, 177; Linford, "Establishing and Maintaining Land Ownership," 131; Fox, "Mormon Land System," chapter 5. Two notes of caution are in order, lest the above description make Utahn settlement seem an entirely organized, top-down, autocratic process: first, that some Mormons declined their "calls"; and second, that a great number of Mormon towns (indeed most of them, by the 1880s) "were not colonies but regular settlements founded by families and individuals acting in their own interest" or in the interest of settling among others of similar ethnicity. Farmer, *On Zion's Mount*, 63.

32. Larson, "Land Contest in Early Utah," 313. Jared Farmer describes the historical processes by "several itinerant bands" of mixed-bloods, mixed equestrian/pedestrian groups, and (so-called) Goshutes and Piutes were seen "not [to] qualify as . . . landholding 'tribe[s],'" in Farmer, *On Zion's Mount*, 19–35, 50–53 (citations at 50).

33. Larson, "Land Contest in Early Utah," 314; Arrington, *Brigham Young*, 212, 468n9. The speaker was either Young or Heber C. Kimball.

34. On Walkara's interests in Mormon trading—which included selling stolen Indian children to Mormons—see Farmer, *On Zion's Mount*, 50-51, 77-80. See also Mueller, *Race and the Making of the Mormon People*, 155, 171-74.

35. On Mormon theology with respect to Indians, see Farmer, *On Zion's Mount*, 55-62, 81 ("The church hierarchy generally cared more about the redemption of the Lamanites than did the laity," but "even the authorities were not monolithic" in their "belie[f] in Lamanism"); Mueller, *Race and the Making of the Mormon People*, chapters 5 and 6; Mauss, *All Abraham's Children*, chapters 3-5; and Lindell, "Mormons and Native Americans." On Joseph Smith's, Brigham Young's, and other Mormons' Indian policies, see further Ronald W. Walker, "Seeking the Remnant" and "Toward a Reconstruction of Mormon and Indian Relations." A much-debated (and subsequently retranslated) Book of Mormon passage, 2 Nephi 30:6, prophesies that Lamanites' "scales of darkness shall begin to fall from their eyes; and many generations shall not pass away among them, save they shall be a white and a delightsome people." (The third edition of the Book of Mormon substituted the phrase "pure and ... delightsome" for "white and ... delightsome," but the original wording persisted in subsequent printings.)

36. Arrington, *Brigham Young*, 217-18. On federal Indian policies and the promotion of agriculturalism, see, classically, Prucha, *Great Father*, esp. parts 3 and 5.

37. *CG*, H.R., 35th Cong., 1st Sess., March 11, 1858, 1086. See chapter 1 for discussion.

38. Dimick Huntington, as cited by Farmer, *On Zion's Mount*, 96. Literature on the Mountain Meadows Massacre is extensive. The fullest and most recent contribution to the historiography is Ronald W. Walker, Turley, and Leonard, *Massacre at Mountain Meadows*. On the massacre's relation to the 1857-58 Utah Expedition, and on politicians' fears about Mormon-Indian alliances generally, see also Furniss, *Mormon Conflict*; and Rogers, *Unpopular Sovereignty*, chapter 3.

39. Farmer, *On Zion's Mount*, 77-78.

40. John Turner, *Brigham Young*, 217. See also Arrington, *Brigham Young*, 217, 214; Farmer, *On Zion's Mount*, 87; and Reeve, *Making Space on the Western Frontier*, 101-2.

41. Parenthetical citations: JH, July 31, 1847; Minutes of meeting at Walker's tent, Utah Valley, May 22, 1850, as cited in Arrington, *Brigham Young*, 11 (see also Farmer, *On Zion's Mount*, 79). On LDS petitions for Indian removal and the revocation of Indian land titles (as recognized according to the 1790 Indian Intercourse Act), see Larson, "Land Contest in Early Utah," 316-17; Arrington, *Brigham Young*, 214; and Farmer, *On Zion's Mount*, 100. Later memorials to Congress include William H. Hooper, "Memorial of Utah Citizen Asking Benefit of Certain Laws," Utah Territory Territorial Papers, box N.A. 103 of T.P. 325, folder for March 19, 1860, HR36A.

42. "Uinta Not What Was Represented," *DN*, September 25, 1861; Larson, "Land Contest in Early Utah," 316. President Lincoln set aside the Uinta Reservation in 1861, and Congress confirmed the act in 1864.

43. Arrington, *Brigham Young*, 169, 168, 184-90; Arrington, *GBK*, 112-30. See also Reeve, *Making Space on the Western Frontier*.

44. Arrington, *GBK*, 64-79.

45. On these settlements' deviations from the Plat of Zion or Salt Lake City templates, see Thomas Carter, *Building Zion*.

46. Larson, "Land Contest in Early Utah," 316–17; Arrington, *Brigham Young*, 214; Farmer, *On Zion's Mount*, 100; Hooper, "Memorial of Utah Citizen."

47. John Pierce, as cited in Linford, "Establishing and Maintaining Land Ownership," 137.

48. Linford, "Establishing and Maintaining Land Ownership," 137–39; Larson, "Land Contest in Early Utah," 319–20. The death of Dr. Robinson became a cause célèbre among non-Mormons, and details remain unclear. For two very different accounts of Robinson's eviction and beating, see Beadle, *Life in Utah*, 206–10; and Brigham H. Roberts, "History of the Mormon Church," 453–56. That Robinson laid claim to a resort area is significant, for pleasure-retreats were much-contested places; see chapters 4–6 of the present work for further discussion.

49. Brigham Young, as cited by Linford, "Establishing and Maintaining Land Ownership," 138.

50. Linford, "Establishing and Maintaining Land Ownership," 140.

51. George A. Smith to Jesse N. Smith, May 6, 1869, in HOLC.

52. Amos Milton Musser Journal, December 1, 1869. See also Linford, "Establishing and Maintaining Land Ownership," 142; and Sauder, "State v. Society." Salt Lake City was granted a special exemption for its size and population, and city properties continued to be described in terms of lot, block and plat. Paul Reeve explores the ways in which government surveyors and land agents sought to override Mormon and Southern Paiute settlement systems in southern Utah—and to replace them with policies favorable to Gentile miners and absentee owners—in *Making Space on the Western Frontier*.

53. George A. Smith to Bro. Jacob G. Bigler, May 19, 1869, in HOLC.

54. Whereas the functional trusteeship of a mayor or probate judge occurred in accordance with federal Townsite Act regulations, such mechanisms of distribution were unusual and unauthorized. Nevertheless, federal officials often looked the other way when faced with technical infractions and "ordinary subterfuges" of this sort. (The phrase "ordinary subterfuge" is from Sauder, "State v. Society," 72.)

55. J. T. Little to George Ryndus, December 26, 1871, in Feramorz Little Letter Book, 163. For complaint, see, e.g., "Mormon Land Monopoly," *New York Times*, February 2, 1880.

56. Musser Journal, December 1, 1869.

57. George A. Smith to Albert Carrington, June 30, 1869, in HOLC.

58. Arrington, *GBK*, 236. This and the following section are guided by Arrington's groundbreaking study of Mormon-railroad relations.

59. *JD* 12:54. Leonard Arrington speaks of Young's 1862 stock purchase—presumably undertaken on behalf of the church generally, with Young acting as trustee-in-trust—and his 1865 board appointment in *GBK*, 236–37. Thomas Stevens notes that Brigham Young provided men and supplies to help the UP conduct a survey of the Great Basin area in 1864, one year before his appointment to the board of directors, and that "Young's assistance with the survey netted him $4,692.69 which he had applied to his stock subscription" ("Union Pacific Railroad and Mormon Church," 10–11). The UP's chief surveyor, Samuel Benedict Reed, spoke of the "butter, eggs, milk, and plenty of fresh mutton" provided "by order of President Young" in a

letter dated June 12, 1864 (Samuel Benedict Reed, Letters). George Francis Train on several occasions praised Young for having supported UP surveys, purchased stock, and assumed a position of leadership on the company board during an early stage of transcontinental planning; see Bitton, "George Francis Train and Brigham Young." D. Michael Quinn, citing Maury Klein (*Union Pacific*, 52, 175), stresses that—the ceremonial nature of Young's directorship notwithstanding—he was no mere figurehead, having taken an active role in such early surveys and planning discussions (*Mormon Hierarchy*, 80–81). Later LDS presidents *were* appointed to the same board strictly as ex officio figureheads, but that fact is significant in its own right, indicating the degree to which the UP came to value the history, substance, and appearance of LDS cooperation under Young and his contemporaries.

60. Louisa Sanger to Dear Cousins, April 6, 1868, in Eliza Ann Graves Rich Correspondence, folder 1. Doctrine and Covenants 133:27, referring to Isaiah 11:16 ("And there shall be a highway for the remnant of his people, which shall be left, from Assyria; like as it was to Israel in the day that he [the Lord] came up out of the land of Egypt"), says that "highway will be cast up in the midst of the great deep" for the lost tribes to come to Zion. "Time is no longer" refers to Revelation 10:6.

61. Arrington, *GBK*, 239.

62. Cannon, as cited by Arrington, *GBK*, 239–40.

63. Arrington, *GBK*, 250. Many of the endeavors described in this section were associated with, and overseen by, the so-called School of the Prophets, a semipublic cultural committee that counted Amos Milton Musser, George A. Smith, and other leading Saints among its membership. Brigham Young linked the railroad, Perpetual Emigrating Fund, and Word of Wisdom thus, in his already cited speech on the railroad: "We want to hear the iron horse puffing through this valley . . . [t]o bring our brethren and sisters here. 'But,' says one, 'we shall not have any money.' Yes, we shall, if you and I observe the Word of Wisdom, we shall have plenty of it." *JD* 12:54, May 26, 1867.

64. Arrington, *GBK*, 250.

65. Amos Milton Musser to Young, December 17, 1868, Musser to Young, March 23, 1867, and Office of Walker Brothers to Young, December 31, 1867, in BYOF, Incoming Correspondence.

66. Smith to Carrington, June 30, 1869; George A. Smith to Hannah P. Butler, July 29, 1860, in HOLC.

67. "The Mormon Women and Gentile Fashions," *Crofutt's Western World* 2, no. 1 (July 1872): 6.

68. Brigham Young's instructions to his wives and daughters, November 1869; *DN*, December 6, 1867; and Susa Young Gates, *History of the Young Ladies' Mutual Improvement Association*—as cited in Arrington, *GBK*, 252, 251, and 253, respectively. See also "Young Ladies' Department of the Ladies' Cooperative Retrenchment Association, Resolutions, May 27, 1870," in Derr et al., *First Fifty Years of Relief Society*, 353–57.

69. Arrington, *GBK*, 253.

70. *DN*, January 19, 1870. Utahn women were the first to enact suffrage in America; Wyoming passed a suffrage act earlier than Utah, but Utah held elections before Wyoming. On women's work and activism in Mormonism, the operations of the Relief Society and predecessor organizations in Utah, and the history of Utahn suffrage,

see, e.g., Ulrich, *House Full of Females*, esp. chapters 12, 14–15; Claudia L. Bushman, *Mormon Sisters*; Carol Cornwall Madsen, *Battle for the Ballot*; Van Wagenen, "Sister-Wives and Suffragists"; Claudia Lauper Bushman and Ulrich, *Special Issue, Dialogue*; Alexander, "Experiment in Progressive Legislation"; and Foster, "From Frontier Activism to Neo-Victorian Domesticity."

71. "The Suffrage in Utah," *DCR*, June 10, 1871; "Woman Suffrage Fails," *Corinne Daily Reporter*, December 8, 1871; "Who Are Voters," *Corinne Daily Reporter*, January 30, 1872; "What the Junction Knows about Woman Suffrage," *DCR*, September 25, 1872.

72. Ronald W. Walker, *Wayward Saints*, 98.

73. JH, July 3, 1869.

74. JH, October 3, 1868; Arrington, *GBK*, 248–49. One attendee of the railroad conference characterized the announcement thus: "There was measures entered into to cease supporting the gentiles merchants that was in our midst that was endeavoring to lay a foundation for our overthrow and destruction. The plan was to cease to trade with them and let them alone severly" (Esia Edwards, Journal, November 22, 1868).

75. Bliss, *Merchants and Miners*, 350–51; Arrington, Fox, and May, *Building the City of God*, 91–110; "Constitution and By-Laws of the Zion's Co-operative Mercantile Institution," in Arrington, Fox, and May, *Building the City of God*, app. 3.

76. George A. Smith to Jesse N. Smith, October 23, 1868, in HOLC. Smith reported some $150,000 in subscriptions already in October. For a list of shareholders and capital contributions around March 1869, the first official month of operation, see Arrington, Fox, and May, *Building the City of God*, 93–95.

77. Office of Walker Brothers to Young, December 31, 1867, in BYOF, Incoming Correspondence. The list of jobs and goods provided by the Walkers is taken from their letterhead of this year.

78. Bliss, *Merchants and Miners*, 160.

79. J. K. Trumbo, auctioneer and commission merchant, was among them; see Brigham D. Madsen, *Corinne*, 142.

80. *JD* 13:22–29. George A. Smith predicted a similar fate for Corinne one week later: "Expectations and anticipations are . . . indulged in that Corinne will be permanent and will make a great city, tho I fail to perceive the basis on which any such ideas are founded. The probability is that Corinne will settle down into a small station for way business: for the hundreds of workmen and hangers on who now sustain dram drinking, gambling and brothel keeping will float off to White Pine or other mining localities, or else be compelled to establish some business which will make them producers; but there is little probability that men acquainted with farming in the Mississippi valley will ever do much in that line here where irrigation is necessary unless their religion or other tie equally strong should bind them, to the locality" (Smith to N. S. Elderkin, April 14, 1869, in HOLC). They were not wrong. And to anticipate the arguments of following chapters: Corinnethians went on to attempt 'ties' of religious tourism and irrigated agriculture.

81. Thomas Durant, Telegraph to Young, May 6, 1868, and Young, Telegraph to Durant, May 6, 1868, in BYOF, Incoming Correspondence. Reed wrote of the need to show Brigham Young "the greatest respect" during preliminary contract negotiations in a letter dated May 20, 1868 (Samuel Benedict Reed, Letters). On contract

terms themselves, see Samuel Benedict Reed Correspondence. Items 12, 20, 23, 34, 37, 48, 54, 56, 65, 80–83, 87, 123, 126, 136, 144, 146, 153, 155, and 163 trace the development of Mormon construction contracts and subcontracts. See also Arrington, *GBK*, 261 (which estimates the contract's worth at $2,125,000); Stevens, "Union Pacific Railroad and Mormon Church," 11–19, 60 (which calculates the contract's worth—before additional expenses—at $2,313,957); Athearn, "Contracting for the Union Pacific"; and Reeder, *History of Utah's Railroads*, 30–32.

82. Arrington, *GBK*, 264. See also Stevens, "Union Pacific Railroad and Mormon Church," 17–19, for contract terms and immigration programs. Among Young's subcontractors was non-LDS businessman Joseph F. Nounan, who nonetheless received aid and hands through Brigham Young; see George A. Smith to Carrington, November 4, 1868, in HOLC.

83. Franklin Wheeler Young, Journal, entries for June 8–9 and September 1868, notes difficulties "get[ting] hands" in Cache Valley after laborers had departed for railroad work; and Helena Rosbery, "History," which faults the LDS Church for having sent her husband to work at considerable distance from their home and for failing to support her family during his absence or after his death on the job. Regarding delays in payment, see also Athearn, "Contracting for the Union Pacific," 24–27.

84. Mill operator Esia Edwards noted that "green backs is becoming plenty and the prices of every thing is that we have to sell is a good price" (Journal, January 3, 1869); and teamster Samuel Porter delighted in the high wages and "money harvest" brought by the railroad, though he feared also their transience and the possibility that some Mormon laborers would be left "no better off financially & some worse off spiritually" by close contact with Gentiles ("Journal"). See also Smith to Elderkin, April 14, 1869.

85. Durant to Young, May 6, 1868.

86. *JD* 13:22–29 [April 7, 1869].

87. See again Franklin Wheeler Young, Journal, and Porter, "Journal"; compare "Camp at Devil's Gate," *Deseret Evening News*, June 23, 1868.

88. DN, July 22, 1868, as cited in Reeder, *History of Utah's Railroads*, 33–34.

89. DN, August 12, 1868, as cited in Reeder, *History of Utah's Railroads*, 35–36. For variants of this song, see also "Echo Canyon" or "Hurray, Hurrah, the Railroad's Begun" in Fife Mormon Collection, series I, vol. 4, no. 571, and vol. 3, no. 414.

90. Elijah Malin Weiler to Dear Brother, June 15, 1868, in Elijah Malin Weiler Papers.

91. Klein, *Union Pacific*, 155, 170; George A. Smith to Carrington, September 16, 1868, in HOLC. See Klein, *Union Pacific*, 154–56, 170–71, on arguments among UP officers regarding the relative merits of northern and southern routes.

92. Arrington, *GBK*, 260. Leland Stanford and other CP agents, wishing to maintain positive relations with Mormons, alerted them when anti-Mormon groups tried to secure work contracts along the line. See, e.g., T. B. H. Stenhouse to Young, October 13, 1868, in BYOF, Incoming Correspondence, describing a competitive overture made by Patrick E. Connor.

93. George A. Smith reported on the status of the CP contracts in: Smith to Mrs. Hannah P. Butler, July 29, 1869, in HOLC. As of July 1869 the CP had paid approximately $800,000 and still owed $200,000.

94. As cited by Klein, *Union Pacific*, 175.

95. George A. Smith to Carrington, September 16, 1868, Smith to Carrington, November 4, 1868, and Smith to Elderkin, April 14, 1869, in HOLC. See also Reeder, *History of Utah's Railroads*, 45–46; and Arrington, *GBK*, 263. On contract figures and payments, see further Arrington, *GBK*, 265–70; and Smith to W. H. Hooper, April 3, 1869, in HOLC. On the transcontinental railroad companies as agents and exemplars of modern bureaucratic inefficiency, see White, *Railroaded*.

96. For payment negotiations and details, see esp. Stevens, "Union Pacific and Mormon Church," 55–75; Young to Oliver Ames, April 27, 1870, C. G. Hammond to Ames, May 11, 1870, and Hammond, Telegraph to Ames, May 28, 1870, in UPRC, subgroup 2, series 1, box 8; also statements of July 15 and 18, 1870, in "Statements of Brigham Young's contracting accounts with UP, July–Oct 1870," UPRC, subgroup 5, series 1, box 198, folder 358, the latter of which notes that the UP had provided some $26,000 in emigrant transportation costs before the Boston settlement. I acknowledge that the *Deseret News* often expressed anti-UP sentiments during this time, including charges of gross mistreatment, but—while granting genuine hardships among some subcontractors and workers—I read them partly as an inducement to ever-more-favorable payment terms and timetables by the company, that is, as a shrewd negotiating tactic. For the good relations that belied *Deseret News* rhetoric, see Stevens, "Union Pacific and Mormon Church," 49. See also Arrington, *GBK*, 265–70; Athearn, *Union Pacific Country*, 100–112, 265–69; and Klein, *Union Pacific*, 246–47.

97. Smith to Elderkin, April 14, 1869.

98. Ibid.

99. Saxey [E. L. Sloan], "Promontory, near Cedar City," dated March 25, 1869, in *DN*, April 7, 1869. Emphasis (*civilized*) added to first clause; emphasis in second clause (*developing* . . .) is original.

100. The junction point was not officially fixed at Ogden until 1874, for the federal resolution stated only that it would be "at or near Ogden"; but for all intents and purposes it was always thus. Several LDS officials did attend the Promontory celebrations in Brigham's stead, among them the subcontractors Benson, Farr, and West and the photographer C. R. Savage. Francis A. Hammond—a LDS worker on Benson, Farr, and West's CP contract—may have been one of the men pictured centrally in photographs of the joining ceremony, reaching across the gap between the two engines, holding a bottle (Adamson, *Francis Asbury Hammond*, 77–78; John J. Hammond, pers. comm., September 23, 2016). See image on page 81 of the current work. On UP-CP rail joining celebrations, see Klein, *Union Pacific*, chapter 11. On Mormons' variously frustrated and optimistic reception thereof, see Arrington, *GBK*, 265–70; and Athearn, *Union Pacific Country*, 98–100.

101. On the construction of the Utah Central, see Reeder, *History of Utah's Railroads*, chapter 3; and Arrington, *GBK*, 270–75. See also Utah Central Railroad, Day Book, 1869, in UPRC, subgroup 130, vol. 2.

102. *DN*, January 11, 12, 1870; see Arrington, *GBK*, 273; and Reeder, *History of Utah's Railroads*, chapter 3.

103. Musser Journal, November 16, 1868.

Chapter Three

1. *DN*, May 11, 1869.

2. The excommunication featured condemning testimony by Brigham Young and Apostles Orson Pratt, Wilford Woodruff, and George A. Smith. "The True Development of the Territory" had appeared in *Utah Magazine*, October 16, 1869. See E. L. T. Harrison, "An Appeal to the People," *UM*, October 30, 1869, 406–48, for an account of the ecclesiastical trial. See also chapter 9 of Ronald W. Walker's *Wayward Saints*, a collective biography of Godbeite leaders and the fullest account of the New Movement to date. Musser's recollections are from Amos Milton Musser Journal, December 1, 1869. Godbe recalled the circumstances of his excommunication in "Statement of William S. Godbe, September 2, 1884."

3. Ronald W. Walker, *Wayward Saints*, 43.

4. In naming these five figures especially, I follow the example of Ronald W. Walker, whose *Wayward Saints* points to general trends as well as discrete differences within their speeches, writings, and actions. The Stenhouses' mid-1870s writings and hosting efforts are discussed in later chapters of the current work.

5. E. L. T. Harrison, "We Are Nothing, If Not Spiritual," *UM*, October 23, 1869, 390.

6. Tullidge, "The Godbeite Movement," *Tullidge's Quarterly Magazine* 1, no. 1 (October 1880): 14–64, at 31, 17; Harrison, "Appeal to the People." By reaffirming Young's presidential rights and Utah's pride of place, Godbe, Harrison, and Tullidge distanced themselves from other Mormon groups that had rejected outright the elections of Young and Utah, making clear their play for the LDS mainstream. Compare groups described in D. Michael Quinn, "Mormon Succession Crisis of 1844."

7. Tullidge, "The Reformation in Utah," *Harper's New Monthly Magazine* 43, no. 256 (September 1871): 602–10, at 604.

8. Max Weber, *General Economic History*, 275–78.

9. Tullidge, "Godbeite Movement," 18 (emphasis in original), 17.

10. The *Utah Magazine* (1868–69) was later reorganized as the *Mormon Tribune* (1870) and the *Salt Lake Tribune* (1870–73, albeit with titular variations). The *Tribune* was reorganized in 1873 under different ownership.

11. E. L. T. Harrison, "Our Workmen's Wages," *UM*, August 28, 1869; and W. S. Godbe, "A Card by W. S. Godbe," *UM*, October 30, 1869.

12. "True Development of the Territory."

13. Musser Journal, December 1, 1869. Granted, the Godbeites wanted gold rushes little more than Brigham Young did. But they argued that effective organization and capitalization would obviate placer mining practices and preclude their demographics (read: poor, single, desperate, and transient laborers), meaning that Utah could have stable companies, company towns, and quartz or depth mining from the start. Such enterprises could be managed mainly by Utahn residents, but Godbeites thought it advantageous, still, to hire and consult outside, non-LDS partners. Here again they treaded ecclesiastically and politically contentious terrain, for the church feared the contagions of a Corinnethian ethos, if not the Corinnethian contingent itself. ("True Development of the Territory.")

14. George Darling Watt to Martha Watt, n.d., in G. D. Watt Letters, emphasis added. The *Deseret Evening News* had already denounced the *Utah Magazine* on

October 26, 1869, the day after its publishers' excommunication. The direct questioning of *Salt Lake Tribune* subscribers was a subsequent campaign. Watt himself was excommunicated for Godbeite affiliation in 1874.

15. Tullidge, "Godbeite Movement," 28.
16. Harrison, "We Are Nothing, If Not Spiritual."
17. Harrison, "Appeal to the People"; Tullidge, "Godbeite Movement," 26, 36.
18. This was not Colfax's first visit to the Mormon city; he had visited also in 1865 with Massachusetts reporter Samuel Bowles. See Bowles, *Across the Continent*, 83–84.
19. George A. Smith to George Francis Train, October 11, 1869, in HOLC; Schuyler Colfax, as cited in Ulysses S. Grant, *Papers*, 105–6; Colfax, "Speech of Vice-President Schuyler Colfax"; "Colfax among the Mormons," *New York Times*, October 16, 1869; Bowles, *Across the Continent*, 83. Ovando James Hollister married Caroline Vroom Matthews, half-sister of Schuyler Colfax, on December 1, 1869. In 1886 Hollister published *Life of Schuyler Colfax*. At the time of Colfax's visit, Hollister resided in Salt Lake City, where he held the post of U.S. tax collector; but he still owned land and property in 'downtown' Corinne, straddling the railroad tracks.
20. Colfax, "Speech of Vice-President Schuyler Colfax," 3–4.
21. "I know you claim that a subsequent revelation annulled all this," Colfax continued. Indeed the Utahn church claimed that Joseph Smith's 1843 revelation on polygamy had overruled such imperatives and, moreover, that the revelation itself was anticipated by a second passage in Jacob 2, in which God withholds the right to "command my people . . . otherwise." But Colfax wished "to show [Mormons] that the Congressional law, which you denounce, only enacted what was the original and publicly proclaimed and printed creed on which your church was founded." Colfax, "Speech of Vice-President Schuyler Colfax," 4. See Book of Mormon, Jacob 2:24, 30.
22. On the 'Josephite' mission to Utah, Idaho, and the greater West in 1869, see Avery, *From Mission to Madness*, chapter 5, esp. 93–113; *Utah Weekly Reporter* (Corinne), August 7, 1869; Douglas [O. J. Hollister], "Utah," *Chicago Tribune*, August 8, 1869; "The Mormon Fermentation," *Utah Weekly Reporter*, August 14, 1869; David H. Smith, editorial, dated August 13, 1869, in *Utah Weekly Reporter*, August 14, 1869; "The Mormon Row," *Utah Weekly Reporter*, August 21, 1869; "Editorial Correspondence," *Utah Weekly Reporter*, August 28, 1869; David H. Smith, "Extracts from Elder David H. Smith's Journal," *True Latter Day Saints' Herald* (Plano, Ill.), November 15, 1869; and W. W. Blair's letters printed in the *True Latter Day Saints' Herald*, December 15, 1869, January 1, 1870, and February 15, 1870. The Church of Jesus Christ of Latter Day Saints (note differences in capitalization and punctuation relative to the Utah-based Church of Jesus Christ of Latter-day Saints) added the term 'Reorganized' in 1872. The 'RLDS' changed its name to the Community of Christ in 2001.
23. Ulysses S. Grant, *Papers*, 105–6.
24. Smith to Train, October 11, 1869.
25. Colfax, "Speech of Vice-President Schuyler Colfax," 5.
26. Tullidge, "Godbeite Movement," 55.
27. T. B. H. Stenhouse, as cited in Tullidge, "Godbeite Movement," 55–56. The story was reproduced in Bancroft, *History of Utah*, 656. On Stenhouse's audience with Lincoln, see chapter 1 of the current work.
28. Edward W. Tullidge, "Do We Fear Civilization?," *UM*, November 20, 1869, 454–55.

29. On Mormonism and spiritualism's relations, especially with reference to Godbeitism, see Ronald W. Walker, "When the Spirits Did Abound"; Bitton, "Mormonism's Encounter with Spiritualism"; and Homer, "Spiritualism and Mormonism." On spiritualism as site and datum for religious definition more broadly, see David Walker, "Humbug in American Religion."

30. W. S. Godbe and E. L. T. Harrison, "Manifesto from W. S. Godbe and E. L. T. Harrison," *UM*, November 27, 1869; "Spiritualism and Priesthood," *UM*, January 18, 1869.

31. *New York Herald*, January 2, 1870, 8; Godbe and Harrison, "Manifesto." On the 1868 "New York Epiphany," see Ronald W. Walker, *Wayward Saints*, chapter 7.

32. Brigham Young, JH, February 2, 1870.

33. See Ronald W. Walker, *Wayward Saints*, 205–7. Among Godbeites, T. B. H. Stenhouse was the most persistent in comparing Joseph Smith with spiritualist mediums. He was also the most willing to cast Smith as a lesser party in some such comparisons. See T. B. H. Stenhouse, *Rocky Mountain Saints*, 521; and Bitton, "Mormonism's Encounter with Spiritualism," 44.

34. "Salt Lake Correspondence," *DUR*, June 26, 1870.

35. As cited in Tullidge, *History of Salt Lake City*, 491; and in Tullidge, *Tullidge's Histories*, 309. Although the name "Liberal Party" was not fixed until July 1870, I use the term more broadly and with earlier application, here, not only for the sake of clarity, but in recognition of erstwhile shared discourses of liberalism among coalition partners. On the Liberal Party, see also Brigham D. Madsen, *Corinne*, chapter 4.

36. Ronald W. Walker, *Wayward Saints*, 217.

37. Orson F. Whitney, *History of Utah*, 385–86; Ronald W. Walker, *Wayward Saints*, 217–18. The People's Party was named in jest, referencing the Liberals' invitation to "the people of Salt Lake City."

38. Tullidge, *History of Salt Lake City*, 491.

39. "Invitation," *DUR*, June 7, 1870; "The Right Man," *DUR*, June 17, 1870.

40. "Our Convention," *DUR*, July 17, 1870.

41. "Salt Lake Correspondence," *DUR*, June 26, 1870.

42. Douglas [O. J. Hollister], "Utah," *Chicago Tribune*, July 11, 1870.

43. Douglas [O. J. Hollister], "Utah," *Chicago Tribune*, February 12, 1870.

44. Douglas [O. J. Hollister], "Utah," *Chicago Tribune*, March 24, 1870.

45. "The Political Situation," *DUR*, July 16, 1870; "Our Convention," *DUR*, July 17, 1870; Brigham D. Madsen, *Corinne*, chapter 4.

46. "Political Situation." For his part, Beadle came later to appreciate a certain logic and strategy in supporting the New Movement. In his 1870 *Life in Utah* he applauded Godbeites for advancing "the most sensible and promising set of principles from any of the recusant [Mormon] sects," including the antipolygamous Josephites. Beadle particularly—and predictably—approved of Godbeites' arguments that "the mines should be developed, and trade free and unrestricted with all classes." Nevertheless he remained wary of their "claim to be good Mormons, maintain[ing] polygamy and every man's right to revelation." At best Beadle hoped that "[Godbeites] are sufficiently crazy to outdo Brigham in fanaticism" and that, by means of spiritualism or otherwise, they would "carry the matter through," splintering Mormonism—and perhaps sacrificing themselves—for the sake of "liberal principles." Regime change

effected, Corinnethians would fill the power vacuum and emerge triumphant (*Life in Utah*, 433-34).

47. For discussions of the Cullom Bill with reference to Godbeitism, Corinne, and antipolygamy legislative histories more generally, see, respectively, Ronald W. Walker, *Wayward Saints*, 214-15, 219-21; Brigham D. Madsen, *Corinne*, 93-96; and Arrington, *GBK*, 357.

48. This and subsequent Cullom Bill citations are from H.R. 1089, "A Bill in Aid of the Execution of the Laws in the Territory of Utah, and for other purposes," 41st Cong., 2nd Sess., February 3, 1870. See also an earlier (but quickly abandoned) form of the bill, H.R. 696, 41st Cong., 2nd Sess., December 21, 1869; and the final form of the bill, H.R. 1089, as passed by the House of Representatives and introduced in the Senate, 41st Cong., 2nd Sess., March 24, 1870. Despite its multiple authorship, I use "Cullom" as shorthand for the bill's authors below.

49. Without stating outright opposition to women's voting in America, the Cullom Bill assumed that it would be an especially counterproductive and pernicious practice in Utah, where most women were Mormon and where all electoral processes were monitored by LDS churchmen. No loyal Mormon could be trusted to recognize his or her own best interests, by logic of the Cullom Bill, let alone vote for them. This was a problem of voter intimidation and vote tampering (hence another provision of the bill: that all ballots be unnumbered and anonymous), but it was also a problem of mental capacity and education. In any case, Cullom said, information required a kind of corrective paternalism, a federal counterbalance to Utah's local patriarchy.

50. Ronald W. Walker, *Wayward Saints*, 214-15.

51. Beadle's testimony, reproduced in "Laws in Utah: To Accompany Bill H.R. No. 1089," H.R. Rep. 21, part 2, 41st Cong., 2nd Sess., 7-15, was given February 9, 1870 (hereinafter cited as H.R. Rep. 21, part 2). See also "Execution of the Laws in Utah: To Accompany Bill H. R. No. 1089," H.R. Rep. 21, 41st Cong., 2nd Sess. (hereinafter cited as H.R. Rep. 21, part 1); and "Laws in Utah: To Accompany H. R. No. 1089," H.R. Rep. 21, part 3, 41st Cong., 2nd Sess. (hereinafter H.R. Rep. 21, part 3). Other key witnesses were R. N. Baskin, Salt Lake City lawyer; John P. Taggart, United States assessor for Utah Territory; Alexander Major, dealer of lumber in southern Idaho; and Franklin Head, former superintendent of Indian affairs in Utah. Original copies of their testimony are housed in Utah Territory Territorial Papers, boxes N.A. 102 and 103 of T.P. 325, folders marked February 3, February 14, and March 10, 1870.

52. R. N. Baskin, in H.R. Rep. 21, part 1, 17.

53. Beadle, *Life in Utah*, 523-24. On Beadle's pro-Cullom lobbying efforts, see also Brigham D. Madsen, *Corinne*, 94-96.

54. H.R. Rep. 21, part 2, 12. This was one of Buckley's favored questions. Two days later he asked a version to John P. Taggart: "Do you think Mormonism can sustain itself when brought into contact with *the institutions of civilization*, by means of railroads, &c?" When set for publication, the clause "the institutions of civilization" was replaced by the presumptively equivalent phrase "American institutions." Compare ibid., 6, with testimony in Utah Territory Territorial Papers, box N.A. 102 of T.P. 325, folder for February 14, 1870.

55. H.R. Rep. 21, part 2, 12. The manuscript testimony suggests "thirty or forty" years, whereas the printed version reads "twenty or thirty." Compare ibid. with

testimony in Utah Territory Territorial Papers, box N.A. 102 of T.P. 325, folder for February 14, 1870.

56. J. H. Beadle, "Correspondence," *DUR*, June 11, 1870.

57. H.R. Rep. 21, part 3, 5. Head testified before Congress on February 28, 1870, nineteen days after Beadle.

58. Ibid., 3–4.

59. Tullidge, "Godbeite Movement," 58. On Tullidge's appeal for Godbeite-LDS reconciliations, see Ronald W. Walker, *Wayward Saints*, 308–9.

60. On congressional bureaucracy and lobbying activity in the Gilded Age, see Thompson, *"Spider Web."* Thompson describes congressmen in terms almost antithetical to Max Weber's description of "the trained official, the pillar of both the modern State and of the economic life of the West," master of systematic thought and specialized expertise (Max Weber, *Protestant Ethic and the Spirit of Capitalism* [Parsons trans.], 16).

61. Hooper delivered a lengthy speech in the House of Representatives on March 22–23, 1870, arguing—with evidence from scripture, biblical interpretation, Christian sacramentalism, American constitutional law, and the history of Mormonism—that Mormon marriages were legitimately religious and thus legally protected. "Polygamy in Utah: Speech of Hon. W. H. Hooper, of Utah, in the House of Representatives, March 22 and 23, 1870," *CG*, 41st Cong., 2nd Sess., March 22–23, 1870, app., 173–79.

62. See Aaron A. Sargent's speech regarding the Pacific railroad, as reproduced in *CG*, H.R., 37th Cong., 2nd Sess., January 31, 1862, 599–603. Sargent was not always the unanimous darling of railroad leadership; on controversy among CP personnel respecting Sargent's 1885 senatorial candidacy, when Leland Stanford advanced himself as a competitor, see White, *Railroaded*, 259–62. Thomas Fitch was a short-term congressman but a lifelong politician. He wrote a series of "Recollections and Reflections" about his personal and political life for the *San Francisco Call* in 1903–4; these have been republished as Fitch, *Western Carpetbagger*.

63. *CG*, February 23, 1870, 1517, 1519.

64. [Hollister], "Utah," *Chicago Tribune*, February 12, 1870.

65. "Modification of the Cullom Bill," in Tullidge, "Godbeite Movement," 59–61, at 60; see also "Opinions of the Press on the Cullom Bill," *DN*, April 27, 1870.

66. "Modification of the Cullom Bill," 60. On this front the Godbeites were in full agreement with a reporter for the *DN*, who nicknamed the Cullom Bill "An Act to Replenish Brothels" (*DN*, May 2, 1870).

67. See *CG*, H.R., 41st Cong., 2nd Sess., March 23, 1870, 2180–81.

68. See *CG*, S., 41st Cong., 2nd Sess., May 18, 1870, 3571–82.

69. The phrase "put religion into discourse" evokes Michel Foucault's discussion of sex being "put into discourse" in *History of Sexuality*, 11.

70. "Cullom a Mormon Missionary," *DN*, April 27, 1870.

Chapter Four

1. J. H. Beadle, Letter dated September 29, 1868, in *Cincinnati Commercial*, October 17, 1868; "Great Enterprise!," *Salt Lake Daily Reporter* [December 11, 1868], in JHBS.

2. "Great Enterprise!"

3. "Brigham Correspondence," dated February 21, 1869 [*Salt Lake Weekly Reporter*, February 27, 1869], in JHBS.

4. Withey, *Grand Tours and Cook's Tours*, 29, 43. See also Buzard, *Beaten Track* and "Grand Tour and After"; and Sweet, *Cities and the Grand Tour*.

5. Europeans and Americans alike had long been interested in visiting biblical lands, hoping there to uncover and understand biblical truths; bolstered by new steamboat services, guidebooks, and organized group tours, such travel boomed in the 1860s. One major promoter of Egyptian and Palestinian tourism was Thomas Cook, a British Baptist and temperance advocate who organized 'moral tours' in collaboration with early steamboat and railroad companies. Withey, *Grand Tours and Cook's Tours*, chapter 8; Ben-Arieh, *Rediscovery of the Holy Land*; Said, *Orientalism*, esp. 166–97; Vogel, *To See a Promised Land*; Obenzinger, *American Palestine*; Brendon, *Thomas Cook*.

6. Sears, *Sacred Places*; McKinsey, *Niagara Falls*; Bendixen and Hamera, *Cambridge Companion to American Travel Writing*, part 1; Shaffer, "'See America First'" and *See America First*; Pomeroy, *In Search of the Golden West*; Withey, *Grand Tours and Cook's Tours*, chapter 4. On the rising popularity of beach going and sanitarium trips among an (also rising) American middle class in the mid-nineteenth to early twentieth century, see also Aron, *Working at Play*. The classic sociological statements on the leisure class and its tourist practices are Veblen, *Theory of the Leisure Class*; and MacCannell, *Tourist*.

7. "Brigham Correspondence," dated February 21, 1869.

8. 'Douglas' [O. J. Hollister], "Utah," *Chicago Tribune*, July 8, 1869. On the scheduling of Ogden layovers, see "The Future of Our Train," *Trans-Continental* 1, no. 12 (July 4, 1870). The regular one-way fare from Ogden to Salt Lake City (or vice versa) in 1870 was $2.50. Travelers returning the same day via the accommodation train paid only the one-way fare, and travelers willing to ride in a mixed passenger/freight car paid less than half the regular fare. In March 1870, total passenger and freight receipts for the Utah Central were $3,307 and $2,937, respectively. See Reeder Jr., *History of Utah's Railroads*, 90–92, 94, which, however, offers no breakdown of earnings from touristic versus local travel and no data for the number of Mormon ex-laborers traveling at reduced fares. For the UP, passenger fares also outstripped freight earnings in 1870 and periodically thereafter; see Fifer, *American Progress*, 191.

9. "Our Water Privilege," *DUR*, June 17, 1870; *DUR*, July 17, 1870. Many people took notice of the *Kate Connor*'s relaunch, including historian Hubert Howe Bancroft, who clipped and filed the following notice among his reference notes: "The Pioneer Steamer on Salt Lake and Bear River. . . . It would be a good idea to run regular excursion trips from Corinne to the neighborhood of Salt Lake City. It would be possible to land passengers within four or five miles of the Mormon capital, and tourists would gladly avail themselves of the chance of a trip on a lake, which is one of the great natural curiosities of our continent." "Utah, 1869, First Steamer, Corinne, July 17, 1869," in Bancroft Reference Notes for the Western States, carton 24, folder 5.

10. "Salt Lake City," *DUR*, August 9, 1870. Beadle was accompanied on his journey by Presbyterian minister E. E. Bayliss and other Corinnethians.

11. T. B. H. Stenhouse, *Rocky Mountain Saints*, chapter 56; Bliss, *Merchants and Miners*, 167–76; Brigham D. Madsen, *Glory Hunter*, 184–87. Madsen reports that between

August and October 1870, Connor and the Walker brothers, who paid $10,000 for the Silveropolis mine, "had shipped 500 sacks of ore, worth from $50 to $100 per sack" (186).

12. "A Steamboat," *DUR*, December 2, 1870.

13. "From Corinne to Lake Point," *DCR*, May 16, 1871; "All Together Now," *DCR*, May 24, 1871; Brigham D. Madsen, *Corinne*, 164, 160; "From Ophir," *DCR*, April 14, 1871. See also reports in the *DCR* of May 13 and 19 and June 13 and 16, 1871.

14. Brigham D. Madsen, *Corinne*, 158–61, and *City of Corinne*; "From Corinne to Lake Point"; *SLH*, May 19, 1871. Opportunistic Mormon doctor, justice of the peace, and businessman Jeter Clinton (who later supported Mormon resorts with equal vigor), anticipating an influx of Gentile traders and excursionists at Lake Point, built a "Lake House" resort there in 1870. See "Lake Navigation," *DCR*, August 11, 1870; Morgan, *Great Salt Lake*, 353–54; "From Ophir"; and "The Utah Mines," *DCR*, April 17, 1871. Corinnethians also toyed with the idea of setting up their own lakeside swimming area and heath resort, but plans for "Lake View" were quickly abandoned. See "A Road to Salt Lake," *DUR*, August 19, 1870; and "Lake View," *DUR*, August 22, 1870.

15. "The Tourists Elysium," *DCR*, June 15, 1871.

16. "Finishing the Work," *DCR*, May 24, 1871; "The 'City of Corinne,'" *DCR*, June 21, 1871; Morgan, *Great Salt Lake*, 300. See also coverage in the *DCR* of May 18, 19, and 22 and June 5, 12, and 14, 1871.

17. Brigham D. Madsen, *Glory Hunter* (187), *Corinne* (164), and *City of Corinne*, which notes that "financially, the new steamboat service was a failure, probably because the ship could not get over the mud bar at the mouth of Bear River with a full load of ore." The boat floated more in the salty water of the lake than it did the fresh water at the outlet of the Bear River. See also Morgan, *Great Salt Lake*, 300.

18. Brigham D. Madsen, *Corinne*, 164; Arrington, *GBK*, 275; Reeder, *History of Utah's Railroads*, 94–95.

19. William Birelie Hyde to Mattie Hyde, June 14, 1871, in William Birelie Hyde Papers, box 1, folder 1. Hyde longed for the day when "the across the lake trip will be one of the most delightful in the whole of The Great Overland."

20. Hübner, *Ramble round the World*, 118–19.

21. U.S. Census for Box Elder County, June 1870; E. Bayliss to Sheldon Jackson, 17 May 1870, in SJP, box 1, folder 13; "Brigham Correspondence," dated March 11, 1869 [*Salt Lake Weekly Reporter*, ca. March 13, 1869], in JHBS; Toponce, *Reminiscences*, 195–96; Brigham D. Madsen, *Corinne*, chapter 2; Corinne City Council Minutes, 1870.

22. Brigham D. Madsen, *Corinne* (272–76), *Shoshoni Frontier* (chapters 10 and 11), and *Northern Shoshoni* (esp. 34–40, 48–56, 58–64, 90–92).

23. *Utah Reporter*, April 21 and November 17, 1870; Brigham D. Madsen, *Corinne*, 274–75.

24. Brigham D. Madsen, *Northern Shoshoni*, 90, and *Corinne*, 275; Corinne City Council Minutes, August 1–2, 1870. The Corinnethians' petition claimed that Indians spread pestilence and odor in the city.

25. Hübner, *Ramble round the World*, 118–19.

26. Ibid., 122. On this cultural fascination with American Indians—a fascination epitomized by the later writings of Karl May—see Penny, *Kindred by Choice*.

27. Hübner, *Ramble round the World*, 122–23.

28. The literature on displaying and playing Indian(ness) is vast. Important works include Philip J. Deloria, *Playing Indian*; Hoxie, *Final Promise*; Fowler, *Laboratory for Anthropology*; McFeely, "Palimpsest of American Identity"; Dilworth, *Imagining Indians in the Southwest* and "Tourists and Indians in Fred Harvey's Southwest"; Wenger, *We Have a Religion* and "Modernists, Pueblo Indians, and the Politics of Primitivism"; and Warren, *Buffalo Bill's America*, chapters 13 and 14.

29. Joseph Hill, son of George W. Hill, as cited in Ralph O. Brown, "Life and Missionary Labors of George Washington Hill," 62; and Christensen, *Sagwitch*, 98.

30. Marvin Mikesell coined the terms "frontier of inclusion" and "frontier of exclusion" when describing Spanish American and Anglo-American colonial policies, respectively, in "Comparative Studies in Frontier History," 65. See also David J. Weber, "Turner, the Boltonians, and the Borderlands."

31. *DCR*, June 27, 1871.

32. The Corinne station on the CP opened for business December 4, 1869. For legal discussions regarding subsidy bonds for lands and construction between Promontory and Ogden, see Correspondence of July–December 1869, in UPRC, subgroup 8, series 1, box 294, folder 12; Correspondence of June 1870, in UPRC, subgroup 2, series 1, box 6, folder 32; Caleb Cushing to O. Ames, July 10, 13, and 19, 1869, in UPRC, subgroup 2, series 1, box 3, folder 38; and UP, "Claim for Bonds Between Ogden and Promontory Summit," in UPRC, subgroup 2, series 1, box 3. For Corinnethian reports and frustrations, see "Railroad Lots, Churches, Etc.," *DUR*, September 8, 1870; "Union Pacific Town Lots," *DUR*, September 9, 1870; "[Re:] 'Railroad Lots, Churches, Etc.,'" *DUR*, September 9, 1870; "Water," *DCR*, May 9, 1871; "Land Decision," *DCR*, May 24, 1871; Corinne City Council Minutes, entries for June 16 and August 1, 1870, and June 10 and December 6, 1871; and Toponce, *Reminiscences*, 186–87. For an earlier report on Stanford's unwillingness to commit the CP to the Corinnethian cause, see also ". . . And All along the R. R. Line," *DN*, May 5, 1869. On the CP's general policy of noninvestment in northern and western Utahn lands, and on the related unclarity of titles there, see Orsi, *Sunset Limited*, 74–75, 79. Very few references to Corinne station and its surrounding lands survive in the CP corporate archives, for instance in the 1880 Station Plan Book, Salt Lake Division, CP Railroad Collection; and CP Earnings and Expenses Ledger Book, 1869–71, Gilbert H. Kneiss Collection, box 44.

33. *DCR*, July 1, 1871.

34. "The Coming Celebration," *DCR*, June 30, 1871; "Grand Excursion," *DCR*, June 30, 1871.

35. "Ode on Independence Day, Written For and Read at the Celebration by the Liberal Party at Salt Lake City, on the Fourth of July, 1871, by Nat Stein, Esq., of Corinne," Nat Stein Collection. Stein's poem was printed (in slightly edited form) as a broadside by the *Corinne Daily Journal*.

36. "Coming Celebration."

37. MacCannell, *Tourist*, 13, italics omitted. Other works connecting travel (albeit not necessarily of the leisure-class sort) and the work of cultural or religious theory include Clifford, "Notes on Travel and Theory"; and Tweed, *Crossing and Dwelling*. For introductions to anthropological and religious studies approaches to tourism, see Valene L. Smith, *Hosts and Guests*; Norman, *Spiritual Tourism*; Stausberg, *Religion and Tourism*.

38. MacCannell, *Tourist*, 9.

39. George A. Smith to George Francis Train, October 11, 1869, in HOLC. See chapter 3 for discussion.

40. Coffin, "Diary of a Visit to Salt Lake City." Compare Coffin, *Our New Way round the World*, chapter 61. Most of Coffin's book treated travel and culture in Europe, India, and East Asia, but the concluding section covered California, Utah, and the Pacific Railway. Beadle published descriptions of the Endowment House and its (supposed) rituals in *Life in Utah* (1870), 242, and chapter 20. On the Endowment House, see Lisle Brown, "Temple Pro Tempore."

41. Coffin, "Diary of a Visit to Salt Lake City"; 'Carleton' [Coffin], "Round the World Sketches" [no. 5], *Boston Journal*, January 30, 1869; Coffin, *Our New Way round the World*, 500. On the popularity of Wait's 1866 book *The Mormon Prophet and His Harem*, see also Campbell, *Charles Ellis Johnson and the Erotic Mormon Image*, 95.

42. Coffin, "Diary of a Visit to Salt Lake City"; 'Carleton' [Coffin], "Round the World Sketches" [no. 3], *Boston Journal*, January 16, 1869.

43. 'Carleton' [Coffin], "Round the World Sketches" [no. 2], *Boston Journal*, January 9, 1869. On the tabernacle buildings, see Robison with Dixon, *Gathering as One*, esp. chapters 4–8; and Thomas Carter, *Building Zion*, 210–14. On some LDS leaders' reticence to allow outsiders into the tabernacles and, in time, their embrace of the New Tabernacle as an outwardly facing "stage for high culture," see Hafen, "City of Saints, City of Sinners," 363–64, 372–73. The New Tabernacle is elsewhere and hereafter called also the Salt Lake Tabernacle or simply the Tabernacle.

44. 'Carleton' [Coffin], "Round the World Sketches" [no. 2].

45. 'Carleton' [Coffin], "Round the World Sketches" [no. 6], *Boston Journal*, February 6, 1869.

46. Angela G. Ray, *Lyceum and Public Culture*, 144. On Dickinson's career generally, see Gallman, *America's Joan of Ark*.

47. 'Douglas' [Hollister], "Utah," *Chicago Tribune*, July 8, 1869.

48. Dickinson, "Mormonism"; "Anna Dickinson's Lecture on Sunday Evening," *San Francisco Chronicle*, September 7, 1869; "Parker Fraternity Lectures," *Boston Daily Journal*, October 13, 1869; "Whited Sepulchres," *Brooklyn Daily Eagle*, November 20, 1869. The first publication contains Dickinson's lecture notes, whereas the others are partial transcriptions of her lecture by attendees and reporters. The phrase "whited sepulchres" is itself drawn from Matthew 23:27 (KJV): " Woe unto you, scribes and Pharisees, hypocrites! for ye are like unto *whited sepulchres*, which indeed appear beautiful outward, but are within full of dead men's bones, and of all uncleanness."

49. I have opted not to refer to Helen Hunt by her better-known name, partly because it would be anachronistic to do so and partly because the author herself attributed the work to "H. H.," even in printings antedating her marriage. *Bits of Travel at Home* was published in its entirety in 1878 but recalls a trip taken in 1872. The author married Sharpless Jackson in 1875.

50. H. H. [Helen Hunt], *Bits of Travel at Home*, 17–18.

51. Ibid., 20, 21–22.

52. Ibid., 26.

53. Ibid., 27.

54. Brigham Young, as cited in Arrington, *GBK*, 252. See chapter 2 of the present work for commentary.

55. Mrs. T. B. H. [Fanny] Stenhouse, *Exposé of Polygamy*. Charles Carleton Coffin met briefly with T. B. H. Stenhouse during his 1868 tour, but he recorded only that Stenhouse was "proprietor of Daily Telegraph. Met him in S. L., has two wives" (Coffin, "Diary of a Visit to Salt Lake City and Travel to Chicago"). The Stenhouses formally requested excommunication from the LDS Church in the summer of 1870. On Fanny Stenhouse's *Exposé* and other works by the Stenhouses after this date, see DeSimone, "Introduction"; and Ronald W. Walker, *Wayward Saints*, 295–306.

56. Mrs. T. B. H. [Fanny] Stenhouse, *Exposé of Polygamy*, 111, 73.

57. Ibid., 146, 87.

58. Ibid., 154. Stenhouse here also addresses a (satirical but nonetheless biting) suggestion made by Mark Twain: that multiple marriage was an act of benevolent selflessness, on the part of Mormon men, because Mormon women were unattractive. Twain's *Roughing It* recalls an 1860s stagecoach trip, but it was published in 1872 to capitalize on the new market for travelogues.

59. Advertisement, *Salt Lake Tribune*, April 28, 1871; "Millinery and Dressmaking," *SLH*, June 20, 1871.

60. Mrs. T. B. H. [Fanny] Stenhouse, *Exposé of Polygamy*, 155.

61. Ronald W. Walker, *Wayward Saints*, 298, 301.

62. "The Lecture Last Night," *Corinne Daily Reporter*, November 3, 1872.

63. Beadle moved to Indiana in late 1872, but he returned to Utah in 1874, then resided in Salt Lake City for a few more years, before moving back to Indiana (again) ca. 1878.

64. This was the guidebook's title by 1871, in its third year of publication. It was first published in 1869 with the main title *Great Trans-Continental Railroad Guide*. By late 1870—its second of many reprints and revisions—it was renamed the *Great Trans-Continental Tourist's Guide*; and in 1871 (through 1876) it became *Crofutt's Trans-Continental Tourist's Guide*, all the while retaining the same basic subtitle. Crofutt's cowriter and co-compiler was H. Wallace Atwell, but for simplicity I use "Crofutt" as shorthand for the guidebook and its authors. On Crofutt and his guidebooks, see Fifer, *American Progress*, which discusses also the novelty of the term "trans-continental" (as opposed to "overland" or "pacific") at 168–70. Crofutt was himself a one-time resident of Salt Lake City, where, after working briefly as a freighting operator, he had a hand in the publication (with E. L. Sloan) of *The Salt Lake City Directory and Business Guide for 1869*, which contained a short history of Mormonism, a description of Pacific Railway legislation, and a twenty-two-page section on "Chicago: Its Growth and Trade." The only mention of Corinne there is a paid advertisement for the *Corine* [sic] *Daily Reporter*, offering "Job Printing of Every Description, Executed on the Shortest Notice, and at the Lowest Cash Prices" (ibid., 148).

65. Fifer, *American Progress*, 171, 181, 186. Chromolithographs of John Gast's 1872 painting were copyrighted and offered for sale beginning in 1873.

66. *Crofutt's Trans-Continental Tourist's Guide* [1871], 97, 109. The text regarding Corinne had been in place since the 1869 publication. The main difference between the 1869 and 1871 reports was their population estimates: the 1869 edition said that

Corinne "contains about 2,500 inhabitants," while the 1871 deflated that number to a still-optimistic 1,000. Compare *Great Trans-Continental Railroad Guide* [1869], 129.

67. *Crofutt's Trans-Continental Tourist's Guide* [1869], 106–8; *Crofutt's Trans-Continental Tourist's Guide* [1871], 98, italics omitted.

68. *Crofutt's Trans-Continental Tourist's Guide* [1871], 104. The context of this quotation is a discussion of the Utah Central Railroad (which Crofutt takes to be a positive public good) and Brigham Young's other public works.

69. On the Danites, see Rebecca Foster Cornwall and Arrington, "Perpetuation of a Myth"; Gentry, "Danite Band of 1838"; and Ronald W. Walker, Turley, and Leonard, *Massacre at Mountain Meadows*. On Hickman, see Hilton, *"Wild Bill" Hickman and the Mormon Frontier*.

70. Neither Young nor Hickman nor the others were brought to trial on these charges. Brigham Young was, however, briefly confined to house arrest while federal officers pursued the case against him.

71. Hickman [and Beadle], *Brigham's Destroying Angel*; Arrington, "Kate Field and J. H. Beadle"; Kate B. Carter, "Notes on the Life of 'Bill' Hickman."

72. Hickman [and Beadle], *Brigham's Destroying Angel*, 195.

73. "It is idle to talk of any compromise" while the church "claim[s] absolute temporal power within its jurisdiction," Beadle maintained. See, respectively, ibid., 219, 10, 24, 11, 15–16, 205, 16. Beadle pursues also some of his earlier lines of comparative religion here, as familiar from his 1870 publication *Life in Utah*. He calls Mormonism "Mohammedanism Yankeeized," on account of its passionate excess and temporal tyranny, and he likens it to Munster Anabaptism, Shakerism, Free-Love-ism, and Communism, on account of their followers "imagin[ing] they alone had a right to the favor of God" (ibid., 16, 9–10).

74. Beadle himself became one such roving reporter later in 1872. His six-part series detailing a trip through New Mexico and Navajo country, titled "Across the Continent: The Irrepressible Beadle on a Mule," was published in the *Crofutt's Western World* issues of May 1872 (letter no. 1, 74), June 1872 (no. 2, 82–83), August 1872 (nos. 3 and 4, 18, 26–28), September 1872 (no. 5, 44–45), and October 1872 (no. 6, 59–60). See also "Beadle on a Mule," *Crofutt's Western World* 1, no. 3 (March 1872): 40. With respect to the current narrative, the most salient feature of this series is Beadle's comparison of "Navajoe theology" with Mormonism: "Like most savage races, [Navajo] theology is principally superstition. *Chinday*, the devil, is a more important personage in all their daily affairs than *Whaillahay*, the *god*. Like the Mormons, Shakers, and other white schismatics, they attribute everything they don't like in other people to the personal agency of the devil; and about the only value of their *god* is to protect them from the devil. . . . Their moral code is extremely vague; whatever is good for the tribe or band is in general right; whatever is not *pro bono public[o]* is wrong" (Beadle, "Across the Continent: Letter Number Four: The Irrepressible Beadle on a Mule," *Crofutt's Western World* 2, no. 2 [August 1872]). Such comparisons would soon be developed further by his fellows back at Corinne.

75. *Crofutt's Western World*, published in San Francisco and New York, ran from 1872 to 1874. Crofutt's biographer estimates a peak circulation of nine thousand to ten thousand in 1873; see Fifer, *American Progress*, 197. None of the above is meant to imply that *Brigham's Destroying Angel* was slighted by its publisher. To the contrary,

Crofutt's Western World ran numerous full-page advertisements for it, along with lengthy reviews and excerpts. (See "Mormonism and Its Latest Exposure," *Crofutt's Western World* 1, no. 2 [February 1872]: 17–18; and "Wm. A. Hickman, Brigham Young's Destroying Angel," *Crofutt's Western World* 1, no. 1 [January 1872]: 16.) The point that I am making here is that Crofutt promoted it mainly in that particular venue. By contrast there appeared in his 250-page 1872 *Tourist's Guide* only an engraving of Hickman and a short note under the heading "Uintah Station": "Near this station, on this broad bottom, in 1862, was the scene of the Morrissite Massacre, related by Bill Hickman, in his confession, recently published, and which lays bare some of the most fearful crimes ever committed in the name of religion in *this* or *any* age of the world" (*Crofutt's Trans-Continental Tourist's Guide* [1872], 96–97). The tone was arguably consistent, but the tense was different, and so too was the terrain; the *Guide* did not speak of present Latter-day atrocities or the persistent plague of Mormonism.

76. Brigham D. Madsen, *Glory Hunter*, 187, 204; *Utah Mining Journal*, November 14, 1872. The new owner was Christopher Layton, of Kaysville.

77. Morgan, *Great Salt Lake*, 354, also 300. See also Brigham D. Madsen, *Corinne*, 167–68; *SLH*, April 16, 1872; and *Deseret Evening News*, May 20, 1872. John W. Young describes the purchase of the *City of Corinne* in a letter to George W. Thatcher and John N. Pike, November 6, 1874, in John W. Young Papers, box 2, folder 11.

78. Brigham D. Madsen, *Corinne*, 166. See "Steamer Excursion on the Lake," *DN*, May 1872. The article reports an "agreeable ride on the U.C.R.R.," bringing "the party to Lake Side," whereupon excursionists set foot on the *City of Corinne*. "We understand the original intention was to steam from Lake Side to Lake Point, land there for a while, re-embark, and return to Lake Side," but the *Deseret News* reporter was pleased to find that "this intention was relinquished in favor of a voyage clear round the Island," thus avoiding the Gentile dock at Lake Point.

Chapter Five

1. Codman, *Mormon Country*, 1–2.

2. Ibid., 3, 7; Hamilton, *Gail Hamilton's Life in Letters*, 715–16, 721. Gail Hamilton was the penname of Mary Abigail Dodge.

3. Pullman's grandmother was a member of the Mormon Church for a time in Nauvoo, and he may have been motivated by a measure of familial feeling, beyond corporate interest, to see and support the Saints. However I have found little evidence to that effect. Pullman told George Q. Cannon about his grandmother's church affiliation during a later visit in Chicago, but they seem to have spoken mostly about systems of town planning and communal responsibility in Nauvoo and the Chicagoan neighborhood of Pullman (which Pullman founded in the 1880s). See GQCJ, September 7, 1893. Pullman didn't tell Cannon as much, but his wife's aunt Louisa Sanger had also been a member of the original Nauvoo Relief Society, though she refused to move to Utah and became a critic of 'Brighamite' Mormonism.

4. Hamilton, *Gail Hamilton's Life in Letters*, 721. James Townsend brought the idea of opening a "Publick House" to Brigham Young in 1857: Townsend to Young, July 3, 1857, in BYOF, General Letters, 1840–1877. The hotel was built shortly after the Civil War—the *Deseret News* first advertised it in December 18, 1867—and by 1868 it was well established as Salt Lake City's premier hotel. Located one block from the

downtown Temple Block, the hotel also appealed to Gentile visitors because of its proprietors' polygamy. Indeed, according to one 1870 guest who complained bitterly about flies and subpar food there, the Townsend House's good reputation "is based less on its intrinsic merits than on the circumstance that it is kept by a Mormon, and that, consequently, it affords the inquisitive stranger an opportunity of learning something as to the practical working of the peculiar institution in which Mormons glory." Many tourists engaged in their first on-site conversations about Mormon marriage and domestic life with the Townsend family, and their hosts were happy to speak on its behalf, often over breakfasts of disputable quality. Rae, *Westward by Rail*, 104. See also Hafen, "City of Saints, City of Sinners," 363.

5. On the Utah Southern and Utah Western, see Arrington, *GBK*, 277–82; Reeder, *History of Utah's Railroads*, chapter 4; and Athearn, *Union Pacific Country*, 270–71, 274. The Utah Southern was organized in January 1871 with Joseph A. Young as principal shareholder, but Brigham Young became the principal holder in 1872. The UP bought construction bonds in May 1871 and again in September 1872, paying for them with rolling stock and track materials. The second purchase was made after John Sharp traveled to the East, to deliver the message that he "would be pleased to have our personal friends as individuals of the U.P. company—who have befriended us before—join us in the farther construction of the U.S.R.R. for I know it to be a safe investment." See Sharp to E. H. Rollins, December 18, 1872, in Account Records for the Utah Central and Utah Southern Railroad, for accounts with the UP, 1872, in UPRC, subgroup 8, series 1, box 302, folder 459.

6. Codman, *Mormon Country*, 4.

7. Reeder, *History of Utah's Railroads*, 257–89, quotation at 278. The Utah Western was originally founded in 1872 as the Salt Lake, Sevier Valley and Pioche Railroad, with the chief stockholders: Patrick E. Connor, of southern Utah; H. S. Jacobs, of Salt Lake City; and John Leisenring, A. W. Leisenring, William Lilley, and John Thomas, of Mauch Chunk, Pennsylvania. John W. Young bought the line when this predominantly Gentile project folded. See also Brigham D. Madsen, *Glory Hunter*, chapter 13.

8. On the Utah Central and its arrangements with the UP, see Athearn, *Union Pacific Country*, 269–74; and Reeder, *History of Utah's Railroads*, 103. Another of John W. Young's projects, to be discussed further below, was the Utah Northern, which ran north of Ogden. The Utah Northern was founded in 1871 and reorganized by UP agents in 1877 as the Utah & Northern. See Reeder, *History of Utah's Railroads*, chapter 6. Before the UP's involvement, a major financier of the Utah Northern was Joseph Richardson of New York, with whom John W. Young maintained close business relations. It was in response to Bishop W. B. Preston of Logan's concerns about the involvement of non-Mormon financiers that Brigham Young promised "[they] do not seek the control" (as cited in ibid., 217–19). Young assured him that there was a corporate relationship between churchmen and capitalists whereby railroad operations would be maintained according to Saints' interests, if not under their direct management. Preston was one of thirteen company directors for the Utah Northern; the others, beyond John W. Young and two New York capitalists, Richardson and Le Grand Lockwood, were bishops, authorities, and other ranking members of the LDS Church in Utah. Utah Northern Railroad, Articles of Association, August 23, 1871,

in Utah and Northern Corporate Records, UPRC, subgroup 191, box 725. See also Arrington, *GBK*, 283–85.

9. Morgan, *Great Salt Lake*, 354; Brigham D. Madsen, *Corinne*, 166; John W. Young to George W. Thatcher and John N. Pike, November 6, 1874, in John W. Young Papers; "A Capital Enterprise," *SLH*, June 5, 1870; "Lake Side! Look Out for the School Train" (advertisement), *SLH*, June 8, 1870; "Lake Side," *SLH*, June 9, 1870; "The Excursion Yesterday," *SLH*, June 12, 1870; "Ho! For Lake Side," *DN*, June 15, 1870; "Excursion Party," *DN*, June 29, 1870; "Steamer Excursion on the Lake," *DN*, May 1872; "Lake Side Excursion," *SLH*, July 31, 1873.

10. On Corinnethian hopes for Lake Point, see the preceding chapter. Later in the decade Lake Point would become a popular Mormon-friendly destination. Jeter Clinton, an opportunistic Mormon doctor, justice of the peace, and businessman who built a guest- and bathhouse there in 1870 and later built much more impressive versions of the same in 1874, was evidently willing to run it as either a Corinnethian- or a Mormon-friendly establishment. See also McCormick and McCormick, *Saltair*, 5–6.

11. Arrington, *GBK*, 283–85, citation at 283. See also Brigham D. Madsen, *Corinne*, 170, 295–309; Reeder, *History of Utah's Railroads*, chapter 6; "Utah Northern Railroad," *DN*, October 2, 1872; George A. Smith to Albert Carrington, September 12, 1873, HOLC; *JD* 16:63–71 [June 28, 1873]; and Utah and Northern Corporate Records, UPRC, subgroup 191. Among journal accounts of trade by and among Cache County residents, see Franklin Wheeler Young, Journal, March 1, 1872; Samuel Rose Parkinson, Diary; and Bear, "Autobiography of Elder John Bear."

12. Athearn, *Union Pacific Country*, 270–71, 274. See also Reeve, *Making Space on the Western Frontier*, 91–92.

13. Codman, *Mormon Country*, 5–7; Hamilton, *Gail Hamilton's Life in Letters*, 722; Willard Richards, as cited in Hafen, "City of Saints, City of Sinners," 363; "The Future of Our Train," *Trans-Continental* 1, no. 12 (July 4, 1870). In 1873 the regular Ogden–Salt Lake City fare was two dollars, with a round-trip ticket costing three dollars. For more on guidebook encouragements, see chapter 6 of the present work.

14. Codman, *Mormon Country*, 5–6.

15. Ibid., 6, 162–63.

16. Smith to N. S. Elderkin, November 11, 1869, and Smith to Dr. H. Gould, June 20, 1871, in HOLC. In the earlier of these letters, Smith also talks about railroads' positive effect on emigration numbers, costs, and experiences: "This season's immigration to the territory amounts to about four thousand souls. The contrast experienced by our immigrants in crossing the plains, which is now accomplished by rail-road in four days in very great when compared with our ox team trains which in former years took one hundred days."

17. Rae, *Westward by Rail*, 142–43.

18. Ibid., 142.

19. *JD* 6:277–83; 3:328–33; 22:297–312; 6:18–27.

20. The debate is reproduced in pamphlet form: Orson Pratt and Newman, *Bible and Polygamy*. See also *New York Tribune*, August 19 and 22, 1870; and Tullidge, *History of Salt Lake City*, 470–79.

21. "Methodists and Mormons," *DCR*, November 18, 1871.

22. Codman, *Mormon Country*, 6–7.

23. George A. Smith to N. S. Elderkin, November 11, 1869. As Thomas K. Hafen rightly notes, "the Mormon Tabernacle Choir evolved more slowly as a tourist attraction than the tabernacle organ" did ("City of Saints, City of Sinners," 372). Indeed, tourist references to the choir are relatively infrequent until around 1890, when the church hired a new director and promoted it more actively. See also J. Spencer Cornwall, *A Century of Singing*; and Hicks, *Mormon Tabernacle Choir*.

24. Ross, *10,000 Miles*, 61–70; Boller, *Among the Indians*, 401. Ross describes having entered on a Utah Central car "crowded" with "travelers anxious to see the 'peculiar institution' to the best advantage" who therefore "aim[ed] at spending Sunday in the capital of Mormondom" (58, 61–62). On Tabernacle displays, see also Ronald W. Walker, "Salt Lake Tabernacle."

25. Jackson, "Mormon Experience"; see also Farmer, *On Zion's Mount*, chapter 3.

26. Ross, *10,000 Miles*, 67–68. The most widely known and distributed version of the "Utah's Best Crop" image—featuring babies' heads arranged as if blossoming in a field—was designed by Charles R. Savage, Mormon photographer and documenter of transcontinental construction. On Savage's work and career, see Richards, *Savage View*; and Wadsworth, *Set in Stone, Fixed in Glass*, chapter 3. On the Deseret Agricultural and Manufacturing Society, which hosted agricultural fairs in the city and praised the arguably simple, peaceful farming orientation of the Mormon people—and which supported Tabernacle displays to that effect—see Arrington, *GBK*, 226–28; Utah State Fair Association, *History of the Utah State Fair Association*; Deseret Agricultural and Manufacturing Society, Minute Books.

27. Rae, *Westward by Rail*, 108; Ross, *10,000 Miles*, 70. For discussions of the theater and related performances in early Utah, see Lindsay, *Mormons and Theatre*; Horace Whitney, *Drama in Utah*; Maughan, *Pioneer Theatre in the Desert*; Scanlon, "Buffalo Bill in a Boiled Shirt"; Lamar, *Theatre in Mormon Life and Culture*; and Sowell, "Theatrical Dancing in the Territory of Utah." Some visitors made analogies between the theater and the (as yet unbuilt) temple: Dixon, *New America*, 209. Theater managers sometimes timed openings to correspond with Tabernacle conferences and events: Lindsay, *Mormons and Theatre*, 33, 41, and elsewhere.

28. Lindsay, *Mormons and Theatre*, 23. The Salt Lake Theatre would be built with funds raised from reselling materials left behind by U.S. troops following the Utah War.

29. Moore, *Selling God*, 97, 99.

30. Stout, *Divine Dramatist*, xviii.

31. Maughan, *Pioneer Theatre in the Desert*, 84.

32. Lindsay, *Mormons and Theatre*, 66–68. This is a summary of Young's words.

33. Ibid., 25; Brigham Young, as cited in Maughan, *Pioneer Theatre in the Desert*, 84.

34. On the October 1868 conference and Cannon's speech on October 7, see Arrington, *GBK*, 239–40, and chapters 1 and 2 of the present work. The Salt Lake Theatre presented *Under the Gaslight* on October 7, 1868, as well as in June–July 1868, December 1868–January 1869, and May 1869, and on a few occasions between 1870 and 1873. See Salt Lake Theatre Program Broadsides. Promotional text taken from the Salt Lake Theatre's newsletter, *The Curtain*, December 25, 1868 (copies at CHL).

35. Salt Lake Theatre Program Broadsides; "Theatrical," *DN*, May 10, 1869.

36. Smith to Erminia F. Kinney, n.d., HOLC. See also Amos Milton Musser Journal, January 10, 1870.

37. Cast descriptions, as cited by Saxton, "Blackface Minstrelsy and Jacksonian Ideology," 26–27; "Extra!," *Footlights*, December 21, 1871; *New York Times*, March 1, 1871, as cited by Scanlon, "Buffalo Bill in a Boiled Shirt," 159. Black Cloud is spurred on by an Anglo villain named Adderly.

38. "Theatre," *Footlights*, December 22, 1871. In this respect, the production and reception of *Across the Continent* was comparable to Mormon stagings of and enthusiasm for blackface minstrel shows, as described in Hicks, "Ministering Minstrels." Although one of the first troupes invited to the theater after the completion of the transcontinental railroad was a San Francisco–based minstrel troupe, most such stagings occurred in smaller local venues, until the late 1870s and 1880s.

39. *DN*, March 7, 1873; Lindsay, *Mormons and Theatre*, 155, 51; "Theatre," *SLH*, April 9, 1873; "Theatre," *SLH*, March 5, 1873. The classic work on comedic types in American drama is Rourke, *American Humor*.

40. "Theatre," *SLH*, March 5, 1873; Frederick Jackson Turner, "Significance of the Frontier in American History."

41. Scanlon, "Buffalo Bill in a Boiled Shirt," 243–44.

42. Lindsay, *Mormons and Theatre*, 3. On plays in this period, see ibid., chapters 16 and 17; Salt Lake Theatre Program Broadsides. These production numbers were especially impressive given that 1873 was a 'down year' for the theater; the nationwide Panic of 1873 discouraged some theatrical troupes from cross-country travel then, and attendance numbers in the Salt Lake Theatre were depleted by rumors of smallpox infections there. See Hicks, "Ministering Minstrels," 57.

43. See Homer, *On the Way to Somewhere Else*, 182. Some guest performers were charmed by the city and its theater, and they carried a good word with them for the rest of their tour. "Delighted with SL & everything I have seen in it," reported one actor, and "I think that the builders of this city will go down to posterity for many hundred years." Daniel E. Bandmann, note in Visitors' Register, May 7, 1871, in BYOF.

44. Hamilton, *Gail Hamilton's Life in Letters*, 721; 'Carleton' [Charles Carleton Coffin], "Round the World Sketches" [no. 5], *Boston Journal*, January 30, 1869.

45. Rae, *Westward by Rail*, 113; "Anna Dickinson's Lecture on Sunday Evening," *San Francisco Chronicle*, September 7, 1869. See also Mrs. T. B. H. [Fanny] Stenhouse, *Exposé of Polygamy*, 195–96; and A London Parson, *To San Francisco and Back*, 121–22.

46. J. J., "That Crusade," *Latter-day Saints' Millennial Star*, October 20, 1869. A *Deseret Evening News* editorial also reported on September 16, 1869, that Dickinson "makes willful misrepresentations" about the theater.

47. Train, as cited in Bitton, "George Francis Train and Brigham Young," 415.

48. W. W. Ritter, "Correspondence," in *Deseret Evening News*, January 18, 1870.

49. "Salt Lake Theatre: Lightening Express Train!," *DN*, July 21, 1870.

50. "Mr. Train's Lecture on Saturday Evening," *DN*, July 27, 1870.

51. Granted, not all theatrical defenses of Mormonism by non-Mormons were so obviously underwritten by corporate interests. Augusta St. Clair's lecture "Six Months in Utah" was another perceived counterpoint to Dickinson's "Whited Sepulchres," insofar as (from the LDS perspective) it did justice to the generous treatment she received during a lengthy stay in Salt Lake City, rather than betraying her hosts

by misrepresenting their families and facilities. At the Salt Lake Theatre in November 1869, and in San Francisco before that, St. Clair praised Mormon women for nursing her daughter during a fatal case of mountain fever, and she expressed gratitude also to Brigham Young, who spoke at her funeral. Hers was a heartfelt defense of people whom she considered horribly misrepresented in anti-Mormon exposés and lectures like Dickinson's. However the title of her talk, evoking captivity narratives, shows recognition of the need to incorporate their style, even in the act of defense. The evocation and incorporation of criticism was and would remain a common theme in all Mormon attempts to manage public perceptions of the church among transcontinental audiences. "Theatrical," *DN*, November 23, 1869; "Utah News," *Latter-day Saints' Millennial Star*, December 22, 1869; Orson F. Whitney, *History of Utah*, 307.

52. Ulrich, *House Full of Females*, xi–xiii.

53. Mrs. Miner and Eliza R. Snow, in "Proceedings in Mass Meeting of the Ladies of Salt Lake City," 8, 4.

54. "Proceedings in Mass Meeting of the Ladies of Salt Lake City," 2, 5.

55. Ulrich, *House Full of Females*, xiii, 383–84; Eliza R. Snow, Discourse, July 24, 1871 [with notes], in Derr et al., *First Fifty Years of Relief Society*, 365–72; Van Wagenen, "Sister-Wives and Suffragists." Stanton and Anthony's primary guide in Salt Lake City seems to have been Daniel Grant, real estate agent for the Tribune Buildings and agent of the Union Mining Company: "Notes about Women," *Revolution*, June 29, 1871. See also Elizabeth Cady Stanton's "Overland Letters" in the *Revolution*, July 13 and 20, 1871.

56. Urry, *Tourist Gaze*.

57. Brigham Young also claimed that Dickinson had misquoted Mrs. Townsend, of the Townsend House hotel, and that she fabricated stories about interactions with other Mormon families. "Remarks," *DN*, February 2, 1870.

58. "Distinguished Guests," *Trans-Continental* 1, no. 5 (May 30, 1870); Hamilton, *Gail Hamilton's Life in Letters*, 721.

59. Visitors' Registers, 1868–69 and 1869 May–1871 August, in BYOF. Even J. H. Beadle visited Young's office, on August 24, 1869. Beadle seems to have been acting as a guide (presumably in the key of atrocity tourism) to a group of Illinois politicians and lawyers, at the time.

60. Visitor numbers from May 14, 1869 (the first day of the register), through May 10, 1871 (two years after the joining of the rails at Promontory), are drawn from Visitors' Register, 1869 May–1871 August, in BYOF (for which total period there were about 2,300 parties). NB: On occasions where persons were clearly traveling together or in a group, I have counted them as a single party. By contrast to these numbers for May 1869–May 1871, logs record only 173 groups visiting in the seven months before the completion of the transcontinental line: Visitors' Register, 1868–69, in BYOF.

61. Visitors' Register, 1869 May–1871 August, in BYOF.

62. Brigham Young, as cited in Arrington, *Brigham Young*, 398. See also Hafen, "City of Saints, City of Sinners," 370.

63. Hübner, *Ramble round the World*, 90–91. Hübner signed Brigham Young's visitor log on June 5, 1871 (Visitors' Register, 1869 May–1871 August, in BYOF).

64. Francesco Varvaro Pojero, as cited in Homer, *On the Way to Somewhere Else*, 183, emphasis added; Hafen, "City of Saints, City of Sinners," 370–71.

65. Victor-Henri Rochefort (discussing interaction with T. B. H. Stenhouse), as cited in Homer, *On the Way to Somewhere Else*, 176.

66. Francesco Varvaro Pojero, as cited in Homer, *On the Way to Somewhere Else*, 182–84.

67. Barfoot, "Brief History of the Deseret Museum." "Professor" Barfoot managed the museum until his death in 1882.

68. Sloan, *Gazeteer of Utah*, 178; Barfoot, "Brief History of the Deseret Museum."

69. George Washington Hill to Brigham Young, May 6, 1873, in BYOF, Incoming Correspondence; George Washington Hill, "A Brief Acct of the Labors of G W Hill"; Christensen, *Sagwitch*, chapter 3; Ralph O. Brown, "Life and Missionary Labors of George Washington Hill."

70. Richard H. Pratt, "Advantages of Mingling Indians with Whites," 46; John Wesley Powell, 1880 correspondence, as cited in Hoxie, *"Final Promise,"* 24.

71. Brigham D. Madsen, *Northern Shoshoni*, 93. See also Brigham D. Madsen, *Corinne*, 277–78; and Christensen, *Sagwitch*, 79–81.

72. Brigham D. Madsen, *Northern Shoshoni*, 94–95.

73. Hill to D. B. Huntington, October 27, 1873, in BYOF, Incoming Correspondence; George Washington Hill, Indian Vocabulary, George W. Hill Papers.

74. Barfoot, "Brief History of the Deseret Museum"; Deseret Museum Items; "Menagerie and Museum," *DN*, November 3, 1869; "Local and Other Matters," *DN*, October 26, 1870.

75. Barfoot, "Brief History of the Deseret Museum." Barfoot's description of Mormon settlements as *the first settlements* (without qualification) is a good example of the colonial practice of "firsting" described in O'Brien, *Firsting and Lasting*.

76. "Menagerie and Museum," *DN*, November 3, 1869; Barfoot, "Brief History of the Deseret Museum"; Deseret Museum Items.

77. Codman, *Mormon Country*, 6–7, also 91.

78. Barfoot, "Brief History of the Deseret Museum."

79. Beyond the bounds of the current study—but certainly worthy of extended analysis—are the touristic routes by which Mormons came to self-understanding as a historical, American, and religious community. Certainly the Deseret Museum took root as one such attraction, and so too, as we shall see later, did certain bathing resorts. But if Mormons themselves took excursions to the Deseret Museum in order to reflect upon the richness of their Utahn environs, the hardships of pre-Utahn life, or the differences between Saints and other religious Others, they also built networks of community and corporate self-awareness at another site linked, in part, to the efforts of John W. Young. The Logan Temple, located in the heart of Cache Valley—for which John W. Young ceremonially broke ground in 1877 and which opened officially in 1884—was accessible to Salt Lake residents via Young's Utah Northern railroad. (Indeed the Utah Northern and Utah & Northern offered reduced fares for temple-bound Saints, as well as for Cache County residents bound for the beaches of Salt Lake.) At the Logan Temple, Mormons in good standing partook in special ecclesiastical rituals with others, of course. But they also recollected the spaces between that particular temple and others: temples both original (as in Jerusalem or, in Mormon history, at Kirtland and Nauvoo) and anticipated (as at Salt Lake City, opened 1893). Among and between their temples Saints created mental

maps of Mormon sites and regions and also material routes for their visitation, along with bureaucratic networks for their administration. Indeed temple tours were major events for nineteenth- as well as twentieth- and twenty-first-century Saints, and each opening—especially that of the Salt Lake City Temple in 1893—was an occasion for celebration, travel, and thought. On the emergence of Mormon heritage tourism in the post-1893 era, see, briefly, Neilson, *Exhibiting Mormonism*, 205–6; and Michael H. Madsen, "Sanctification of Mormonism's Historical Geography."

80. Joseph Henry to John W. Young, November 22, 1870, in Deseret Museum Items.

81. P. T. Barnum to John W. Young, April 23, 1871, in Deseret Museum Files, box 1, folder 1.

82. Hamilton, *Gail Hamilton's Life in Letters*, 722.

83. Codman, *Mormon Country*, 11.

84. Hogan, "History of Goudy Hogan," entry for 1871.

85. Brigham D. Madsen, *Corinne*, 169–74.

86. Codman, *Mormon Country*, 22–23, 57.

87. Codman, *Round Trip*, 210–11; Codman, "Mormonism"; Codman, "Mormonism in Idaho," *Bedford's Magazine* 5, no. 26 (July 1890): 169–78. An earlier articulation of Josephite support is in Codman, "Through Utah," *Galaxy* 20, no. 4 (October 1875). See also Joseph Smith III to John Codman, December 15, 1884, Joseph Smith III Letter Press Book.

88. Reeder, *History of Utah's Railroads*, 230–32.

89. Codman, *Mormon Country*, 79. Codman continued in a mocking (but not altogether inaccurate) tone: "For this purpose churches and grog-shops were to act in harmony. Therefore there had been opened three of the former and twenty of the latter. The churches are supported by home missionary societies; the grog-shops are maintained by the voluntary system."

90. See Toponce, *Reminiscences*, 147, 148, 153, 157, 200; and "The Corinne Cattle Stealing Case," *DN*, January 15, 1873.

91. Codman, *Mormon Country*, 79–81.

92. Toponce, *Reminiscences*, 181–82.

93. Ronald W. Walker, Turley, and Leonard, *Massacre at Mountain Meadows*; Turley, "Clash of the Legal Titans"; *Corinne Mail*, August 9, 10, 11, and 12, 1875; Brigham D. Madsen, *Corinne*, 282–83; Brigham D. Madsen, *Northern Shoshoni*, 97; Christensen, *Sagwitch*, 120–22.

94. Hill to Brigham Young, August 12, 1875, and Indian John, Address to All White Men, as recorded in Hill to Brigham Young, August 31, 1875, in BYOF, Incoming Correspondence. "Indian John" was a member of Sagwitch's band of Northwestern Shoshoni.

95. Brigham D. Madsen, *Corinne*, 283, and *Northern Shoshoni*, 97.

96. *Ogden Junction*, August 14, 1875; *DN*, August 18, 1875; Brigham D. Madsen, *Northern Shoshoni*, 97–98.

97. Codman, *Mormon Country*, 137, 147–49, 162–63.

98. Ibid., 158, 160, 128, 211; Codman, "Through Utah," *Galaxy* 20, no. 3 (September 1875). In the earlier work Codman quoted a Mormon woman as suggesting that "when the last rail was spiked" by "that great missionary, the Union Pacific Railroad," "universal toleration echoed to the sound of the hammer; and now all past

bickerings and persecutions should be forgotten, and different Christianities and civilizations allowed to work themselves out side by side." Codman expressed doubt about much of what she said, but this sentiment was not too far from his own (*Mormon Country*, 91).

99. Codman, *Mormon Country*, 225.

100. Stanford Family Library Collection, box 20.

Chapter Six

1. Charles Francis Adams Jr. to Edwards Roberts, July 3, 1888, in UPRC, subgroup 2, series 2, vol. 44; Roberts to Adams, July 4, 8, and 24, 1888, in UPRC, subgroup 2, series 1, box 71. Compare Edwards Roberts, "Glimpse of Utah" (quoted adjectives at 41), to Edwards Roberts, *Shoshone*, esp. chapter 5. The latter reflects the changes discussed in the previously cited letters. Roberts's introductory section warned his reader that "he will find less barbarism than he expected" in Salt Lake City and throughout the West (Edwards Roberts, *Shoshone*, 4).

2. Edwards Roberts, *Shoshone*, 132.

3. Toward the end of his study of anti-Mormon genres, J. Spencer Fluhman notes the "dramatically" benign character of references to Mormonism in many railroad pamphlets, given "the [anti-Mormon] protests still raging in other quarters." Railroad boosters accented "familiarly" while still "preserving enough mystery to pique readers' curiosity." Thereby they "suggested a template for Mormon/non-Mormon cooperation at the turn of the century" (*"Peculiar People,"* 145–46). The present chapter develops this theme via emphasis on railroads' multifront participation in religious template-building, relative to Mormonism.

4. The best single source on tourism in late nineteenth-century Salt Lake City is Hafen, "City of Saints, City of Sinners." My analysis assumes Hafen's, in certain respects, even as it deploys similar data toward different arguments about Mormon imagination and religious tourism. I agree with Hafen regarding certain indicators of interaction among Mormons, railroads, and tourists, for instance, the forefronting of cultural and agricultural refinements, the opening of the Tabernacle, and the establishment of Saltair. Where I differ from Hafen is, first, with respect to the invitational verbiage of early tourism literature; where he sees early guidebooks reiterating the alarmist claims of anti-Mormon exposé literature—by his account, Gentile authors ushered Gentile visitors to the private "back regions of Mormonism" so as to gain unique insights, there, into Mormons' polygamous and barbarous secrets—I see railroad-backed literature avoiding such language, even in the late 1860s and early 1870s, by inviting observation and consideration of things public, material, and geographic, and by thus allocating most acts and initiatives for interior speculation to the off-page prerogatives of visitors. Where Hafen sees a slow and somewhat begrudging accommodation of tourists by LDS officials and businessmen, too, I find relatively enthusiastic Mormon participation and mediation in most sectors of postrailroad tourism.

5. Many such groups—not just Mormons—engaged in projects of cultural reformation or presentation, along with industrialists and travel agents, to religiously constructive ends. For descriptions of railroad and tourism companies' attempts to package Native American cultures and religions for public observation, see Dilworth,

Imagining Indians in the Southwest; Weigle and Babcock, *Great Southwest*; and McLuhan, *Dream Tracks*. Compare discussion of black Americans' religious negotiations vis-à-vis railroads in Giggie, "'When Jesus Handed Me a Ticket.'"

6. J. Spencer Fluhman has described the rather ironic process by which anti-Mormon polemics, in forging (what I have called) a triangular signification among polygamy, patriarchy, and religious primitivism—and, then, in making of polygamy the singular "symbolic stand-in for all of Mormonism's faults," thereby "reduc[ing] Mormonism to that single practice alone"—rendered Mormonism capable of being "substantially defanged by [polygamy's] renunciation," thus clearing the path to Utahn statehood, much to some politicians' continued irritation (*"Peculiar People,"* 124–25).

7. On this legal terrain and its effects on church economics and political power, see Gordon, *Mormon Question*, 147–220; Firmage and Mangrum, *Zion in the Courts*, 160–260; and Arrington, *GBK*, 353–79.

8. Arrington, *GBK*, 359.

9. Larson, *"Americanization,"* 115–206. Much to the chagrin of federal officials, "The Pen" was a place itself immortalized, even romanticized, in the letters and paintings of Mormon loyalists. Leonard Arrington estimates that some 1,004 people were convicted/or imprisoned for unlawful cohabitation (a crime carrying a maximum sentence of six months) under the Edmunds Acts between 1884 and 1893 (*GBK*, 359). See also Gordon, *Mormon Question*, 155.

10. Arrington, *GBK*, 362–79. Woodruff's journal entry (as cited in ibid., 377) was dated September 25, 1890. This was the same day that he published his "Manifesto" to the church, in which he declared "that my advice to the Latter-day Saints is to refrain from contracting any marriage forbidden by the law of the land" (Woodruff, "Official Declaration," *Deseret Weekly*, September 25, 1890; LDS Church, Official Declaration 1, *Doctrine and Covenants*).

11. Sidney Dillon to Shellabarger and Wilson, March 10, 1882, and Charles Francis Adams to Grover Cleveland, December 1, 1885, in UPRC, subgroup 2, series 2.

12. John W. Young to F. D. Richards, February 12, 1866, in John W. Young Letterbooks Collection, book 1. On Young's lobbying efforts overall, see Watson, "John Willard Young and the 1887 Movement for Utah Statehood"; and Keller, "Promoting Railroads and Statehood."

13. Watson, "John Willard Young," 59; John W. Young, as cited in ibid., 60.

14. E. A. Mudgett to John Taylor, April 9, 1884, in John Taylor Family Papers, box 1A. The Denver & Rio Grande, Denver & Rio Grande Western, and Rio Grande Western companies built and operated lines in Utah in the 1880s and afterward. Their entry into Utah was precipitated by conflict over more southerly routes with the Atchison, Topeka and Santa Fe line; and they proceeded to compete with the UP over Utahn routes, connections, and business. Rio Grande and UP interests were seldom identical, but they nevertheless developed a commensurate mode of reportage, and in time they shared images and promoted mixed-line package tours. On the Rio Grande and its divisions, see Athearn, *Denver and Rio Grande Western Railroad*.

15. GQCJ, Mar 13, 1882, and April 2, 1884.

16. GQCJ, July 1, 1887 (including correspondence between Young, Cannon, and James Jack dated June 30–July 2); Watson, "John Willard Young," 76–77; Keller, "Pro-

moting Railroads and Statehood," 304-6. The First Presidency was not opposed to such methods, necessarily, but Young's lavish expenditures (and his reticence to account for them) were a source of friction between them.

17. John W. Young, Telegram to James Jack, January 14, 1887, as contained in GQCJ, January 15, 1887. Young does not provide names, but Democratic politicians and railroaders John A. Logan, David L. Yulee, and William Kimmel all died in 1886; and Charles H. Sherrill, a lobbyist for the UP, died in early 1887.

18. The most famous of scandals concerned the Crédit Mobilier, a subcontracting company owned by the UP in which prominent politicians were given stock in return for legislative favors. Charles Francis Adams Jr. was known as a reformer of railroad excesses and a critic of backroom politics, but after he became president of the UP, he too became involved in such practices. See Klein, *Union Pacific*, 285-305, 373-84; and White, *Railroaded*, 62-87, chapters 3 and 5.

19. Franklin S. Richards, as cited in Keller, "Promoting Railroads and Statehood," 298. On the amendment and related debates, see Watson, "John Willard Young," 80-89.

20. Watson, "John Willard Young," 80, 85-86. See also Taylor and George Q. Cannon to C. W. Penrose and F. S. Richards, February 19, 1887, copy in D. Michael Quinn Papers, box 1, folder 3; but compare GQCJ, January 15, 1887, in which he expressed support for "Scott's amendment and any other amendment which will defeat object of the enemy."

21. GQCJ, September 15, 1885. On Fitch's pitch, see George Q. Cannon to George Reynolds, April 24, 1872, George Reynolds Papers, L. Tom Perry Special Collections, Harold B. Lee Library, Brigham Young University, copy in D. Michael Quinn Papers, box 1, folder 1.

22. GQCJ, September 15, 1885.

23. Lyman, *Political Deliverance*, 80-85, 92. I am grateful to Edward Leo Lyman for having shared with me several of the primary sources on which he based this account, including the following letters: H. B. Clawson to John W. Young, May 9, 1887 (which speaks of "strong influential friends in San Francisco"); 'Emigrant' [George Q. Cannon] to Young, July 21, 1887 (which speaks of the "very valuable aid from undoubted influential source [that] has been proffered in aid of Statehood movement"); Cannon and Joseph F. Smith to Leland Stanford, July 27, 1887 (a letter of introduction for Clawson); Cannon and Smith to Clawson, July 27, 1887 (which instructs Clawson to "learn, if you can, what S[tanford] considers would be a proper recognition for what he and company have done," noting that "mention is made of 'Judges favorable to them'"); Clawson to James Jack, August 4, 1887 (which reports that he has "had interview with Governor Stanford" and that "he will help us if press can be secured to help. Thinks that absolutely necessary. I will know probable cost of each paper"); and Clawson to Jack, August 7, 1887 (which reports that an "answer from the East has come. The newspapers we want both East and here will work for us; if the price they each name is satisfactory"), all from collections since renamed and closed to research, CHL. Several of Lyman's sources are verifiable through other means; for instance, a transcription of Cannon and Smith's letter of July 27, 1887, to Clawson, who acted as agent for the church in these negotiations, is contained also in GQCJ, July 27, 1887. See also Watson, "John Willard Young," 160-61 (citing Clawson letters)

and 174 (citing Heber J. Grant's journal). On the LDS Church's discouragement of association with the Knights of Labor and other unions ca. 1886–1896 (and beyond), see Davies, "Mormonism and the Closed Shop."

24. GQCJ, April 17 and 24, 1889.

25. Minutes of the Apostles, September 25, 1890, and January 28, 1891; James S. Clarkson to Wilford Woodruff, July 11, 1894; I. Tobias [Trumbo] to Solomon [Joseph F. Smith], October 2, 1890, in Joseph F. Smith Papers, General Correspondence. On Trumbo's actions generally, see Lyman, "Isaac Trumbo and the Politics of Utah Statehood."

26. Carlton, *Wonderlands of the Wild West*, 66–67, 330–33.

27. Tobias [Trumbo] to Solomon [Joseph F. Smith], October 2, 1890. See *Deseret Weekly*, October 11 and 25, 1890, for such announcements and summaries of national coverage. The Articles of Faith, as circulated by Trumbo, were: "1. We believe in God, the Eternal Father, and in His Son, Jesus Christ, and in the Holy Ghost. 2. We believe that men will be punished for their own sins, and not for Adam's transgression. 3. We believe that, through the atonement of Christ, all mankind may be saved, by obedience to the laws and ordinances of the Gospel. 4. We believe that these ordinances are: First, Faith in the Lord Jesus Christ; second, Repentance; third, Baptism by immersion for the remission of sins; fourth, Laying on of hands for the Gift of the Holy Ghost. 5. We believe that a man must be called of God, by 'prophecy, and by the laying on of hands,' by those who are in authority, to preach the Gospel and administer in the ordinances thereof. 6. We believe in the same organization that existed in the primitive church, namely, apostles, prophets, pastors, teachers, evangelists, etc. 7. We believe in the gift of tongues, prophecy, revelation, visions, healing, interpretation of tongues, etc. 8. We believe the Bible to be the word of God, as far as it is translated correctly; we also believe the Book of Mormon to be the word of God. 9. We believe all that God has revealed, all that He does now reveal, and we believe that He will yet reveal many great and important things pertaining to the Kingdom of God. 10. We believe in the literal gathering of Israel and in the restoration of the Ten Tribes. That Zion will be built upon this continent. That Christ will reign personally upon the earth, and that the earth will be renewed and receive its paradisiacal glory. 11. We claim the privilege of worshiping Almighty God according to the dictates of our own conscience, and allow all men the same privilege, let them worship how, where, or what they may. 12. We believe in being subject to kings, presidents, rulers, and magistrates, in obeying, honoring, and sustaining the law. 13. We believe in being honest, true, chaste, benevolent, virtuous, and in doing good to ALL MEN; indeed, we may say that we follow the admonition of Paul, 'We believe all things, we hope all things,' we have endured many things, and hope to be able to endure all things. If there is anything virtuous, lovely, or of good report or praiseworthy, we seek after these things.—JOSEPH SMITH."

28. Clarkson to Woodruff, July 11, 1894.

29. Ibid.; GQCJ, August 17, 1894; Clarkson to Clawson, in Minutes of the Apostles, September 1, 1894; George Q. Cannon, "Interview with General Clarkson and Colonel Trumbo," in Minutes of the Apostles, September 25, 1894; "Defended by Trumbo," *San Francisco Call*, June 26, 1895, and "The Political Arena," *SLH*, June 29, 1895, as saved in Isaac Trumbo Scrapbook.

30. *JD* 22:53-58.

31. Lyman, *Political Deliverance*, 92.

32. Burton's account of his 1860 Utahn travels—*The City of the Saints*—was first published in London (1861), and then in the United States (1862). Hereinafter references pertain to the American version.

33. Burton, *Personal Narrative* and *Book of the Thousand Nights and a Night*; Burton, *City of the Saints*.

34. Burton, *City of the Saints*, 397-98. Burton was not alone in his notion that one could learn much about ancient (especially Semitic) religions and/or religious developments by visiting modern-day 'tribes.' Later in the century, Eduard Meyer argued that scholars could learn more about culturally Semitic and religiously Muslim peoples from studies of Mormonism, in *Ursprung und Geschichte der Mormonen*.

35. Beadle compiled—or cribbed—a similar list of resonances in 1870, albeit with decidedly different argumentative framing and intent: *Life in Utah*, 312, 327-28.

36. Burton, *City of the Saints*, 212-14.

37. The classic work on the Western fears and fantasies about the East that constituted Orientalism is Said, *Orientalism*. On Burton as a particular type of Orientalist, see ibid., 191-97. On Orientalism as critique, see also Pennington, *Was Hinduism Invented?*, chapter 4, which further describes also some Orientalists' interest in affective geographies; Nance, *Arabian Nights*; and Makdisi, *Making England Western*. "The Islam of America" is the subtitle of a 1912 book by Bruce Kinney, *Mormonism*.

38. Especially in nineteenth-century Germany, romantic nationalisms and academic geography carefully documented and posited the interrelations among geographic environments and the cultures they hosted. See Kohn, "Romanticism and the Rise of German Nationalism"; and Livingstone, *Geographic Tradition*.

39. Fluhman, *"Peculiar People"*; also Givens, *Viper on the Hearth*, 130-33; Givens, "Caricature as Containment"; and, with more attention to irony, Marr, *Cultural Roots*, 185-218.

40. Fluhman, *"Peculiar People,"* 127.

41. Eric A. Eliason has similarly explored Burton's *City of the Saints* as an instance of literary mediation between genres of exposé and apology, in his "Curious Gentiles and Representational Authority in the City of the Saints." If Eliason focuses there on *The City of the Saints*'s significance as presage to a later ethnographic mode and method—one composed of participant observation, respectful engagement, and analytical detachment—then I focus here on its representation of a materially and geographically attentive subdivision thereof.

42. Ross, *10,000 Miles by Land and Sea*, v-vi. See also Bryant, *Picturesque America*, 187.

43. Burton, *City of the Saints*, 193.

44. *Pacific Tourist*, 134, 120. See also Nelsons' Pictorial Guide Books, *Salt Lake City*, 23; and James, *Utah*, 11.

45. Nelsons' Pictorial Guide Books, *Salt Lake City*, 23, 7.

46. I do not mean to imply that this descriptive combination—sublime, curious, and weird—was unique to Utahn literature; it can be found in other travel literature as well, including romances and apocalypses. I am instead pointing to the ways in which railroad guides and agents inhabited such motifs while inhabiting Utah,

that is, how they yoked them to industry and deployed them en route to the (re)production of religion in the modern West. On literary and religious descriptions of nineteenth-century American landscapes, especially those deemed tourist attractions, see Sears, *Sacred Places*.

47. Rideing, *Pacific Railroads*, 48; *Pacific Tourist*, 119; Nelsons' Pictorial Guide Books, *Salt Lake City*, 9–10. See also Buel, *Glimpses of America*, 94–96.

48. One guidebook expressed frustration at the thought that travelers would overlook the sublime in favor of the curious, thus: "While the curious erosions of Echo Cañon are still in mind, we are inclined" to comment on "the unsatisfying enjoyment which the phenomenal in Nature affords. It is to be granted that a mere curiosity will attract the multitude, when a thing of beauty passes unnoticed and people who could gaze on one of the empurpled peaks of the Wahsatch range, or on one of the terrific cliffs of Echo, without a touch of feeling, go into ecstasies in the contemplation of a bizarre rock. . . . It would be a pity to overlook [such rocks], as they are especially characteristic of the West; but they soon weary the better taste, and it is a still greater pity when they are allowed to monopolize the whole attention." People were predictably unpredictable, even when faced with objective beauty. Rideing, *Pacific Railroads*, 51.

49. The Pulpit Rock myth, in its railroading iteration, dates as early as 1869, with the descriptive text accompanying William Henry Jackson's stereoview photograph "No. 104. Pulpit Rock—mouth of Echo Canon where it is said Brigham Young preached his first Sermon in Utah" (see figure 11). Jackson was commissioned by the UP to document its construction and operations, and this photograph of his, re-rendered as a lithograph, was published and republished often in western travel literature. See *Crofutt's Trans-Continental Tourist's Guide* [1871], 91. So too was some variation of the accompanying text published often, as in [UP], *Sights and Scenes in Utah* [1888], 35; and [UP], *Description of the Western Resorts* [1889], 86. Pulpit Rock was also sometimes called Hanging Rock and the Sphinx. The rock was not a point of special concern or interest among prerailroad Mormon emigrants, under any name, in any case. By contrast, Mormon emigrants did name and occasionally mention the Witches Rocks or Witches Bluffs, albeit without assigning them specific historical or religious significance either. Piercy, *Route from Liverpool to Great Salt Lake Valley* [1855], 101–2.

50. *Trans-Continental* 1, no. 12 (July 4, 1870), and no. 5 (May 30, 1870). In 1887 the UP introduced special "Pullman Vestibuled" cars on its "Overland Flyer" passenger train, advertising them as especially useful for Echo and Weber Canyon sightseeing.

51. [UP], *Sights and Scenes in Utah* [1888], 35.

52. Schivelbusch, *Railway Journey*, 61.

53. On the railroad as a place of "public domesticity," see Richter, *Home on the Rails*.

54. Railroads' role in the construction of a reading public is perhaps most dramatically evident in the 1870 publication and distribution of an on-train periodical, for a group of transcontinental travelers representing the Boston Board of Trade. The *Trans-Continental* primed readers for upcoming sites, providing certain historical details and/or summarizing the accounts of contemporaneous guidebooks, and

then summarized the experience of having seeing them, a day or two later. Anticipatory and post hoc coverage of Echo Canyon ran in *Trans-Continental*, 1, no. 4 (May 28, 1870): 1, and no. 5 (May 30, 1870): 1–2. With respect to Utahn reporting, it is relevant that the *Trans-Continental* often cribbed whole passages from *Crofutt's Trans-Continental Tourist's Guide*—an already rather evenhanded document, as described in chapter 4 of the current work—if anything only further excising from them any content that might be considered critical of Mormonism. See, e.g., *Trans-Continental* 1, no. 5 (May 30, 1870), and compare [Crofutt], *Great Trans-Continental Tourist's Guide* [1869], 117, 129–30. Among other changes, the *Trans-Continental* omitted Crofutt's description of Corinne as a "perfect thorn in the side of the Mormons."

55. On stereography and religion, see Lindsey, *Communion of Shadows*, chapter 5. Lindsey focuses on the sensory experience of stereoscope-assisted Holy Land viewing, but Mormon-themed stereoviews also combined travel, history, and religion.

56. *Crofutt's Trans-Continental Tourist's Guide* was unusual among railroad-promoted guidebooks in that it acknowledged—and indeed called attention to—the Utah War fortifications in Echo Canyon, calling them "evidence of a people's folly" ([1869], 114). Later guidebook generations—and especially ones directly penned or produced by railroad agents—tended rather to overlook or hurry past them, in favor of Pulpit Rock.

57. On Echo City as refueling center, see Mikkelsen, "Growing Up Railroad," 350.

58. "Diary of a Voyage from New York to California"; Nevins, "Diary of a Trip."

59. James G. Hunt, 1883 Railroad Scrapbook, UPRC, subgroup 197, series 2, vols. 4–5, 51. Hunt evidently compiled his travel scrapbook in 1893, pasting into it several newspaper clippings from the time of his trip (1883) along with numerous images dating to the late 1880s or 1893. The books from which Hunt derived images and narratives are: [UP], *Sights and Scenes in Utah* [1893]; *Pacific Tourist* [1881 or later]; and [UP], *Description of the Western Resorts* [1888 or later]. Some 77 percent of Hunt's sentences were transcribed verbatim or nearly verbatim from these guidebooks. Of the sentences not directly derived from these books, the vast majority are differently unoriginal, recounting only his times of arrival and departure for different locations. There was one notable exception, to be discussed below.

60. Bryant, *Picturesque America*, 180.

61. Ferris, *Our Native Land*, 91; Lambourne, "Sketches of Utah Scenery," 163.

62. Bryant, *Picturesque America*, 87, 184, 187. William Fraser Rae offered a similar analysis in 1870. "Before the railway made the journey comparatively easy," he wrote, emigrants' tendency to "fall on their knees in an ecstasy of admiration and shed tears of joy" upon glimpsing valleys below Wasatch canyons was more understandable. This was precisely the ecstasy described by Richard Francis Burton, of course, and it was the impression outlined also by the railroads, when priming their passengers for similar sensations at and after Pulpit Rock. Against them Rae argued that neither tourists nor travel guides had legitimate business perpetuating the notions of righteous, persistent, and topographically determined "enthusiasm" in Utah, no matter whether it be among Mormons or non-Mormons, for the railroads themselves had rendered the Utahn journey easy and the Mormon city "less fascinating" (*Westward by Rail*, 113–15).

63. Bryant, *Picturesque America*, 180–82; [UP], *Sights and Scenes in Utah* [1888], 38, 33–34. For his part, J. H. Beadle tried to rebrand Pulpit Rock as the site of an egregious Mormon murder, and he retitled one of Crofutt's lithographs to that effect, but neither Crofutt nor other guidebooks followed suit. See Hickman [and Beadle], *Brigham's Destroying Angel*, 169.

64. Burton, *City of the Saints*, 193.

65. Kathryn Lofton writes similarly about decidedly different data, thus: "It *is* the case that Oprah viewers will and do make of her what they will, responding critically and borrowing ad hoc. But we do a disservice to patterns in production and to the pervading, prescribing influence of corporate structures when we fail to account for the mass media's effect on religious life, on the ways this formats *against* improvisation" (*Oprah*, 16–17).

66. Lévi-Strauss, *Savage Mind*, 18–19. "The elements which the 'bricoleur' collects and uses are 'pre-constrained' like the constitutive units of myth, the possible combinations of which are restricted by the fact that they are drawn from the language where they already possess a sense which sets a limit on their freedom of manoeuvre" (ibid., 19).

67. I have written elsewhere about how Marietta Walker, a member of the 'Josephite' RLDS Church, recognized that even the most casual or critical acts of scrapbook clipping and stereocard viewing in Echo Canyon had profound effects in the history of religions, insofar as they still positively imagined Utah as the 'right place' for the rise (and now tracking) of Mormonism's arguably wrong religiosity. David Walker, "Railroading Independence."

68. Edwards Roberts, *Shoshone*, 125.

69. Edwards Roberts, "Glimpse of Utah," 41. Compare Edwards Roberts, *Shoshone*, 131, where this paragraph is omitted amid an otherwise fully reproduced discussion of the Tabernacle. Adams to Roberts, July 3, 1888.

70. *Pacific Tourist*, 150.

71. This stands in contrast to Adams's and Roberts's utter lack of regard for or commitment to Shoshoni representation at Shoshone Falls. Indigenous groups were substantially absent from Roberts's text, except as implicit referents or supposed sources for certain place-names. Indeed it may only be because of their presumed or prescribed absence that nominal references were deemed romantically appealing. On the politics of white people's 'Indian' place names in and around Idaho, see Farmer, *On Zion's Mount*, chapter 7.

72. GQCJ, February 1, 1888. On this and other business ventures by Heber J. Grant, see Ronald W. Walker, "Young Heber J. Grant."

73. Cook, *Joseph C. Kingsbury*, 237–38, 249n1. Henry Charles Barrell described his work as Temple guard on the back of a photograph, showing him surrounded by tourists at the top of the scaffolding: "The Fulfillment of a Dream" (1892). The church invited some outsiders to tour the Salt Lake Temple before its official opening in 1893.

74. *Crofutt's Trans-Continental Tourist's Guide* [1871], 100; Edwards Roberts, *Shoshone*, 128–29; [UP], *Sights and Scenes in Utah*, 8, 14, 21.

75. Edwards Roberts, "Glimpse of Utah," 42; Edwards Roberts, *Shoshone*, 132.

76. Edwards Roberts, *Shoshone*, 127–28; [UP], *Sights and Scenes in Utah*, 10–11.

77. On LDS Church financial arrangements in the Edmunds-Tucker era, see Arrington, *GBK*, 362–79. On Grant's role, see First Presidency Office Journals, January 18 and 20, 1887, in D. Michael Quinn Papers; and Ronald W. Walker, "Young Heber J. Grant," 103–6. The government retained control of the Gardo House through 1893, and it raised the church's monthly rent to $450 in 1890. Heber J. Grant (LDS president, 1918–45) is known to historians of Mormonism as an influential promoter of a "middle way" or "Grant synthesis" between the gospel of wealth, a semilibertarian drive for monetary accumulation, and the concern for communitarianism and mutual support among Saints (Bowman, "Liberty and Order," 123–26). Though Grant's presidency postdates the era of current concern, I would suggest that this synthesis was born of the railroading moment and, moreover, that Grant's experience in the livery business—undertaken while some LDS leaders were 'underground,' hiding from federal marshals—trained him in the necessary art of counterbalancing concealment with selective acts of public display and touristic invitation.

78. The Utah car was officially donated by the Utah Central, a branch of the UP, by arrangement with LDS bishop John Sharp. John W. Young and other prominent Mormon businessmen were officers of the chamber of commerce, but so too were ex-Mormons like the Walker brothers. The Salt Lake City Chamber of Commerce was thus both product and promoter of touristic common grounds in Utah. The language of mission and conversion is deployed in H. L. A. Culmer, "The Tale of the Car," *Salt Lake Journal of Commerce*, July 1, 1888; W. H. H., "The Exposition Car," *SLH*, August 18, 1888; and C. R. Savage, "Doing the West for the Picturesque," *DN*, July 11, 1888. On chapel cars, see Taylor and Taylor, *This Train Is Bound for Glory*.

79. "The Utah Exposition Car," *Salt Lake Journal of Commerce*, June 15, 1888; Salt Lake City Chamber of Commerce, *Western Wonderland!* and *Salt Lake City*; Edwards Roberts, "The Scenery around Salt Lake City," in *Salt Lake Journal of Commerce*, January 1, 1888 (original source: Edwards Roberts, *Salt Lake City and Utah By-Ways*, 34–37).

80. H. L. A. Culmer, "The Tale of the Car," *Salt Lake Journal of Commerce*, July 15, 1888; M. J. Forhan, "Our Special Advantages," *Salt Lake Journal of Commerce*, January 1, 1888.

81. W. H. H., "Exposition Car"; "How Others View It," *SLH*, August 24, 1888.

82. [UP], *Sights and Scenes in Utah*, 27–29; "Giant's Cave at Garfield Beach," *Salt Lake Journal of Commerce*, April 15, 1889.

83. See sources cited in note 82, above; and Nelsons' Pictorial Guide Books, *Salt Lake City*, 30–31.

84. Ochs, *Heart of the Rockies*, 134.

85. Donan, *Utah*, 25.

86. Ludlow, *Heart of the Continent*, 327–28, 331–32.

87. Ibid., 331–32. See also [Rio Grande Western], *Pointer to Prosperity*, 15 ("Utah occupies a central position in the arid region and its details of irrigation possess unusual interest; the farmers having introduced methods of their own and achieved success"); [UP], *Sights and Scenes in Utah*, 9 ("Mormons did not come to Deseret . . . to 'prospect' or to create a 'boom.' They came to build their homes, and it is, perhaps, for this old-fashioned reason that there seems something exotic to the dry Great Basin in the development of the city of the Latter-Day Saints"); Donan, *Utah*, 25. See further UP, *Irrigation*; and Bowles, *Across the Continent*, 89–90. On perceptions and

myths of Mormon irrigation, compare Arrington and May, "'Different Mode of Life'"; and Worster, "Kingdom, Power, and Water."

88. Culmer, *Resources and Attractions of Utah*, 19; Salt Lake City Chamber of Commerce, *Salt Lake City*, 5, 15.

89. H. L. A. Culmer, "The Tale of the Car," *Salt Lake Journal of Commerce*, July 1, 1888.

90. Ochs, *Heart of the Rockies*, 134. See also Donan, *Utah*, 90, with map at 82. The "Promised Land" map was sometimes subtitled "A Striking Comparison," "Comparative Cut," or "The Holy Land and Utah" over some twenty years of use, as at, respectively: [Rio Grande Western], *Pointer to Prosperity*; Denver & Rio Grande Railroad, *What May Be Seen Crossing the Rockies*; and [Rio Grande Western], *Utah*. Thomas K. Hafen rightly describes such comparisons of the Salt Lake Valley with the Holy Land: while "early Mormon settlers had noticed the geographic correspondence" without attempting to "use the resemblance to try and attract visitors[,] Easterners involved in western tourism first employed these similarities to entice commercial travelers during the railroad era" ("City of Saints, City of Sinners," 352). Jared Farmer too has recognized that "it was the Union Pacific and the Denver & Rio Grande—not the LDS Church—that most forcefully advanced the Utah–Holy Land comparisons," in *On Zion's Mount*, 163. Consider, along these lines, that the previously cited John Codman expressed considerable surprise during his 1873 tour that Mormons spoke so little about (what he saw to be) a "geographical similarity" between Lake Utah and the Sea of Galilee, and between the Great Salt Lake and the Dead Sea. "Perhaps, if it is not too late, [Brigham Young] may take the hint even from an unbelieving Gentile," renaming Utahn landforms after Palestinian ones in order to attract the attention of other Mormons and Gentile observers (*Mormon Country*, 136). Railroads, hoping to attract more tourists like Codman, took that hint well before Brigham Young did.

91. [Rio Grande Western], *Pointer to Prosperity*; Denver & Rio Grande Railroad, *What May Be Seen Crossing the Rockies* (see note above). See also "The Progress of Western America," *Irrigation Age* 6, no. 5 (May 1894): 183. Reflecting on Jonathan Z. Smith's well-known dictum that "map is not territory," Pamela E. Klassen has rightly noted that, in the context of railroad mapping and settler colonialism, "maps are crucial in the work of turning land into territory" insofar as they "both erase and create stories" (*The Story of Radio Mind*, 97). The literature on 'Holy Land' pilgrimage and the artistic and textual representation of the Middle East is extensive; and so too is the historiography of Americans' participation therein. See Le Beau and Mor, *Pilgrims and Travelers to the Holy Land*; Withey, *Grand Tours and Cook's Tours*, 223–62; Obenzinger, *American Palestine*; Long, *Imagining the Holy Land*; and Davis, *Landscape of Belief*. I have little interest in distinguishing tourism from pilgrimage here. Classic theories have differentiated them generally in terms of participant commitment, soteriological mandate, insider/outsider status, or the industrial access and mass marketing of goods. The assumption here is that all such types of mobile consideration operate within spaces set up by the social differentiation of things 'original' and things 'duplicative,' 'expansive,' or 'representative'; and that, within those spaces, people reflect upon the distance between differentiated things and the values contained in their differentiation. That is: such rituals are born out

of the relation between originals and representations, and they occupy the space between them, in order that they might enable reflection upon that very relationship, on that very space, and on the very nature of the things distinguished. Rituals create value for ostensible 'originals,' by this account, only in a somewhat complicated way: by creating even more value for, and even more significance in, the act of ritual reflection itself and the products of disjointed assemblage it enables. Compare Victor Turner and Edith L. B. Turner, *Image and Pilgrimage in Christian Culture*, with MacCannell, *Tourist*, 48–49. The assumption here is also that, in their attempts to identify themselves or others from (or, as) tourists, travelers, or pilgrims, people perform similar and commensurate theoretical work, attending to social differentiations and revaluing cultural 'originals' or 'developments.' None of these terms—pilgrims, tourists, travelers—was static or uncontested, after all; and the fact of cross-, self-, and mutual criticism was crucial to the discursive and material creations of religion. These things being said, here I am interested primarily in a literature of Gentile appeal and circulation, rather than in intra-Mormon invitations to pilgrimage or tourism.

92. Davis, *Landscape of Belief*, 3.

93. See ibid., 53–97. See also Lindsey, *Communion of Shadows*, chapters 4 and 5.

94. On the displays of the 1904 fair, see Vogel, "Staying Home for the Sights."

95. Ibid., 251.

96. Farmer, *On Zion's Mount*, 108.

97. *Crofutt's Trans-Continental Tourist's Guide* [1871], 104; Adams to Cleveland, December 1, 1885.

98. Promey, "Hearts and Stones," 209; Promey and Brisman, "Sensory Cultures," 180–81. See also McDannell, *Material Christianity*, 4–8.

99. Promey, "Hearts and Stones," 209.

100. MacCannell, *Tourist*, 9; Donan, *Utah*.

101. Staal, "Meaninglessness of Ritual." The above argument might usefully be linked to Sally Promey's work again, too. For I am suggesting that, while tourists and railroads jointly deemed Mormonism a discursive object relevant to Americans' religious and (therefore also) secular self-understandings, they belied implications of singular comprehension with verbose ambivalence, in part by engaging, vocationally, in (what Promey has provocatively called) the "constant oscillation[s]" of significance vis-à-vis religious materials ("Hearts and Stones," 209).

102. Rae, from whom we have also read criticisms of guest preachers' Tabernacle addresses, wrote against adjacent celebrations of Mormons' agricultural successes that "no miracle has been wrought here," as "to irrigate the thirsty land is here the merest child's play" (*Westward by Rail*, 115–16).

103. [Denver & Rio Grande and Rio Grande Western], *Sight Places and Resorts in the Rockies*, 52; Rio Grande Western Railway, *Utah*.

104. See sources cited in note 103, above. "The old and the new are strangely blended in Salt Lake City," reported the 1900 Rio Grande Western pamphlet *Salt Lake City*, 8.

105. James G. Hunt, 1883 Railroad Scrapbook, UPRC, subgroup 197, series 2, vols. 4 and 5, 63.

106. After promoting it for several years, the UP assumed direct control of Garfield Beach in 1887.

107. W. W. Riter to Adams, March 12, 1888, Pacific Hotel Company to T. J. Potter, January 11, 1888, and Riter to Potter, January 18, 1888, in UPRC, subgroup 2, series 1, box 71; [UP], *Sights and Scenes in Utah*, 18–29; McCormick and McCormick, *Saltair*, 9.

108. Edwards Roberts, *Shoshone*, 133. Roberts expanded his section on Garfield Beach per C. F. Adams's suggestion. Utah & Nevada Railway, *Descriptive and Historical Sketch*, 23. Muir had been speaking of an 1877 trip on the Utah Western to bathe at Lake Point, but the railroad altered his words to promote the Utah & Nevada and Garfield Beach; see John Muir, "Notes from Utah," *Daily Evening Bulletin* [San Francisco], June 14, 1877.

109. For more on Barnum's perceptions of Mormonism, see P. T. Barnum to *New York Tribune*, n.d., 1870, as reproduced in JH, September 3, 1870, 2–3, and *Latter-day Saints' Millennial Star*, October 25, 1870. On Barnum's promotional techniques, see Harris, *Humbug*; and David Walker, "Humbug in American Religion."

110. *Pacific Tourist*, 152.

111. See Colborn, *Glimpse of Utah*, 9.

Conclusion

1. Toponce, *Reminiscences*, 200. Bear Lake and River Water Works and Irrigation Company, *Description of Location, Works, and Business*, 32–33. On Bear River Canal history, see further Thomas, *Development of Institutions under Irrigation*, chapter 12; and Brough, *Irrigation in Utah*, 63–66. Company surveys are housed (partly) in the James N. Holdaway Papers and in Nephi Anderson, Box Elder County Survey Collection.

2. The company was invited to participate in the fair by Jeremiah Sanborn, the Gentile president of the new Agricultural College of Utah in Logan (Cache County). For Sanborn's communication with the company, see Jeremiah Sanborn Presidential Papers, Utah State University Special Collections and Archives, Logan.

3. Bancroft, *Book of the Fair*, 359–60; E. A. McDaniel, "Secretary's Report, Utah World's Fair Commission, Read in Legislature February 1, 1894," in *Utah at the World's Columbian Exposition*. According to McDaniel, "The irrigation relief map was a wonderful attraction, and gave the Utah Agricultural exhibit a great deal of prominence. Thousands of visitors went to the Agricultural Building especially to see this feature alone" (ibid.). Utah Irrigation Commission, *Irrigation in Utah*, 9, 123, and appended advertisements.

4. Thomas, *Development of Institutions under Irrigation*, 211–12.

5. Neilson, *Exhibiting Mormonism*. See also Konden Rich Smith, "Appropriating the Secular." On the expanded membership, repertoire, and public relations mission of the Mormon Tabernacle Choir around 1890, see J. Spencer Cornwall, *A Century of Singing*; Hicks, *Mormon Tabernacle Choir*.

6. The Bear River Irrigation and Ogden Water Works Company, *Bear River Valley*.

7. Culmer, *Resources and Attractions of Utah*; Utah Irrigation Commission, *Irrigation in Utah*. The latter publication had a full-page advertisement for the Bear River Irrigation and Ogden Water Works Company.

8. GQCJ, August 28, September 1, 1893.

9. GQCJ, September 6–7, 1893. It was during this trip that Cannon learned of George Pullman's Mormon family members; Pullman noted that "my father's mother, my grandmother, was a Mormon and lived at Nauvoo." Pullman seems not to have expressed any special affinity or familial feeling for Mormons (of either the Utahn or midwestern sorts), in conversation with Cannon, but he did liken the orderly arrangement of Mormon settlements to his own planned community of Pullman.

10. GQCJ, September 7, 1893.

11. GQCJ, September 8 and 10, 1893. The lack of "ornamentation" (for instance, at the Utah Pavilion) was noted by another Mormon reviewer when justifying lukewarm audience reactions at different demonstrations, in "Utah at Chicago," *DN*, June 9, 1893.

12. The Midway Plaisance was of course famous for its 'exotic' displays of cultural 'Others' (see Burris, *Exhibiting Religion*, chapter 4), and Cannon described seeing a "very good" model volcano and hearing "four half-bloods s[i]ng some native songs" there. GQCJ, September 14, 1893.

13. Studying the later works of the Salt Lake City photographer Charles Ellis Johnson, art historian Mary Campbell has offered a commiserating argument: that Johnson's variously buttoned-up (formal) and dressed-down (erotic) portraits were both representative of national interests in Mormonism and component to Utahn integration in America. See Campbell, *Charles Ellis Johnson and the Erotic Mormon Image*.

14. Saltair's principal historians note that "the Mormon church ... held half of the company's 2500 shares," and "Mormon church leaders and prominent Mormon businessmen held the other shares and were company officers" (McCormick and McCormick, *Saltair*, 19). Two members of the First Presidency, George Q. Cannon and Joseph F. Smith, were president and vice president, respectively. Wilford Woodruff, then president of the Church of Jesus Christ of Latter-day Saints, served on the board of directors. Isaac A. Clayton and Nephi W. Clayton, Mormon businessmen and officers of the Brigham Young Trust Company, were secretary and treasurer and general manager, respectively. Ibid.; *Poor's Manual of the Railroads of the United States*, 346. Morgan, *Great Salt Lake*, chapter 18, gives an overview and history of Salt Lake resorts generally; see also Arrington, *GBK*, chapter 13.

15. *DN*, June 9, 1893; as cited in McCormick and McCormick, *Saltair*, 21, 23.

16. GQCJ, April 22, 1893; *DN*, June 17, 1893; Rio Grande Western Railway, *Utah*.

17. GQCJ, December 28, 1893.

18. For (sometimes contentious) discussions of Trumbo and Clarkson's efforts to leverage the Salt Lake and Los Angeles Railway and Saltair to church economic and political benefit, see GQCJ, February 2, April 28, May 17, and August 17, 1894; James S. Clarkson to Wilford Woodruff, July 11, 1894; Clarkson to Hiram B. Clawson, in Minutes of the Apostles, September 1, 1894; George Q. Cannon, "Interview with General Clarkson and Colonel Trumbo," in Minutes of the Apostles, September 25, 1894; and Clarkson to George Q. Cannon and Associates, in Minutes of the Apostles, September 26, 1894. Frustrated with Trumbo and Clarkson's efforts, Cannon brought a different potential investor to Saltair in May 1894 (CQCJ, May 17, 1894).

19. Isaac W. Hoffman, Railroad Scrapbook. "A Host Enraptured: The City's Guests Entertained in Splendid Style" was printed in the *Deseret Evening News*, April 20, 1894. The images of an "irrigated cabbage field near Ogden, 8000 heads to acre,"

and a "Celery Field. Ogden, Weber Co." are from Culmer, *Resources and Attractions of Utah*, 20, 15. The Ogden collage—from ibid., 92—is featured in such Denver & Rio Grande publications as Donan, *Utah*, but typographical variations indicate that Hoffman cut these pictures from *The Resources and Attractions of Utah*.

20. Pamela Klassen has articulated a different metaphor for the railroad, describing Canada's Grand Trunk Pacific Railway as the "spinal cord of colonialism" in *The Story of Radio Mind*, 9, 97. This is an apt description for American railroads as well, provided that we recognize (to stick with the metaphor) that America's spinal cords manifested particularly severe cases of scoliosis, being overbuilt to the point of near-incoherent saturation, and provided also that we account for both the productive and destructive nature of that overbuilding.

21. Max Weber, *Protestant Ethic and the Spirit of Capitalism* (Parsons trans.), 181–82, 36. By Weber's analysis, the Puritan work ethic, when bound and bent around modern "technical and economic conditions of machine production" and the desire for material goods, convenience, and efficiency, hardened into a "stalhartes Gehäuse," that is, by different translations, an "an iron cage," "shell as hard as steel," or "steel-hard casing." The phrase has been taken as a descriptor of modern bureaucratic rationality in general. On the metaphor and translation of *stalhartes Gehäuse*, see Stephen Kalberg's translation of Weber's *Protestant Ethic*, 397–98n133; and Baehr, "'Iron Cage' and 'Shell as Hard as Steel.'"

22. Regarding Weber's American tour and his St. Louis lecture on "The Relations of the Rural Community to Other Branches of Social Science" (for which only flawed translations survive), see Scaff, *Max Weber in America*; and Ghosh, "Max Weber on 'The Rural Community'" and "Not the *Protestant Ethic*?" Weber had already submitted the first half of *The Protestant Ethic* for publication before his arrival in America.

BIBLIOGRAPHY

Full citations for government publications and nineteenth-century periodical publications are given in the endnotes.

Newspapers and Periodicals

Baltimore Sun
Bedford's Magazine (New York)
Boston Courier
Boston Daily Journal
Boston Journal
Boston Transcript
Brooklyn Daily Eagle
Chicago Tribune
Cincinnati Commercial
Congressional Globe (Washington, D.C.)
Corinne Daily Journal
Corinne Daily Mail
Corinne Journal
Corinne Mail
Corinne Reporter
Crofutt's Western World (San Francisco)
The Curtain (Salt Lake City)
Daily Corinne Reporter
Daily Evening Bulletin (San Francisco)
Daily National Intelligencer (Washington, D.C.)
Daily Utah Reporter (Corinne)
Decatur (Ill.) Republican
Deseret Evening News (Salt Lake City)
Deseret News (Salt Lake City)
Footlights (Salt Lake City)
Haverhill (Mass.) Gazette
Hunt's Merchant's Magazine (New York)
Irrigation Age (Chicago)
Mormon Tribune (Salt Lake City)
New York Herald
New York Times
New York Tribune

Presbyterian (Philadelphia)
The Revolution (New York)
Salt Lake Daily Reporter
Salt Lake Daily Tribune
Salt Lake Herald
Salt Lake Journal of Commerce
Salt Lake Weekly Reporter
Salt Lake Tribune
San Francisco Call
San Francisco Chronicle
The Trans-Continental (published aboard Union Pacific and Central Pacific trains, 1870)
True Latter Day Saints' Herald (Plano, Ill.)
Utah Magazine (Salt Lake City)
Utah Weekly Reporter (Corinne)
Virginia Free Press (Charlestown, W.Va.)
Worcester (Mass.) Aegis

Manuscript Items and Collections

Berkeley, California
  Bancroft Library, University of California
    Bancroft Reference Notes for the Western States, excluding California. Bancroft Collection, MSS B-C 8.
    Barfoot, Joseph L. "A Brief History of the Deseret Museum" (Salt Lake City, 1880), HHB P-F 1.
    Godbe, William S. "Statement of William S. Godbe, September 2, 1884." MS29.
    Stein, Nat. Collection, 1860–1875. MSS 2002/96 z.
Denver, Colorado
  Stephen A. Hart Library & Research Center, History Colorado Center
    Denver & Rio Grande Western Records
    Union Pacific Railroad Collection
Independence, Missouri
  Community of Christ Library-Archives
    Smith, Joseph III. Letter Press Book, P6.
Iowa City, Iowa
  Special Collections Department, University of Iowa
    Reed, Samuel Benedict. Correspondence, June–December 1868. In Levi O. Leonard Papers, MsC 159.
Lincoln, Nebraska
  Nebraska State Historical Society
    Union Pacific Railroad Collection. RG3761.AM.
Logan, Utah
  Special Collections and Archives, Merrill-Cazier Library, Utah State University
    Anderson, Nephi. Box Elder County Survey Collection. COLL MSS 089.
    Arrington, Leonard. Papers, 1839–1999. LJAHA COLL 1.
    Corinne Business Letters, 1867–1870. MSS 241.

BIBLIOGRAPHY 307

   Fife Mormon Collection, 1940–1976. FOLK COLL 4, no. 1.
   Holdaway, James N. Papers. COLL MSS 328.
   Miller, William, and William Patterson. Union Pacific Railroad Correspondence. MSS 374.
   19th Century Western Stereo-Views Collection, 1865–1899. P0349.
   Sanborn, Jeremiah. Presidential Papers.
   Young, Brigham. Financial Records, 1859–1882. MSS 042.
   Young, John W. Papers, 1876–1889. Caine Collection MSS 26.
New Haven, Connecticut
  Beinecke Rare Book and Manuscript Library, Yale University
   Coffin, Charles Carleton. "Diary of a Visit to Salt Lake City and Travel to Chicago." 1868.
   "Diary of a Voyage from New York to California and Return Trip by Train, 1874–1875." WA Mss S-1415.
   King, Frank H. Photographs of Salt Lake City and Great Salt Lake Resorts, Utah, ca. 1892. WA Photos 333.
   Quinn, D. Michael. Papers. Uncat WA MS 98.
   Young, John W. Letterbooks Collection, WA MSS s-15.
Oakland, California
  Oakland Museum of California
   Russell, Andrew J. Collection.
Palo Alto, California
  Special Collections and University Archives, Stanford University
   Hyde, William Birelie. Papers, 1861–1896. M0267.
   Stanford Family Library Collection. SC0010.
Philadelphia, Pennsylvania
  Presbyterian Historical Society
   Sheldon Jackson Papers. RG 239.
Provo, Utah
  L. Tom Perry Special Collections, Harold B. Lee Library, Brigham Young University
   Deseret Museum Items. MSS SC 1383.
   Salt Lake, Garfield & Western Railway Company. Records, circa 1891–1961. MSS 1445.
Sacramento, California
  California State Railroad Museum
   Central Pacific Railroad Collection. MS 79.
   Kneiss, Gilbert H. Collection. MS 17.
Salt Lake City, Utah
  Church History Library, The Church of Jesus Christ of Latter-day Saints
   Historians Office Letterpress Copybooks, 1854–1879. MS 2737.
   Journal History of the Church of Jesus Christ of Latter-day Saints
   Barrell, Henry Charles. "The Fulfillment of a Dream" [May 1892]. PH 67.
   Clarkson, James S., Washington, D.C., to Wilford Woodruff, Salt Lake City, July 11, 1894. Ms 16021.
   Deseret Museum Files. CR 69 2.
   First Presidency (John Taylor). Correspondence, 1877–1887. CR 1 180.

Hill, George Washington. "A Brief Acct of the Labors of G W Hill." October 1, 1876. MS 2481, folder 1.
Hill, George W[ashington]. Papers, 1842–1883. MS 8172.
Historians Office. Letterpress Copybooks, 1854–1879. MS 2737.
Hoffman, Isaac W. Railroad Scrapbook, 1894. MS 12798.
Parkinson, Samuel Rose. Diaries, 1876–1933. MS 1798.
Rich, Eliza Ann Graves. Correspondence, 1851–1877. MS d 5338.
Salt Lake Theatre. Program Broadsides, 1862–1907. M284.3 S176sx.
Smith, Joseph F. Papers, 1854–1918. MS 1325.
Trumbo, Isaac. Scrapbook. MS 8841.
Young, Brigham. Office Files, 1832–78. CR 1234 1.
Young, Franklin Wheeler. Journal. MS 324.
Watt, G. D. Letters, 1867–1875. MS 5206.

Special Collections, J. Willard Marriott Library, University of Utah
Blair, Philip T. Family Papers, 1836–1968. Ms 0120.
Madsen, Brigham D. Papers. Ms 671.
Saltair Beach Resort. Records. Accn 1025.
Salt Lake Theatre. Records. Ms 541.
Taylor, John. Family Papers. Ms 50.
Weiler, Elijah Malin. Papers, 1839–1921. Accn 2216.

Utah State Archives and Records Service
Box Elder County. County Commission Reports, 1894–1908. Series 82954.
Box Elder County. County Court Minutes, 1856–1893. In Box Elder County, County Commission Minutes, 1856–[ongoing]. Series 84093.
Box Elder County. Water Records, 1880–1975. Series 84092.
Corinne City Council. Minutes, 1870–[ongoing]. Series 3659.
Deseret Agricultural and Manufacturing Society. Minute Books, 1863–1874. Series 59925.
Utah Legislative Assembly. Journals, 1851–1880. Series 3145.

Utah State Historical Society
Beadle, John Hanson. "Scrapbook containing editorials and dispatches from the Salt Lake Daily Reporter and the Salt Lake Weekly Reporter, October, 1868–August, 1869." MIC A12.
Corinne Mill, Canal & Stock Company. Records, 1868–1898. MSS B5.
Grant Brothers Livery and Transport Company. Ledgers and Ride Logs, May 1892–April 1893 and April 1894–Oct 1894. In Salt Lake Livery and Transfer Company Records, Mss B 48, box 7.
Musser, Amos Milton. Journal. In Musser Family Papers, 1852–1967. MSS B96.

San Marino, California
Huntington Library
Hogan, Goudy. "History of Goudy Hogan." MSS FAC 1663.
Little, Feramorz. Letter Book. HM 30694.
Mormon File, c. 1805–1995.
Whitaker, John Mills. Papers.
Edwards, Esia. Journal. In Hugh F. O'Neil Papers.

Porter, Samuel. "A Journal of the Life and Travels of Samuel U. Porter, c. 1868–1900." MS FAC 559.
Railroadiana Collection
Nevins, Joseph Allen. "Diary of a Trip from Adams Co., Ill., to California by Union Pacific and Central Pacific, and Back to New York via Isthmus of Panama and Jamaica, Jan 10–April 1, 1874." MSS HM 26339.
Reed, Samuel Benedict. Letters, 1864–1870. MSS HM 66497.
Rosbery, Helena. "History of Helena Rosbery." February 1883. MSS FAC 633.

Washington, D.C.
U.S. National Archives
Utah Superintendency. Records. Bureau of Indian Affairs, RG 75.15.13.
Utah Territory. Territorial Papers, 1857–1871. Records of the United States House of Representatives, RG 233.

Published Sources, Theses, and Dissertations

Acts, Resolutions and Memorials, Passed at the Several Annual Sessions of the Legislative Assembly of the Territory of Utah. Salt Lake City: Joseph Cain, 1855.

Adams, Charles Francis, Jr. *Railroads: Their Origin and Problems.* New York: G. P. Putnam's Sons, 1878.

Adamson, Nathan W., Jr. *Francis Asbury Hammond: Pioneer and Missionary.* Salt Lake City: David H. Allred and West Hammond, 1993.

Alexander, Thomas G. "An Experiment in Progressive Legislation: The Granting of Woman Suffrage in Utah in 1870." *Utah Historical Quarterly* 38, no. 1 (Winter 1970): 20–30.

Ames, Charles Edgar. *Pioneering the Union Pacific: A Reappraisal of the Builders of the Railroad.* New York: Appleton-Century-Crofts, 1969.

Anderson, Edward H. "The Bureau of Information." *Improvement Era* 25, no. 2 (December 1921): 131–39.

Appletons' Hand-Book of American Travel: Western Tour. Embracing Eighteen Through Routes to the West and Far West . . . . New York: D. Appleton, 1872.

Aron, Cindy S. *Working at Play: A History of Vacations in the United States.* New York: Oxford University Press, 1999.

Arrington, Leonard J. *Brigham Young: American Moses.* New York: Alfred A. Knopf, 1985.

———. *Great Basin Kingdom: An Economic History of the Latter-day Saints, 1830–1900.* Cambridge, Mass.: Harvard University Press, 1958.

———. "Kate Field and J. H. Beadle: Manipulators of the Mormon Past." American West Lecture, University of Utah, Salt Lake City, March 31, 1971.

———. "The Transcontinental Railroad and the Development of the West." *Utah Historical Quarterly* 37, no. 1 (Winter 1969): 3–15.

———. "Utah and the Depression of the 1890's." *Utah Historical Quarterly* 29, no. 1 (January 1961): 3–18.

Arrington, Leonard J., and Dean May. "'A Different Mode of Life': Irrigation and Society in Nineteenth-Century Utah." *Agricultural History* 49, no. 1 (January 1975): 3–20.

Arrington, Leonard J., Feramorz Y. Fox, and Dean L. May. *Building the City of God: Community and Cooperation among the Mormons*. Salt Lake City: Deseret Book, 1976.
Asad, Talal. *Formations of the Secular: Christianity, Islam, Modernity*. Stanford, Calif.: Stanford University Press, 2003.
Athearn, Robert G. "Contracting for the Union Pacific." *Utah Historical Quarterly* 37, no. 1 (Winter 1969): 16–40.
———. *The Denver and Rio Grande Western Railroad: Rebel of the Rockies*. Lincoln: University of Nebraska Press, 1977.
———. *Union Pacific Country*. Lincoln: University of Nebraska Press, 1976 [1971].
Avery, Valeen Tippetts. *From Mission to Madness: Last Son of the Mormon Prophet*. Urbana: University of Illinois Press, 1998
Baehr, Peter. "The 'Iron Cage' and the 'Shell as Hard as Steel': Parsons, Weber, and the Stahlhartes Gehäuse Metaphor in the Protestant Ethic and the Spirit of Capitalism." *History and Theory* 40, no. 2 (May 2001): 153–69.
Bancroft, Hubert Howe. *The Book of the Fair*. San Francisco: Bancroft, 1893.
———. *History of Utah, 1540–1886*. San Francisco: History, 1889.
Banker, Mark T. *Presbyterian Missions and Cultural Interaction in the Far Southwest, 1850–1950*. Chicago: University of Illinois Press, 1993.
Barlow, Philip L. *Mormons and the Bible: The Place of Latter-day Saints in American Religion*. New York: Oxford University Press, 2013 [1991].
Beadle, John Hanson. *Life in Utah; or, The Mysteries and Crimes of Mormonism, Being an Exposé of the Secret Rites and Ceremonies of the Latter-day Saints, with a Full and Authentic History of Polygamy and the Mormon Sect from Its Origin to the Present Time*. Philadelphia: National, 1870.
———. *The Undeveloped West; or, Five Years in the Territories: Being a Complete History of That Vast Region between the Mississippi and the Pacific, Its Resources, Climate, Inhabitants, Natural Curiosities, etc., etc. . . .* Philadelphia: National, 1873.
———. *Western Wilds, and the Men Who Redeem Them: An Authentic Narrative*. Cincinnati, Ohio: Jones Brothers, 1878.
Bear, John. "Autobiography of Elder John Bear." *Journal of History* [Lamoni, Iowa] 4, no. 3 (July 1911): 326.
Bear Lake and River Water Works and Irrigation Company. *A Description of the Location, Works and Business of the Bear Lake and River Water Works and Irrigation Co.* Kansas City, Mo.: Hudson-Kimberly, [1889].
Bear River Irrigation and Ogden Water Works Company. *Bear River Valley, Utah*. Chicago: Poole Bros., [1894].
Beecher, Lyman. *A Plea for the West*. Cincinnati, Ohio: Truman and Smith, 1835.
Ben-Arieh, Yehoshua. *The Rediscovery of the Holy Land in the Nineteenth Century*. Detroit, Mich.: Wayne State University Press, 1979.
Bender, Norman J. *Winning the West for Christ: Sheldon Jackson and Presbyterianism on the Rocky Mountain Frontier, 1869–1880*. Albuquerque: University of New Mexico Press, 1996.
Bendixen, Alfred, and Judith Hamera, eds. *The Cambridge Companion to American Travel Writing*. Cambridge: Cambridge University Press, 2009.

Bitton, Davis. "George Francis Train and Brigham Young." *BYU Studies Quarterly* 18, no. 3 (1978): 410–27.

———. "Mormonism's Encounter with Spiritualism." *Journal of Mormon History* 1 (1974): 39–50.

Blackhawk, Ned. *Violence over the Land: Indians and Empires in the Early American West.* Cambridge, Mass.: Harvard University Press, 2006.

Bliss, Jonathan. *Merchants and Miners in Utah: The Walker Brothers and Their Bank.* Salt Lake City: Western Epics, 1983.

Boller, Henry A. *Among the Indians: Eight Years in the Far West, 1858–1866, Embracing Sketches of Montana and Salt Lake.* Philadelphia: T. Ellwood Zell, 1868.

Bowles, Samuel. *Across the Continent: A Summer's Journey to the Rocky Mountains, the Mormons, and the Pacific States, with Speaker Colfax.* Springfield, Mass.: Samuel Bowles, 1865.

———. *Our New West: Records of Travel between the Mississippi River and the Pacific Ocean. . . .* Hartford, Conn.: Hartford, 1869.

Bowman, Matthew. "The Crisis of Mormon Christology: History, Progress, and Protestantism, 1880–1930." *Fides et Historia* 40, no. 2 (2008): 1–25.

———. "Liberty and Order: The Mormon Struggle with American Capitalism." In *The Business Turn in American Religious History*, edited by Amanda Porterfield, John Corrigan, and Darren E. Grem, 108–30. New York: Oxford University Press, 2017.

Brendon, Piers. *Thomas Cook: 150 Years of Popular Tourism.* London: Martin Secker and Warburg, 1991.

Brough, Charles Hillman. *Irrigation in Utah.* Baltimore: Johns Hopkins University Press, 1898.

Brown, Dee. *Hear That Lonesome Whistle Blow.* New York: Touchstone, 1977.

Brown, Lisle G. "'Temple Pro Tempore': The Salt Lake City Endowment House." *Journal of Mormon History* 34, no. 4 (Fall 2008): 1–68.

Brown, Ralph O. "The Life and Missionary Labors of George Washington Hill." M.S. thesis, Brigham Young University, 1956.

Bryant, William Cullen. *Picturesque America; or, The Land We Live In.* Vol. 2. New York: D. Appleton, 1874.

Buel, J. W. *Glimpses of America: A Pictorial and Descriptive History of Our Country's Scenic Marvels, Delineated by Pen and Camera.* Philadelphia: Historical Publishing, 1894.

Burris, John P. *Exhibiting Religion: Colonialism and Spectacle at International Expositions, 1851–1893.* Charlottesville: University Press of Virginia, 2001.

Burton, Richard F. *The Book of the Thousand Nights and a Night.* 10 vols. N.p.: Kama Shastra Society, 1885.

———. *The City of the Saints, and across the Rocky Mountains to California.* New York: Harper and Brothers, 1862.

———. *A Personal Narrative of a Pilgrimage to Al-Medinah and Meccah.* 3 vols. London: Longman, Brown, Green, and Longmans, 1855.

Bushman, Claudia L., ed. *Mormon Sisters: Women in Early Utah.* Logan: Utah State University Press, 1997 [1976].

Bushman, Claudia Lauper, and Laurel Thatcher Ulrich, eds. *Special Issue, Dialogue* 6, no. 2 (Summer 1971).

Bushman, Richard Lyman. *Joseph Smith: Rough Stone Rolling*. New York: Vintage Books, 2005.

Buzard, James. *The Beaten Track: European Tourism, Literature, and the Ways to "Culture," 1800–1918*. Oxford: Clarendon Press, 1993.

———. "The Grand Tour and After (1660–1840)." In *The Cambridge Companion to Travel Writing*, edited by Peter Hulme and Tim Youngs, 37–52. Cambridge: Cambridge University Press, 2002.

Callahan, Richard J., Jr. *Work and Faith in the Kentucky Coal Fields: Subject to Dust*. Bloomington: University of Indiana Press, 2008.

Callahan, Richard J., Jr., Kathryn Lofton, and Chad E. Seales. "Allegories of Progress: Industrial Religion in the United States." *Journal of the American Academy of Religion* 78, no.1 (March 2010): 1–39.

Campbell, Mary. *Charles Ellis Johnson and the Erotic Mormon Image*. Chicago: University of Chicago Press, 2016.

Cannon, Abraham H. *A Hand-Book of Reference to the History, Chronology, Religion, and Country of the Latter-day Saints, including the Revelation on Celestial Marriage, for the Use of Saints and Strangers*. Salt Lake City: Juvenile Instructor, 1884.

Carlton, Ambrose Bolivar. *The Wonderlands of the Wild West, with Sketches of the Mormons*. N.p.: A. B. Carlton, 1891.

Carter, Kate B., ed. "Notes on the Life of 'Bill' Hickman." In *Heart Throbs of the West*, 427–30. Salt Lake City: Daughters of Utah Pioneers, 1945.

Carter, Thomas. *Building Zion: The Material World of Mormon Settlement*. Minneapolis: University of Minnesota Press, 2015.

Central Pacific Railroad Company. *Lands of the Central Pacific Railroad Company in California, Nevada and Utah, January 1, 1877*. [San Francisco: n.p.], 1877.

———. *The Lands of the Central Pacific Railroad Co. of California, with General Information on the Resources of the Country through which the Railroad Takes Its Way*. San Francisco: H. S. Crocker, 1880.

———. *Railroad Lands in California, Nevada, and Utah*. [San Francisco: n.p., 1875].

Chidester, David. *Savage Systems: Colonialism and Comparative Religion in Southern Africa*. Charlottesville: University of Virginia Press, 1996.

Chidester, David, and Edward T. Linenthal. "Introduction." In *American Sacred Space*, edited by David Chidester and Edward T. Linenthal, 1–42. Bloomington: Indiana University Press, 1995.

Christensen, Scott R. *Sagwitch: Shoshone Chieftain, Mormon Elder, 1822–1887*. Logan: Utah State University Press, 1999.

Clark, Ira G., Jr. "The Railroads and the Tribal Lands: Indian Territory, 1830–1890." Ph.D. diss., University of California, Berkeley, 1947.

Clifford, James. "Notes on Travel and Theory." *Inscriptions* 5 (1989): 177–88.

Codman, John. *The Mormon Country: A Summer with the "Latter-day Saints."* New York: United States Publishing, 1874.

———. *The Round Trip: By Way of Panama through California, Oregon, Nevada, Utah, Idaho, and Colorado*. New York: G. P. Putnam's Sons, 1879.

Coffin, Charles Carleton. *Our New Way round the World*. Boston: James R. Osgood, 1869.

Coffman, Elesha J. *The Christian Century and the Rise of the Protestant Mainline*. New York: Oxford University Press, 2013.

Colborn, Edward F. *A Glimpse of Utah: Its Resources, Attractions and Natural Wonders*. Denver, Colo.: Passenger Department, Denver and Rio Grande Railroad, 1906.

Colfax, Schuyler. "Speech of Vice-President Schuyler Colfax, Delivered on the Portico of the Townsend House, Salt Lake City, October 5, 1869." In *The Mormon Question, Being a Speech of Vice-President Schuyler Colfax, at Salt Lake City, [with] a Reply Thereto by Elder John Taylor* . . . . Salt Lake City: Deseret News Office, 1870.

A Complete and Comprehensive Description of the Agricultural, Stock Raising and Mineral Resources of Utah. St. Louis, Mo.: Woodward and Tiernan, 1893.

Cook, Lyndon W. *Joseph C. Kingsbury: A Biography*. Provo, Utah: Grandin Book, 1985.

"Corinne: Its Past, Present and Future." Corinne: Utah Reporter Printers, August 2, 1869.

Cornwall, J. Spencer. *A Century of Singing: The Salt Lake Mormon Tabernacle Choir*. Salt Lake City: Deseret Book, 1958.

Cornwall, Rebecca Foster, and Leonard J. Arrington. "Perpetuation of a Myth: Mormon Danites in Five Western Novels, 1840–90." *BYU Studies Quarterly* 23, no. 2 (Spring 1983): 147–65.

Coyner, John McCutchen. *Hand-Book on Mormonism*. Salt Lake City and Chicago: Hand-Book Publishing Co., 1882.

Crofutt, George A. *Crofutt's Trans-Continental Tourist's Guide* . . . . New York: Geo. A. Crofutt, 1871 [also 1872, 1873, 1874].

———. *Crofutt's Trans-Continental Tourist Guide* . . . . New York: G. W. Carleton; London: S. Low, 1875 [also 1876].

———. *Great Trans-Continental Railroad Guide* . . . . Chicago: G. A. Crofutt, 1869 [also Crofutt and Eaton, 1870].

Culmer, H. L. A. *The Resources and Attractions of Utah, as They Exist Today, Set Forth for the Enquiring Public, Especially for the Midwinter Fair, California, 1894*. Salt Lake City: Geo Q. Cannon and Sons, 1894.

Curts, Kati. "Assembling Fords: A Harrowing History of Religion in the Automobile Age." Ph.D. diss., Yale University, 2016.

Dall, Caroline H. *My First Holiday; or, Letters Home from Colorado, Utah, and California*. Boston: Roberts Brothers, 1881.

Davies, J. Kenneth. "Mormonism and the Closed Shop." *Labor History* 3, no. 2 (1962): 169–87.

Davis, John. *The Landscape of Belief: Encountering the Holy Land in Nineteenth-Century American Art and Culture*. Princeton, N.J.: Princeton University Press, 1996.

Decker, Leslie E. *Railroads, Lands, and Politics: The Taxation of the Railroad Land Grants, 1864–1897*. Providence, R.I.: Brown University Press, 1964.

Deloria, Philip J. *Playing Indian*. New Haven, Conn.: Yale University Press, 1998.

Deloria, Vine, Jr., and Raymond J. DeMallie, eds. *Documents of American Indian Diplomacy: Treaties, Agreements, and Conventions, 1775–1979*. Vol. 1. Norman: University of Oklahoma Press, 1999.

Denison, Brandi. *Ute Land Religion in the American West, 1879–2009*. Lincoln: University of Nebraska Press, 2017.

Denver & Rio Grande Railroad. *Album of Views on the Denver & Rio Grande*. Denver, Colo.: W. H. Lawrence, [ca. 1886].

———. *Among the Rockies: A Complete List and Guide to the Principal Scenic Attractions on the Line of the Denver & Rio Grande Railroad, Scenic Line of the World, as Seen from the Train*. Denver, Colo.: Passenger Dept., Denver & Rio Grande Railroad, 1893 [also 1897, 1901].

———. *"Around the Circle": One Thousand Miles through the Rocky Mountains . . .* . Denver, Colo.: Passenger Dept., Denver & Rio Grande Railroad, ca. 1888 [also 1889, 1890, 1904].

———. *A Journey across the Continent by the Scenic Route: Colorado, Utah, and New Mexico*. [Denver, Colo.: Denver & Rio Grande Railroad, 189–?].

———. *Panoramic Views along the Line of the Denver & Rio Grande Railroad: The Scenic Line of the World*. Denver, Colo.: Denver & Rio Grande Railroad, 1893 [also 1898, 1901, 1904, 1906].

———. *Rocky Mountain Scenery: A Brief Description of Prominent Places of Interest along the Line of the Denver and Rio Grande Railroad*. [New York: Press of the American Bank Note Co., 1888?].

———. *Tourists' Hand Book Descriptive of Colorado, New Mexico, and Utah*. New York: Press of the American Bank Note Co., 1885.

———. *What May Be Seen Crossing the Rockies en Route between Ogden, Salt Lake City, and Denver*. [Denver, Colo.?]: S. K. Hooper, 1905.

[Denver & Rio Grande and Rio Grande Western]. *Sight Places and Resorts in the Rockies: A Brief Preachment of Charming Resorts and Wonderful Sights in the Rocky Mountains with a Galaxy of Useful Hints of How to Reach Them*. 5th ed. [Denver, Colo.: n.p.], 1903.

———. *Valleys of the Great Salt Lake: Describing the Garden of Utah and the Two Great Cities of Salt Lake and Ogden*. Chicago: R. R. Donnelley and Sons, 1890.

A Descriptive Catalogue of the Photographs of the United States Geological Survey of the Territories, for the Years 1869 to 1873, Inclusive. Washington, D.C.: Government Printing Office, 1874.

Derr, Jill Mulvay, et al., eds. *The First Fifty Years of Relief Society: Key Documents in Latter-day Saint Women's History*. Salt Lake City: Church Historian's Press, 2016.

Deseret Museum. *Handbook Guide to the Salt Lake Museum (Established 1869), Opposite the Tabernacle Gates*. Salt Lake City: Juvenile Instructor Print, 1881.

DeSimone, Linda Wilcox. "Introduction." In Fanny Stenhouse, *Exposé of Polygamy in Utah: A Lady's Life among the Mormons*, edited by Linda Wilcox DeSimone, 1–21. Logan: Utah State University Press, 2008.

Dickinson, Anna. "Mormonism." In *The Lyceum and Public Culture in the Nineteenth-Century United States*, edited by Angela G. Ray, 239–50. East Lansing: Michigan State University Press, 2005.

———. "Whited Sepulchres." In *The Lyceum and Public Culture in the Nineteenth-Century United States*, edited by Angela G. Ray, 221–38. East Lansing: Michigan State University Press, 2005.

Dilworth, Leah. *Imagining Indians in the Southwest: Persistent Visions of a Primitive Past*. Washington, D.C.: Smithsonian Institution Press, 1997.

———. "Tourists and Indians in Fred Harvey's Southwest." In *Seeing and Being Seen: Tourism in the American West*, edited by David M. Wrobel and Patrick T. Long, 142–64. Lawrence: University Press of Kansas, 2001.

Dixon, William Hepworth. *New America*. 7th ed. Vol. 1. London: Hurst and Blackett, 1867.

Donan, P. *Utah: A Peep into a Mountain-Walled Treasury of the Gods* [for the Rio Grande Western]. Buffalo, N.Y.: Matthews Northrup, 1891.

Durkheim, Emile. *Professional Ethics and Civic Morals*. New York: Routledge, 1992 [1957; French orig., 1950].

Dwinell, Rev. I. E. *The Higher Reaches of the Great Continental Railroad: A Sermon Preached in the Congregational Church, Sacramento, May 9, 1869, on the Completion of the Overland Railway*. Sacramento: H. S. Crocker, 1869.

Eliade, Mircea. *Patterns in Comparative Religion*. Translated by Rosemary Sheed. New York: Sheed and Ward, 1958.

Eliason, Eric A. "Curious Gentiles and Representational Authority in the City of the Saints." *Religion and American Culture* 11, no. 2 (Summer 2001): 155–90.

Falk, Alfred. *Trans-Pacific Sketches: A Tour through the United States and Canada*. Melbourne, Australia: George Robertson, 1877.

Farmer, Jared. *On Zion's Mount: Mormons, Indians, and the American Landscape*. Cambridge, Mass.: Harvard University Press, 2008.

Ferris, George T. *Our Native Land; or, Glances at American Scenery and Places, with Sketches of Life and Adventure*. New York: D. Appleton, 1882.

Fessenden, Tracy. *Culture and Redemption: Religion, the Secular, and American Literature*. Princeton, N.J.: Princeton University Press, 2007.

Fifer, J. Valerie. *American Progress: The Growth of the Transport, Tourist, and Information Industries in the Nineteenth-Century West, Seen through the Life and Times of George A. Crofutt, Pioneer and Publicist of the Transcontinental Age*. Chester, Conn.: Globe Pequot, 1988.

Firmage, Edwin Brown, and Richard Collin Mangrum. *Zion in the Courts: A Legal History of the Church of Jesus Christ of Latter-day Saints, 1830–1900*. Urbana, Ill.: University of Illinois Press, 1988.

Fitch, Thomas. *Western Carpetbagger: The Extraordinary Memoirs of "Senator" Thomas Fitch*. Edited by Eric N. Moody. Reno: University of Nevada Press, 1978.

Flake, Kathleen. "The Development of Early Latter-day Saint Marriage Rites, 1831–53." *Journal of Mormon History* 41, no. 1 (2015): 77–102.

———. "Ordering Antinomy: An Analysis of Early Mormonism's Priestly Offices, Councils, and Kinship." *Religion and American Culture* 26, no. 2 (2016): 139–83.

———. *The Politics of American Religious Identity: The Seating of Senator Reed Smoot, Mormon Apostle*. Chapel Hill: University of North Carolina Press, 2004.

Fluhman, J. Spencer. *"A Peculiar People": Anti-Mormonism and the Making of*

Religion in Nineteenth-Century America. Chapel Hill: University of North Carolina Press, 2012.

Foster, Lawrence. "From Frontier Activism to Neo-Victorian Domesticity: Mormon Women in the Nineteenth and Twentieth Centuries." *Journal of Mormon History* 6, no. 1 (1979): 3–21.

Foucault, Michael. *The History of Sexuality*, vol. 1, *An Introduction*. Translated by Robert Hurley. New York: Vintage Books, 1990 [1976].

Fowler, Don. *A Laboratory for Anthropology: Science and Romanticism in the American Southwest, 1846–1930*. Albuquerque: University of New Mexico Press, 2000.

Fox, Feramorz Young. "The Mormon Land System: A Study of the Settlement and Utilization of Land under the Direction of the Mormon Church." Ph.D. diss., Northwestern University, 1932.

Francaviglia, Richard V. *Believing in Place: A Spiritual Geography of the Great Basin*. Reno: University of Nevada Press, 2003.

Freed, Clyde H. *The Story of Railroad Passenger Fares*. Washington, D.C.: Clyde H. Freed, 1942.

Furniss, Norman F. *The Mormon Conflict, 1850–1859*. New Haven, Conn.: Yale University Press, 1960.

Gallman, J. Matthew. *America's Joan of Arc: The Life of Anna Elizabeth Dickinson*. New York: Oxford University Press, 2006.

Gardner, Hamilton. "Nauvoo Legion, 1840–1845: A Unique Military Organization." *Journal of the Illinois State Historical Society* 54 (Summer 1961): 181–97.

Gates, Paul W. *The Illinois Central Railroad and Its Colonization Work*. Cambridge, Mass.: Harvard University Press, 1934.

———. *The Jeffersonian Dream: Studies in the History of American Land Policy and Development*. Edited by Allan G. Bogue and Margaret Beattie Bogue. Albuquerque: University of New Mexico Press, 1996.

Gates, Susa Young. *History of the Young Ladies' Mutual Improvement Association of the Church of Jesus Christ of Latter-day Saints, from November 1869 to June 1910*. Salt Lake City: Deseret News, 1911.

Gentry, Leland H. "The Danite Band of 1838." *BYU Studies Quarterly* 14, no. 4 (Summer 1974): 421–50.

GhaneaBassiri, Kambiz. *A History of Islam in America: From the New World to the New World Order*. New York: Cambridge University Press, 2010.

Ghosh, Peter. "Max Weber on 'The Rural Community': A Critical Edition of the English Text." *History of European Ideas* 31, no. 3 (2005): 327–66.

———. "Not the *Protestant Ethic*? Max Weber at St. Louis." *History of European Ideas* 31, no. 3 (2005): 367–407.

Giggie, John M. "'When Jesus Handed Me a Ticket': Images of Railroad Travel and Spiritual Transformations among African Americans, 1865–1917." In *The Visual Culture of American Religions*, edited by David Morgan and Sally M. Promey, 249–66. Berkeley: University of California Press, 2001.

Gill, Sam. "Territory." In *Critical Terms for Religious Studies*, edited by Mark Taylor, 298–313. Chicago: University of Chicago Press, 1998.

Givens, Terryl L. "Caricature as Containment: Orientalism, Bondage, and the

Construction of Mormon Ethnicity in Nineteenth-Century American Popular Fiction." *Nineteenth-Century Contexts* 18, no. 4 (Winter 1995): 385-403.

———. *Viper on the Hearth: Mormons, Myths, and the Construction of Heresy*. New York: Oxford University Press, 1997.

Glover, E. S. [for Corinne and Bear River Valley Immigration Society]. *Corinne and the Bear River Valley, Utah Territory. 1875. Location, Climate, Agricultural and Commercial Advantages Unsurpassed for Actual Settlers and Colonization Enterprises*. Cincinnati, Ohio: Strobridge, 1875.

Gordon, Sarah Barringer. *The Mormon Question: Polygamy and Constitutional Conflict in Nineteenth-Century America*. Chapel Hill: University of North Carolina Press, 2001.

Grant, H. Roger. *Railroads and the American People*. Bloomington: Indiana University Press, 2012.

Grant, Ulysses S. *The Papers of Ulysses S. Grant*, vol. 21, *November 1, 1870–May 31, 1871*. Edited by John Y. Simon. Carbondale: Southern Illinois University Press, 1998.

Green, Steven K. *The Second Disestablishment: Church and State in Nineteenth-Century America*. New York: Oxford University Press, 2010.

Greenberg, Amy S. *Manifest Manhood and the Antebellum American Empire*. New York: Cambridge University Press, 2005.

Hafen, Thomas K. "City of Saints, City of Sinners: The Development of Salt Lake City as a Tourist Attraction, 1869–1900." *Western Historical Quarterly* 28, no. 3 (Autumn 1997): 343-77.

Hamburger, Philip. *Separation of Church and State*. Cambridge, Mass.: Harvard University Press, 2002.

Hamilton, Gail. *Gail Hamilton's Life in Letters*. Vol. 2. Edited by H. Augusta Dodge. Boston: Lee and Shepard, 1901.

Harris, Neil. *Humbug: The Art of P. T. Barnum*. Boston: Little, Brown, 1973.

Hart, Alfred A. [*The Pacific Railway Panoramic Guide:*] *The Traveler's Own Book, a Panorama of Overland Travel* . . . . [Chicago: Horton and Leonard], ca. 1870.

Hawthorne, Nathaniel. *The American Notebooks*. Edited by Randall Stewart. New Haven, Conn.: Yale University Press, 1932.

———. "The Celestial Railroad" (1843). In *Mosses from an Old Manse*, vol. 1, pp. 172-92. London: Wiley and Putnam, 1846,.

Heaton, John W. *The Shoshone-Bannocks: Culture and Commerce at Fort Hall, 1870–1940*. Lawrence: University Press of Kansas, 2005.

Hickman, Bill. *Brigham's Destroying Angel: Being the Life, Confession, and Startling Disclosures of the Notorious Bill Hickman, the Danite Chief of Utah, Written by Himself, with Explanatory Notes by J. H. Beadle, Esq., of Salt Lake City*. New York: Geo. A. Crofutt, 1872.

Hicks, Michael. "Ministering Minstrels: Blackface Entertainment in Pioneer Utah." *Utah Historical Quarterly* 58, no. 1 (Winter 1990): 49–63.

———. *The Mormon Tabernacle Choir: A Biography*. Urbana, Ill: University of Illinois Press, 2015.

Hilton, Hope A. *"Wild Bill" Hickman and the Mormon Frontier*. Salt Lake City: Signature Books, 1988.

Hollister, Ovando James. *Life of Schuyler Colfax.* New York: Funk and Wagnalls, 1886.
———. *The Resources and Attractions of Utah.* Salt Lake City: Tribune, 1882.
Homer, Michael W., ed. *On the Way to Somewhere Else: European Sojourners in the Mormon West, 1834–1930.* Spokane, Wash.: Arthur H. Clark, 2006.
———. "Spiritualism and Mormonism: Some Thoughts on Similarities and Differences." *Dialogue* 27, no. 1 (Spring 1994): 171–94.
Horsman, Reginald. *Race and Manifest Destiny: The Origins of American Racial Anglo-Saxonism.* Cambridge, Mass.: Harvard University Press, 1981.
Hoxie, Frederick E. *A Final Promise: The Campaign to Assimilate the Indians, 1880–1920.* New York: Cambridge University Press, 1989 [1974].
Hübner, Joseph Alexander, Graf von. *A Ramble round the World, 1871.* Translated by Lady Herbert. New York: MacMillan, 1875 [1874].
Humason, W. L. *From the Atlantic Surf to the Golden Gate: First Trip on the Great Pacific Rail Road, Two Days and Nights among the Mormons.* Hartford, Conn.: Wm. C. Hutchings, 1869.
Hunt, Helen. *Bits of Travel at Home.* Boston: Roberts Brothers, 1878.
Jackson, Richard H. "The Mormon Experience: The Plains as Sinai, the Great Salt Lake as the Dead Sea, and the Great Basin as Desert-cum-Promised Land." *Journal of Historical Geography* 18, no. 1 (January 1992): 41–58.
———. "The Mormon Village: Genesis and Antecedents of the City of Zion Plan." *BYU Studies Quarterly* 17, no. 2 (Winter 1977): 223–40.
———. "Myth and Reality: Environmental Perception of the Mormons, 1840–1865, an Historical Geosophy." Ph.D. diss., Clark University, 1970.
———. "Sacred Space and City Planning: The Mormon Example." *Architecture et Comportement / Architecture and Behaviour* 9, no. 2 (1993): 251–60.
Jakobsen, Janet R., and Ann Pellegrini. *Love the Sin: Sexual Regulation and the Limits of Religious Tolerance.* Boston: Beacon Press, 2004.
James, George Wharton. *Utah: The Land of Blossoming Valleys.* Boston: Page, 1922.
Jones, Megan Sanborn. *Performing American Identity in Anti-Mormon Melodrama.* New York: Routledge, 2009.
Kane, Elizabeth Wood. *Twelve Mormon Homes Visited in Succession on a Journey through Utah to Arizona.* Philadelphia: [n.p.], 1874.
Kasson, John. *Civilizing the Machine: Technology and Republican Values in America, 1776–1900.* New York: Hill and Wang, 1999 [1976].
Keller, Charles L. "Promoting Railroads and Statehood: John W. Young." *Utah Historical Quarterly* 45, no. 3 (Summer 1977): 289–308.
Kerber, Linda K. *Toward an Intellectual History of Women: Essays.* Chapel Hill: University of North Carolina Press, 1997.
Kinney, Bruce. *Mormonism: The Islam of America.* New York: Fleming H. Revell, 1912.
Klassen, Pamela E. "Fantasies of Sovereignty: Civil Secularism in Canada." *Critical Research on Religion* 3, no. 1 (2015): 41–56.
———. *The Story of Radio Mind: A Missionary's Journey on Indigenous Land.* Chicago: University of Chicago Press, 2018.

Klein, Maury. *Union Pacific: The Birth of a Railroad, 1862–1893*. New York: Doubleday, 1987.

Knott, Kim. *The Location of Religion: A Spatial Analysis*. London: Equinox, 2005.

Kohn, Hans. "Romanticism and the Rise of German Nationalism." *Review of Politics* 12, no. 4 (1950): 443–72.

Lamar, Howard. *The Theater in Mormon Life and Culture*. Leonard J. Arrington Mormon History Lecture Series, 4. Logan: Special Collections and Archives, Utah State University, 1998.

Lambourne, Alfred. "Sketches of Utah Scenery." *Parry's Monthly Magazine* 6, no. 5 (February 1890): 161–64.

Larson, Gustive O. *The "Americanization" of Utah for Statehood*. San Marino, Calif.: Huntington Library, 1971.

———. "Land Contest in Early Utah." *Utah Historical Quarterly* 29 (October 1961): 309–25.

The Latter Days: Railways, Steam, and Emigration, with Its Consequent Rapid Peopling of the Deserts, also the Present Going To and Fro, and Increase of Knowledge, Foretold by Isaiah, Daniel, and Joel, and Indicating the Rapid Approach of the End of the Latter Days. Dublin: Samuel B. Oldham, 1854.

Le Beau, Bryan F., and Menachem Mor, eds. *Pilgrims and Travelers to the Holy Land*. Omaha, Nebr.: Creighton University Press, 1996.

Leonard, Glen M. "The Mormon Boundary Question in the 1849–50 Statehood Debates." *Journal of Mormon History* 18, no. 1 (Spring 1992): 114–36.

Lévi-Strauss, Claude. *The Savage Mind*. Chicago: University of Chicago Press, 1966 [1962].

Lindell, Jennifer. "Mormons and Native Americans in the Antebellum West." M.A. thesis, San Diego State University, 2011.

Lindsay, John S. *The Mormons and the Theatre; or, The History of Theatricals in Utah*. Salt Lake City: Century Printing, 1905.

Lindsey, Rachel McBride. *A Communion of Shadows: Religion and Photography in Nineteenth-Century America*. Chapel Hill: University of North Carolina Press, 2017.

Linford, Lawrence L. "Establishing and Maintaining Land Ownership in Utah prior to 1869." *Utah Historical Quarterly* 42, no. 2 (Spring 1974): 126–43.

Livingstone, David N. *The Geographic Tradition: Episodes in the History of a Contested Enterprise*. Malden, Mass.: Wiley-Blackwell, 1993.

Lofton, Kathryn. *Consuming Religion*. Chicago: University of Chicago Press, 2017.

———. *Oprah: The Gospel of an Icon*. Berkeley: University of California Press, 2011.

A London Parson [Hervey Jones]. *To San Francisco and Back*. London: Society for Promoting Christian Knowledge, 1878.

Long, Burke O. *Imagining the Holy Land: Maps, Models, and Fantasy Travels*. Bloomington: Indiana University Press, 2003.

Lubetkin, M. John. *Jay Cooke's Gamble: The Northern Pacific Railway, the Sioux, and the Panic of 1873*. Norman: University of Oklahoma Press, 2006.

Ludlow, Fitz Hugh. *The Heart of the Continent: A Record of Travel across the Pains and in Oregon, with an Examination of the Mormon Principle*. New York: Hurd and Houghton, 1870.

Lyman, Edward Leo. "Isaac Trumbo and the Politics of Utah Statehood." *Utah Historical Quarterly* 41 (Spring 1972): 128–49.
———. *Political Deliverance: The Mormon Quest for Statehood*. Urbana: University of Illinois Press, 1986.
MacCannell, Dean. *The Tourist: A New Theory of the Leisure Class*. Berkeley: University of California Press, 1999 [1976].
Madsen, Brigham D. *The City of Corinne*. Salt Lake City: Friends of the University of Utah Libraries, 1973.
———. *Corinne: The Gentile Capital of Utah*. Salt Lake City: Utah State Historical Society, 1980.
———. "Corinne, the Fair: Gateway to Montana Mines." *Utah Historical Quarterly* 37, no. 1 (Winter 1969): 102–23.
———. *Glory Hunter: A Biography of Patrick Edward Connor*. Salt Lake City: University of Utah Press, 1990.
———. *The Northern Shoshoni*. Caldwell, Idaho: Caxton Press, 2000.
———. *The Shoshoni Frontier and the Bear River Massacre*. Salt Lake City: University of Utah Press, 1985.
Madsen, Carol Cornwall, ed. *Battle for the Ballot: Essays on Woman Suffrage in Utah, 1870–1896*. Logan: Utah State University Press, 1997.
Madsen, Michael H. "The Sanctification of Mormonism's Historical Geography." *Geographies of Religions and Belief Systems* 1, no. 1 (October 2006): 51–73.
Maffly-Kipp, Laurie. "Engaging Habits and Besotted Idolatry: Viewing Chinese Religions in the American West." *Material Religion* 1, no. 1 (March 2005): 72–96.
Makdisi, Saree. *Making England Western: Occidentalism, Race, and Imperial Culture*. Chicago: University of Chicago Press, 2014.
Marr, Timothy. *The Cultural Roots of American Islamicism*. New York: Cambridge University Press, 2006.
Marsden, George M. *The Soul of the American University: From Protestant Establishment to Established Nonbelief*. New York: Oxford University Press, 1994.
Marx, Leo. *The Machine in the Garden: Technology and the Pastoral Ideal in America*. New York: Oxford University Press, 2000 [1964].
Mason, Patrick Q. "God and the People: Theodemocracy in Nineteenth-Century Mormonism." *Journal of Church and State* 53, no. 3 (Summer 2011): 349–75.
———. *The Mormon Menace: Violence and Anti-Mormonism in the Postbellum South*. New York: Oxford University Press, 2011.
Masuzawa, Tomoko. *The Invention of World Religions; or, How European Universalism Was Preserved in the Language of Pluralism*. Chicago: University of Chicago Press, 2005.
Mathews, Alfred Edward. *Gems of Rocky Mountain Scenery: Containing Views along and near the Union Pacific Railroad*. New York: A. E. Mathews, 1869.
Maughan, Ila Fisher. *Pioneer Theatre in the Desert*. Salt Lake City: Deseret Book, 1961.
Mauss, Armand L. *All Abraham's Children: Changing Mormon Conceptions of Race and Lineage*. Urbana: University of Illinois Press, 2003.
McCormick, Nancy D., and John S. McCormick. *Saltair*. Salt Lake City: Bonneville Books, University of Utah Press, 1985.

McDannell, Colleen. *Material Christianity: Religion and Popular Culture in America*. New Haven, Conn.: Yale University Press, 1995.
McFeely, Eliza. "Palimpsest of American Identity: Zuni, Anthropology, and American Identity at the Turn of the Century." Ph.D. diss., New York University, 1996.
McKinsey, Elizabeth. *Niagara Falls: Icon of the American Sublime*. Cambridge: Cambridge University Press, 1985.
McLuhan, T. C. *Dream Tracks: The Railroad and the American Indian, 1890–1930*. New York: Harry N. Abrams, 1985.
Memorial of the Citizens of Corinne, Utah, Asking for a Grant of Lands to Aid in Constructing a Canal for Irrigating Bear River Valley. Washington, D.C.: Chronicle, 1871.
Merk, Frederick. *Manifest Destiny and Mission in American History: A Reinterpretation*. New York: Alfred A. Knopf, 1963.
Meyer, Eduard. *Ursprung und Geschichte der Mormonen, mit Exkursen über die Anfänge des Islâms und des Christentums*. Halle, Germany: Max Niemeyer, 1912.
Mikesell, Marvin. "Comparative Studies in Frontier History." *Annals of the Association of American Geographers* 50, no. 1 (1960): 62–74.
Mikkelsen, Robert S. "Growing Up Railroad: Remembering Echo City." *Utah Historical Quarterly* (Fall 1994): 349–62.
Miller, Perry. *The Life of the Mind in America from the Revolution to the Civil War*. New York: Harcourt, Brace, and World, 1965.
Miner, H. Craig. *The Corporation and the Indian: Tribal Sovereignty and Industrial Civilization in Indian Territory, 1866–1907*. Columbia: University of Missouri Press, 1976.
Minutes of the Apostles of the Church of Jesus Christ of Latter-day Saints, 1835–1951. Electronic ed. Salt Lake City: privately published, 2015.
Modern, John Lardas. *Secularism in Antebellum America*. Chicago: University of Chicago Press, 2011.
Moore, R. Laurence. *Selling God: American Religion in the Marketplace of Culture*. New York: Oxford University Press, 1994.
Morgan, Dale L. *The Great Salt Lake*. Lincoln: University of Nebraska Press, 1986 [1947].
Morris, John W. "'That Place Over There': A Journalistic Look at Latter-Day Corinne, the Last Gentile Railroad Boomtown in the Mormon Lands of Utah." M.A. thesis, Utah State University, 1987.
Mueller, Max Perry. *Race and the Making of the Mormon People*. Chapel Hill: University of North Carolina Press, 2017.
Murray, Andrew E. *The Skyline Synod: Presbyterianism in Colorado and Utah*. Denver, Colo.: Golden Bell Press, 1971.
Nance, Susan. *How the Arabian Nights Inspired the American Dream*. Chapel Hill: University of North Carolina Press, 2009.
Neilson, Reid L. *Exhibiting Mormonism: The Latter-day Saints and the 1893 Chicago World's Fair*. New York: Oxford University Press, 2011.
Nelsons' Pictorial Guide Books. *Salt Lake City, with a Sketch of the Route of the Union and Central Pacific Railroads, from Omaha to Salt Lake City, and from Ogden to San Francisco, with Twelve Illustrations from Photographs by C. R. Savage*. New York: T. Nelson and Sons, 1870.

Nibley, Preston. *Brigham Young: The Man and His Work*. Salt Lake City: Deseret News Press, 1936.

Norman, Alex. *Spiritual Tourism: Travel and Religious Practice in Western Society*. New York: Bloomsbury, 2011.

Nugent, Walter. "Where Is the American West? Report on a Survey." *Montana* 42 (Summer 1992): 2–23.

Nye, David E. *America as Second Creation: Technology and Narratives of New Beginnings*. Cambridge, Mass.: MIT Press, 2003.

———. *American Technological Sublime*. Cambridge, Mass.: MIT Press, 1994.

Obenzinger, Hilton. *American Palestine: Melville, Twain, and the Holy Land Mania*. Princeton, N.J.: Princeton University Press, 1999.

O'Brien, Jean. *Firsting and Lasting: Writing Indians out of Existence in New England*. Minneapolis: University of Minnesota Press, 2010.

Ochs, Milton B. *Heart of the Rockies, Illustrated*. [Denver, Colo.]: Passenger Department, Rio Grande Western Railway, 1890.

Orsi, Richard J. *Sunset Limited: The Southern Pacific Railroad and the Development of the American West, 1850–1930*. Berkeley: University of California Press, 2005.

Otto, Rudolph. *The Idea of the Holy*. New York: Oxford University Press, 1958 [1923].

Pacific Coast Land Bureau. *California Guide Book: The Lands of the Central Pacific and Southern Pacific Railroad Companies: Homes for All in California, Nevada and Utah*. . . . San Francisco: Pacific Coast Land Bureau, [188–?].

The Pacific Tourist: Adams and Bishop's Illustrated Trans-Continental Guide of Travel from the Atlantic to the Pacific Ocean. . . . New York: Adams and Bishop, 1881 [also 1884, 1885].

Peet, Volney S. *$13,000 Reward. Bear River Valley, Utah. How to Get There. A Review of the Smoot Inquiry*. Salt Lake City: n.p., 1905.

Pennington, Brian. *Was Hinduism Invented? Britons, Indians, and the Colonial Construction of Religion*. New York: Oxford University Press, 2005.

Penny, H. Glenn. *Kindred by Choice: Germans and American Indians since 1800*. Chapel Hill: University of North Carolina Press, 2013.

Piercy, Frederick. *Route from Liverpool to Great Salt Lake Valley: Illustrated with Steel Engravings and Wood Cuts from Sketches Made by Frederick Piercy*. Edited by James Linforth. London: Latter-day Saints' Book Depot, 1855.

Pitzer, Donald E., ed. *America's Communal Utopias*. Chapel Hill: University of North Carolina Press, 1997.

Pomeroy, Earl. *In Search of the Golden West: The Tourist in Western America*. Lincoln: University of Nebraska Press, 2010 [1957].*Poor's Manual of the Railroads of the United States*. New York: H. V. and H. W. Poor, 1896.

Porterfield, Amanda. *Corporate Spirit: Religion and the Rise of the Modern Corporation*. New York: Oxford University Press, 2018.

Pratt, Orson, and J. P. Newman. *The Bible and Polygamy: Does the Bible Sanction Polygamy? Discussion between Professor Orson Pratt, One of the Twelve Apostles of the Church of Jesus Christ of Latter-day Saints, and Dr. J. P. Newman, Chaplain of the U.S. Senate, in the New Tabernacle, Salt Lake City, August 12, 13, and 14, 1870*. . . . Salt Lake City: Deseret News, 1874.

Pratt, Richard H. "The Advantages of Mingling Indians with Whites." In

Proceedings of the National Conference of Charities and Correction, at the Nineteenth Annual Session Held in Denver, Col., June 23–29, 1892, edited by Isabel C. Barrows, 45–59. Boston: George H. Ellis, 1892.

"Proceedings in Mass Meeting of the Ladies of Salt Lake City, to Protest against the Passage of Cullom's Bill, January 14, 1870." [Salt Lake City: n.p., 1870].

Promey, Sally M. "Hearts and Stones: Material Transformations and the Stuff of Christian Practice in the United States." In *American Christianities: A History of Dominance and Diversity*, edited by Catherine A. Brekus and W. Clark Gilpin, 183–213. Chapel Hill: University of North Carolina Press, 2011.

Promey, Sally M., and Shira Brisman. "Sensory Cultures: Material and Visual Religion Reconsidered." In *The Blackwell Companion to Religion in America*, edited by Phillip Goff, 177–205. Malden, Mass.: Wiley-Blackwell, 2010.

Prucha, Francis Paul. *The Great Father: The United States Government and the American Indians*, 2 vols. Lincoln: University of Nebraska Press, 1984.

Quinn, D. Michael. *The Mormon Hierarchy: Wealth and Corporate Power*. Salt Lake City: Signature Books, 2017.

———. "The Mormon Succession Crisis of 1844." *BYU Studies Quarterly* 16, no. 2 (1976): 187–233.

Quinn, Frederick. "Daniel S. Tuttle: Utah's Pioneer Episcopal Bishop." *Journal of Mormon History* 33, no. 2 (2007): 119–54.

Rae, William Fraser. *Westward by Rail: A Journey to San Francisco and Back, and a Visit to the Mormons*. 2nd ed. London: Longmans, Green, 1871 [1870].

Ray, Angela G., ed. *The Lyceum and Public Culture in the Nineteenth-Century United States*. East Lansing: Michigan State University Press, 2005.

Reeder, Clarence A., Jr. *The History of Utah's Railroads, 1869–1883*. New York: Arno Press, 1981.

Reeve, W. Paul. *Making Space on the Western Frontier: Mormons, Miners, and Southern Paiutes*. Urbana: University of Illinois Press, 2006.

———. *Religion of a Different Color: Race and the Struggle for Mormon Whiteness*. New York: Oxford University Press, 2015.

Remy, Jules. *A Journey to Great-Salt-Lake City . . . With a Sketch of the History, Religion, and Customs of the Mormons*. London: W. Jeffs, 1861.

Report of the Utah World's Fair Commission, Signed R C Chambers, President, Submitted to Governor Heber M. Wells. Salt Lake City: n.p., 1896.

Richards, Bradley W. *The Savage View: Charles Savage, Pioneer Mormon Photographer*. Nevada City, Calif.: Carl Mautz, 1995.

Richardson, Heather Cox. *The Greatest Nation on Earth: Republican Economic Policies during the Civil War*. Cambridge, Mass.: Harvard University Press, 1997.

Richter, Amy G. *Home on the Rails: Women, the Railroad, and the Rise of Public Domesticity*. Chapel Hill: University of North Carolina Press, 2005.

Rideing, William Henry. *The Pacific Railroads, Illustrated*. New York: D. Appleton, 1878.

Rio Grande Western. *A Pointer to Prosperity: A Few Facts about the Climate and Resources of the New State of Utah . . . .* Salt Lake City: [Rio Grande Western Railway], 1896.

———. *Salt Lake City: The "Zion of the New World": An Outline of Its Natural Beauty and Manifold Attractions.* Salt Lake City: [Passenger Department, Rio Grande Western], 1900.

———. *Utah, the Promised Land: A Few Specimen Tours* . . . . Denver, Colo.: Rio Grande Western Railway, 1895.

Robbins, Roy M. *Our Landed Heritage: The Public Domain, 1776–1936.* Princeton, N.J.: Princeton University Press, 1942.

Roberts, Brigham H. "History of the Mormon Church, Chapter 106." *Americana American Historical Magazine* 9 (1914): 429–63.

Roberts, Edwards. "A Glimpse of Utah." *Overland Monthly* 5 (January 1885): 38–45.

———. *Salt Lake City and Utah By-Ways.* Chicago: R. R. Donnelley and Sons, 1883.

———. *Shoshone and Other Western Wonders.* [Preface by Charles Francis Adams.] New York: Harper and Brothers, 1888.

Robinson, Phil. *Sinners and Saints: A Tour across the States, and round Them; with Three Months among the Mormons.* Boston: Roberts Brothers, 1883.

Robison, Elwin C., with W. Randall Dixon. *Gathering as One: The History of the Mormon Tabernacle in Salt Lake City.* Provo, Utah: BYU Studies, 2014.

Rogers, Brent M. *Unpopular Sovereignty: Mormons and the Federal Management of Early Utah Territory.* Lincoln: University of Nebraska Press, 2017.

Rosenberg, Emily S. "Rescuing Women and Children." *Journal of American History* 89, no. 2 (September 2002): 456–65.

Ross, William Wilson. *10,000 Miles by Land and Sea.* Toronto: James Campbell and Son, 1876.

Rourke, Constance. *American Humor: A Study of the National Character.* New York: New York Review Books, 2004 [1931].

Saler, Bethel. *The Settler's Empire: Colonialism and State Formation in America's Old Northwest.* Philadelphia: University of Pennsylvania Press, 2014.

Salt Lake City Chamber of Commerce. *Salt Lake City: A Sketch of Utah's Wonderful Resources.* Salt Lake City: M. J. Forhan; Chicago: Rand, McNally, 1888.

———. *The Western Wonderland! Utah, Her Mineral and Other Resources; Advantages Offered to the Homeseeker, Manufacturer and Capitalist: Mineral, Industrial, Agricultural, Commercial.* [Salt Lake City]: Salt Lake Tribune, [1888].

Sauder, Robert A. "State v. Society: Public Land Law and Mormon Settlement in the Sevier Valley, Utah." *Agricultural History* 70, no. 1 (Winter 1996): 57–89.

Savage, C. R. *Gems of Utah Scenery.* [Salt Lake City: n.p., 189–?].

———. *Reflex of Salt Lake City and Vicinity: Including Letter-press Description and Illustrations of Public Edifices, Hotels, Business Blocks, Churches, Indians, Bathing Resorts, etc.* Salt Lake City: C. R. Savage, 1893.

———. *Views of Utah and Tourists' Guide: Containing a Description of the Views and General Information for the Traveler, Resident and Public Generally, from Authentic Sources.* Salt Lake City: C. R. Savage, ca. 1887.

Saxton, Alexander. "Blackface Minstrelsy and Jacksonian Ideology." *American Quarterly* 27, no. 1 (March 1975): 3–28.

Scaff, Lawrence A. *Max Weber in America.* Princeton, N.J.: Princeton University Press, 2011.

Scanlon, Lee Edward. "Buffalo Bill in a Boiled Shirt: The Salt Lake Theatre, 1869–1874." Ph.D. diss., Brigham Young University, 1979.

Schivelbusch, Wolfgang. *The Railway Journey: The Industrialization of Time and Space in the Nineteenth Century.* Berkeley: University of California Press, 1986 [1977].

Sears, John F. *Sacred Places: American Tourist Attractions in the Nineteenth Century.* New York: Oxford University Press, 1989.

Senatorial Excursion Party over the Union Pacific Railway, E. D.: Speeches of Senators Yates, Cattel, Chandler, Howe, and Trumbull; Hon J. A. J. Creswell, Hon. John Covode, M. C., and Hon. Wm. M. PcPherson, on the Pacific Rail Road Question . . . . St. Louis, Mo.: S. Levison, 1867.

Shaffer, Marguerite S. "'See America First': Re-Envisioning Nation and Region through Western Tourism." *Pacific Historical Review* 65 (November 1996): 559–82.

———. *See America First: Tourism and National Identity, 1880–1940.* Washington, D.C.: Smithsonian Books, 2001.

Shipps, Jan. "Introduction: Religion in the Mountain West: Geography as Destiny." In *Religion and Public Life in the Mountain West: Sacred Landscapes in Transition*, edited by Jan Shipps and Mark Silk, 9–14. Walnut Creek, Calif.: AltaMira, 2004.

———. *Mormonism: The Study of a New Religious Tradition.* Urbana: University of Illinois Press, 1985.

Shipps, Jan, and Mark Silk, eds. *Religion and Public Life in the Mountain West: Sacred Landscapes in Transition.* Walnut Creek, Calif.: AltaMira, 2004.

Shoemaker, S. Todd. "Saltair and the Mormon Church, 1893–1906." M.A. thesis, University of Utah, 1983.

Simpson, James Hervey. *The Shortest Route to California: Illustrated by a History of Explorations of the Great Basin of Utah with Its Topographical and Geological Character and Some Account of the Indian Tribes.* Philadelphia: J. B. Lippincott, 1869.

Sloan, Edward L. *Gazeteer of Utah, and Salt Lake City, Directory.* Salt Lake City: Salt Lake Herald, 1874.

———, ed. *The Salt Lake City Directory and Business Guide for 1869, Compiled and Arranged by E. L. Sloan.* Salt Lake City: E. L. Sloan, 1869.

Smith, Henry Nash. *Virgin Land: The American West as Symbol and Myth.* Cambridge, Mass.: Harvard University Press, 2007 [1950].

Smith, Jonathan Z. *Relating Religion: Essays in the Study of Religion.* Chicago: University of Chicago Press, 2004.

———. *To Take Place: Toward Theory in Ritual.* Chicago: University of Chicago Press, 1987.

Smith, Konden Rich. "Appropriating the Secular: Mormonism and the World's Columbian Exposition." *Journal of Mormon History* 34, no. 4 (Fall 2008): 153–80.

Smith, Marietta V. *Fifteen Years among the Mormons* . . . . New York: C. Scribner, 1858.

Smith, Valene L., ed. *Hosts and Guests: The Anthropology of Tourism.* Philadelphia: University of Pennsylvania Press, 1977.

Soja, Edward W. *Postmodern Geographies: The Reassertion of Space in Critical Social Theory.* New York: Verso, 1989.

Sowell, Debra Hickenlooper. "Theatrical Dancing in the Territory of Utah." *Dance Chronicle* 1, no. 2 (1977): 96–126.

Spude, Robert L. *Promontory Summit, May 10, 1869: A History of the Site Where the Central Pacific and Union Pacific Railroads Joined to Form the First Transcontinental Railroad, 1869* . . . . [Denver, Colo.]: Cultural Resources Management, Intermountain Region, National Park Service, 2005.

Staal, Frits. "The Meaninglessness of Ritual." *Numen* 26, no. 1 (June 1979): 2–22.

Stausberg, Michael. *Religion and Tourism: Crossroads, Destinations, and Encounters*. New York: Routledge, 2011.

Stenhouse, Mrs. T. B. H. [Fanny]. *Exposé of Polygamy in Utah: A Lady's Life among the Mormons*. New York: American News, 1872.

Stenhouse, T. B. H. *The Rocky Mountain Saints: A Full and Complete History of the Mormons . . . and the Development of the Great Mineral Wealth of the Territory of Utah*. New York: D. Appleton, 1873.

Stephanson, Anders. *Manifest Destiny: American Expansion and the Empire of Right*. New York: Hill and Wang, 1996.

Stevens, Thomas M. "The Union Pacific Railroad and the Mormon Church, 1868–1871: An In Depth Study of the Financial Aspects of Brigham Young's Grading Contract and Its Ultimate Settlement." M.A. thesis, Brigham Young University, 1972.

Stolow, Jeremy. "Introduction." In *Deus in Machina: Religion, Technology, and the Things in Between*, edited by Jeremy Stolow, 1–22. New York: Fordham University Press, 2013.

———. "Salvation by Electricity." In *Religion: Beyond a Concept*, edited by Hent de Vries, 668–86. New York: Fordham University Press, 2007.

———. "Wired Religion: Spiritualism and Telegraphic Globalization in the Nineteenth Century." In *Empires and Autonomy: Moments in the History of Globalization*, edited by Stephen Streeter, John Weaver, and William Coleman, 79–92. Vancouver: University of British Columbia Press, 2009.

Strahorn, Robert E. *To the Rockies and Beyond; or, A Summer on the Union Pacific Railroad and Branches*. Omaha, Nebr.: New West, 1879.

Strong, Josiah. *Our Country: Its Possible Future and Its Present Crisis*. New York: Baker and Taylor, 1885.

Stout, Harry S. *The Divine Dramatist: George Whitefield and the Rise of Modern Evangelicalism*. Grand Rapids, Mich.: William B. Eerdmans, 1991.

Sullivan, Winnifred Fallers. *The Impossibility of Religious Freedom*. Princeton, N.J.: Princeton University Press, 2007.

Sweet, Rosemary. *Cities and the Grand Tour: The British in Italy, c. 1680–1820*. Cambridge: Cambridge University Press, 2015 [2012].

Szasz, Ferenc Morton. *Religion in the American West*. Tucson: University of Arizona Press, 2000.

Taysom, Stephen C. *Shakers, Mormons, and Religious Worlds: Conflicting Visions, Contested Boundaries*. Bloomington: Indiana University Press, 2011.

Thomas, George. *The Development of Institutions under Irrigation, with Special Reference to Early Utah Conditions*. New York: Macmillan, 1920.

Thompson, Margaret Susan. *The "Spider Web": Congress and Lobbying in the Age of Grant*. Ithaca, N.Y.: Cornell University Press, 1985.

Toponce, Alexander. *Reminiscences of Alexander Toponce, Written by Himself*. Norman: University of Oklahoma Press, 1971 [1923].
Tullidge, Edward W. *History of Salt Lake City*. Salt Lake City: Star, 1886.
———. *Tullidge's Histories*, vol. 2, *Containing the History of All the Northern, Eastern and Western Counties of Utah . . . .* Salt Lake City: Juvenile Instructor, 1889.
Turley, Richard E., Jr. "Clash of the Legal Titans: The First Trial of John D. Lee, July 20 to August 7, 1875." Thirty-First Annual Juanita Brooks Lecture, St. George Tabernacle, St. George, Utah, March 26, 2014.
Turner, Frederick Jackson. "The Significance of the Frontier in American History." *Report of the American Historical Association* (1893): 197–227.
Turner, John. *Brigham Young: Pioneer Prophet*. Cambridge, Mass.: Harvard University Press, 2012.
———. *The Mormon Jesus: A Biography*. Cambridge, Mass.: Harvard University Press, 2016.
Turner, Victor, and Edith L. B. Turner. *Image and Pilgrimage in Christian Culture*. New York: Columbia University Press, 1978.
Tuttle, Daniel S. *Reminiscences of a Missionary Bishop*. New York: Thomas Whittaker, 1906.
Twain, Mark. *Roughing It*. Hartford, Conn.: American Publishing, 1872.
Twain, Mark, and Charles Dudley Warner. *The Gilded Age: A Tale of Today*. Hartford, Conn.: American Publishing, 1873.
Tweed, Thomas A. *Crossing and Dwelling: A Theory of Religion*. Cambridge, Mass.: Harvard University Press, 2006.
Ulrich, Laurel Thatcher. *A House Full of Females: Plural Marriage and Women's Rights in Early Mormonism, 1835–1870*. New York: Alfred A. Knopf, 2017.
Underwood, Grant. *The Millenarian World of Early Mormonism*. Urbana: University of Illinois Press, 1993.
[Union Pacific]. *A Description of the Western Resorts for Health and Pleasure Reached via the Union Pacific System, "The Overland Route," Compliments of the Passenger Department*. Chicago: Rand, McNally, 1888 [also 1889, 1890, 1891].
———. *A Glimpse of Great Salt Lake, Utah, on the Line of the Union Pacific System, "The Overland Route."* Omaha, Neb.: Union Pacific System Passenger Department, 1891 [also 1892, 1893].
———. *Guide to the Union Pacific Railroad Lands: 12,000,000 Acres Best Farming, Grazing and Mineral Lands in America, in the State of Nebraska and Territories of Colorado, Wyoming and Utah*. Omaha, Nebr.: Land Dept., Union Pacific Railroad Building, 1872.
———. *Irrigation: Its History, Methods, Statistics and Results; Lands Irrigated along the Union Pacific System*. St. Louis, Mo.: Woodward and Tiernan, 1894.
———. *The Resources and Attractions of Utah*. Omaha, Nebr.: Passenger Department of the Union Pacific Railway, 1888.
———. *Sights and Scenes in Utah for Tourists, Compliments of the Passenger Department*. Omaha, Nebr.: Union Pacific Railway, 1888.
———. *The Union Pacific and Utah and Northern Through Rail Route to Montana and Yellowstone Park*. [Omaha, Nebr.]: Omaha Daily Republican, [1881?].

———. *Union Pacific Railroad: The Great National Highway between the Missouri River and California* . . . . Chicago: Horton and Leonard, 1868.

———. *World's Pictorial Line: Birdseye View of the Great Salt Lake Basin Reached via the Union Pacific, the Overland Route*. Omaha, Nebr.: Union Pacific System, ca. 1893.

Urry, John. *The Tourist Gaze: Leisure and Travel in Contemporary Societies*. Thousand Oaks, Calif.: Sage, 1990.

Utah: Her Attractions and Resources, as Inviting the Attention of Tourists and Those Seeking Permanent Homes . . . . Salt Lake City: G. A. Meears, [1881].

Utah & Nevada Railway. *Descriptive and Historical Sketch of the Great Salt Lake, Utah Territory: Issued by Passenger Department*. Salt Lake City: J. C. Parker, 1886.

Utah at the World's Columbian Exposition. Salt Lake City: E. A. McDaniel, Salt Lake Lithographing, 1894.

Utah Board of Trade. *The Resources and Attractions of the Territory of Utah*. Omaha, Nebr.: Republican Publishing House, 1879.

Utah Irrigation Commission. *Irrigation in Utah: Report of the Irrigation Commission to the Third National Irrigation Congress, Held at Denver, September, 1894*. Salt Lake City: Utah Irrigation Commission, 1895.

Utah State Fair Association. *History of the Utah State Fair Association, Golden Jubilee Exposition, 1856–1928*. Salt Lake City: [Utah State Fair Association, 1928].

Van Wagenen, Lola. "Sister-Wives and Suffragists: Polygamy and the Politics of Woman Suffrage, 1870–1896." Ph.D. diss., New York University, 1994.

Vaughan, W. R. *Union Pacific Business Hand Book and Emigrants' Guide from Omaha to Salt Lake and Corinne, Utah*. Council Bluffs, Iowa: Bluff City Book and Job Printing House, 1871.

Veblen, Thorstein. *The Theory of the Leisure Class*. New York: Macmillan, 1899.

Vogel, Lester I. "Staying Home for the Sights: Surrogate Destinations in America for Holy Land Travel." In *Pilgrims and Travelers to the Holy Land*, edited by Bryan F. Le Beau and Menachem Mor, 251–67. Omaha, Nebr.: Creighton University Press, 1996.

———. *To See a Promised Land: Americans and the Holy Land in the Nineteenth Century*. University Park: Pennsylvania State University Press, 1993.

Voss, Robert J. "Railroads and Coal: Resource Extraction in Indian Territory, 1866–1907." Ph.D. diss., University of Nebraska, Lincoln, 2013.

Wadsworth, Nelson B. *Set in Stone, Fixed in Glass: The Great Mormon Temple and Its Photographers*. Salt Lake City: Signature Books, 1992.

Wait, Catherine Van Valkenburg. *The Mormon Prophet and His Harem; or, An Authentic History of Brigham Young, His Numerous Wives and Children*. Cambridge, Mass.: Riverside Press, 1866.

Walker, David. "The Humbug in American Religion: Ritual Theories of Nineteenth-Century Spiritualism." *Religion and American Culture* 23, no. 1 (Winter 2013): 30–74.

———. "Railroading Independence: Pulpit Rock and the Work of Mormon Observation." *John Whitmer Historical Association Journal* 37, no. 1 (Spring–Summer 2017): 29–50.

---. "Transporting Mormonism: Railroads and Religious Imagination in the American West." In *Sensational Religion: Sensory Culture in Material Practice*, edited by Sally M. Promey, 581–603. New Haven, Conn.: Yale University Press, 2014.
Walker, Ronald W. "The Salt Lake Tabernacle in the Nineteenth Century: A Glimpse of Early Mormonism." *Journal of Mormon History* 32, no. 3 (Fall 2005): 198–240.
---. "Seeking the Remnant: The Native American during the Joseph Smith Period." *Journal of Mormon History* 19, no. 1 (1993): 1–33.
---. "Toward a Reconstruction of Mormon and Indian Relations, 1847–1877." *BYU Studies Quarterly* 29, no. 4 (Fall 1989): 23–42.
---. *Wayward Saints: The Social and Religious Protests of the Godbeites against Brigham Young*. Provo, Utah: Brigham Young University Press, 2009 [1998].
---. "When the Spirits Did Abound: Nineteenth-Century Utah's Encounter with Free-Thought Radicalism." *Utah Historical Quarterly* 50, no. 4 (Fall 1982): 304–24.
---. "Young Heber J. Grant, Entrepreneur Extraordinary." *BYU Studies Quarterly* 43, no. 1 (2004): 81–113.
Walker, Ronald W., Richard E. Turley, Jr., and Glen M. Leonard. *Massacre at Mountain Meadows: An American Tragedy*. New York: Oxford University Press, 2008.
Warren, Louis. *Buffalo Bill's America: William Cody and the Wild West Show*. New York: Alfred A. Knopf, 2005.
Watson, Charles W. "John Willard Young and the 1887 Movement for Utah Statehood." Ph.D. diss., Brigham Young University, 1984.
Weber, David J. "Turner, the Boltonians, and the Borderlands." *American Historical Review* 91, no. 1 (February 1986): 66–81.
Weber, Max. *General Economic History*. Translated by Frank H. Knight. London: Allen and Unwin, 1930.
---. *The Protestant Ethic and the Spirit of Capitalism*. Translated by Talcott Parsons. New York: Charles Scribner's Sons, 1958 [1905].
---. *The Protestant Ethic and the Spirit of Capitalism*. Translated by Stephen Kalberg. New York: Oxford University Press, 2011 [1905].
Weigle, Marta, and Barbara Babcock, eds. *The Great Southwest of the Fred Harvey Company and the Santa Fe Railway*. Phoenix, Ariz.: Heard Museum, 1996.
Weinberg, Albert K. *Manifest Destiny: A Study of Nationalist Expansionism in American History*. Baltimore: John Hopkins University Press, 1935.
Welter, Barbara. "The Cult of True Womanhood: 1820–1860." *American Quarterly* 18, no. 2 (Summer 1966): 151–74.
Wenger, Tisa. "Modernists, Pueblo Indians, and the Politics of Primitivism." In *Race, Religion, Region: Landscapes of Encounter in the American West*, edited by Fay Botham and Sarah Patterson, 101–14. Tucson: University of Arizona Press, 2006.
---. *We Have a Religion: The 1920s Pueblo Indian Dance Controversy and American Religious Freedom*. Chapel Hill: University of North Carolina Press, 2009.
White, Richard. *"It's Your Misfortune and None of My Own": A New History of the American West*. Norman: Oklahoma University Press, 1994.
---. *Railroaded: The Transcontinentals and the Making of Modern America*. New York: W. W. Norton, 2011.

Whitman, Walt. "Passage to India." In *Leaves of Grass*, 315–23. Boston: James R. Osgood, 1881–82.

Whitney, Horace. *The Drama in Utah: The Story of the Salt Lake Theatre*. Salt Lake City: Deseret News, 1915.

Whitney, Orson F. *History of Utah, Comprising Preliminary Chapters on the Previous History of Her Founders . . . and the Subsequent Creation and Development of the Territory*. Vol. 2. Salt Lake City: George Cannon and Sons, 1893.

Winsor, Justin, ed. *The Memorial History of Boston . . . , 1630–1880*. Vol. 4. Boston: James R. Osgood, 1883.

Withey, Lynne. *Grand Tours and Cook's Tours: A History of Leisure Travel, 1750 to 1915*. New York: William Morrow, 1997.

Wood, Stanley. *Over the Range to the Golden Gate: A Complete Tourist's Guide to Colorado, New Mexico, Utah, Nevada, California, Oregon, Puget Sound, and the Great North-West*. Chicago: R. R. Donnelley and Sons, 1894.

Worster, Donald. *Encountering Mormon Country: John Wesley Powell, John Muir, and the Nature of Utah*. Leonard J. Arrington Mormon History Lecture Series, 8. Logan: Special Collections and Archives, Utah State University, 2003.

———. "The Kingdom, the Power, and the Water." In *Great Basin Kingdom Revisited: Contemporary Perspectives*, edited by Thomas G. Alexander, 21–38. Logan: Utah State University Press, 1991.

———. *Rivers of Empire: Water, Aridity, and the Growth of the American West*. New York: Pantheon Books, 1985.

INDEX

Page numbers in *italics* refer to illustrations.

Across the Continent (Byron play), 161–62
Adams, Charles Francis, Jr., 185–86, 187–89, 191, 208, 211, 213, 232, 293n18
agriculture: Corinnethian hopes for, 36, 45, 235; Indian displacement and, 20–21, 62, 126; Mormon interests in, 49, 51, 53–54, 62, 64–65, 67, 72, 73, 83, 89, 112, 145, 155–57, 158, 168, 175–76, 213, 215, 218–22, 235–36, 239, 244, 286n26, 301n102; national expansion and, 20–21, 57; touristic reflections on, 155–57, 168, 175–76, 213, 215, 218–22, 235–36, 244. *See also* Indian farms; irrigation
Amelia's Palace. *See* Gardo House
American Progress (Gast painting), *20–21*, 141
Anthony, Susan B., 167, 169
Anti-Bigamy Act, 12–19; Cullom Bill and, 92, 102, 103, 104, 105, 108; death knell thesis and, 16–19, 33, 105, 188; Edmunds-Tucker Act and, 187; exegesis and, 93; Pacific Railway Act and, 18, 19, 23–24, 62, 109; religious comparison and, 14–15, 16–17, 197; religious freedom and, 15–16; terms of, 18
Arrington, Leonard J., 60, 69, 151, 252–53n6, 253n9, 264n20
Articles of Faith, 192, 232, 294n27
Asad, Talal, 25, 258n45
Associated Press, 191

Badlam, Alex, 191
Bancroft, Hubert Howe, 236, 277n9
Bannocks, 62, 124, 171. *See also* Bear River Valley: Indians in
Baptists, 29, 37, 154
Barfoot, Joseph L., 289n67
Barnum, Phineas T., 177, 230–31, 232
Barrell, Henry Charles, 298n73
Barrett, J. R., 23
Baskin, R. N., 103, 275n51
Bayliss, E. E., 260n59, 277n10
Beadle, John Hanson: Corinnethian promotions by, 1–2, 33–34, 36–41, *42–44*, 65, 80, 104–5, 115–23, 124–25, 127–34, 135–36, 138, 141–44, 175, 225, 226, 235; Cullom Bill and, 104–5, 106, 107, 111; death knell thesis and, 36–37, 44, 105, 106, 107, 130, 138, 142, 247; departure from Corinne, 180; exposés and histories of Mormonism by, 34–35, 111, *132*, 143–44, 147, 182, 211, 213, 298n63; Godbeites and, 99–100, 101, 104, 106, 107, 274n46; Josephites and, 93; Liberal Party campaign by, 99–100; on a mule, 282n74; Protestant ecumenism of, 37–39, 155; as Salt Lake City guide, *130–33*, 134, 175, 212, 213, 225, 226, 288n59
Bear Lake & River Water Works and Irrigation Company, 235–37
Bear River: Corinnethian plotting at, 43–44; freshwater resources of, 1, 36, 43, 278n17; irrigation and, 235; Shoshonis and, 124–25, 171, 173; steamboats on, 43, 117, 127, 278n17. *See also* Bear River Massacre;

Bear River (*continued*)
  Bear River Valley; *City of Corinne*; Corinne; *Kate Connor*
Bear River City, Wyo., 79
Bear River Irrigation & Ogden Water Works Company, 237
Bear River Massacre, 36, 62, 124–25, 252n1. *See also* Shoshonis
Bear River Valley: Gentile promotion of, 1–5, 36–37, 38, 43, 44, 45, 58, 62, 98, 104–5, 117, 124–25, 235–37; Indians in, 1, 4, 33, 36, 62, 124–27, 171, 173–74, 180–82; Mormons in, 171, 173, 179, 180, 237–38; natural resources of, 1, 36, 43, 104–5; railroad construction in, 43, 44, 45, 127–28, 179–80. *See also* Corinne
Beecher, Lyman, 29, 197
Beehive House, 168–69, 214
beliefs, as related to acts, 16, 92, 103, 111, 194, 225, 255n14
Benson, Farr & West, 77–78, *81*, 271n100
Blaine, James G., 148, 152–53, 163, 178, 193
Blair, Francis Preston, Jr., 22
Boston Board of Trade, 168, 296–97n54
Bothwell, John R., 235–36, 237
Box Elder, Treaty of, 125
Box Elder County, 63, 99, 104, 151. *See also* Bear River Valley; Corinne
Boyce, William Waters, 16–18, 34, 61
bricolage. *See* scrapbooks
Brigham City, 171, 179
Brighamites. *See* Young, Brigham
Brigham's Destroying Angel (Hickman), 143–44, 147, 298n63
Bryant, William Cullen, 205–9, 227, 232
Buchanan, James, 13
Buckley, Charles Waldron, 105, 106, 275n54
bureaucracy: Congress and, 88–89, 104, 107–8, 243, 247; Mormonism and, 2, 3–5, 9–10, 13, 51, 52, 56, 66–67, 73, 77–78, 84, 87–89, 102–3, 108, 111, 191, 210, 236, 243, 245–47; railroads and, 9, 56, 73, 77–78, 88–89, 191, 243, 246–47; rationality/irrationality of, 77–78, 101–2, 107–8, 247; religious formations of, 2, 3–5, 27, 56, 84, 88–89, 101–3, 107–8, 209–10, 243, 245–47
Burton, Richard Francis, 195–200, 207, 221, 224, 230, 242, 297n62

Cache Valley, 63–64, 66–67, 126, 151, 171, 178–79, 235, 270n83, 289–90n79
Callahan, Richard J., Jr., 258n45
Campbell, Mary, 303n13
Camp Douglas, 181
Cannon, George Q., 68–69, 133–34, 160, 191–92, 193, 238–39, 240–41, 242–43, 283n3, 303n13
capitalism: Congress and, 18, 19, 20–21, 23–24; Corinnethian faith in, 1–2, 4, 5, 7–8, 9, 36, 37, 101, 105, 121, 245–46; Godbeites and, 8, 83–84, 87–88, 89, 94–95, 96, 101; Mormons (LDS) and, 9, 74, 83–84, 87–88, 149–50, 182, 183, 195, 226, 238, 243, 246–47; Orientalism and, 196. *See also* death knell thesis; mining; Young, Brigham: railroad contracts and negotiations by; Young, John W.
Carter, Charles W., *169*
Carter, Thomas, 262n4, 263n15
Catholicism/Catholics, 14, 25, 29, 33–34, 38, 137, 165, 192, 225
Central Pacific Railroad: charter of, 19; Corinne and, 1, 34, 40, 42–43, 44–45, 48, 80, 116, 125, 127–29, 135–36, 144; death knell thesis and, 21, 44, 65, 175–76; land office and, 65; lobbying by, 108, 190, 191–92, 193–94; Mormon contracts with, 47–48, 59, 77–78, 79, 80; Ogden and, 42–43, 45, 47–48, 79, 80–81; Promontory joining with Union Pacific, 80–*81*; route of, 30, 34, 42–43, 44–45, 47–48, 73–74, 76–77, 79, 80; tourist provisions and promotions of, 119, 127–29, 135, 141, 194, 203, 205. *See also* Pacific Railway Act
chapel cars, 215
Chicago, Rock Island & Pacific Railroad, 189

INDEX

Chinese: in Corinne, 33, 124; Mormon contracts and, 74; theatrical depictions of, 161
Church of Jesus Christ of Latter-day Saints (LDS), 252n2. *See also specific entries related to Mormons/Mormonism*
Church of Zion, 96–98. *See also* Godbeites
church-state relations, secularity and, 4, 9, 91. *See also* First Amendment; theocracy; theodemocracy
City of Corinne (boat), 121–24, *122*, 127–29, 135–36, 144–45, 150, 228
Civil War, 1, 18, 19, 20, 23, 27, 33, 34, 118, 256n28
claim jumping, 64–65, 66
Clark, Horace F., 148–49, 152, 168, 178
Clarkson, James S., 192–93, 242–43
Clawson, Alice Young, 163
Clawson, H. B., 191
Cleveland, Grover, 188, 194
Clinton, Jeter, 278n14, 285n10
Codman, John, 147–50, 152–53, 155, 156, 163, 168, 170–71, 175–76, 177, 178–80, 182–84, 192, 227, 232, 300n90
Cody, William "Buffalo Bill," 238–39
Coffin, Charles Carlton, 131–34, 135, 153, 163–64, 281n55
Colfax, Schuyler, 43, 91–96, 100, 102, 106, 107, 119, 130
colonial resource, Mormonism as, 222, 242–43
colonizing companies, 59–60, 62–64
communalism/communitarianism, 48, 49, 50, 54, 55, 56, 59, 86, 97, 157, 176, 195, 220, 299n77
Congregationalism/Congregationalists, 29–30, 34, 152, 154,
Connor, Patrick E., 36, 37, 62, 72, 92, 115, 116, 121, 123, 124–25, 143, 145, 149, 150, 176, 260n64, 270n92
Cook, Thomas, 277n5
Corinne: Central Pacific interests in, 45, 127–29, 135, 279n32; Chicago World's Fair and, 2, 235–36; Cullom Bill testimony respecting, 104–5, 106, 111; demographics of, 33–34, 124–25, 260n59; Episcopalians in, 33–34, 39, 133, 180, 261n68; founding vision of, 1–2, 3, 7–8, 9, 11–12, 33–34, 36–38, 40–41, 42–44; Godbeites and, 84, 88, 96, 97–102, 104, 106, 109–10, 111, 112, 138, 140–41, 144; Indians and anti-Indianism in, 1, 33, 36, 62, 124–27, 171, 180–82; Josephites in, 93; Liberal Party in, 99–101; mining and freighting concerns in, 1, 2, 36, 42, 43, 99, 115, 116, 121, 123, 127, 150, 151, 176, 182; Mormon responses to and measures against, 5–6, 8, 67, 72–73, 77, 80, 144–45, 150–52, 178, 179, 180, 182, 228; Mormon women and, 69–70, *71*, 140–41; naming of, 36, 43–44, 252n4; Ogden and, 42–43, 45, 48, 67, 77, 80, 88, 99, 181, 237, 252–53n6; Presbyterians in, 29, 33, 37, 38–41, 42, 44, 124, 180, 260n59, 277n10; Protestantism and, 4, 5, 9, 37–39, 42, 88, 128, 130, 155, 182, 235; railroad bypassing of, 2, 8, 45, 48, 80; secular aspirations and models of, 4, 9, 38, 88, 98, 99, 100–102, 182, 245–46, 247; tourist aspirations of, 8, 43, 115–24, 127–30, 134, 140–41, 144–45, 183, 228; tourist impressions of, 123–24, 125–26, 148, 178, 179–80, 182, 247; Union Pacific interests in, 42, 43–44; Walker Brothers and, 72, 98; whiteness and, 36, 62, 124, 125, 162. *See also* Beadle, John Hanson; Hollister, O. J.; Toponce, Alexander
Corinnethians (term), 252n4
Crofutt, George A., 141–44, 194, 213, 297n56, 298n63. *See also American Progress; Brigham's Destroying Angel*; guidebooks
Crofutt's Trans-Continental Tourist's Guide. See Crofutt, George A.
Cullom, Shelby, 103. *See also* Cullom Bill

Cullom Bill, 102–13; Corinnethians and, 104–5, 106, 107, 110, 111, 123; Godbeites and, 92, 102–3, 104, 106–8, 109–11, 112, 138; irony and, 107–8, 109–10, 111, 112–13; legislative genealogy of, 92, 102, 103, 187; railroad lobbyists and, 102, 108–9, 165–66, 188; terms of, 103–4; women's indignation meeting against, 166–67
Culmer, H. L. A., 215–17, 221, 237. *See also* Utah Exposition Palace Car
Curtis, Samuel, 22

Danites, 143
Davis, Jefferson, 22
death knell thesis: basic terms of, 7–8, 11–12; congressional articulations of, 16–19, 22–24; Corinnethian articulations of, 36–37, 44, 101–2, 130, 133, 137–38, 140, 142, 236, 245, 247; Cullom Bill contest between Corinnethian and Godbeite evocations of, 102–3, 105–7, 109, 110; Mormon addresses of, 68–69, 80, 88, 138, 140, 160; and the Protestant mainline, 29–30, 33; railroad lobby and, 109, 138, 188; tourism and, 130, 133, 137–38, 140, 142, 176, 183. *See also* secularization thesis
Denver & Rio Grande. *See* Denver & Rio Grande Western
Denver & Rio Grande Western, 189, 211–12, 219, 222–23, 227, 229–31, *230*, 237, 240, 243–44, 292n14
Deseret, 52–53, 63, 222
Deseret Agricultural & Manufacturing Society, 83, 286n26
Deseret Museum, 170–77, *172*, 178, 180, 213, 215, 218, 228, 230, 239, 289n79
Dickinson, Anna, 134–35, 136, 137, 138, 139, 164–65, 166–67, 168, 218, 227
Diefendorf, Fox, 121, 145,
Dillon, Sydney, 188, 189
Dodge, George W., 173–74, 180
Dodge, Grenville, 77–78,

Dodge, Mary Abigail. *See* Hamilton, Gail
Donation Land Claim Act, 264n18
Douglas, Stephen, 22
Durant, Thomas, 47–48, 73, 78, 82
Durkheim, Émile, 265n29

Eastern Shoshonis, 124. *See also* Shoshonis
Echo Canyon, *75*, *210*; fortifications in, 13, 22, 203–4, 297n56; railroad construction in, 47, 73, 75–76, *77*, 203; railroad representations of, 198–201, 204–8, 298n67. *See also* Pulpit Rock
Echo City, 47, 200, 203, 207
Edmunds Act, 187
Edmunds-Tucker Act, 187–88, 189, 190, 193, 194, 208, 214, 230
Edwards, Esia, 269n74, 270n84
Eliade, Mircea, 265,n27
Eliason, Eric, 295n41
Ellinwood, Frank F., 33
Emigration Canyon, 198, 204
Emporium of Fashion, 139–40
Endowment House, 131, *132*, 138–39, 152, 213
Episcopalianism/Episcopalians, 29–30, 33–34, 39, 133, 154, 180

Farmer, Jared, 224, 300,n90
farming. *See* agriculture; Indian farms; irrigation
fashion, 12, 69–70, 137–38, 139–40
Fessenden, Tracy, 25
First Amendment, 15–16, 153. *See also* church-state relations
Fitch, Thomas, 108–10, 191
Fluhman, J. Spencer, 187, 197, 291n3
Folson, William H., 158
Foote, George W., 39, 133
Fort Hall Reservation, 124, 173–74, 180, 181
Foucault, Michel, 176n69
Fox, Feramorz Young, 49, 54, 55,

Gardo House, 214, 215
Garfield Beach, 217, 228–31, 229, 239
General Garfield (boat), 122, 228. See also *City of Corinne*
Gentiles (term), 252n4
Giant's Cave, 217–18, 221, 228
Givens, Terryl, 254–55n13
Godbe, Anthony, 99
Godbe, William S.: early orthodoxy and prerailroad concerns of, 84–87; excommunication of, 83–84, 89–90, 91, 96, 112; testimony regarding Cullom Bill, 104, 106, 107. *See also* Godbeites
Godbeites: capitalism and liberalism of, 83–84, 85–86, 87–88, 89, 91, 94, 95, 96, 98, 102, 112; Church of Zion and spiritualism of, 96–98; Corinnethians and, 84, 88, 96, 97–102, 104, 106, 109–10, 111, 112, 138, 140–41, 144; Cullom Bill and, 92, 102–3, 104, 106–8, 109–11, 112, 138; Josephites and, 94–95; leading figures, 84–85; Liberal Party and, 98–102; mining and, 83–84, 85, 86, 88, 89–91, 96, 101, 111–12, 140, 142, 151–52, 157, 221; political capital of, 88–89, 101, 102–3, 109, 111, 221; polygamy and, 85, 94–95, 100, 101, 106, 109–10, 138–40; Protestantism of, 84, 85, 88, 95, 98, 100, 112; railroad arrival as occasion for, 8, 83–84, 86, 87, 88, 91–92, 94–96, 102, 109, 111–12; as tour-guides, 138, 167, 170. *See also* Stenhouse, Fanny
Goshutes, 265n32
Grand Tour, 117–18, 129
Grant, Daniel, 288n55
Grant, Heber J., 212, 214, 299n77
Grant, Ulysses S., 43, 92, 93, 107
Grant Brothers Livery Co., 211–12, 213–14
Great Salt Lake, *x*; comparison with Dead Sea, 118–19, 222, 241; comparison with Great Lakes, 122; healthful climate of, 119, 122–23, 240; possible transcontinental routes around, 73–74, 76–77, 78; railroad construction along, 30, 34, 42, 44–45, 47, 73–74, 77, 149; sublimity of, 120, 122, 198. *See also City of Corinne*; Garfield Beach; *General Garfield*; Giant's Cave; *Kate Connor*; Lake Park; Lake Point; Lake Side; Saltair
Grow, Henry, 99
guidebooks: genres of, 143, 144, 183–84, 194, 195, 203, 209, 211, 215, 217; influence of Richard Francis Burton on, 195–200, 242; material and geographical foci of, 156–57, 194–95, 198–201, 206, 210, 211, 213–14, 217–23, 224–28, 231, 232–34, 243–44; mediating role of, 141–42, 156–57, 183–84, 185–87, 194, 198, 207–8, 226–27, 230–34; railroad officials' editorial influence on, 184, 185–87, 211, 232; railroad production and promotion of, 141, 203, 207, 211, 215, 222–23, 228, 243–44; tourist transcriptions and reproductions of, 204–5, 208–10; *See also* scrapbooks; tourism

Hafen, Thomas K., 291n4, 300n90
Hamilton, Gail, 148–49, 152, 153, 163–64, 168, 170–71, 178
Harrison, E. L. T., 83–84, 85–87, 88–89, 91, 96–98, 100, 106, 161
Hawthorne, Nathaniel, 26, 28
Head, Franklin, 106–7, 108, 109, 110
Hickman, William "Wild Bill," 143. *See also Brigham's Destroying Angel*
Hill, George Washington, 171–74, 180, 181
Hinduism/Hindus, 23, 92, 110, 131, 135, 174, 195
Hoffman, Isaac W., 243–44. *See also* scrapbooks
Hollister, O. J., 92, 93, 99, 100–2, 110, 129, 130, 134
Holy Land: comparison of Utah with, 9, 217, 219, 222–25, 223, 227, 231, 237, 300n90; tours of, 9, 118, 223–24
home manufactures, 62–63, 70, 83, 111–12, 155, 166, 168, 175–76, 215, 237

Homestead Act, 3, 20–21, 34, 65, 67, 103, 261n77, 264n18
homesteading. *See* Homestead Act
Hooper, William H., 108, 148–49
House, J. E., 262n79
Hübner, Baron Alexander von, 123–26, 170, 171, 180
Hudson River, 118, 122
Hughes, Melancthon, 32, 39–41, 42
Hunt, Helen, 136–38, 139–40
Hunt, John G. 205, 208–10, 228, 230
Huntington, Dimick, 61
Hurt, Garland, 61

Indian farms, 60–61, 62, 171–73, 174, 181. *See also* agriculture
Indian John, 181
Indians/Indigenous peoples: Anti-Bigamy Act and, 17, 173–74; in Bear River Valley and Corinne, 1, 4, 33, 36, 62, 124–27, 171, 173–74, 180–82; fear of Mormon collaboration with, 17, 61, 62, 173–74, 180–81; federal Indian agents and, 61, 106, 124–25, 173–74, 180; geography and, 57, 218, 221–22, 223; and Mormon claims to indigeneity, 223; in Mormon-Muslim comparisons, 17, 242; Mormon missions to, 59, 60–61, 171–74, 180, 181; Mormons compared with, 143–44, 171, 174, 176, 216–18, 221–22, 223, 228, 242; Mormon settlements and, 53, 60–62, 171; Mormon violence against, 61, 62, 63, 218; Pacific Railway Act and, 19–21, 22, 174; Presbyterian missions to, 30; reservations and, 61, 62, 124–25, 136, 173–74, 180, 181; sovereignty and aboriginal title of, 19, 21, 60, 61–62; theatrical depictions of, 161–62, 238; touristic depictions of, 125–27, 171–73, 174, 176–77, 217–18, 221–22, 223, 228, 298n71; Utah War and, 22, 61. *See also* Bannocks; Bear River Massacre; Goshutes; Piutes; Shoshonis; Utes
indignation meeting, 166–67

Ingalls, G. W., 174, 180
International Association of Ticket Agents, 243
iron cage, 245–47. *See also* Weber, Max
irrigation: Corinne and, 235–36; Mormons and, 53, 55–56, 59, 63, 64, 154, 156, 235–36, 237–38; myth of Mormon origins, 219–20; touristic focus on, 156, 194, 217, 218–22, 233, 235–36, 237–38, 244. *See also* agriculture; water
Islam/Muslims: comparison of Mormonism with, 14–15, 16–17, 34, 143, 174, 183, 196–98, 221, 230, 242, 247. *See also* Orientalism

Jackson, Helen Hunt. *See* Hunt, Helen
Jackson, Richard H., 53
Jackson, Sheldon, 29–33, 37, 38–41, 42, 44, 45, 80, 197, 225
Jackson, William Henry, *200*, 204, 296n49
Johnson, Charles Ellis, *212*, 303n13
Jordan River, 116, 227
Josephites, 93–94, 175, 238, 252n2, 263n13, 274n46, 298n67
Judaism/Jews, 14, 33–34, 38, 252n4; comparison of Mormonism with, 183, 195, 198, 221

Kate Connor (boat), 115–17, 119–21, 123, 131, 144–45
Kimball, Heber C., 53, 55
Kimball, Heber P., 99
Kimball, Sarah N., 166
Kingsbury, Joseph, 212–13, 214
Klassen, Pamela E., 25, 300n91, 304n20
Kletting, Richard K. A., 240–41

Ladies Retrenchment Association, 69–70
Lake Park, 229–30, 240
Lake Point, 121, *122*, 123, 144–45, 150, 228, 302n108
Lake Side, 145, 150, 228
Lake View, 278n14

INDEX

Lamanites, 60. *See also* Indians/Indigenous peoples
Land-Grant College Act, 20–21
land grants: Corinne and, 44, 104–5, 127–28, 261n77; federal initiatives respecting, 19–21, 103, 255–56n24; Indian dispossession through, 19, 20, 53, 60; Mormon municipal planning and, 49, 53, 55–56, 104; Mormon-railroad connections through, 47–48, 67, 80; railroads and, 19, 21, 27–28, 31, 42, 44, 47–48, 67, 80, 127–28; religion and, 3, 8, 9, 10, 19, 21, 27–28, 31, 49, 56–57, 58–59
land office, 54–55, 62, 64–66, 67
Land Ordinance of 1785, 21, 49, 255n24
Latham, Milton, 23
Lawrence, Henry W., 106–7
Lee, John D., 181. *See also* Mountain Meadows Massacre
leisure, work of, 118. *See also* tourism
Lévi-Strauss, Claude, 209
Liberal Party, 98–102, 106, 110, 128, 191
Lincoln, Abraham, 18–19, 95
Lindsay, John, 163
Lion House, 135, 147, 168, *169*, 214, 233
lobbying. *See* railroad lobby
Lofton, Kathryn, 258n45, 298n65
Logan, 178, 289–90n79. *See also* Cache Valley; Utah Northern
Lyman, Amasa, 97
Lyman, Edward Leo, 191–92, 193–94

MacCannell, Dean, 129–30, 226
Madsen, Brigham H., 145, 252–53n6
mainline: in connection with Mormonism, 2, 6, 8, 78, 84, 99, 102, 116, 144, 184, 185–87, 194, 232–33, 239, 246, 247; railroad-era etymology and Protestant evocations of, 29–31, 259n48. *See also* death knell thesis; guidebooks; tourism
manifest destiny, 20–21, 24–25, 54, 109, 162
Marx, Leo, 27, 257–58n41

Mason, Patrick, 51
Methodism/Methodists, 29–30, 31, 34, 37, 154–55
mining: Gentile interests in, 2, 11, 22, 30, 36, 72, 100, 101, 115, 116, 121, 123, 124, 127, 140, 142, 151–52, 178, 180, 227; Godbeites and, 83, 85, 86, 88, 89–91, 96, 101, 111–12, 140, 142, 151–52, 157, 221; legislation respecting, 55–56, 62; Mormon (LDS) concerns about, 63, 85, 89, 151, 157; Mormon (LDS) connections to and benefits from, 63, 123, 144, 149, 150, 151–52, 157, 176, 178, 182, 220–21, 242; touristic reframings of, 142, 171, 172, 175–76, 177, 215, 220–21, 222, 227, 231
Modern, John, 25, 258n42
Modus Operandi, 65–67, 69, 79, 80, 81, 128, 220–21
Moore, R. Laurence, 158
Mormonism (term), 252n2
Mormon railroads. *See individual company names*
Mormon Tabernacle Choir, 237, 238–39, 286n23
Morrill, Justin S., 12–13, 14–16, 17, 18, 34, 55, 197, 254n11. *See also* Anti-Bigamy Act
Mountain Meadows Massacre, 61, 180–81
Muir, John, 228
Muslims. *See* Islam/Muslims
Musser, Amos Milton, 66–67, 69, 73, 82, 83–84, 89, 99, 268n63

Neilson, Reid L., 236–37
Newman-Pratt debate, 154–55
New Movement. *See* Godbeites
Northwestern Shoshonis. *See* Shoshonis
Northwest Ordinance (1787), 21
Nye, David, 27, 257–58n41

Ogden: Corinne and, 42–43, 45, 48, 67, 77, 80, 88, 99, 181, 237, 252–53n6; guidebook depictions of, 243–44; land grants in, 47–48, 67, 80, 103; layovers at,

Ogden (*continued*)
  119, 147, 152; Mormon emigrants to, 69; Mormon labor in, 73–74; Mormon plans for a branch line to, 47, 77, 78, 81–82; Mormon settlements in, 63, 66–67, 79, 103; tourists in, 119, 136, 147, 148, 152, 168, 178; as transcontinental terminus and hub, 42–43, 45, 47–48, 67, 79–81; travel time to, 69, 202. *See also* Utah Central; Utah Northern
Old Tabernacle, 133
O'Neil, John, 43, 44
Orientalism: in anti-Mormonism, 15, 16–17, 35, 131–33, 197, 247; as critique of Protestantism, 196; Mormon iterations of, 174, 240–42, 247; tourism and, 9, 196–98, 218–19, 222–23, 224, 229–31, 240–42, 247
Orth, Godlove S., 23
Otto, Rudolph, 26

Pacific Railway Act, 19–24; Anti-Bigamy Act and, 18, 19, 23–24, 62, 108, 109; Indians and, 19, 20–21, 22, 62; land grants and, 19–21; Mormonism and, 21–22, 23–24, 62, 68, 109, 162; Protestantism and, 24, 29; sectionalism and, 20, 23, 256n28; terms of, 19
Pacific Railway Survey, 256n28
Palace Cars. *See* Pullman Palace Car Company; Utah Exposition Palace Car
panoramas, 202, 224
Pennsylvania Railroad, 189, 259n48
People's Party, 99
Perpetual Emigrating Fund Company, 59, 63, 69–70, 72, 74, 82
pilgrimage. *See* tourism
Piutes, 173, 265n32
Plat of Zion, 48–50, 52, 53, 79, 237
polygamy: Corinnethian evocation of, 1–2, 12, 34–35, 38, 43, 69–70, 131–33, *132*, 137–38, 140, 155; exposés of, *132*, 138–41; First Amendment and, 15–16, 92, 153; Godbeites and, 85, 94–95, 100, 101, 106, 109–10, 138–40; Islam and, 15, 131, 183, 196; Judaism and, 14, 153, 183; Moorish architecture and, 229–31, 240–42; Mormon adoption of, 13; Mormon concessions respecting, 3, 187, 188, 190–93, 195, 241–42; Mormon sects and, 93, 94; Mormon women's defense of, 166–67; Newman-Pratt debate of, 154–55; patriarchy and, 13–14; prostitution and, 166, 254n8; railroads as death knell for, 12, 17, 69–70, 133, 137–38, 139–40, 183, 188; scriptural considerations of, 14, 15, 92–93, 94, 106, 152–53, 183; as slavery, 13–14, 70, 135, 143; touristic observations and representations of, 131, 133, 134–37, 138, 140–41, 152–53, 163–66, 167, 168–69, 179, 183, 185, 196, 198, 213, 229–31, 231, 232, 240–42; Utah statehood and, 188, 190–93, 195, 233. *See also* Anti-Bigamy Act; Cullom Bill; Edmunds-Tucker Act
Powell, John Wesley, 173–74, 180
Pratt, Orson, 153, 154–55
Pratt, Richard Henry, 173
Presbyterianism/Presbyterians: anti-Mormonism and, 29–31, 33, 40–41, 44; in Corinne, 37, 38–41, 42, 44, 124, 180, 260n59, 277n10; railroads and, 29–33, 37, 38–39, 40; at Tabernacle, 153–54
priesthood: Godbeites and, 85–86, 88, 90, 100, 111–12; Mormon offices of, 48, 50–51, 52, 111–12, 220; and Mormon responsibilities concerning land and labor, 56, 63, 67, 74, 220
Promey, Sally M., 225, 301n101
"Promised Land, The" (map), 222–*23*, 233, 237
Promontory/Promontory Summit, 44, 45, 77, 80–*81*, 82, 116, 127, 160
Protestantism: as compared to Catholicism, 25, 29, 38, 225, 254n11; Corinne and, 5, 9, 33–34, 37–39, 42, 44, 88, 128, 130, 155, 182, 235, 245, 257n10; Gentility as, 38, 252n4; Godbeite claims to, 84, 85, 88, 95, 98, 100, 112; Holy

Land tourism and, 224; mainlines of, 29–30; manifest destiny and western fixations of, 15, 21, 24–25, 29–30, 197; materiality and, 225–26; Max Weber on, 25, 245, 246; Mormon likenesses and LDS overtures to, 52, 182, 183, 192; nonsectarianism and, 21, 155; Orientalism and, 15, 196; railroads and, 24–25, 26, 27–30, 42, 44, 84, 88, 95, 245, 246; Salt Lake Theatre displays of, 162–63; secularity and, 4, 5, 9, 25, 28–29, 38, 84, 88, 135, 225, 245–46, 257–58nn40–41, 258n42; Tabernacle displays of, 153–55; technology and, 24–29, 245–46, 257–58nn40–41, 258n42. *See also* secularization thesis; *individual denomination names*

Provo, 189

Pullman, Albert B., 168

Pullman, George M., 148, 152, 168, 178, 238

Pullman Palace Car Company, 119, 120, 168, 202–3, 238, 296n50. *See also* Utah Exposition Palace Car

Pulpit Rock, 58, 199–202, *200*, *201*, 203–8, *210*, 211, 219, 221–22, 228, 230–31, 239, 296n49. *See also* Echo Canyon

race: in acts of Mormon-Muslim comparison, 15; in acts of Mormon-Muslim-Indian comparison, 17, 61, 242; as applied to Indians, 126, 171, 217–18; as benefiting Mormon reception, 161–62, 218, 242. *See also* whiteness

Rae, W. F., 154, 157, 164, 227, 297n62

Raid, the, 187–88

railroad lobby, 5, 6, 10, 28, 101, 236; Cullom Bill and, 102, 104, 108–9, 111, 112, 113, 138, 165; Edmunds-Tucker Act and, 188–90, 194; Godbeites and, 102, 109, 112, 138; Utah statehood and, 190, 191–95, 242

"railroad problem," Mormon conference on, 68–69, 71, 133

railroads. *See* death knell thesis; guidebooks; mainline; Pacific Railway Act; railroad lobby; tourism; *individual company names*

Reconstruction, 23, 91, 104, 108, 111

Reed, Samuel Benedict, 73, 76–77, 267–68n59

Relief Society, 50, 52, 69–70, 155

Reorganized Church of Jesus Christ of Latter Day Saints (RLDS). *See* Josephites

resorts. *See individual resort names*

Richardson, Joseph, 284n8

Rio Grande Western. *See* Denver & Rio Grande Western

Roberts, Edwards, 185–86, 187, 194, 207, 208, 211–12, 213–14, 215, 227

Robinson, J. King, 64

Rogers, Brent M., 256–57n37

Ross, W. W., 156–57, 158, 211

Rowe, William H., 237

sacred space, 8, 9, 56–59

Sagwitch, 290n94

Saltair, 239–44, *240*, *241*

Saltair Railway, 240

Salt Lake. *See* Great Salt Lake

Salt Lake, Sevier Valley & Pioche Railroad, 284n7

Salt Lake & Fort Douglas Railway, 189

Salt Lake & Los Angeles Railway, 240, 242

Salt Lake City: Corinnethians in, 92, 98–99, 120, 128–29, 130–33, 180, 288n59; Denver & Rio Grande connection with, 109; federal land policy and, 54–55, 62, 64–66, 67; Gentile merchants in, 71–72, 96; guidebook depictions of, 141–43, 185–87, 194–95, 208, 210–11, 213–14, 215, 218, 219–25, 227–29, 230–34, 239, 241, 243–44; Mormon settlement of, 53–56, 59, 64–67; possible transcontinental route through, 68, 73, 76–77, 79; steamboat connections to, 115–17, 120, 127–29, 144–45; tourists in, 91–95,

Salt Lake City (*continued*) 115–17, 118–20, 128–29, 130–38, 144, 147–49, 152–58, 159–60, 163–66, 167–71, 174–77, 185–86, 208, 210–14, 215, 227–34, 239–42, 243–44; Union Pacific agents in, 73, 77, 148–50, 152, 165–66, 168, 178. *See also individual building and site names and names of branch railroads*

Salt Lake City Chamber of Commerce, 215, 217, 220, 222

Salt Lake Tabernacle. *See* Tabernacle

Salt Lake Temple, *169*, *210*, *212*, 53, 213, 214, 215, 219, 227, 228, 231, 233, 240, 243–44, 286n27, 289–90n79, 298n73

Salt Lake Theatre, 157–66, 168, *169*, 170, 177, 239; architecture and interior design of, 158, 161, 163–64; defenses of Mormonism at, 164–66; highbrow representation at, 158, 163; ideology and mission of, 159–60; people-watching at, 158, 163–64; precedents for, 158–59; railroad-themed events at, 160–63, *161*; relationship to Tabernacle, 157–58, 159

salvage ethnography, 126, 173, 174

Sanger, Louisa, 283n3

Sargent, Aaron A., 108–9, 110

Savage, Charles R., *81*, *230*, 237, 271n100, 286n26

Schivelbusch, Wolfgang, 202

School of the Prophets, 268n63

Scott amendment, 190

scrapbooks, *210*, *244*; bricolage and, 208–10, 228, 244, 245; Corinne in, *33*, 42; Mormon constitution through, 243–45; Pulpit Rock in, 202, 204–5. *See also* guidebooks

Seales, Chad, 258n45

secular, the, 4–5, 9; Corinne and, 34, 38, 88, 98, 99, 100–2, 106, 182, 245–46, 247; Godbeites and, 84, 88, 91, 96, 98, 100–3, 106; industry/technology and, 25–29, 245–47, 257n40, 258n42; Mormon (LDS) success in, 56, 84, 103, 203, 226–27, 232, 246, 247; Protestantism and, 25, 28–29, 38, 84, 88, 135, 225, 245–46, 257n40, 258n42, tourism and, 56, 112, 135, 156–57, 211, 225–27, 232, 246, 247

secularization thesis, 6, 9, 88, 225, 245. *See also* death knell thesis

Seward, William H., 23

Sharp, John, 78, 148, 149, 284n5, 299n78

Shipps, Jan, 264–65n26, 265n27

Shoshonis: Bear River Massacre of, 36, 62, 124–25; Corinnethians and, 1, 36, 124–27, 180–82; Indian agents and, 61, 125, 173–74, 180; Mormons and, 53, 60–62, 171–73, 174, 181; touristic displays and depictions of, 125–27, 218, 298n71

Sights and Scenes in Utah for Tourists (guidebook), 207–9, 213, 214, 217, 218, 228, 297n59

Silveropolis, 121, 123

Silver Palace Car Company, 119

Sloan, E. L., 162–63, 281n64

Smith, Alexander Hale. *See* Josephites

Smith, Bathsheba W., 166

Smith, David Hyrum. *See* Josephites

Smith, Emma Hale. *See* Josephites

Smith, George A., 55–56, 66, 67, 69, 71–72, 73, 77, 78, 79–80, 92, 94, 136, 153–54, 155–56, 160–61, 268n63, 269n80

Smith, Henry Nash, 258n42

Smith, Hyrum, 175

Smith, Jonathan Z., 58, 263n12., 300n91

Smith, Joseph, Jr., 48–51, 53, 54, 85, 86, 93, 97, 158, 175, 192, 252n2, 273n21

Smith, Joseph F., 192, 293n23, 303n14

Smith, Joseph, III. *See* Josephites

Smithsonian Institution, 173, 176–77

Smoot, Reed, 3

Snow, Eliza R., 70, 166–67

Soda Springs, Idaho, 151, 178–79, 182

spiritualism, 24, 96–98, 100, 101, 274n46

Staal, Frits, 226

Stage and Steam (Sloan), 162–63

Stanford, Leland, 78, 82, 184, 191–92, 193–94, 270n92, 279n32

Stanton, Elizabeth Cady, 134, 167, 169
St. Clair, Augusta, 287–88n51
steamers. *See individual boat names*
Stein, Nat, 99, 128
Stenhouse, Fanny, 85, 88, 138–41, 144, 147, 182, 213
Stenhouse, T. B. H., 18–19, 85, 88, 95, 138, 170, 274n33
stereographs/stereoviews, 200, 202–3, 204–5, 206, 209, 241, 296n49
Stevens, Aaron F., 23
Stevens, Thomas, 267n59
St. Louis World's Fair, 224, 246
Stout, Harry S., 158
Strong, Josiah, 29–30
suffrage. *See* women's suffrage
Sullivan, Winnifred F., 25
surveys: for railroads, 43, 67, 77, 80, 256n28, 267–68n59; for settlement, 43, 49, 52, 53–54, 55, 63, 64, 66, 67

Tabernacle, 169, 210; agricultural displays in, 155–57, 158, 175, 219–20, 222, 230, 237, 239; Mormon sermons and discourses in, 85, 133, 152–53, 192, 193, 211; organ in, 133, 155–56, 211; railroads discussed in, 5, 68–69, 71–73, 133–34, 160; Salt Lake Theatre and, 157–58, 159, 167–68; staged encounters and debates in, 152–56, 176, 177; as tourist attraction, 133, 147–48, 152–58, 167–68, 170–71, 177, 178, 211, 212–13, 214, 215, 219–20, 221–22, 227, 230–31, 233, 291n4. *See also* Mormon Tabernacle Choir; Old Tabernacle
Taylor, John, 148, 154, 188, 189, 190–91
Taysom, Stephen C., 262n4
technological sublime, 26–29, 206
Temple Block (Salt Lake City), 53, 131, 133, 212–14, 221–22, 228, 283–84n4. *See also* Endowment House; Salt Lake Temple; Tabernacle
theater, 158–59, 196. *See also* Salt Lake Theatre
theocracy, 1–2, 11, 13, 15, 25, 33, 34–35, 36–37, 38, 51, 105, 130, 143, 183, 195, 223. *See also* theodemocracy
theodemocracy, 48, 51, 52–53, 60, 65, 86. *See also* theocracy
Toohy, Dennis J., 99–101, 121, 123, 127–29, 155
Toponce, Alexander, 180, 235
tourism: ambiguity and the incorporation of critique in, 112–13, 177, 207–9, 213–14, 230–31, 239–42; economic interests in, 43, 119, 127–28, 148, 150, 164–65, 185–87, 188, 204, 211–12, 228, 229–30, 232, 239–40, 242–43, 247; heritage tourism (LDS), 289–90n79; leisure and the religious work of, 118, 202–3; motives for and types of, 117–19, 129–30, 148; the mutual gaze of, 167–68, 170, 233; pilgrimage and, 300–301n91; politics of, 187–88, 193–95, 208, 214, 230, 232–33; religious placement and social-structural discernment in, 56, 129–30, 186–87, 197–202, 204–6, 207, 210, 211, 218–23, 224–28, 231, 232, 233–34, 247; ritual and, 202–3, 226–27; structure and agency in, 208–10, 227; and the terms of Utahn incorporation, 194–95, 217, 221–22, 227–28, 231–33, 241–43, 246; as western religious concern, 57, 58–59, 129, 186–87. *See also* guidebooks; *specific entries related to tourism*
Townsend House, 92, 149, 156, 170, 288n57
Train, George Francis, 165–66, 267–68n59
Trans-Continental (periodical), 296–97n54
Trumbo, Isaac, 192–94, 242–43
trusteeship, 54, 55, 56, 60, 61, 66–67, 68–69, 236
Tullidge, Edward W., 85, 87–88, 90, 95–96, 99, 100, 107
Turner, Frederick Jackson, 162
Tuttle, Daniel S., 261n68
Twain, Mark, 26, 28, 281n58

Under the Gaslight (play), 160–61
Union Pacific Railroad: Brigham Young's stock in, 68; charter of, 19; Corinne and, 1, 34, 40, 42–45, 80, 127–28; death knell thesis and, 21, 23, 33, 44, 80, 175–76, 188; investments in Mormon branch railroads by, 78, 81–82, 148–50, 188, 228; lobbying efforts by, 188–90, 191, 194; Mormon contracts with, 47–48, 73–74, 76–78, 81–82, 144, 148, 149–50, 203, 211–12; Mormon labor camps and, 74–76, 203; Mormon land grants and, 47–48, 67, 80, 81, 220; Ogden and, 45, 47–48, 67, 77, 79–81; photographic corps of, 157, 296n49; as Presbyterian mission ground, 30–33, 39; Promontory joining with Central Pacific, 80–*81*; route of, 30, 34, 42–43, 44–45, 47–48, 73–74, 76–77, 79, 80; Salt Lake City visits by agents of, 73–74, 76–77, 148–50, 152, 165–66, 168, 178; strikes and, 171; tourist provisions and promotions by, 119, 141, 185–86, 187, 194, 199–*201*, *200*, 203–5, 207–9, *210*, 211–12, 213–*16*, 217–18, 220, 228–29, 230–31, 238
Unitarians, 38
United Order, 48, 49–50, 54, 55, 71
Utah & Nevada. *See* Utah Western
Utah & Northern. *See* Utah Northern
Utah Central Railroad, 78, 79, 81–82, 83, 115–16, 119, 120–21, 123, 127, 128, 129, 136, 141–42, 144, 145, 148, 149–50, 156, 160, 168, 171, 175–76, 188, 286n24, 299n78
Utah emigration: as aided by trains, 68, 69, 74, 189; Deseret Museum displays of, 174–75, 176; Mormon contestations of, 52, 93, 175; railroading imaginations of, 198, 199–201, 204, 205–6
Utah Expedition. *See* Utah War
Utah Exposition Palace Car, 215–22, *216*, 228, 230, 239
Utah Irrigation Commission, 237–38
Utah Lake, 53, 149

Utah Northern, 151, 178, 179–80, 181, 188, 284n8
Utah Penitentiary, 188
Utah Southern, 149–50, 168, 170, 188
Utah Territory, governance and legislative acts of, 13, 52–53, 54–56, 59, 61–62, 64, 66, 68, 70, 103, 181
Utah War (1857–58), 1, 13, 15, 22, 36, 61, 63, 64, 73, 142, 143, 158, 162, 203, 207, 209, 286n28
Utah Western, 149–50, 188
Utes, 53, 60–62, 171, 217–18, 260n59

Waite, Catherine Van Valkenburg, 131
Walkara, 60
Walker, Marietta, 298n67
Walker, Ronald W., 71, 272n4
Walker Brothers, 72, 96, 98, 121, 176, 299n78
Wasatch Mountains, 13, 22, 45, 53, 198–99, 208, 215, 219, 297n62. *See also* Echo Canyon; Pulpit Rock; Weber Canyon
water: Corinnethian claims to, 1, 36, 43; Mormon claims to, 13, 55–56, 59, 63, 64–65; as sacrament, 152, 166; as tourist resource, 115, 118–19, 127, 178, 198, 228–29; as western religious concern, 57–58. *See also* Bear River; Great Salt Lake; irrigation; *individual boats and resorts*
Watt, George Darling, 90
Weber, Max, 9, 25, 87–88, 245–47, 276n60
Weber Canyon, 42, 68, 73, 198–200, 205, *210*, 213. *See also* Wasatch Mountains
Wells, Daniel H., 72–73, 75, 159
West, the: land and regional religious concerns of, 57–58
Western Railroad Corporation (Mass.), 26, 27, 28
Western Shoshonis, 124. *See also* Shoshonis
White, Richard, 19–20
whiteness: Corinne and, 36, 62, 124–25, 162, 260n59; Mormonism and, 14, 15,

30, 36, 60, 62, 162–63, 180, 218, 242, 260n59. *See also* race
Whitman, Walt, 26–27, 28
Wild West shows, 126, 238–39
Williamson, James A., 43–44
Wind River Reservation (Wyo.), 124, 173,
Witches Rocks, 199, 296n49. *See also* Pulpit Rock
Wodziwob, 173
women's suffrage, 13, 35, 70–71, 103–4, 111, 134–35, 148, 167
Woodruff, Wilford, 53–54, 188, 191–92, 238, 303n14
Woodruff Manifesto, 3, 188, 192, 214, 233, 242
Word of Wisdom, 69
work camps: demographics of, 73, 74–75; Mormons in, 69, 74–76, 203; rule and misrule of, 30, 37, 69, 74–75, 79
World's Fair (Chicago, 1893), 2, 235–39

Young, Amelia, 164, 178, 214
Young, Brigham, *169, 244*; anti-Mormon portrayals of, 1, 11–13, 36, 40–41, 131–33, 135, 143–44, 173, 181; death and grave of, 179, 213–14, 228, 231; guidebook representations of, 142, 183, 199–200, 204–5, 214, 220–21, 233, 243; home of, 135, 147, 168, *169*, 233; "ideology of play" and, 158–59, 239; Indians and, 60–62, 171, 173, 181; mining and, 63, 83, 85, 86, 89, 91, 111–12, 142, 151–52, 157; and Mormon critiques of 'Brighamite' policies, 52, 84, 86, 87–88, 93, 175, 252n51; prerailroad anticipation and planning by, 5–6, 8, 47–48, 65–70, 71–73, 84, 86, 88; railroad contracts and negotiations by, 47–48, 73–78, 80, 81–82, 87, 105, 149–50, 165; resource distribution and land grants by, 13, 47–48, 53–56, 59, 60, 64–65, 67–68, 73, 80, 87, 103, 104, 220–21; and Salt Lake Theatre, 158–60, 161, 163–64, 165–66; and Soda Springs, 178; at Tabernacle, 5, 85, 152–53, 154; as territorial governor, 13, 52–53, 54–56, 59, 61–62, 68; as tour guide, 148, 149–52; tourist audiences and office meetings with, 148, 167–70; tourist sightings of, 147, 163–64; as trustee-in-trust, 54, 67, 267n59; and Utah colonizing companies, 59–60, 62, 63
Young, Brigham, Jr., 74
Young, John W.: as architect of Utahn tourist industries, 144–45, 150, 170–73, 174–77, 183, 215, 221, 228, 230, 239–40; as Corinnethian foe, 144–45, 150–52, 180, 181–83; as lobbyist, 188–91, 193; mining and, 149, 150, 151–52, 157, 175–76, 178, 182, 220–21; as railroad builder, 149–51, 178, 179, 180, 181, 182, 183, 220–21, 228; as railroad subcontractor, 74, 175; as tour guide, 148–49, 150–51, 156, 170, 178–79, 182, 183
Young, Joseph A., 74, 78, 81, 284n5

Zion's Cooperative Mercantile Institution (ZCMI), 71–72, 74, 82, 83, 86, 97, 111, 237

www.ingramcontent.com/pod-product-compliance
Lightning Source LLC
Chambersburg PA
CBHW032013300426
44117CB00008B/1014